How to Make Animated Films

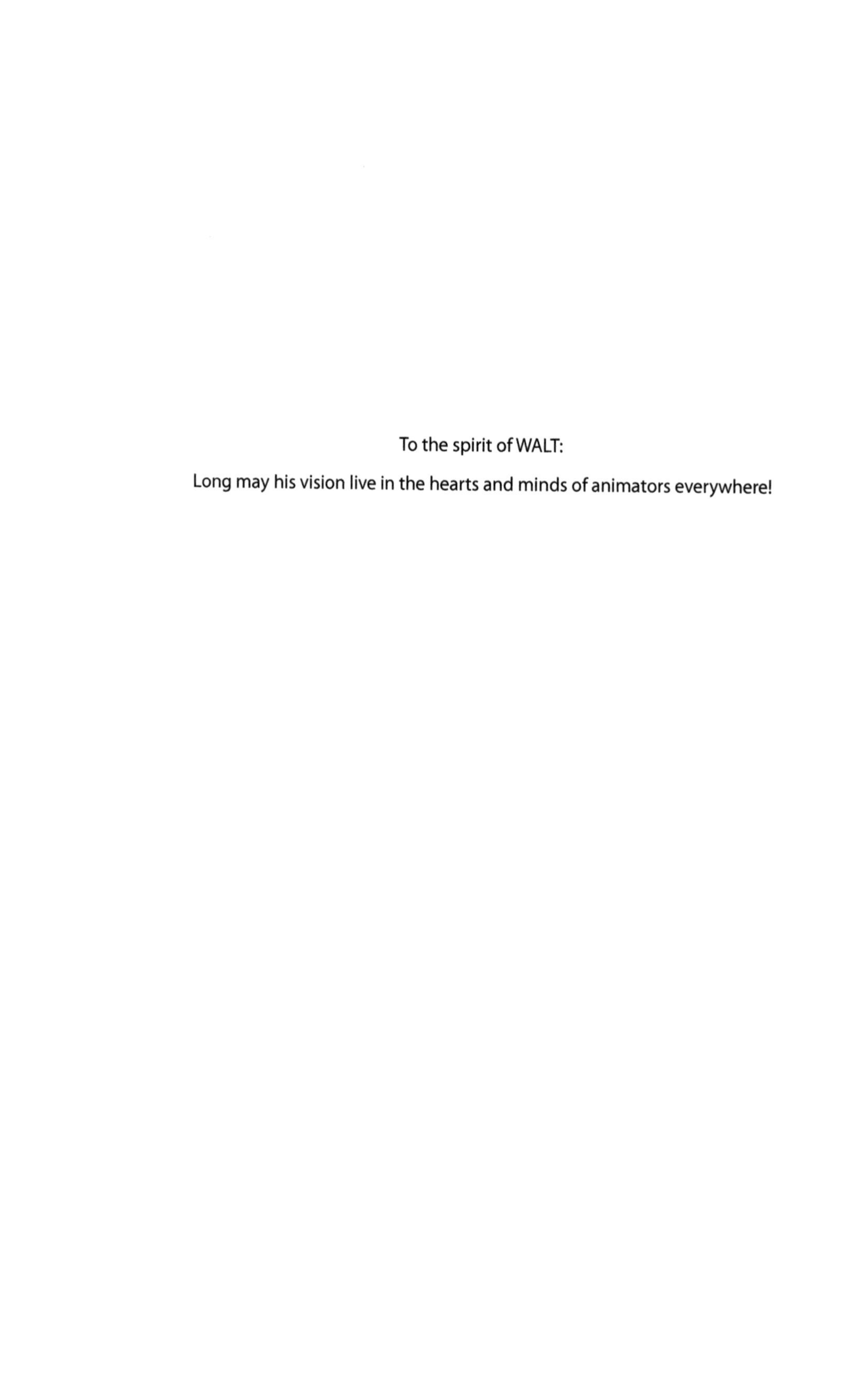

To the spirit of WALT:

Long may his vision live in the hearts and minds of animators everywhere!

How to Make Animated Films

Tony White's Complete Masterclass on the Traditional Principles of Animation

Tony White

An animation apprenticeship—
the way the pros used to do it!

LONDON AND NEW YORK

First published 2013 by Focal Press

Published 2019 by Routledge
2 Park Square, Milton Park, Abingdon, Oxon OX14 4RN
52 Vanderbilt Avenue, New York, NY 10017, USA

Routledge is an imprint of the Taylor & Francis Group, an informa business

Library of Congress Cataloging-in-Publication Data
White, Tony, 1947-
How to make animated films : Tony White's complete masterclass on the traditional principles of animation / Tony White.
p. cm.
"An animation apprenticeship-the way the pros used to do it!"
Includes bibliographical references and index.
ISBN 978-0-240-81033-1 (pbk. : alk. paper) 1. Animated films—Technique. 2. Animation (Cinematography) I. Title. II. Title: Tony White's complete masterclass on the traditional principles of animation. III. Title: Masterclass on the traditional principles of animation.
NC1765.W49 2009
741.5′8—dc22

2009005710

British Library Cataloguing-in-Publication Data
A catalogue record for this book is available from the British Library.

ISBN: 978-0-240-81033-1 (pbk)
ISBN: 978-0-080-92784-8 (ebk)

Contents

Preface

We are in an era where there are probably more books about animation than there ever were. So you would presume that with all that information out there, a young and aspiring student of animation would have more than enough to choose from. However, if you objectively look around at all those books offered, you will find one or two truly great books, but the rest tend to regurgitate the same old material over and over again, much of it losing its value and accuracy in translation and through imitation. Many people also refer to the classic age of "cartoon films," without ever really acknowledging that the great cartoon industry we once knew in "the good old days" has effectively been long, long gone! The actual core principles of animation never change of course—they are timeless and eternal, and will forever be so. However, the obsessive presentations that still hark back to an era where rubbery characters, slapstick gags, and the inevitable "squash and stretch" chase scenes proliferate ad infinitum are totally misleading. The animation that once was, is no more, and the classic industry of cartoon filmmaking is now merely an illusion.

I am often criticized for being so pedantic about this knowledge, and for insisting that there is one way to do something and no other. In reality, animation can be approached in any way that you wish to. And may it forever be so, for variety is the spice of life! However, I write what I write with a knowledge that if you want to animate well and you want to animate in keeping with the requirements of the modern production age, you will find it so much easier and so much better to adhere to the core principles that grace every era of the world of animation. Today, there is a new animation industry to conquer—arguably as powerful as it ever was in the cartoon days. Games animation proliferates, as well as Web animation, TV animation, and also still a little Hollywood-style theatrical animation. Yet each one of these can take the art form to previously unconquered heights, and there is still huge cause for optimism.

As a veteran who spans four decades of animation's expression, covering eras old and new, I still very much believe that what I have learned and experienced are still worthy of sharing and still of value to modern student and professional animators, whatever form of animation they pursue. In truth, my heart lies with the independent animated filmmakers, who spend hours, days, weeks, months, and even years on a project that they believe has something to say outside of the more predictable mainstream animation, and with those who believe that new and wonderful forms of animated expression can be found. My writing speaks to these valiant folk too, because I believe there may still emerge a true renaissance of what animation as an art form is and what it may still be. I, therefore, humbly lay out before you what animation can do through my own experiences and hope that this book will assist you to discover finer and more assured ways of finding your voice.

Some, but sadly not nearly enough, amazing innovative movies of note have graced our screens in recent years, such as Hayao Miyazaki's *Spirited Away* and Silvan Chomet's *Triplets of Belleville*. These films seem cut from a different cloth from the classic films, and it really shows. They keep my belief in real and vital animated storytelling—well made, alive! Beyond films like these, Hollywood seems to regurgitate the same tired, old script and visual formulas ad infinitum, and already the dominant three-dimensional (3D) animation industry offerings are beginning to find a creative rut in the mainstream. The only exception to this trend is the mercurial and ever-innovative Pixar studio, the most recent film of which, *Wall-e*, took a definite turn toward something even more innovative. But beyond that cherished shrine for "good things," there is very little of the classic world that is around and that offers anything new and exciting for the professional animator with any degree of consistency.

Therefore, we have to consider new ground for exploration—that is, if the industry is to grow and thrive and the animators of tomorrow are to find a career worthy of the name. One area that has most definitely grown and thrived, of course, is the games-based animation industry. It now represents the most immediate and approachable source of income for an aspiring, young animator, and as an industry, it well outpaces the languishing world of the more traditional cartoon-based production world (i.e., movies, TV, and Web-based animation). In fact, I am told that the games industry is now rapidly approaching the music industry for the world's largest producer of consumer-targeted media entertainment!

So what constitutes a "professional" animator in this day and age? Certainly, modern animators need to be more chameleon and even somewhat schizophrenic when it comes to their chosen career path. Contemporary animators tend to be more nomadic as well, often having to travel far and wide to where the work is for much of the time. They have to be significantly more versatile too—working in the games industry one moment, the Web animation industry the next, and on feature film entertainment when they are lucky. Occasionally an animated commercial will become an opportunity, but production in that field is a pale shadow of what it was in the 1970s and 1980s, when I was able to perfect my craft and both volume and creativity reached a kind of golden age in the United Kingdom through the work of remarkable animators such as Richard Williams, Oscar Grillo, Eric Goldberg, and, of course, the remarkable folks in my own Animus Productions studio, as it once was called.

Artistic ability in cartoon styles alone doesn't cut it anymore. Modern animators, whether they use two-dimensional (2D), 3D, clay, or cut-out styles, seem to be most in demand if they have an outstanding additional ability in drawing or classical art. The most prized animators can also demonstrate a clear design capability and have a firm grasp of color theory, anatomy, and the classical art notions of perspective, form, and tone. Many are quite amazing classical artists in their own right. Even the students who enter my classroom at DigiPen in Redmond, WA, arrive with classical art skills that often lie far beyond their reach or that of their admiring teacher's reach! Consequently, I believe the future is very bright for the noncartoon horizons of animation. Yes, contemporary animators may be working in a cartoon style on occasion, and it is still a joy to behold this style some of the time; however, the professionals of the future will more likely be required to work in more "mature," "illustrative" styles as well.

Those who prefer to animate their own films have complete liberty toward what they can and want to create. Advertising, too, can sporadically offer opportunities that can break the mold. Yet the signs show that things are quickly changing. In my own experience in the Pacific Northwest, the main employment opportunities for animators is the blossoming games industry from Microsoft, Nintendo, and ArenaNet, and others. These opportunities are beginning to go immediately to students who have an education based on hard-won traditional principles—that is, art training with an emphasis on drawing and hand-drawn animation. This is proving to be a shrewd and wise investment for young artists (or their parents, who usually pay for their education), who wish to enter the modern world of professional animation. Consequently, to be ahead of the curve it is essential that present and future student animators begin to embrace the hardcore principles of animated movement that have been handed down through many decades of amazing expression and accomplishment!

I have tried to make this course of instruction the complete package based on this requirement. It is, I believe, the first-ever comprehensive, structured course set in the requirements of the modern animation world. It is structured to give you just about everything you'll ever need to know to become competent as a professional-level animator for this day and age. With all you'll find written within the pages of this book, as well as the additional filmed lectures and demonstrations on the accompanying DVD, you'll have at your fingertips a virtual degree-level academy of instruction that is a comprehensive and realistic introduction to what I believe is the most wonderful art form the world has ever known. It will not teach you how to draw or paint, however, and it will certainly not instruct you on the art of drawing "cartoons." (Those things I urge you to do anyway—even drawing cartoons alongside the more classic-based artistic subjects.) Neither will this book necessarily give you a deep appreciation for art or the history of art, or provide you with knowledge of all the great classic principles of anatomy, perspective, and color. All these things you need to bring to the table with you if you want to compete with the top professional animators of today.

Of course there can be no substitute for a well-structured and comprehensive animation school education, such as the truly inspired program we provide at the DigiPen Institute of Technology. (And as demonstrated by the outstanding student work shown in this book and on the DVD … lest there be those who have doubt!) However, if you don't have such an outstanding animation program of education where you are, or you quite simply can't afford one in this current economic climate, this book will be an answer to all your prayers! It should provide you with the most comprehensive book/disk–based course ever, covering the core principles of classic animated movement, but with a contemporary, professionally targeted slant that addresses the modern reality of the animation world. Additionally, as well as teaching you how to become an animator, it also guides you through the animation production process too, so you have the capability of turning each one of your film- or games-based dreams into a reality. (Note: The actual production process of creating animated work for both film and games is pretty similar overall. Consequently, an understanding in one strongly prepares you for a sound application in the other!)

How to Make Animated Films has been planned for several years and is the final part of the instructional trilogy I set out to create many years ago. *The Animator's Workbook* kicked off this process as the definitive "beginner's guide to animation," which, through the test of time, has established itself as one of the principal textbooks for teaching in the professional and academic industries. *Pencils to Pixels: Classical Techniques for Digital Animators* more recently took this instructional material to the next level, by providing the more ambitious animator with just about everything he or she might need to know about the tools, techniques, and practices of their subject. Finally, this book rounds off this entire process by tying everything together in the form of a comprehensive educational package that will work for everyone, whether they are raw high school beginners or evolving professional animators in the games, Web, or film industries. All you need to add is your own talent, commitment, enthusiasm, and tenacity!

Additionally, should you wish to take your home-schooling ambitions to the next level, you might want to visit my Desktop Academy website (*www.desktopacademy.com*) where, for a little extra investment, you can receive my personal critiques and feedback for the work you submit from the stage-by-stage assignments I offer in this book. You can even be graded for these, earning credits toward my own "Certificate of Animated Excellence," which is awarded to all students who successfully complete the coursework provided in this book. This does not mean, however, that you cannot study the material in this book alone. Far from it! What is contained here should give you all the information and instruction you will ever need to become a solid animator and filmmaker in your own right, as well as reach a competence that can be embraced by the film, TV, or games industries as a whole.

So, if you dream of becoming an animator in this modern day and age, why not take this book home and jump straight into your studies! I cannot, of course, guarantee that this course will absolutely give you a job at Pixar or Disney (or at Nintendo, ArenaNet, or Blizzard), as clearly a great deal depends on the talents you bring to your work, the tenacity you apply in sticking with it, and the personality you project when you eventually apply for positions. However, what I can assure you is that if you follow the stage-by-stage instructions contained here, you will have a professional-level knowledge in animation. To make things as easy as I can, I will talk you through all the core techniques and approaches you will need in a way that is simple to understand and methodical in its process. I will give you tangible onscreen examples of everything you need to achieve, as well as instruct you on the process of putting this all together in the form of an animated production. *How to Make Animated Films* will make the entire process of learning the principles of animation and filmmaking so much more accessible to you in your home-based environment, and you'll even be able to make good, old-fashioned "cartoon" films if that still remains your ambition at the end of it all!

Supplementary Resources Disclaimer

Additional resources were previously made available for this title on DVD. However, as DVD has become a less accessible format, all resources have been moved to a more convenient online download option.

You can find these resources available here: www.routledge.com/9780240810331

Please note: Where this title mentions the associated disc, please use the downloadable resources instead.

Introduction

First … A Reality Check

There is a popular misconception that animation is easy. It is not. In reality, the process of animation is far from easy! Becoming an animator demands a great deal of focus, tenacity, commitment, and determination, as well as the ability to simply sit still, in one place, for a long period of time, until you achieve what you are determined to achieve. It also requires initial capable artistic ability. That said, if you can commit all these qualities to your studies, and you can confidently wield a pencil (or a mouse or Wacom pen) to achieve what is required here, and you can be patient in everything you do and seek to do, there is absolutely no reason whatsoever why you cannot become an expert animator and/or filmmaker in the fullness of time! Easy, it ain't. (But what in this world is worth having if it isn't hard to achieve?) At the same time, who said anything about not being easy couldn't be fun! What lies ahead is most definitely fun—that is, if you have the heart, the will, and the passion to see the hard parts through to the very end!

Your Own Personal Animation Course

Welcome to your very own animation textbook and DVD classroom! Within the covers of this book you should find just about everything you'll ever need to study to master the art of animated movement for the modern world. You will also discover that once you have mastered the core principles of animated movement, you will even learn how to make a film, contribute to a game, or create a project of your own if you like. Unlike going to a recognized school, you will be learning on your own, at your own pace, and at the times that best suit you. An added bonus is that it will be far cheaper for you to learn animation this way, although I stress that the path is somewhat harder if you don't have a knowledgeable, experienced professional teacher to guide you.

(And yes, sometimes to bully you along, whenever that is necessary!) That said, with all the course work laid out in this book, you should just about be able to find an answer to pretty much every question you're ever likely to ask about the techniques and production process of animation. If you should want further professional-level feedback, however, you will be able to obtain online critiques of your assignment work, and even receive published recognition at the successful completion of your degree-level assignment work, if you so choose. (Details of this can be obtained in Appendix 2.)

2D Or Not 2D?—That Is the Question

The first thing you note as you look through your own degree-level course in animation is that most of the primary lessons and assignments are approached from a traditional two-dimensional (2D) animation viewpoint. That is okay, don't panic! Although drawing 2D animation may seem like an unnecessary challenge, and many people these days erroneously suggest that traditional 2D animation is a lost art form, I would advise you that the very best schools of animation still teach traditional animation as a core foundation that everything else is built on. This is for a justifiable reason.

Traditional 2D animation techniques are still the best way of studying the core principles of movement. Two-dimensional animation's inherent disciplines really underline the process of frame-by-frame movement, and once a student learns the process of animation through having to draw every exercise assignment, he or she will undoubtedly never forget them!

It is not a coincidence that the formative work of the great Pixar studio was founded by traditional 2D animators who where taught what software buttons to push so they could weave their traditional magic through the digital art form. Indeed, many companies—both film-based and games-based—prefer to hire 3D computer animators with traditional 2D animation skill sets before they hire computer-skilled-only animators, simply because they know that they have a more comprehensive understanding of the medium, and with an artistic foundation to their work, they become more versatile members of the company's animation team. Remember, purely "button-pushing" animators are severely limited in terms of their artistic range and versatility when faced with the more aesthetic and broadly ranged production challenges that are invariably required in the demanding and competitive world of animation today.

However ...

Even though the core material in this book is composed of primarily 2D-based material, every effort has been made to respect the essential 3D processes that contemporary animators need to know when considering a career in the modern animation world. Consequently, in many cases, students can substitute 3D animation for the 2D animation assignments given. The intention is not to penalize potentially wonderful animators if they do not have any facility for drawing in the first place! In truth, the ability to demonstrate a comprehensive knowledge of all the principles and techniques of animated movement, whether they are created in a 2D or 3D environment, should be enough to convince a potential employer that the animator before them does indeed "know their stuff." That said, an animator who can demonstrate an ability in both 2D and 3D animation is of a higher premium these days than an animator who is myopic in his or her approach.

Prerequisites for Study

All serious academic courses require certain prerequisites on the part of students before they begin, and this book course is no different! Although this kind of home-based study is far less formal and organized than a regular, structured college education, the prerequisites for study on behalf of the students for this course will be no less real than others. Therefore, before you begin your studies, it might help for me to go over the ideal prerequisites you will need if you are to maximize the effectiveness of the course material presented here. Of course, these prerequisites do not mean that you *have* to have them in order to complete the course. But, being aware of the ideal circumstances and attitudes when approaching your studies will help you better cope with what is to follow.

Drawing Ability

It goes without saying that any course that is dedicated to top-quality animation techniques, especially the 2D-based examples presented in this book, would ideally require students to have some degree of drawing ability. It might be that you are at the very beginning of your journey as an artist and that you have not yet been taught how to draw, or even properly learned the rudiments of drawing technique. You should certainly be aware of which end of a pencil is which and therefore be able to minimally draw the simple characters defined in this book to an acceptable level of consistency.

The better you draw, the better it will be for you to address the requirements of this course. If you don't know how to draw, I certainly recommend you take some classes in the subject before you go too far with what follows, because the artistic demands increase as the process is further explored and executed.

When all is said and done, animation is all about drawing—you cannot escape that fact, whether you want to be a 2D or 3D animator. The very best of Pixar's and Disney's animators as well as those in other major film or game studios, will acknowledge that fact. Indeed, many of the finest among them come from a traditional art or animation background before they arrived! (Actually, many of these top studios provide drawing and other art-based instruction sessions within the company solely to improve the artistic skills of their workforce and make them more effective animators as a result!) The fact that to understand a character in all its dimensions, you ideally need to visualize and replicate it from a number of viewpoints and at a number of repeatedly changing angles, is testimony to this requirement. Drawing it out beforehand, even in a thumbnail sketch form, assists this process, even if your ultimate output is through a 3D environment. Consequently, you will be significantly hindered if you do not have drawing capability, and the better your drawing ability is, the better it will work for you as an animator.

Consequently, it is my most earnest suggestion that as a supplement to the coursework contained in this book, you should at least keep a separate sketchbook with you to draw, draw, and draw from life around you at every possible opportunity! Better still, if you are currently a raw rookie in the art of drawing, at least buy yourself a good book on basic drawing and observational techniques, such as Betty Edward's *The New Drawing from the Right Side of the Brain* (Tarcher; Rev Exp edition, Spetember 6, 1999), and immerse yourself in the desire to be a better artist. Also, if you can take classes in drawing too, your studies will only benefit as a result. Certainly your animation will be of a much higher order if you develop a good drawing capability, especially if you ultimately intend to be a professional animator in the modern world.

A Basic Knowledge of the Classic Principles of Art

A knowledge of the classic principles of art really finishes off where the initial drawing training begins. If your ambition is to be at the top of the totem pole professionally, then you cannot possibly become an accomplished animator without first being an accomplished artist in some way or another. By being an "accomplished" artist, I mean immersing yourself in the traditional principles of art technique and appreciation and being able to respect and replicate them to some degree through your own work. At a very minimum, you should at least study and understand classic art principles such as perspective; human and animal anatomy; light, tone, and color; layout and composition; and perhaps with a more contemporary slant, "filmmaking

101" techniques if you want to make your own productions too. All these disciplines are crucial in order to use your fullest expressions as an animator, for even a rudimentary glance at the capabilities of the world's top 2D and 3D animators will reveal a knowledge of classic art principles.

A certain appreciation of the wide spectrum of dance, mime, music, and drama significantly adds to your cause too! Fundamentally, you cannot possibly express yourself fully in a visual medium like animation without first having a knowledge and grasp of the principles that support the process of that visual medium. Animation is totally a visual medium, and even though it is invariably viewed on a screen and not on a sheet of paper, it does intrinsically rely on the principles contained in all other traditionally based art forms to make it work. Therefore, if you fully wish to reap the potential that this book offers you, you are advised to study the rudiments of all of the abovementioned before you start in earnest as an animation student. If you don't have this knowledge or these skills at the very beginning of your journey, then you certainly should have them available at your fingertips at its conclusion, especially if your ambition is to be a top professional in your own right!

Patience, Commitment, and Tenacity

Animation is a slow, focused, painstaking process, and you're fooling yourself if you think otherwise. Good animation, or indeed great films, are not made overnight. It takes months … maybe years … to perfect something in animation, whether that be a collection of repeatable animator skills or an animated film that really expresses itself to its full potential and capability. Consequently, to be a significant animator you need to be a dedicated and somewhat patient individual. You also need to have a determined commitment to see through whatever you start. Finally, you need to have the tenacity to hang in there when all seems to be failing, or the world seems to be against you fulfilling your dream (as it most certainly will over such a period of time). If you're a video game player and you think that what you see in the game is easy to accomplish … think on! If you believe animation is easy, then you are misguided! If you think animation is something you can pick up, then put it down, pick it up again, and put it down again, ad infinitum … you're wrong!

Great animation is effectively a great obsession. Only the truly obsessed—or to put it more delicately, the more dedicated—will ever fully succeed with it as pure animators. It takes an iron will, blood and sweat, and some tears sometimes to see it through to its fullest conclusion. It is not for the faint-hearted or for the easily distracted. It is totally involving and demands as much dedication and commitment from you than if you were studying to be a great lawyer, surgeon, or scientist. Yes, it is still all about having fun with what you love to do. But, if you want to be as fine as the great master animators of the past, or as accomplished as the greatest of the Pixar-level animators of the present, then you do have to accept the sacrifice of the long, hard road that lies ahead of you.

As I suggested earlier, nothing worth having in this world is easy, and animation is no exception. Professionally, the world is extremely competitive. Great schools like the DigiPen Institute of Technology and even popular online courses such as Animation Mentor are turning out professional-level animators of the highest capability, and the employment market is not infinite and all-absorbing. Consequently, if you're ambitious for a serious career in animation and think this book is a shortcut to your professional ambitions, then you're wrong. The competition is so stiff these days that you will almost have to err on the verge of total obsession with these exercises if you hope to compete with each new generation of highly trained, wannabe animators. That said, what is presented here is everything about the core principles of movement that you'll ever need to know to be a good animator, as long as you develop the focus, temperament, and commitment to see it through to its ultimate conclusion. At the other end of the spectrum, if you're just looking for fun ways to make your cartoon drawings move, or want to know how to make a short film on your own for friends and family, then you'll find more than you need with what follows!

Equipment

Okay, so you want to be an animator and are itching to start your first day of school. So what kind of equipment will your home-based campus need?

The first requirement is that you'll need to be able to execute everything that is required of you throughout the coursework. That means that if you're taking the purely 2D route, you'll need a lightbox. Animators of a 3D persuasion will of course need a computer with suitable 3D animation software that can also render work to movie files. But let's look more at the equipment requirements in greater detail.

Two-Dimensional Animation Lightbox

The traditional animator's lightbox has evolved over decades of practice and experience and really provides the ideal drawing setup for a new animator to work with. Lightboxes can come in all shapes and sizes, from the wonderfully grandiose Disney classics that can fill the good part of a small room, to the simple crafting boxes that easily sit on the top of even the smallest of tables or your lap if space is a premium. A good animator's lightbox, however, will ideally have an adjustable working surface with a rotating circle cut into it, so that that animator can find the best angles to comfortably draw anything he or she needs to draw and be able to turn the drawings accordingly.

The crucial thing about any animator's work surface, however, is that it has to be composed of some kind of translucent material that enables a backlight to shine through several layers of animation paper at a time; thus, the term *lightbox*. The rotating disk in the surface of the lightbox can be either a circular, translucent sheet of Plexiglas sunk into a wooden surface, or, alternatively, the whole disk can be made entirely of Plexiglas and the circular disk cut out of it and installed in such a way that it can rotate but not fall through the hole. A really top-grade professional will have a custom-made, metal disk that not only includes a Perspex surface within it, but it will also have a number of other animated "gizmos" built into it, such as slideable top and bottom panning peg bars. However, for the purposes of the course work in this book, none of that will be necessary. I would recommend to the cash-strapped student that it is perfectly acceptable to use one of the inexpensive crafting lightboxes that many stores carry these days for home hobbyists. A perfect example of one of these is the LightTracer II.

Peg Bar

A 2D animation lightbox is not entirely complete unless you have an animation peg bar attached to it. All animation paper is punched with holes that ensure perfect registration from drawing to drawing. The peg bar is the means by which these punched sheets of animation paper can be kept in perfect alignment with one another as they are being worked on upon the lightbox surface. The professional standard Acme peg system is the most universally used system today. An Acme peg setup contains a circular central peg with two horizontally elongated ones on either side of it, engineered to specific measurements. However, cost-conscious students can alternatively buy a simple three-circular-peg plastic peg bar, which is quite inexpensive but will enable them to use paper that is punched using a standard three-hole office punch. Inexpensive three-hole peg bars can be obtained online from Lightfoot Limited (*www.lightfootltd.com*).

Animation Paper

Most online animation stores, such as Lightfoot Limited, Cartoon Color Company (*www.cartooncolour.com*), and Chromacolour International (*www.chromacolour.com*), will have all kinds of animation supplies on order, including prepunched or unpunched animation paper. There are three major paper sizes that you can consider: student-size paper and 12-field- and 16-field-size paper.

Student-Size Paper

Student-size paper is the simplest and cheapest paper. It can be ultratranslucent (to avoid the need for a really bright lightbox, and, in some cases, no lightbox at all) or else standard opaque white bond paper that is used in most desktop printers or photocopiers. The standard student size in the United States is 8.5 × 11 inches and elsewhere it will probably be A4. Although this is a very cheap and easy-to-obtain paper size, it does significantly limit the dimensions of the drawing surface area, especially if a large-screen film production is being attempted. Its huge advantage, however, is that when it comes to the final scanning stages of a film production, this paper size perfectly fits most standard, and therefore far more inexpensive, scanners without any cutoff around the edges.

12-Field–Size Paper

This is the smallest of the professional animation papers. Measuring approximately 10.5 × 12.5 inches, this paper size is what most commercial-based studios will use when creating animation for games, Web, TV, or direct-to-DVD/video distribution. It is also the most recommended size for the more seriously minded student, although its disadvantage is that it is more expensive than the standard office letterhead-size paper, and will require a larger, and therefore more expensive, scanner to ensure the whole drawing area is covered.

16-Field–Size Paper (15-Field in the United Kingdom)

This is the largest of the two professional animation paper sizes used. It is the size that is predominantly used in large-screen, theatrical movies, although many professional animators prefer to work with this size on all projects because it maximizes the drawing area and therefore the detail they can put into their drawings. Clearly, this is much more costly to obtain than any of the other paper sizes and requires a more expensive flatbed scanner that can cover a minimum of an 11 × 17–inch image area when working on a film production.

Animation Pencils

Pretty much all pencils will work for animation, but there are ones that are preferred by most animators. The industry standard norm is Sanford's Blue (*not* the nonphotographic blue!) Col-erase pencils. These pencils have an excellent drawing lead in them and are provided with an eraser at the end, which, although it wears down pretty quickly (often more quickly than the pencil lead, unfortunately) is a one-stop shop for serious animators. A number of the old Disney studio animators would also have used Sanford's Red Col-erase pencils since a number of their animators preferred the slightly softer lead that the red version provides.

Red and blue pencils are quite often used for the rough and clean-up stages of work, however, if a strong black, scanner-friendly pencil-style line is required for clean-up, then Tombo's Mono is usually the preferred pencil to use. They use graphic-based leads in them, which provides for an excellent high-density look. Sometimes cleaned-up drawings need to be created with an even black line for premium scanner copying and digital coloring. In these cases, using a mechanical pencil with replaceable leads (the softer rather than harder variety), black fiber-tip pens such as PaperMate's Flair, or Pigma's Micron range of pens (which are my favorite inking pens) are more useful.

Pencil Sharpener

If you are using pencils to animate, then you will definitely need some kind of mechanical pencil sharpener. In the old days, pencils were sharpened by finely honed knives. But with the volume of work an animator was required to get through, hand-turned pencil sharpeners became the norm. Today, true professional animators will have a strong and reliable electric pencil sharpener beside their lightboxes. There are a number of excellent ones out there, but I tend to find that Xacto's Powerhouse is the one that has least let me down. However, always make sure before you buy one that the point on the pencil is acceptable for detailed animation drawings, as some of the cheaper varieties can create a stumpy point, which is really not ideal.

Field Guide

Although the above equipment enables animators to work, they do need to define a required area to work in. Consequently, transparent plastic field guides are required to identify the "field" (or viewable screen area) that the animation is to be seen in. Field guides come in various sizes but the normal standard ones are 12 field and 16 field (15 field in the United Kingdom). These come in either regular "academy" size (3:4 screen ratio) or else more rarely in a widescreen format (1.75:1 screen ratio). Available from most online animation stores, the field guide (known as a *graticule* in some places) is an essential piece of 2D animation equipment when filmmaking is the ultimate objective. Many of the exercise details in this book, however, do not require a field guide.

Miscellaneous Two-Dimensional Equipment

Most of the other equipment an animator uses is not just standard to animation stores, but can be purchased from art stores pretty much anywhere. As will be recognized later, it is always advisable to have a ruler and a small tape dispenser close at hand. I also strongly advise getting a good-size, adjustable desktop lamp, as quite often the lighting in a room is not sufficiently bright enough to illuminate the drawing surface and therefore some kind of local light is needed. A stopwatch is also an invaluable item for animators who need to work out action and timings in their head. Inexpensive digital ones can be obtained from chain stores such as Radio Shack.

Paperwork

It's strange to think of an animator requiring paperwork other than just the paper for drawing on, but it is true that paperwork is needed. The key administrative paperwork that 2D animators specifically will need is a pad or two of exposure sheets. Exposure sheets (also called *X-sheets* or *dope sheets* in some places) are crucial to animators who are organizing their thoughts and plotting their movements and layers.

We will discuss this in detail later, but suffice it to say, it is important that animators are equipped with exposure sheets at the onset of their more advanced work. It is possible to either print them from a standard template (available from Desktop Academy, at *www.desktopacademy.com*) or else purchase them from one of the excellent online animation stores on the Web. If you are an intended filmmaker too, you will need to consider scene production folders, which will contain both exposure sheets and animation drawings when the work is completed. These too can be printed from templates available at the Desktop Academy site, or created individually according to design and taste. Another downloadable paperwork item is an animator's progress chart, which we'll deal with later in more detail.

Technology Requirements

If you are to take the process of animation seriously, you will want to make sure you have the means of not only drawing your animation, but also filming and playing it back for inspection and critique. This is universally known as a *pencil test*. Consequently, you will need some kind of image-capture device and software that will allow you to do this. The most inexpensive approach would be to purchase a simple golfball-style webcam from a local computer store and hook it up to your computer that has something like Digicel's Flipbook or the more recent addition to the pencil-test software community, ToonBoom Technology's Pencil Check. Although the basic webcam setup gives soft and slightly blurry pencil test images, it is perfectly usable for any animators who draw their animations in strong, dark lines (i.e., soft, tentative lines tend not to show up on the webcam's lens resolution level).

Of course, a higher-level video camera with high-resolution capabilities will give a much better picture. For both my own production work and my teaching work I use Lightfoot Limited's Teacher Demo Station (*www.lightfootltd.com*), which has an excellent lightbox, as well as filming and teaching capabilities all combined into one unit. However, unless you are teaching (or writing a book about animation teaching!), this is definitely overkill for most student, novice, and even professional animation requirements. The Flipbook, ToonBoom, and Premier software will enable you to adjust your individually shot images into a suitable playback speed and order, and also give you the option of saving the moving sequence as avi, mov, and Flash-based movie clips too.

Production Scanners and Software

Once an animation is pencil tested and approved, it will need to be cleaned up and taken to the next level if it is to be part of a finished film production. Here, each individual drawing will be scanned as individual files, then digitally colored, and then composited together with a suitable piece of background artwork, adding whatever special effects may be required on a scene-by-scene basis. To initiate this process, you will obviously need a suitable flatbed scanner. If you're working at a basic student level with 10 field–size paper (i.e., 8.5 × 11 inches), then the standard, inexpensive flatbed scanners that can be found in most computer or technology stores will be all you need. However, if you're working more professionally—that is, at the 12 field or 16 field paper level—you will need to get a larger, much more expensive scanner that can scan areas up to 11 × 17 inches. If you already have a "super-duper," high-resolution video camera for pencil testing, however, you can use that to capture your final line images. (But this does have to be a high-level professional camera with an exception lens to make this really workable.)

As previously mentioned, animation software will make digitally coloring your scanned images very easy. The software should also enable you to composite and final render your scanned files onto any film medium too. The most exciting developing software in recent years is the collection of animation-centric applications that ToonBoom Technology is putting out ... especially "ToonBoom Studio" and "Animate" for the desktop-based more serious animator, down to the fabulous, fun program for beginners of ages 5–50, "Flip Boom". With the company's recent acquisition of the pioneering "Animo" company, and their total dedication to the 2D-animated art-form, there are clearly even greater things to come from ToonBoom in the future! (Watch this space … http://www.toonboom.com).

Audio Requirements

Sound can be a huge factor in an animated production, but the equipment you need for it should be kept to a minimum, as it often can be both complicated and expensive to acquire. When filmmaking, it is always best to record your soundtrack elements professionally—that is, if you want the film to look professional. I would not recommend, however, buying professional equipment to do this because it will be a huge expense and something that you will rarely use. Consequently, if you can beg, borrow, or steal (not literally!) the services of a professional studio for your recorded tracks, you will be in better financial shape. This applies to both dialog- and music-based tracks. If you are using dialog in your work, you will definitely need some kind of sound breakdown technology. A *sound breakdown* is where you take your final audio track and break down all the phonetic sounds it contains on a frame-by-frame basis. Some of the software previously mentioned does this, but I have always found the standalone Magpie program, produced by Third Wish Software (*www.thirdwishsoftware.com*), to be my long-term favorite.

With Magpie, you can import the soundtrack and then manually (or automatically) analyze its sounds frame by frame, checking visually as you go along. You can also import your own lip-sync (or phoneme) mouth sets, so you can actually watch the mouth moving as you play back your sound breakdown attempts. Finally, you will ultimately need to mix (balance) your various audio tracks (i.e., dialog, music, sound effects, etc.) onto one master audio track. Software such as Adobe's Premiere enables you to do this to some degree, as do other animation-targeted software designed for this purpose. (But always check the specs of any software before you buy it, to see if it has all the specific elements you require.) Audio-specific software, such as Sony's Sound Forge or Adobe's Audition, will also allow you to do this, but again this is an added expense that most animators will not need to take on. (Remember, too, that official full-time students or teachers at approved institutions can obtain software at significantly large discounts through online stores such as *www.academicsuperstor.com*, *www.journeyed.com*, and *www.campustech.com*.)

Three-Dimensional Equipment

Pretty much everyone has access to a good computer these days, but you should be aware that the programs you'll need for 3D animation will need a significant amount of RAM storage and a large hard drive to contain the inevitably large files that animation movie files require. Most software packages will reveal the minimum requirements, including a fast-operating motherboard for faster speed rendering. Many very ambitious animated filmmakers might want to hook up several computers to create a "render farm," which will enable them to access a great deal of rendering power if time becomes an issue.

Three-Dimensional Software

Much to the annoyance of large companies such as Softimage, effectively the "big two" software titles of 3D animation are Maya and 3DMax. In the past, it was said that 3DMax dominated the games industry and Maya dominated the film industry. Now both brands are actually owned by Autodesk (*www.usa.autodesk.com*), and the gaps between them are beginning to narrow. I am advised by many working professional 3D animators and educators that Maya tends to be the preferred software of animators, whereas 3DMax is the preferred modeling platform. However, as I say, the gap is closing, both in capability and application, and in time, we will probably see this balance change further. Raw beginners with a limited purchasing power, however, should seriously look at Animation Master (*www.hash.com*) as a software to begin with. It is a highly impressive starter program that costs only a few hundred dollars (as opposed to professional-level software that costs many times that). I have seen some amazing work created on Animation Master and the owner, Martin Hash, of Hash Inc., speaks with the soul of an animator. Consequently, I am more than happy to support their commitment and their superb program with this free endorsement.

Let the Fun Begin!

Now that we've established what you need to start to learn animation, let's now start the adventure of what needs to be learnt....

Acknowledgments

I cannot express enough the indebtedness I have toward all who have supported me in my obsessive mission to bring sound animation knowledge to all who seek it. In more recent times, I thank Claude Comair for having the vision and selfless commitment of creating something as unique and wonderful as the DigiPen Institute of Technology, as well as being able to use the DigiPen student art in this book. Also, to Raymond Yan for making my journey at DigiPen so pleasantly inspirational. I thank, too, the faculty of DigiPen for their support, ideas, and inspiration—each one of them is an amazing artist in his or her own right and teachers par excellence, who somehow teach me something new and important each and every day.

I thank friends and family, near and far, who have tolerated my passive-obsessiveness, and especially Ken Rowe for being a stalwart friend and colleague, who has helped me keep the flames of my Animaticus Foundation and 2D Or Not 2D Animation Festival dreams alive. I sincerely thank, too, all those kind and generous folks at Focal Press, who for some reason or other seem keen to publish my ramblings and who have helped focus the diffuse and vague into the tangible.

And finally, with all my heart, I thank you dear Saille, for you have somehow managed to endure all of this without a single complaint! Even though I have driven myself to exhaustion and isolation in pursuit of everything at times, you still manage to give reason for my smiles and keep my sagging spirits alive. Thank you, dear Saille. Even when I have been mentally and physically lost through the distractions and challenges of creating this book, you have kept me going through your unconditional love and understanding. Truly, without you, none of this could have ever happened!

PART 1

How to Be an Animator

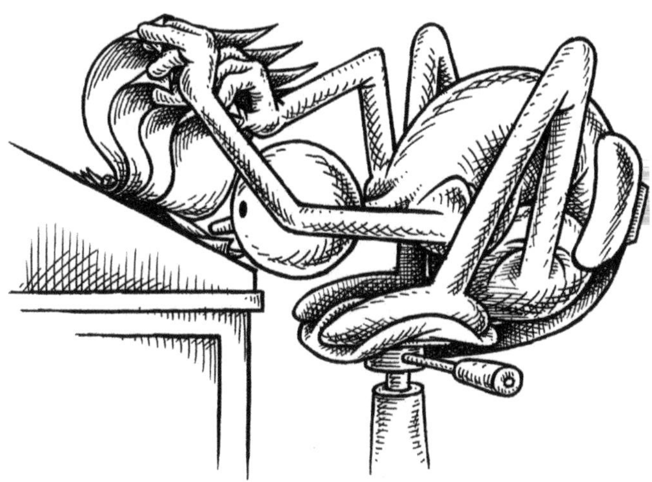

10-Step Foundation Course

Through this 10-step foundation program you will learn the essential core principles of movement that will be the foundation of all your future work in animation, whether that animation is two dimensional (2D), three dimensional (3D), professional, enthusiastic independent filmmaker, or otherwise. As with a regular school curriculum I have broken down the key principles into 10 clearly definable master-class lessons, MC 1–MC 10. It is very important, however, that you don't jump the sequence in any way. Start with MC 1 and don't begin any other exercises until you have mastered that one first.

Note

If you want further one-on-one feedback on anything you are doing by the author, please read Appendix 2.

Either way, if you follow the lectures, guidelines, and assignments as indicated, you should find the process of learning to be an animator easier and more comprehensive.

Animation Basics

Class objective: To learn the underlying principles and disciplines of animation technique.
Equipment required: Lightbox, pencil, and paper.

Key, Breakdown, and In-Between Positions

All animation can be broken down into definable stages. In general terms, these stages are *key positions*, *breakdown* or *passing positions*, and *in-between positions*. Key positions are effectively the major positions in an action where that action ceases or changes direction in some way. The two key positions for walking, for example, will be the full-stride positions—one with the right leg forward and the other with the left leg forward.

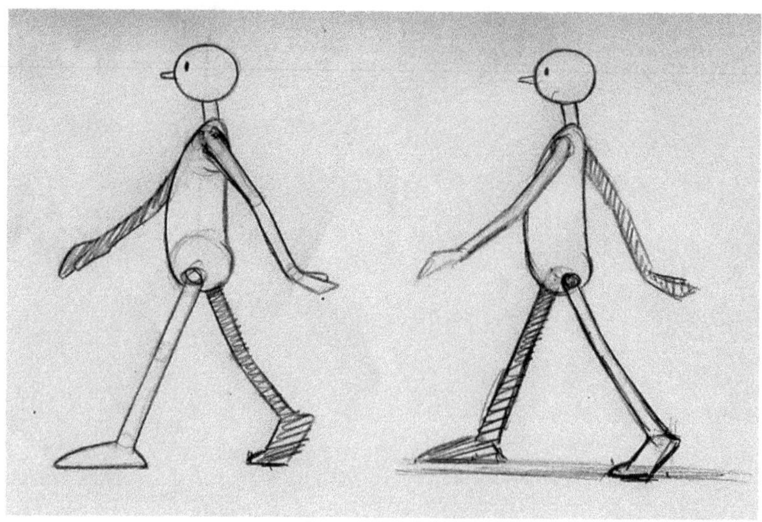

The two key positions for walking—left leg/right arm forward and right leg/left arm forward.

A better example might be a swinging pendulum, where one key position is the highest point of one side of the swing and the other key position is the opposite high position.

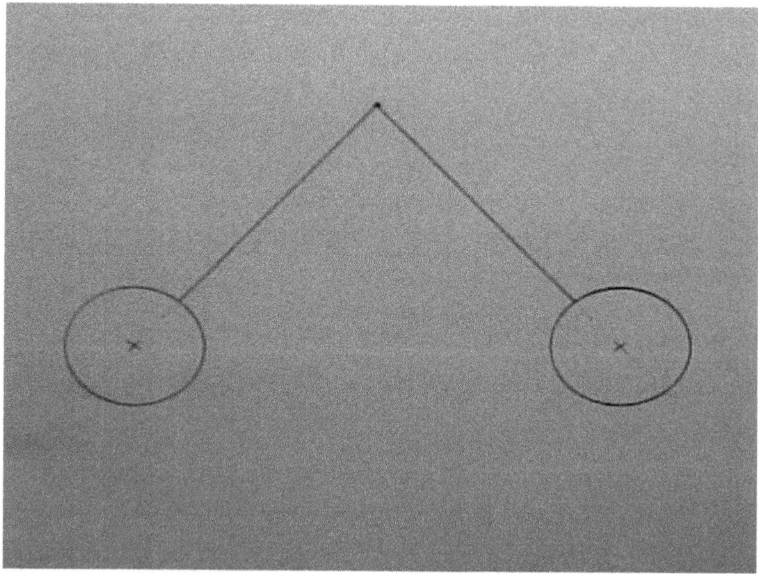

The two key positions for a pendulum— drawings "1" and "17"—extreme swing to the left and an extreme swing to the right.

The breakdown position is the position precisely midway between the two key positions. In the case of the pendulum, it is the perfectly vertical position in the middle of the swing.

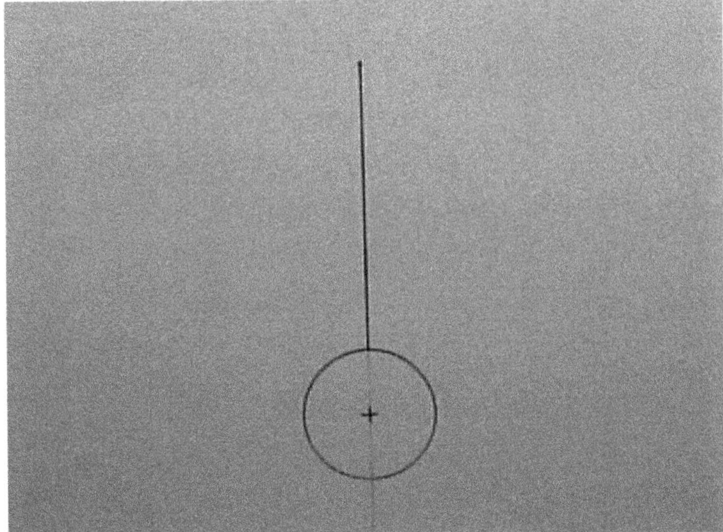

Drawing 9 shows the breakdown position.

Finally, the in-betweens are those secondary positions that fall between the key positions and the breakdown position.

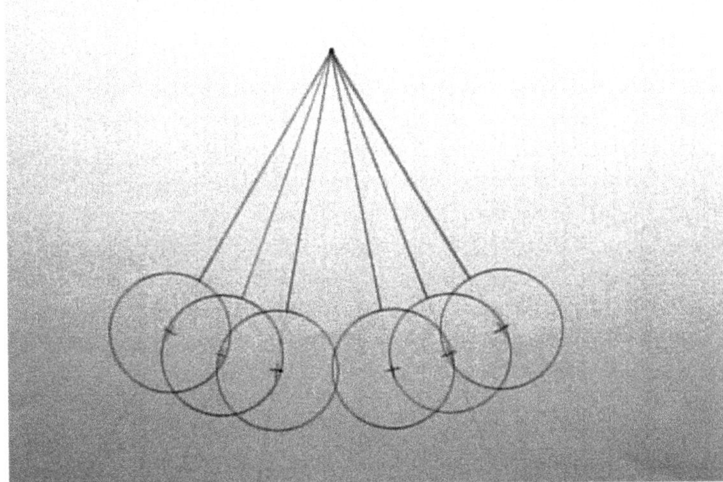

The two sets of in-betweens—three from drawing 1 to drawing 9 and three from drawing 9 to 17.

In the case of the pendulum, we will have two key positions, one in-between position, and three in-between positions on either side, giving us nine drawings (or positions) in total for one swing.

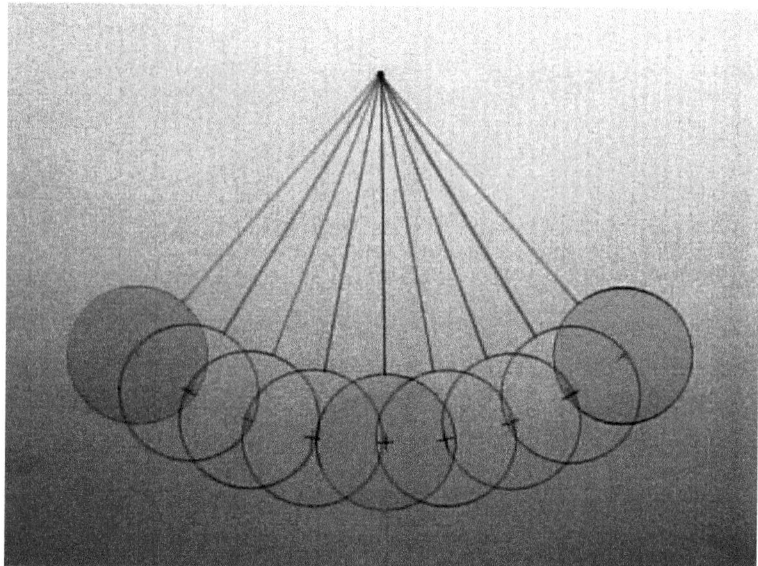

The full set of drawings for the pendulum swing, including the key and breakdown positions, which are shaded.

Creating Key Positions

With the understanding that we need key, breakdown, and in-between positions to create a sequence of animation, we should now look at the process of *in-betweening*, which applies as much to the breakdown drawing as it does to the in-betweens. Let us return to our swinging pendulum and consider the way to approach it. First, using a fresh sheet of animation paper, select a fulcrum (or point) from which the pendulum will swing. The best location to place this will be along the central/vertical line of the field guide, which can be placed beneath the paper with the lightbox on. Put a single dot somewhere along this line, which will represent the point from which the pendulum will swing.

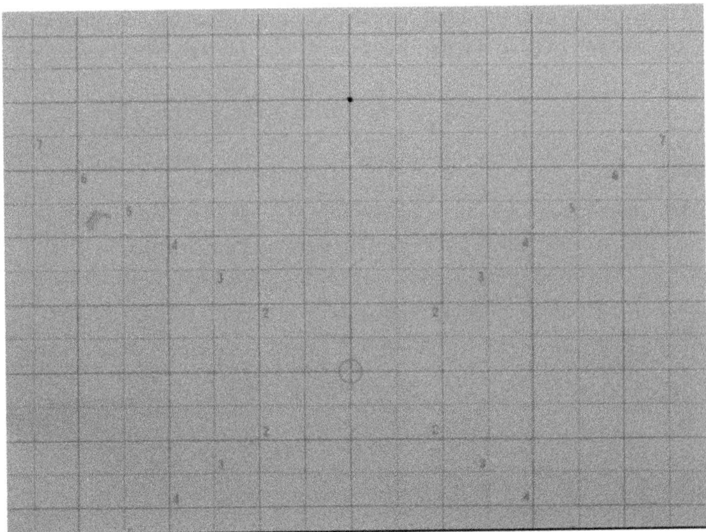

The pendulum's pivot point located on a gridded graticule.

Remember, this point needs to be in a position that allows the pendulum to swing fully left and right and still fit into the field area when it is in the vertical "passing" position.

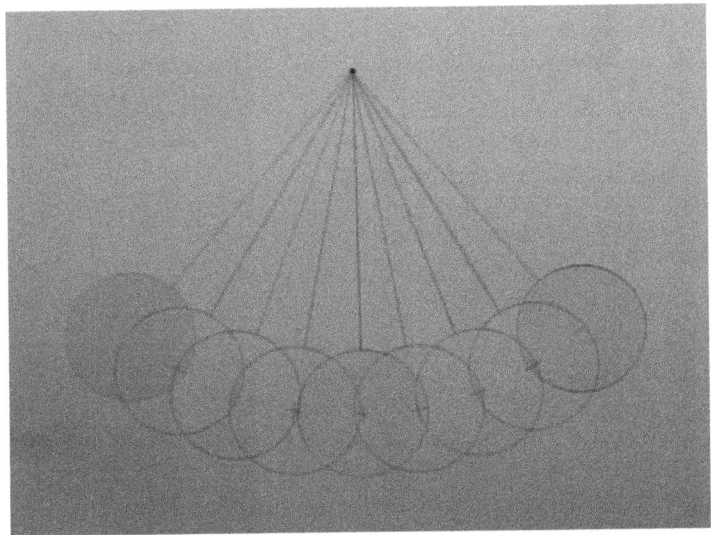

The entire swing, showing that the pendulum safely fits into the entire required screen area.

Now take a piece of paper, lay it over the top, and using the pivotal point on the lower sheet, draw in the pendulum with its maximum swing to the left (west).

Note

When dealing with directions on the screen or on a field guide, left is described as west, up as north, right as east, and down as south. The middle of the field guide is known as center. If you are using a 10 field guide, it is termed a 10 field center, a 12 field guide is a 12 field center, and a 16 field guide is a 16 field center.

Drawing 1 is the left key drawing.

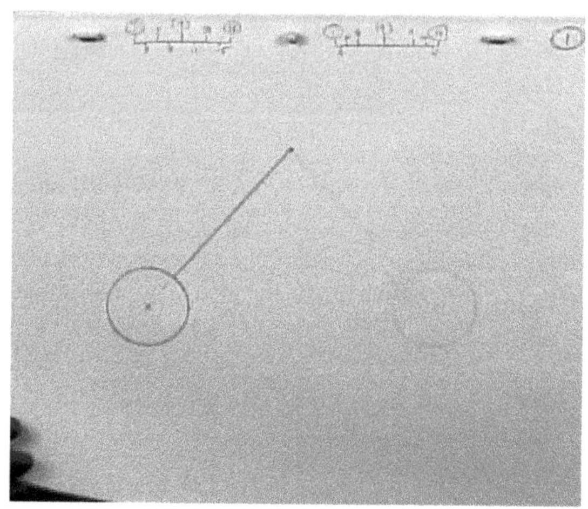

A standard 12 field guide for top pegs animation.

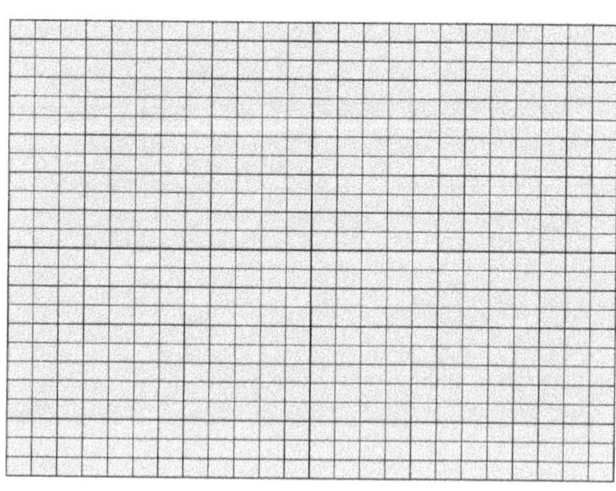

With the key drawing of the westward swing of the pendulum complete, it is necessary to complete the right swing. A good tip here is to place a clean sheet of paper over the previous two, trace the pivotal point as before, and then roughly trace the eastward swing angle of the pendulum to get its maximum swing in the other direction.

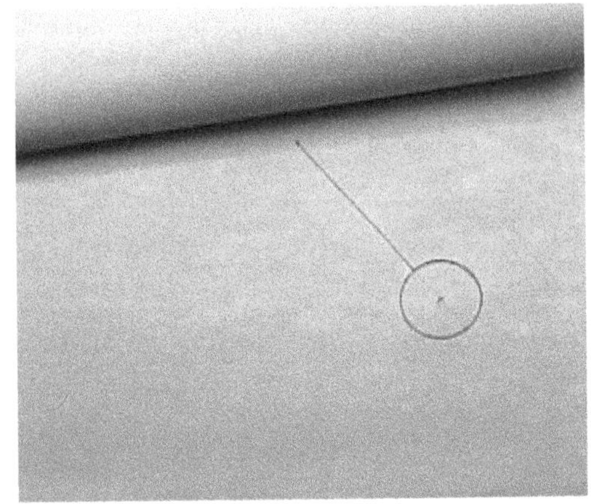

Drawing 17 shows the right pendulum key drawing.

Now take all the sheets of animation paper off the pegs and just work with the first key sheet and the new one you are attempting to create. With the lightbox on, put the first key sheet down and then lay the second (newer) key sheet over it, lining up the pivotal points of both and the line of the pendulum previously lightly sketched in. Now you can trace the new pendulum from the old one, guaranteeing that the length of the pendulum is the same length and size on both keys.

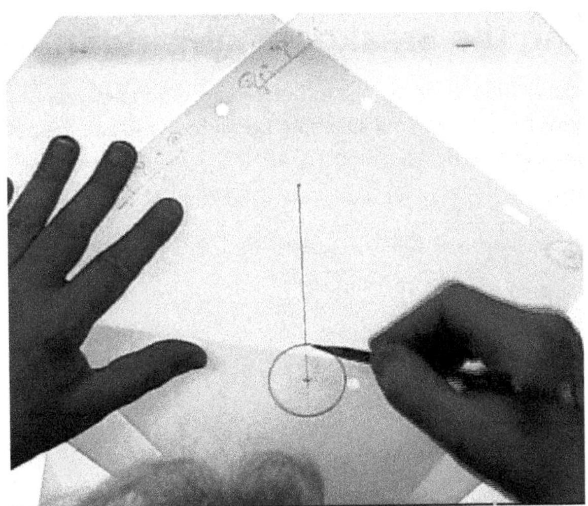

Tracing the second key drawing.

Note

The entire sequence that follows the key creation is demonstrated on the accompanying DVD in the Introduction to In-Betweening section.

Now put both keys together on the pegs and you will see that you have successfully completed the two keys of the action—the furthermost key position swings to the left (west) and the furthermost key position swings to the right (east).

Drawings 1 and 17 show the two extremes of the pendulum swing movement.

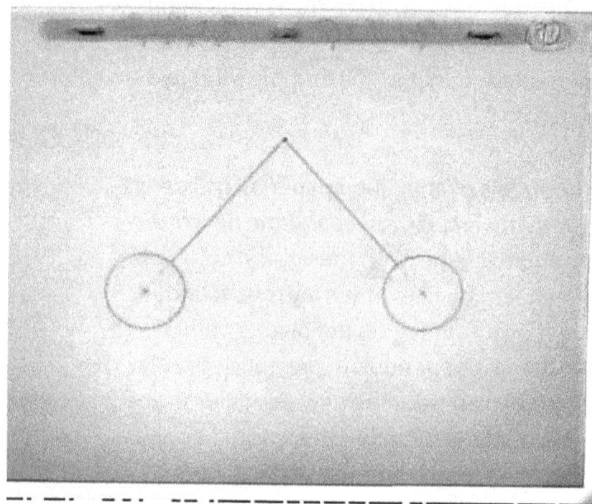

Creating the Breakdown Position

The breakdown position is the first in-between position between two key positions. Consequently, in our swinging pendulum it will be the pendulum seen in a perfectly vertical position.

The breakdown position is the position that is midway (and vertical) between the two key positions.

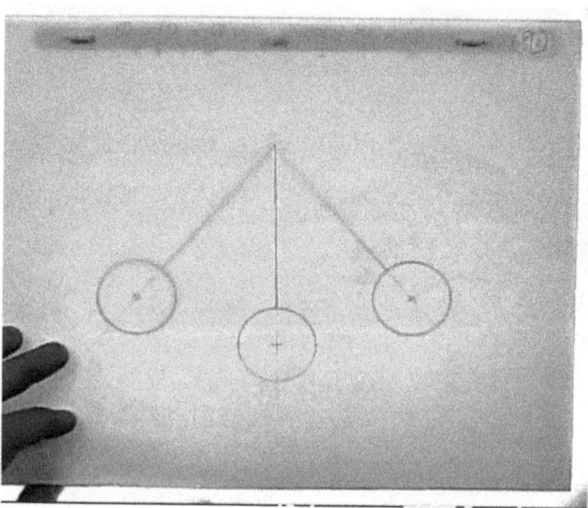

To achieve the breakdown position, we almost copy the same process as for the key positions. With the two key positions on the pegs, place a new sheet of animation paper over them and trace the pivotal point. With a ruler, you can lightly draw in a vertical line traveling down (south) from the point.

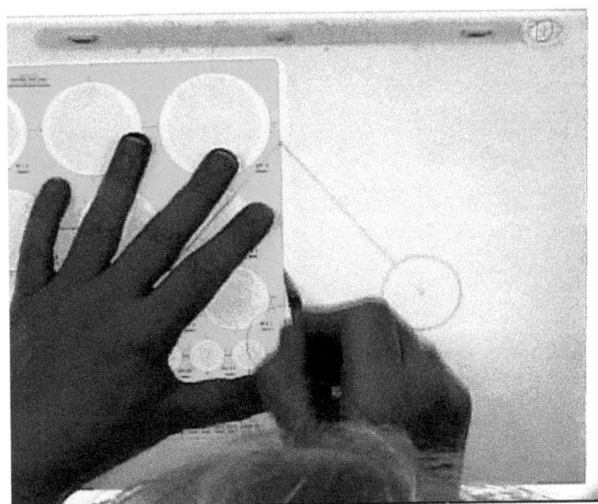

Drawing the vertical shaft of the pendulum. Normally I would use a ruler to do this, but as the circle guide is perfect for drawing the circular pendulum's head, it can be used for a dual purpose in this particular instance!

Now take all the sheets of paper off the pegs and line up the two key drawings over the lightbox with it switched on. Now lay the third (breakdown) drawing sheet over them, lining it up with the pivotal points and line of the arm emanating from them. Now you can trace the breakdown drawing, making sure that you accurately position the line of the arm and the volume of the ball at the end. This process is called *superimposition*, which we'll discuss later.

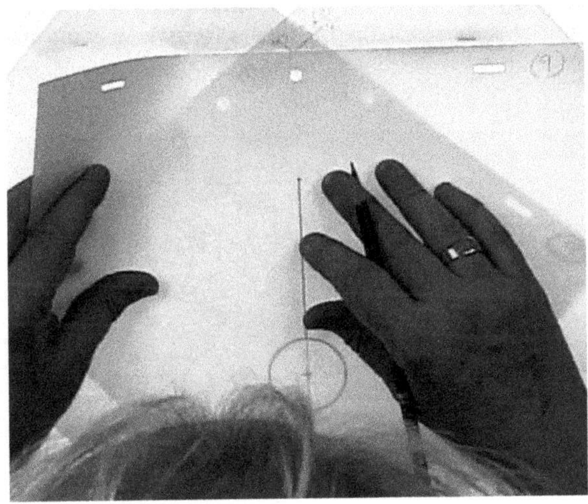

Superimposing is the most valuable skill you can learn for creating accurate in-betweens!

Put the drawings back on the pegs in the order of the first key position, the breakdown position, then the second key position, and roll them backward and forward.

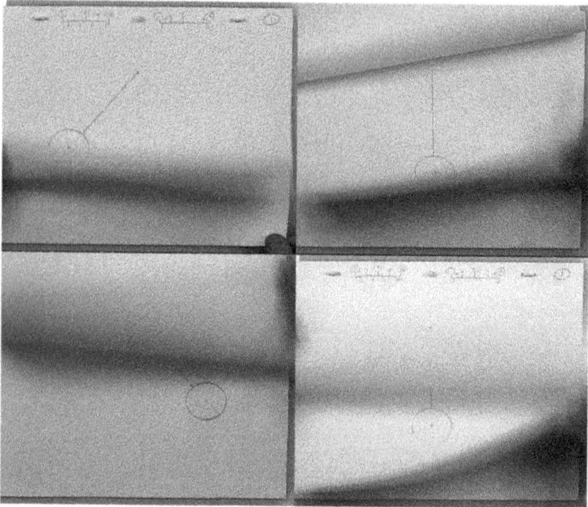

By flipping (or rolling) the drawings, one after the other, you will get a very clear idea of how well your animation is working.

Rolling is a process of placing your fingers between the drawings and rolling them in order forward and backward so that you see each drawing one after the other in sequence. This should give you a very rough sense of the pendulum swinging from one side to the other, although this will be very crude and broad at this stage. However, to make it smoother we will need to add in more in-between drawings. To prepare for this, let us number the drawings 1 (first key drawing), 9 (breakdown drawing), and 17 (second key drawing.)

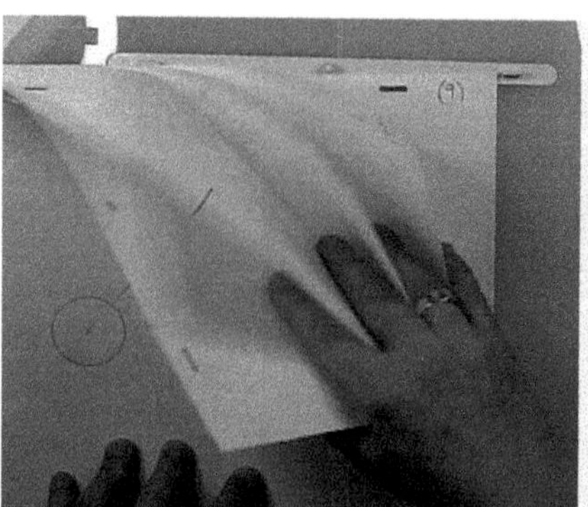

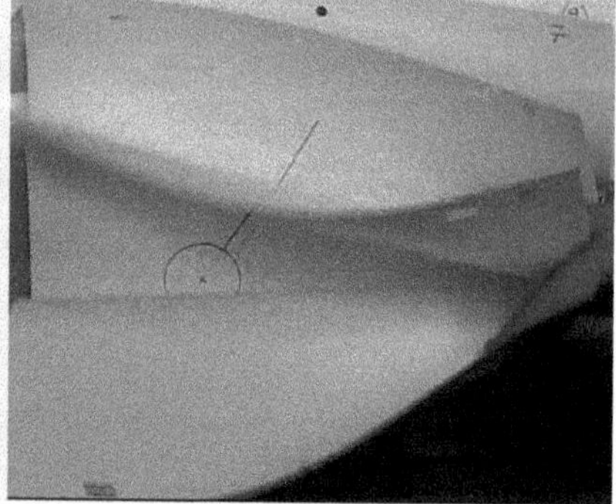

The technique for hand placement and flipping for bottom pegs animation.

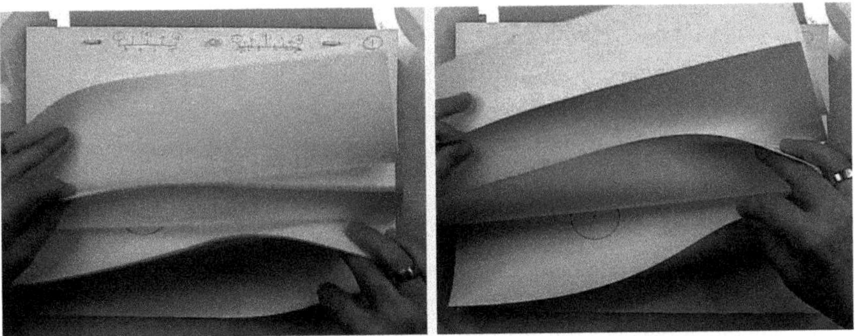

The technique for hand placement and flipping for top pegs animation.

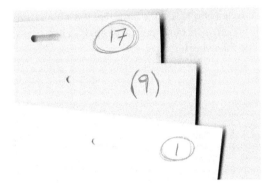

I use top pegs when animating, so I always number my drawings in the top-right corner of each sheet of animation paper.

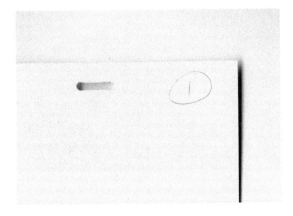

Always circle key drawing numbers and put parenthesis around breakdown drawing numbers.

Important!

Please get into the habit of putting a circle around every key drawing number and a parenthesis around every breakdown drawing number. In-between drawing numbers are written with nothing around them.

I'll explain the numbering choices soon, but suffice it to say you can number the drawings anything you like in practice, as long as you leave enough spare numbers between the first key drawing and the breakdown drawing, and then the breakdown drawing and the second key drawing, so that three in-betweens can go between each key drawing.

Now, with our drawings numbered correctly we need to create an action chart from drawing 1 to drawing 17. On the basis that the in-between movement from key to key is even in its movement, we can draw a chart on the first key that looks like the following figure.

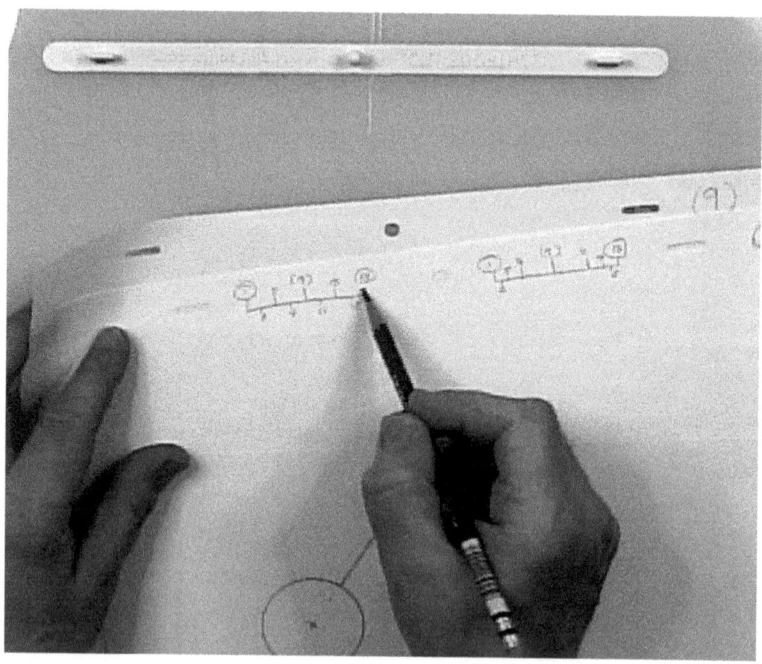

Being a top pegs animator, I always write my chart clearly between the peg holes at the top of my lowest-numbered key animation drawing. The chart indicates just how many in-betweens are needed and how they will be spaced between this first and the next key drawing.

Top Pegs/Bottom Pegs

You will see that I put my numbers to the right of the pegs and the chart between the peg holes at the top of the sheet. This is because I am a top pegs animator.

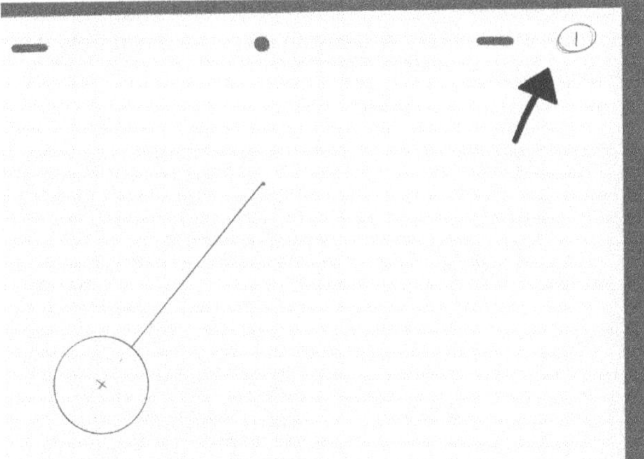

With top pegs animation the drawing number is always found in the top-right corner.

Bottom pegs animators prefer to have their peg holes at the bottom of the sheet. In all honesty, most animators these days tend to use bottom pegs, but I argue extensively in my book *Pencils to Pixels* (pp. 361–365) why I believe top pegs are preferable. However, if you choose to use bottom pegs for your animation, you should place the drawing numbers to the right of the bottom peg holes and charts between the peg holes.

Bottom pegs animators place the drawing number in the bottom-right corner.

Charting Explained

Now that you have the first chart drawn, let's talk about what it represents. Taking the numbers from the first key drawing (1) and the breakdown drawing (9), you will see the numbers 3, 5, and 7 evenly spaced between them. This shows the way that you need to draw the in-betweens. Similarly, the numbers from the breakdown drawing (9) to the second key drawing (17) are also equally spaced.

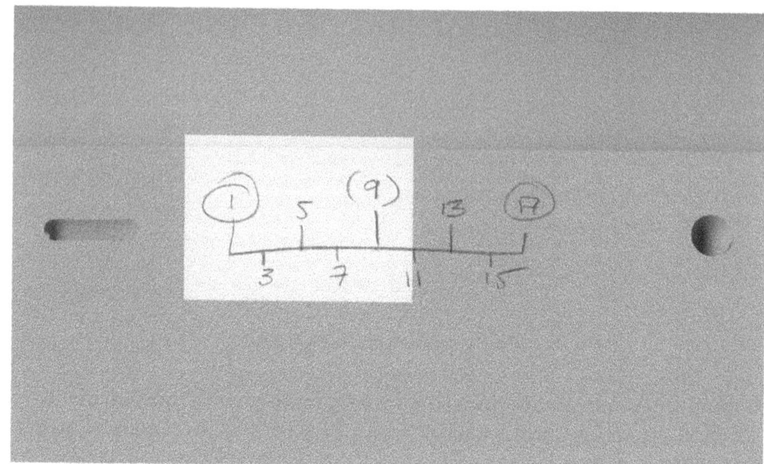

This clearly indicates that the drawings from 1 to 9 need to have *even* in-betweens.

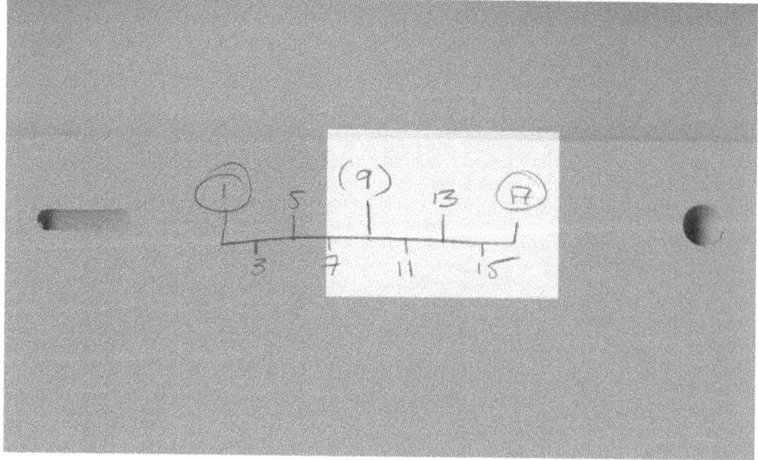

The same evenly spaced in-betweens are required between drawings 9 and 17.

Now let's get down to creating the in-between drawings that are indicated on the chart.

In-Betweening

Looking at the first half of the chart (i.e., 1–9), we can see that drawing 5 is exactly in the middle. This means that we have to create this in-between first. So, place only drawings 1 and 9 on the pegs with the lightbox on, then place a new sheet of paper on the pegs, and trace both the pivotal position and lightly draw in a straight line that dissects the two arm lines of the previous drawings.

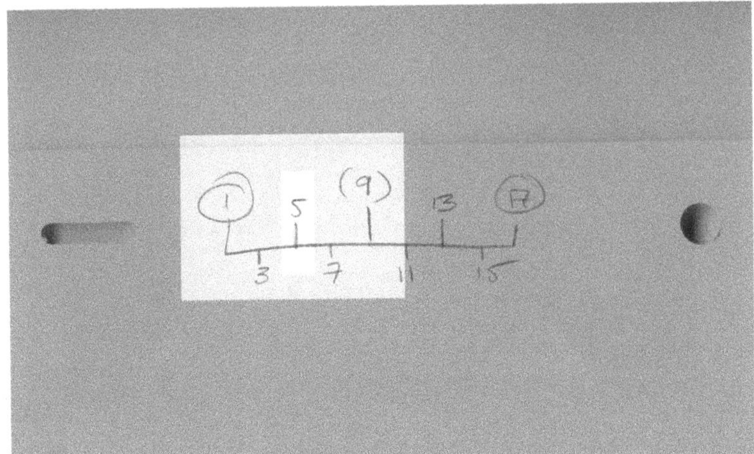

The first in-between drawing to tackle in this case is drawing 5.

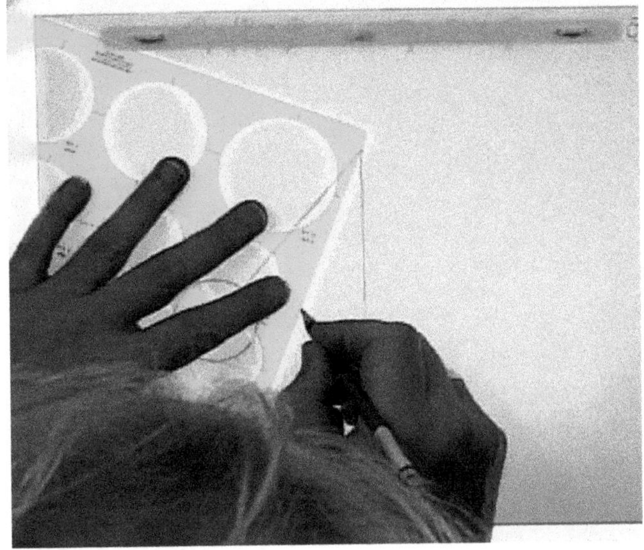

Once you have ascertained the midposition for the shaft of the pendulum, you should draw a light, straight line from the pivot point to use as a superimposition guide.

Now, as before, superimpose all three sheets of paper over one another, making sure the pivotal points and the arm lines are in perfect alignment before tracing the full pendulum onto the new in-between drawing sheet (5).

It is important to have accurate guidelines when superimposing drawings, as well as to make sure that you line up everything very carefully. Make sure that the paper doesn't slip out of position as you're working too!

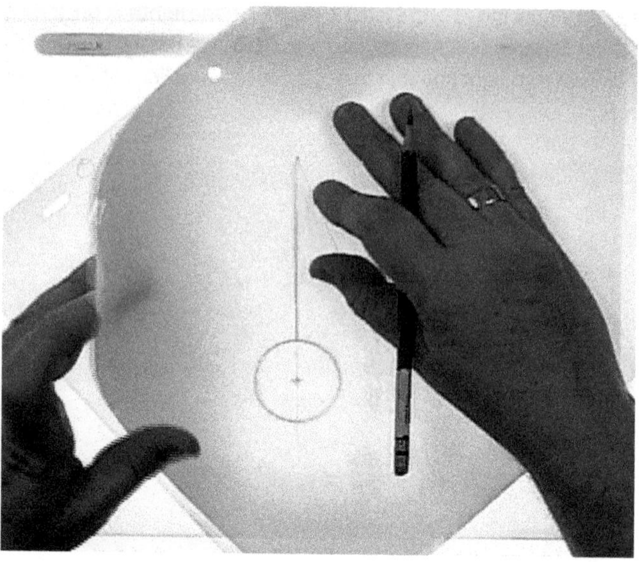

Next, put all these three sheets back onto the pegs in their numerical order, with the lowest number on the bottom, and flip them backward and forward as before.

Teach yourself the art of good flipping (rolling)—it will reward you handsomely as you get further and further into the principles of animation!

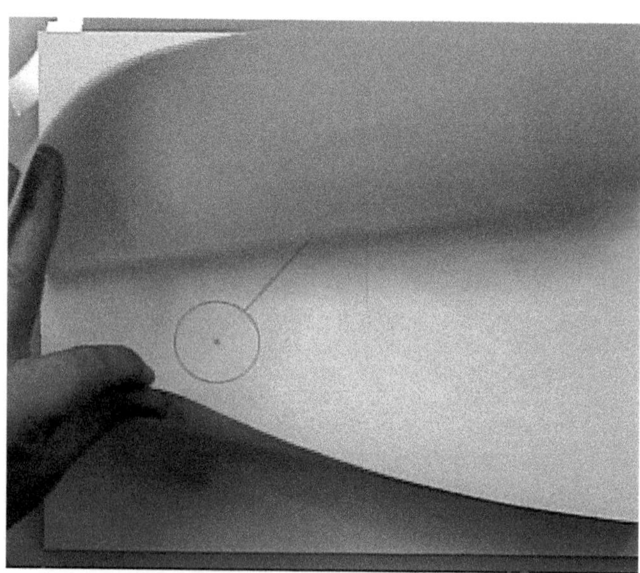

Now you will see that the pendulum swings to the halfway (breakdown) position and back more evenly and clearly. If this works fine, you now need to put in the remaining in-between drawings using the same technique. However, to create in-between 3, you need to accurately place it midway between drawings 1 and 5; then, to create in-between 7, you need to accurately place it between drawings 5 and 9.

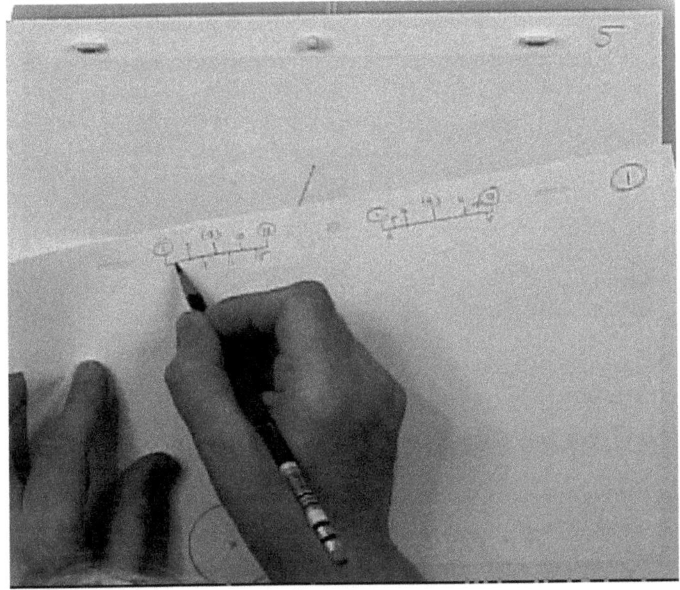

Always refer to the chart before you start each in-between, and make sure you *correctly* number the drawing before you start!

Place all five of these drawings back onto the pegs and roll them in order, with the lowest-number drawing on the bottom and the highest-number drawing on the top. This should give you a much smoother, slower action to the midway point on the pendulum swing.

If this works fine (which it should if you have followed these instructions carefully), you can now do in-between drawings 11–15. This time, however, you have to produce drawing 13 first, accurately drawing it between drawings 9 and 17, followed by in-between drawing 11 between drawings 9 and 13, and then in-between drawing 17 between drawings 13 and 19. Remember to make sure that all the pivotal points are precisely on the same spot each time, and that all the arms of the pendulum are exactly in the middle of the two containing drawings around the pivotal point when you create it. If you don't, the pivotal point of the pendulum will wriggle around, or the swing will not be smooth and even.

Always check the drawings on the pegs when you've completed each set of in-betweens, just in case there is something out of place or poorly drawn.

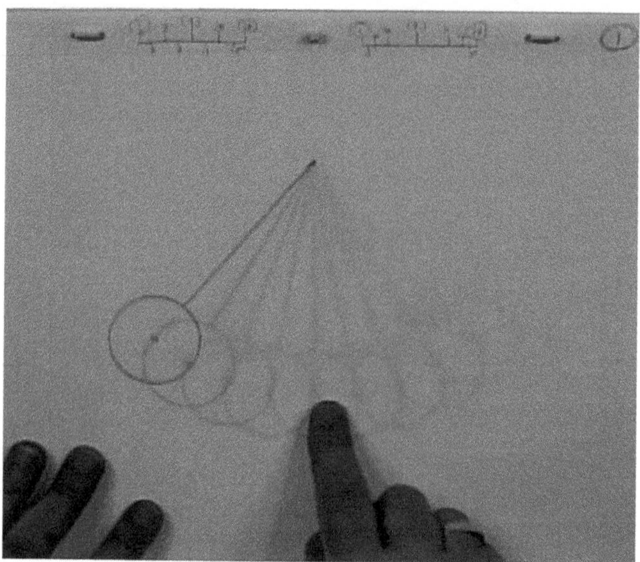

Flipping as Opposed to Rolling

Now you should have more drawings in the sequence than you have fingers to roll them. So, next you need to learn how to "flip" the drawings in order so that you can see them move. As before, place the drawings together in reverse order, the lowest number on the bottom and the highest number on the top. Now, fan them a little so that the lower drawings are more inward at the bottom and the uppermost drawings are more forward. Grip the top of the paper pile firmly with one hand and then "flip" them from the bottom up, as if you are flipping through the pages of a book. You should see the pendulum swing from one side to another more clearly and smoothly.

Repeat the process several times and get used to seeing movement in this way. Flipping is a major tool in testing and correcting your animation, so a skill in this department goes hand in hand with being a good animator.

Arcs and Paths of Action

Now that you have seen the pendulum successfully swing from side to side, let us cover a very important thing that you must remember when animating any action. Nothing in life moves in a perfectly straight line, unless of course it is a machine that is made up of fixed-length elements. Everything moves in curves or arcs, whether it is a leaf falling from a tree, a ball flying through the air, or the torso and limbs of a walking character.

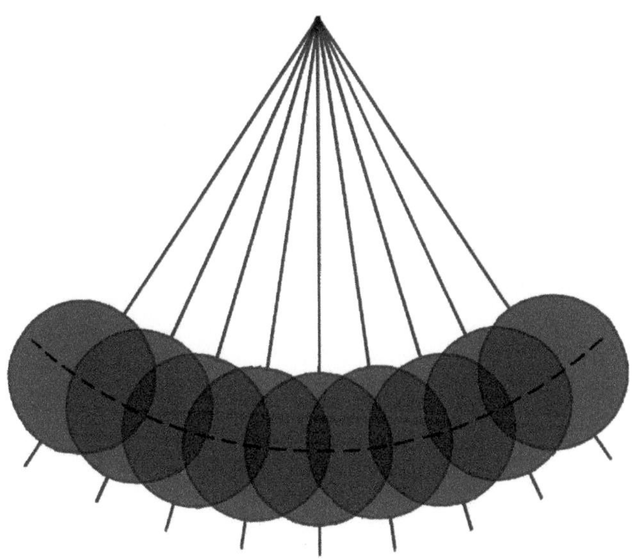

Our completed and colored pendulum swing indicates a clear arc as it moves from one side to the other.

Consequently, you have to remember this whenever you are animating anything. You can see the principle best if you mark the center of the pendulum ball on every one of the drawings, and then on a separate sheet of paper trace them out, one by one. You will end up with a series of positions that are in an arc, which perfectly describes the swing of the pendulum.

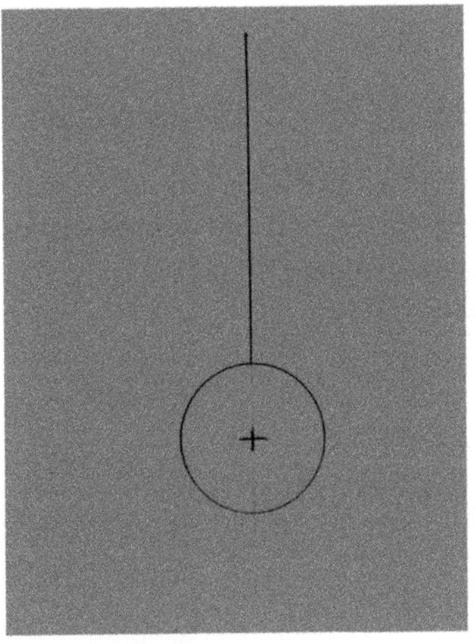

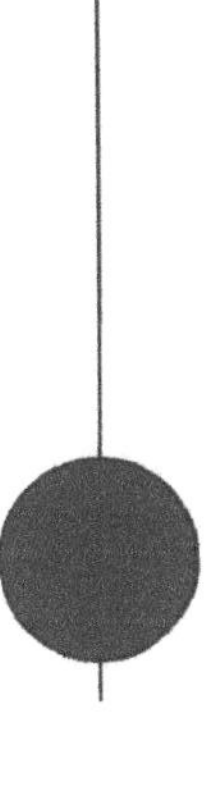

The original animation drawings for the final pendulum frames can have the centers marked to show the arc that the head of the pendulum makes as it swings from side to side.

This arc can also be described as the *path of action* of the swinging pendulum ball, a term that animators use to describe the central, core movement in any animated action figure.

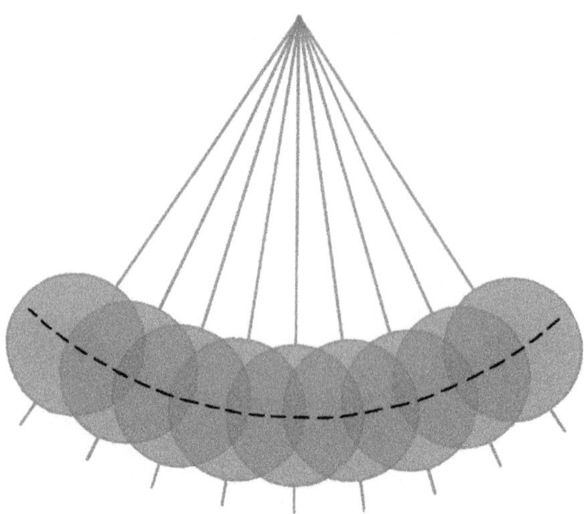

The arc that is described by the center of the pendulum's head as it swings backward and forward.

The path of action or the arc of any movement is something that should never be forgotten by any animator, whether they are creating key poses or simply putting in in-betweens for any extended movement. We will refer to arcs and paths of action as we move through the class curriculum detailed in this book.

Timing and the Spacing of Drawings

It will take students and animation beginners some time to appreciate just how many and how far each charted in-between needs to be. That is where the hard-won experience of a master animator comes in. However, there are a couple of pointers that the learner should know.

More Means Slower

The main thing to remember about all animated action is that the *more* drawings there are, the *slower* the action will appear on the screen when the final action is seen.

It will still be a process of trial and error for beginners to appreciate it, but, by rule of thumb, it should be remembered that if an action needs to be slow, the animator will have to put many more drawings between the key drawings of the action than if the action needs to appear fast. Fewer in-betweens mean a faster action between the key drawings.

Here are silhouettes of all the drawings required for a character walking with a limp. Because the time spent on the strong leg (upper animation) is much slower and longer in screen time than that of the weaker leg (lower animation), there are clearly more drawings required.

Speed Varies in Any Action

The next thing to remember with any action is that its speed is not constant. An arrow fired from a bow will be fast at first but it will slow down as wind resistance works on it. It will also arc upward then downward as the loss of velocity, as well as gravity, exert an effect on it.

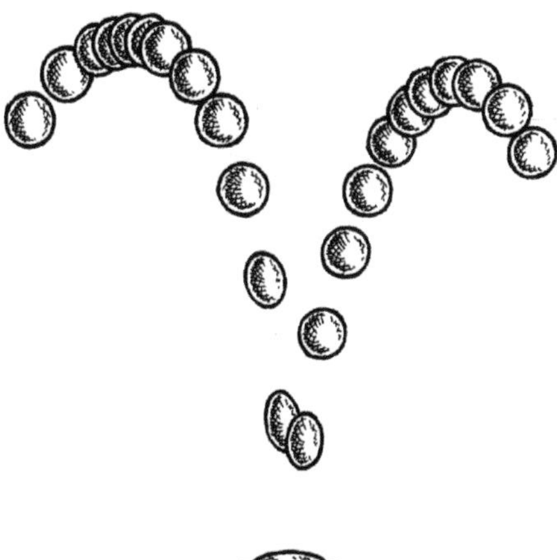

Just like an arrow flying through the air, a bouncing ball will slow down at the top of each bounce apex, meaning that there will have to be more drawings positioned there than elsewhere.

Alternatively, a big heavy train starts slowly at first, increases speed as it builds up momentum, and then slowly decelerates before it comes to its next stop. Consequently, the animator has to take this into consideration when charting out the in-between action from key drawing to key drawing. This brings us to the most valuable technique of all for the positioning of drawings—slowing-in and slowing-out.

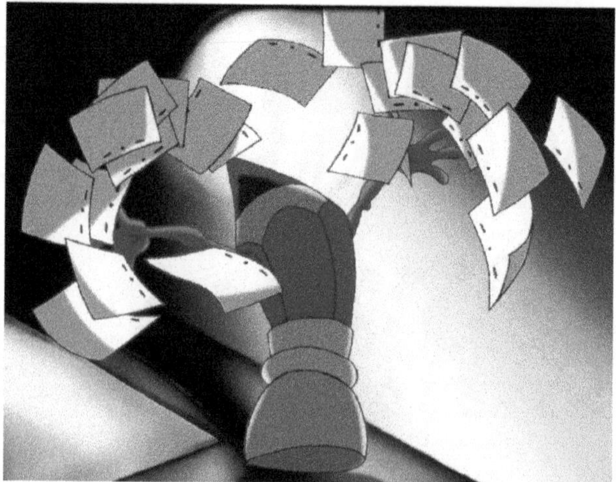

With this animation, I had to add more drawings at the top of the paper drop than at the bottom, meaning that, following the bouncing ball principle, the paper will accelerate as it drops.

Slowing In and Slowing Out

If you really look at a real pendulum action in life, you will note that the speed of the action is never constant. Watch a child on a playground swing and you will notice that as he or she reaches the high spot of the arc—front swing or back swing—there is a definite slowing of movement. Then, as the swing returns from one high point to the next, it will accelerate downward before hitting the low spot and begin to decelerate as it goes up to the next high spot.

You can imagine that to slow the child down at the top part of the swing in each direction there needs to be more drawings closer to the key positions than the breakdown position.

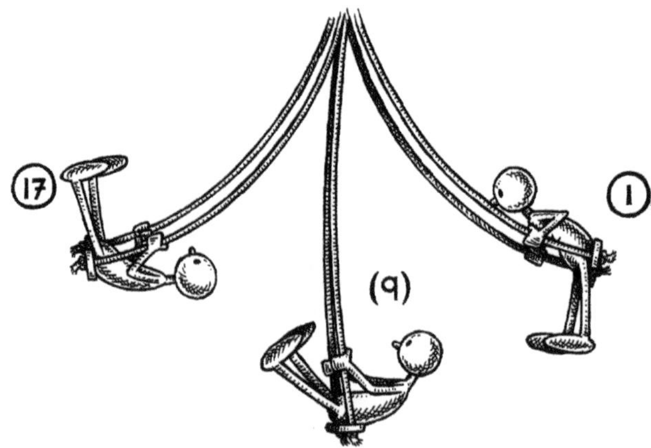

Consequently, the speed of the swinging action is never constant—it is either in a process of speeding up or slowing down. How might we better show this in our previously drawn pendulum sequence? The first thing is to go back and look at our chart positioning.

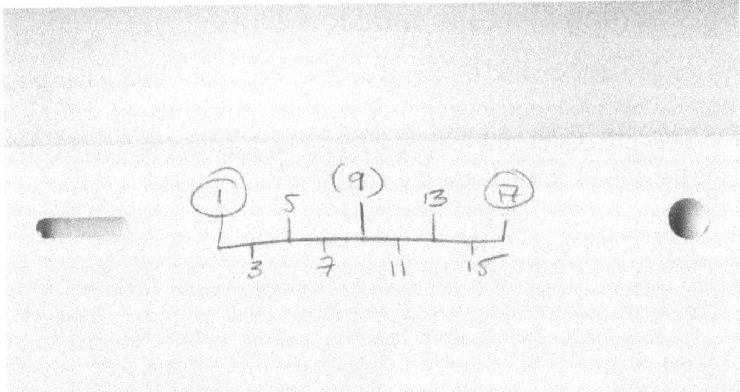

A reminder of what our even positions chart looks like.

On the basis that if we put more drawings in the action it will slow down, and if we take more drawings out the action will speed up, we can rethink the way we chart our in-betweens. As we know, the nearer to the high spots of the pendulum swing (the key positions in our case), the more the swing will decelerate, and then the farther we move away from the high-spot positions, the more it will accelerate. Therefore, if we place more drawings nearer to the key positions and less around the breakdown position, the more we will replicate this slowing-down and speeding-up action.

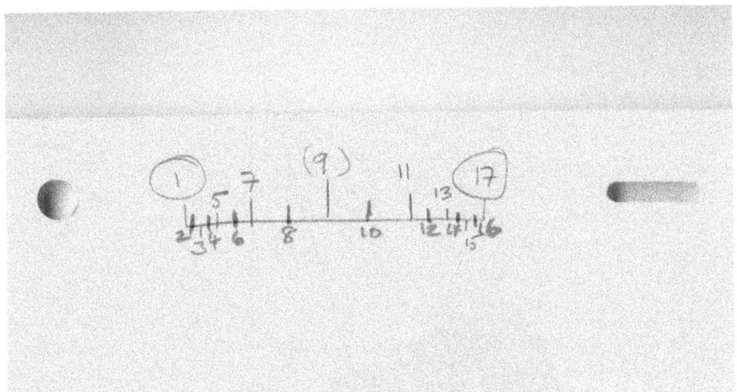

Note the drawing placement differences between this and our even positions chart from earlier. I have also added an indication of the additional in-betweens in red, which when shot on 'ones' will give the entire action a much smoother action.

So, if we rechart our numbers as shown in the figure, we will achieve the desired result. Note that there are now more and closer-positioned drawings to the high points of the swing and less at the low point. On the principle that more means slower and less means faster, we will achieve the acceleration and deceleration that we are looking for. This process of charting is known as slowing-out (accelerating) and slowing-in (decelerating).

In-Betweening Slow-Ins and Slow-Outs

In-betweening slow-ins and slow-outs needs a little more focus when placing and approaching the sequence of in-betweens to be attempted. With our new slow-in/slow-out chart in the following figure, notice that the first in-between drawing between 1 and 9 is now drawing 7.

Clearly, drawing 7 in this slowing-out part of the chart is midway between drawing 1 and drawing 9.

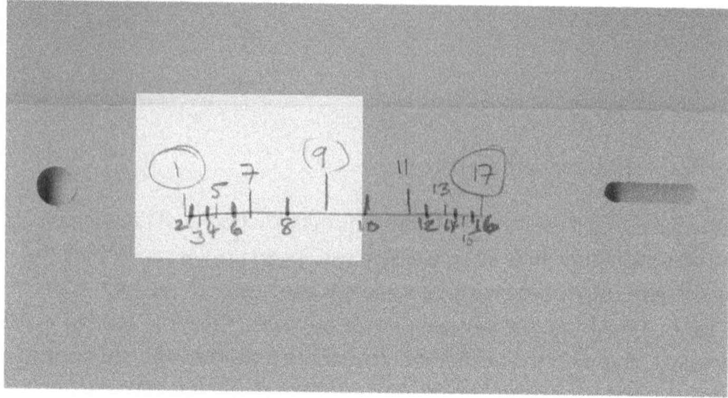

Consequently, this is the first in-between drawing you will need to do when attempting this slowing-out section of the chart.

See how the positions of a pendulum swing with a slowing-out action are closer together at the beginning, then widen as gravity causes the pendulum to accelerate.

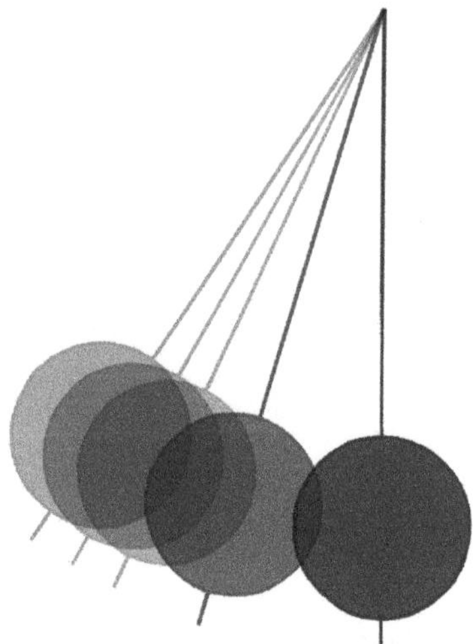

Once drawing 7 is successfully complete, you will see that drawing 5 is the next in-between position, so it should be completed next, positioned between drawings 1 and 7. Finally, with drawing 5 done, drawing 3 has to be completed between 1 and 5.

When approaching the slowing-in part of the chart, from drawing 9 to key drawing 17, you will see that the first drawing to be completed this time is in-between drawing 11. Consequently, drawing 11 is placed accurately between drawings 9 and 17.

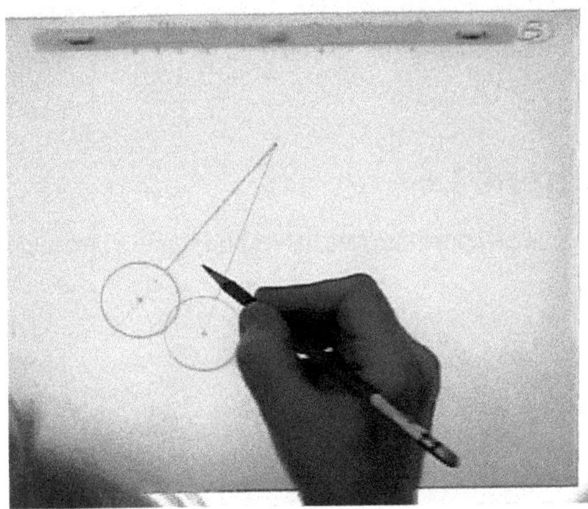

The more slowing-out or slowing-in there is with an action, the more accurately you will need to be when plotting in the guideline positions before superimposition.

After drawing 11 comes in-between drawing 13, which is created by positioning it precisely between drawings 11 and 17. Finally, drawing 15 needs to complete the action by drawing it precisely between drawings 13 and 17. This should give you a complete accelerating/decelerating swing to the pendulum, which you should be able to see by flipping all the drawings as previously described.

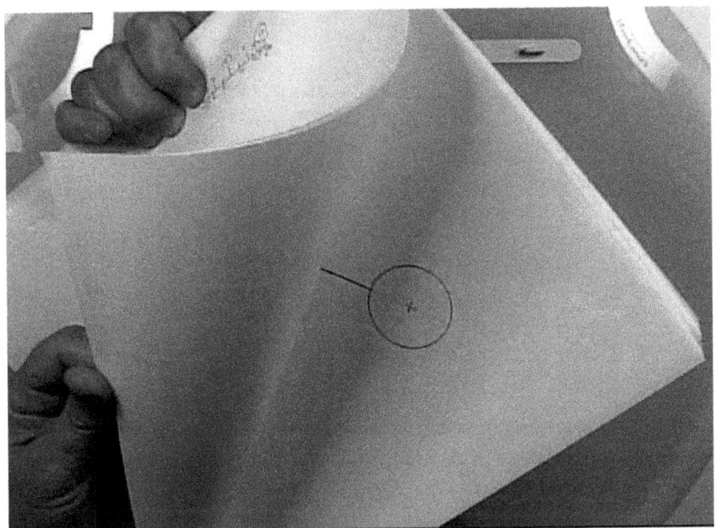

With a good number of finished drawings to work with, it is much easier to flip a long sequence of animation drawings using a handheld flipbook approach.

Suggested Reading

White, T. *The Animator's Workbook*. New York: Watson-Guptill, 1988, pp. 24–34, 38–43 and 112–117.

White, T. *Animation from Pencils to Pixels: Classical Techniques for Digital Animators*. Boston: Focal Press, 2006, pp. 210–226, 332–357 and 360–365.

DVD lecture: "Introduction to Inbetweening".

Assignment 1

Divide the animation paper into two halves and create a pendulum swing on either side.

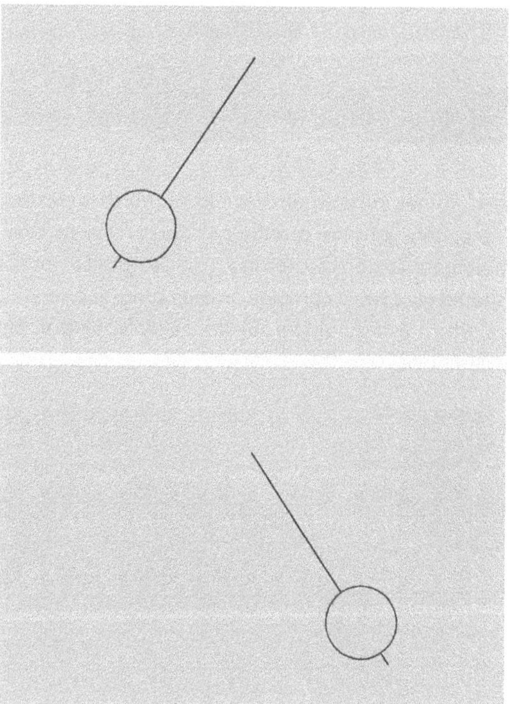

Your two key drawings, 1 and 17, will need to look something like this.

However, you are required to produce two versions of the swing. In version A, use even in-betweens, and in version B, use slowing-in and slowing-out techniques. Note that the key numbers remain the same but the in-between positioning and timing is different in both cases.

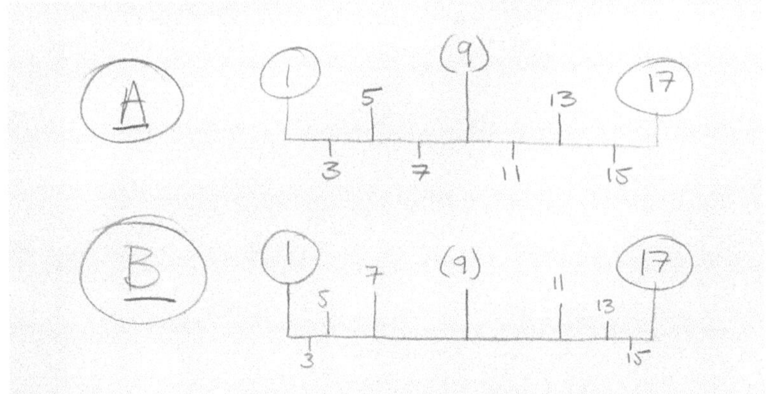

Here are the two different charts that you have to work with for assignments A and B.

When you have completed your assignments, shoot them both as separate pencil tests, repeating the action forward and backward three times without any break. (Shoot your drawings: 01, 03, 05, 07, 09, 11, 13, 15, 17, 15, 13, 11, 09, 07, 05, 03, 01, 03, 05, 07, 09, 11, 13, 15, 17, 15, 13, 11, 09, 07, 05, 03, 01, 03, 05, 07, 09, 11, 13, 15, 17, 15, 13, 11, 09, 07, 05, 03, 01 to create three repeats on each.) Also, shoot one set of each on *two's*, meaning that you hold each drawing for two frames each. Then shoot them both on *one's*, meaning that you shoot each drawing for one frame each. This means that you should ultimately end up with four pencil tests—two repeating for three complete return swings on two's and then two others for three complete return swings on one's.

Film Projection Rates

In general, film is either projected at 24 frames per second (fps) in the cinema or at 30 fps on TV or the Web. (Actually, British [PAL] TV projects film at 25 fps, but that is another story, too long to explain right now—see the *Animation from Pencils to Pixels* book for further clarification!) Therefore, if our pendulum animation is shot on one's in the first test, one swing forward and back will appear half as fast on the screen as the drawings shot on two's. The 25 drawings shot on one's for three swings on the pendulum will last a tiny fraction over one second, whereas if these same drawings are shot on two's, they will appear on the screen for just over two seconds.

The Bouncing Ball

Class objective: To get a sense of spacing, timing, weight, and flexibility in motion.
Equipment required: Lightbox, pencil, and paper.

Now that we have established the principles of key, breakdown, and in-between positions in an action, it is now possible to go further and tackle something a little more advanced. The principle of the bouncing ball has been around since animation began, and it's very tempting to think it cliché to work with it here.

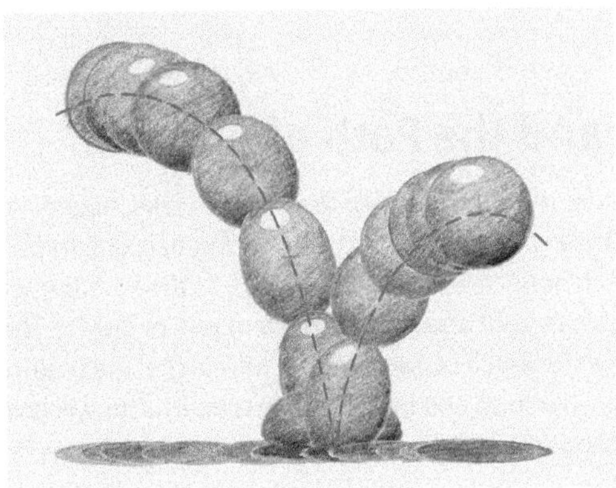

The core frames that comprise a bouncing ball action.

However, there is no better exercise for the beginner to attempt, as it covers all the major principles of animation—namely, the importance of key, breakdown, and in-between positions; as well as arcs, paths of action, slowing-in and slowing-out, weight, gravity, and timing. But, first things first.

Weight, Mass, and Flexibility

Before we can discuss the actual bouncing of the ball, we have to first ascertain the weight and density of the ball to be bounced. For example, a soft, rubber bouncy ball will move in a far different way than a heavy, solid rubber ball. A ping-pong ball will bounce in a far different way than a soccer ball. It is all about weight, mass, and flexibility, and this always has to be borne in mind with any animated object or character, quite aside from the rubber ball challenge. You will find in my other books adequate descriptions of the varying types of bouncing ball effects, so I won't go over them again here. Suffice it to say, let us assume that we are going to work with a standard bouncy, rubber ball, the kind that any kid will kick around in their house or yard.

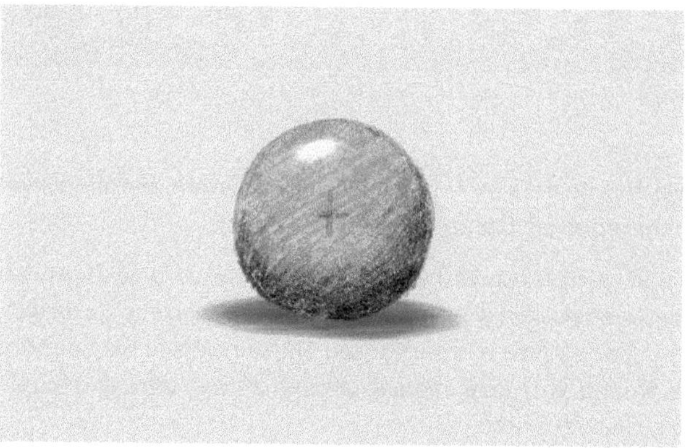

A basic rubber ball.

Gravity and the Path of Action

First let's consider the path of action the ball is to take. Gravity will always exert an effect with all things. With the bouncing ball, gravity will merely ensure that each bounce will get less and less, as the kinetic energy within the ball is unable to fight against the constant pull of gravity. Therefore, as the ball moves forward with a certain amount of velocity, the bounces of that ball will increasingly diminish and be less and less apart. This will give us a path of action for our bounce.

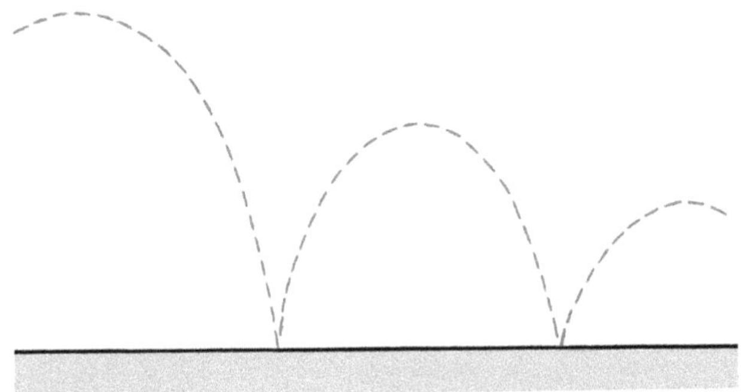

Note that a ball will require increasingly diminishing bounces that become lower and lower before it comes to a halt, possibly preceded by it rolling.

Key Positions

Next we need to establish our key positions along the designated path of action. In the illustration below they are numbers '1', '11', '19', '27' and '31'. With any bouncing action, the main key positions will be at the contact point with the ground and at the apex of the upward arc. However, if we leave our key ball positions in the air and on the ground perfectly round, there would be no life or rubbery feel to the ball—it would merely appear like a cut-out shape moving up and down across the screen, with no life at all. Consequently we need to apply the age-old principles of squash and stretch.

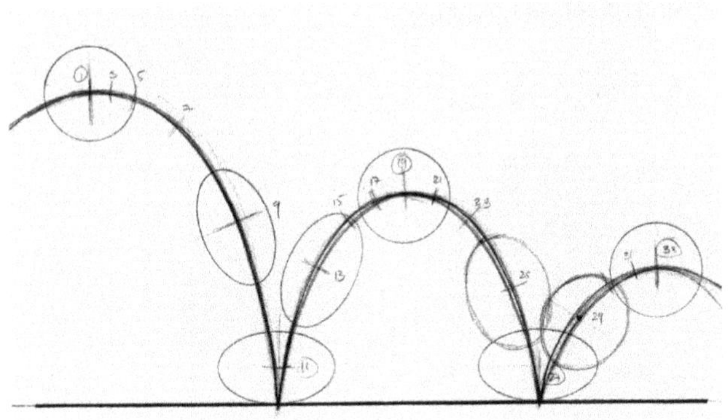

I always like to sketch my key positions first. I may modify them as I begin to animate, but this does at least give me a reliable ground plan to work with. Here I have added the linking positions too, just to indicate the nature of the transitions from one key position to the next.

Squash

Remember that the ball we are dealing with is rubber, and therefore it is subject to shape changes. Rubber is flexible. If the ball were a metal cannonball, it would not be subject to shape shifting and that gives the animator the means to define the nature of the ball's mass. When a flexible, rubber ball hits the solid ground it will distort in shape. In other words, it will "squash." The harder the ground and the faster the velocity the ball contains before it hits the ground will define the amount of squash exerted on it. Therefore, the higher the bounce and the further the ball travels from bounce to bounce, the more the squash distortion will appear. In considering the path of action we have already defined for ourselves, I would suggest the key squash position in the following figure would be reasonable.

This does have sufficient squash to suggest that it is a standard rubber ball. Other balls, such as a soccer ball or a cannonball, would behave differently, of course.

Note, however, that the apex positions of the ball in the figure do not squash, as they are not subject to any contact with a hard surface like the ground, or are even being distorted by velocity.

The beginning and end, up, (north) positions of our bounce.

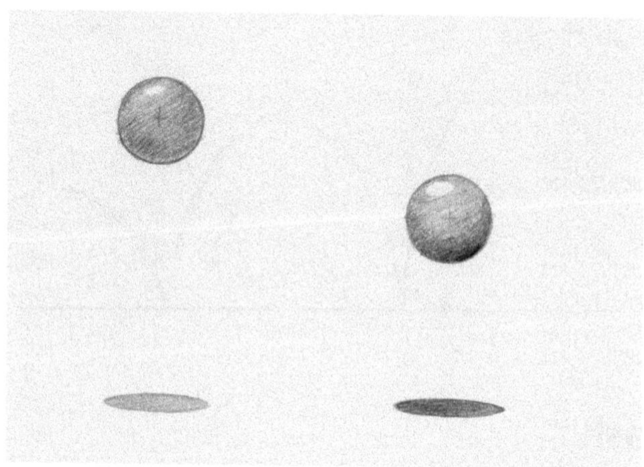

What is meant by this is that at the apex of a bouncing arc the ball is momentarily at a zero point of movement and impact. Here, the ball has slowly ground to a halt, as the kinetic energy from the previous bounce has run out, and yet the forces of gravity have not taken hold quite yet. Consequently, our rubber ball returns to its natural, circular shape. This is not true, however, of its shape on the way up or the way down.

Stretch

If you freeze a movie sequence of a moving shape you will notice that it will actually appear as a blur. This is because at the regular film speed of 24 fps the shutter is not fast enough to capture a sharp image of the moving object, thus the motion blur it presents. In animation, specifically drawn 2D animation, it is not easy to emulate the blur look. Consequently, the animator has to distort, or "stretch," the object to give the illusion of this fast-action blur. This is especially so with the action of our ball when it is on the way up and on the way down.

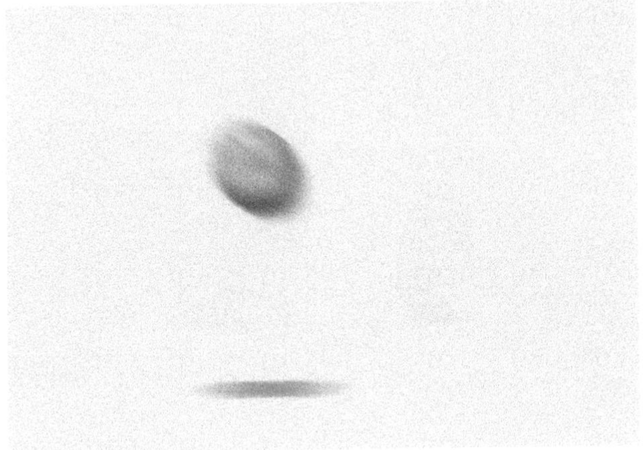

A simulated-motion blur effect to emulate the real-world appearance of a ball moving fast through space.

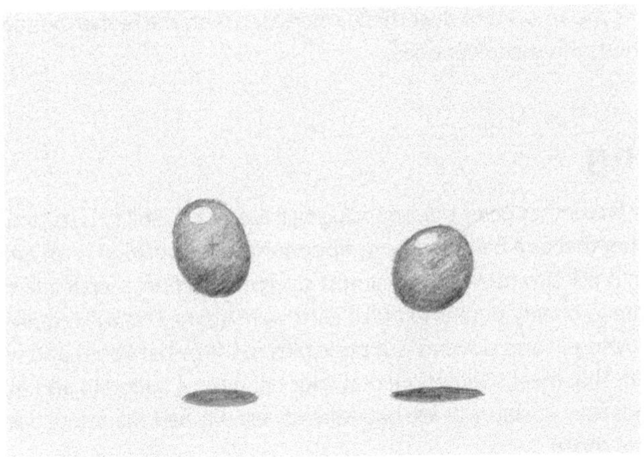

The dropping-down and rising-up stretch effects on the ball, which are separated by the moment when it actually hits the ground.

The amount of stretch is dependent on the degree of flexibility within the object being animated and the speed or velocity it is moving at. For example, our rubber ball will distort significantly as it moves at speed, whereas a metal cannon ball will not stretch very much. Also, the degree of stretch will vary in accordance to the amount of distance covered and the speed the ball is moving. In our reducing-bounce path of action, the distortion of the bounce will therefore look like the following figure as we block-in the breakdown positions.

The stretched ball on the left is longer because the gravity-assisted, downward velocity gives it greater speed. The stretched distortion of the ball on the right is not quite as extended, as it has just hit the ground and therefore has lost a great deal of its earlier velocity.

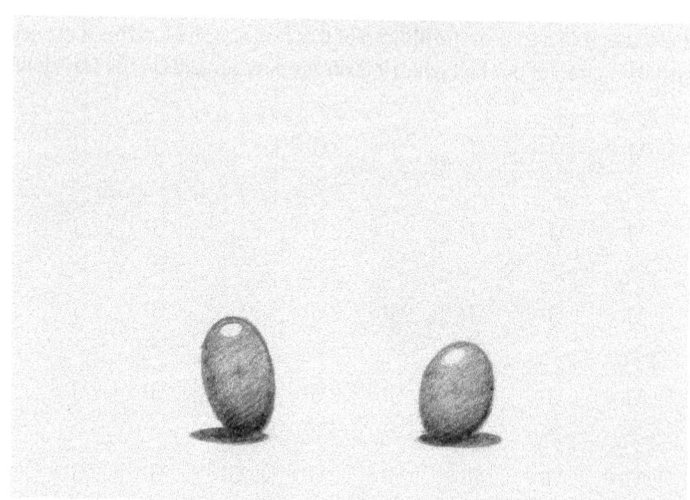

Note how the amount of distortion is increased with the higher bounces and diminished with the lower ones.

Timing

Another factor that gives our bouncing ball action credibility is its timing. Remember that as a ball reaches its uppermost apex position in an arced path of action it will slow down to an almost stopped position, then it will begin to accelerate as gravity begins to pull it earthward again. This will require that we apply slowing-in and slowing-out principles to the in-betweens and we chart them out. That means that more drawings need to be added to and from the uppermost key position, as we have already established that more drawings mean less speed.

If we assume that our two up key positions on the ball are 1 and 21, and the down (squash) position is 11, then these charts clearly show that the ball will accelerate downward at the beginning and decelerate to the next up position at the end.

The actual impact moment on the ground is pretty instantaneous when the high-velocity ball hits, and the bounce back upward again is fast too, depending on the height and speed of the bounce before it. Therefore, the in-betweens at this point need to be minimal (i.e., less drawings mean more speed).

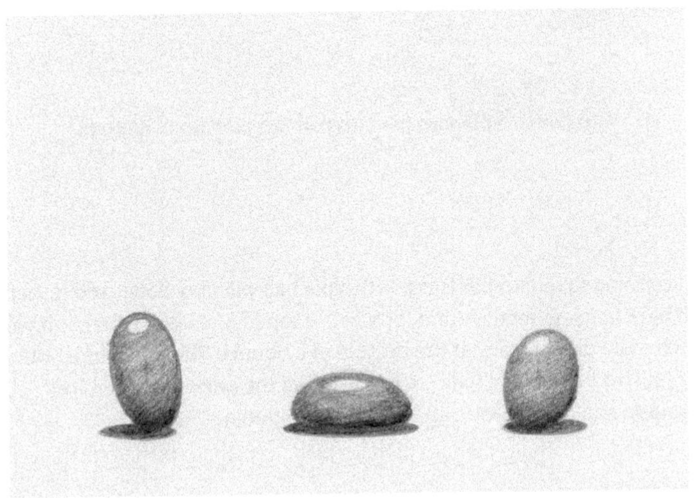

Note that no in-betweens are required during the "hit" positions—the stretched ball effectively squashes on the next frame then stretches up again on the frame immediately after that.

Consequently, we might now suggest the numbering and in-between charting of our bouncing ball. See the following figures.

Based on our slowing-out/slowing-in charting, the two frames in and out of the hit position (11) are effectively breakdown drawings.

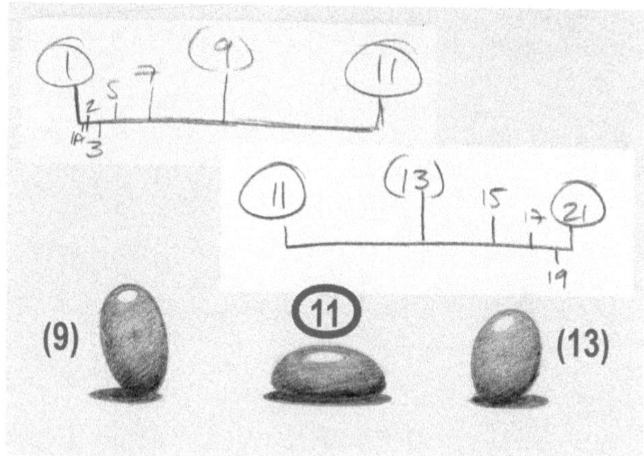

Note that these drawings are separated out to the right to make the action clearer to see. In reality, they would be closer together and overlapping, with the second ball position on the left effectively located directly on top of the first squash position.

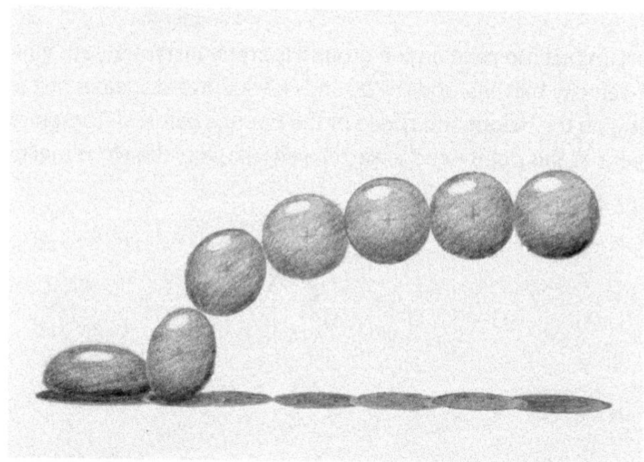

The key thing to remember is that a flexible ball will slow down and reshape itself back to its perfectly round form at the top of a bounce, whereas it will stretch more dramatically at the bottom of a bounce. This is why the bouncing ball is such a good exercise for demonstrating the principles of timing, slowing-in and slowing-out, and squash and stretch.

Weight

Of course, if our ball was not rubber and bouncing, but was heavy and inflexible or light and much more flexible, the actions would look far different. Following are three different examples of balls with varying weights and mass.

Three very different kinds of balls: a ping-pong ball, a standard rubber ball, and a cannonball. They will clearly all bounce very differently!

In-Betweening the Bouncing Ball

Let us now return to our key and breakdown positions for the bouncing ball along its path of action. Here we have to take some things into consideration before we do the in-betweens. Cleary the ball's path of action is moving along an arc, so straightforward in-betweens from one position to another will not be accurate because this will give us angular peaks and troughs, as opposed to the smooth arcing action we are seeking.

Note the curved nature of the bouncing ball's path of action, caused by a combination of forward velocity and gravity.

My approach to handling these eccentric in-betweens is to first mark the center of gravity within each ball drawing and then mark the in-between center of gravity positions for the in-betweens as charted. This will give us the following positional guidelines.

When creating the new in-betweens, always check the numbering and order of their placement before you begin.

In-Betweening the First Part of the Bounce

The next stage is to take a fresh sheet of animation paper and create our first slow-in in-between. For example, if I am going to create the breakdown drawing (9) between keys drawings 1 and 11, I will first mark the center point for the new drawing by placing it over the curved path of action guide and lightly trace its center position.

A good tip to remember is that a movement always looks smoother if there is a slight overlap from position to position on each frame. Therefore, when creating each in-between, place the center point in a position where this overlap can occur wherever possible. In order to achieve this it might be that each in-between is not exactly in the middle of the previous two, as indicated in the chart, however, you will still need to respect the slowing-out placement requirement regardless.

I would then take drawings 1 and 9 and superimpose them center of gravity over center of gravity on the lightbox, which should now be switched on. When the centers of gravity are all lined up between the new drawing and the other two, the new ball inbetween can now be more easily and accurately completed.

Make sure the in-between is accurate and that the superimposed sheets do not shift out of line while you are drawing.

Then, separate the three drawings and place them on the pegs (now with the lightbox off) so you can now roll the drawings to make sure the action is correct.

Note the close overlap between drawings 9 and 11. Clearly 9 does not overlap drawing 1, but when all the other in-betweens are in, you will find that they do all indeed overlap each other.

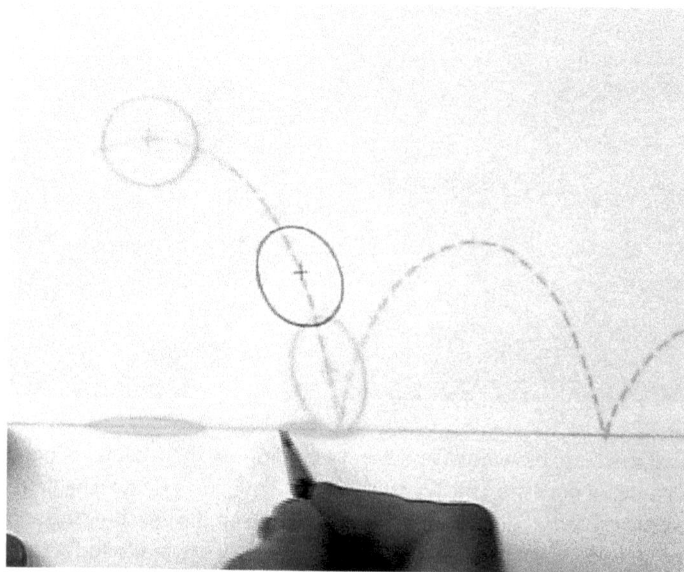

Move on to drawing 7 and do the same thing between 1 and 9. Finally, create drawing 5 between drawings 3 and 2 (I added an extra in-between here and numbered it with an even number, although it should still be shot on two's). Having done all this, you will have completed the first slow-in sequence to the first half of the action. As a last check, flip the drawings on the pegs to see if all is moving well.

In-Betweening the Second Part of the Bounce

Remember that there will be no in-betweens between the breakdown drawing coming into the squashed hit or the breakdown drawing coming out of it. This is because not doing so will ensure a nice snappy bounce. Consequently, we will have to imitate the stretch position we created in drawing 9, although this time we will have to angle it away from the hit position along the path of action. It should also not be quite so elongated in shape, as the velocity (and therefore the speed distortion) has been reduced by the ball hitting the ground.

Note that the length of the stretch coming out is not as long as the stretch coming in of the key hit position.

The rest of the in-betweens should be created in exactly the same way as you produce them in the first part of the bounce—that is, first establish the breakdown position and then create the in-betweens in accordance with the chart requirements.

As with the first half of the action, you will first need to accurately superimpose each drawing over each other, center of gravity lined up with center of gravity, before you create the required in-between drawing.

You will, of course, have to use some personal judgment with regard to the size, stretch, and shape of the new breakdown position (drawing 13) when you create it. You also have to respect the path of action that the ball is about to be projected up and along. I do additionally advise you to add shadows to the ground beneath the ball. This gives a wonderful grounding to the action.

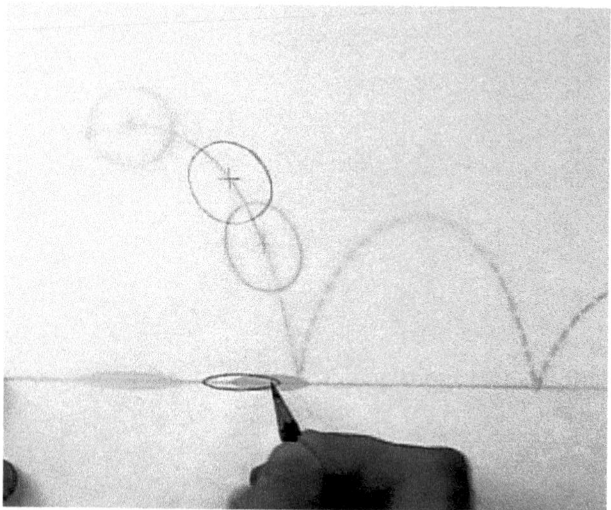

Including shadows on the ground always give a greater sense of contact when the ball hits and rises.

Distorting Mass and Volume

Remember when applying squash and stretch to any object, character, or in this case ball, you can only distort the shape in accordance with that object's inherent volume and mass. As mentioned before, a solid metal cannonball will hardly distort, whereas a very soft, rubber ball will distort significantly because its mass will enable it to do so. The volume of objects do not change when you apply squash and stretch to their shape. An acutely squashed or stretched ball cannot increase or decrease its volume just because it is changing shape. Therefore, when you apply distortion to a shape, make sure that its size, mass, and volume remain plausible in the shape you choose to make it.

Keep consistent volumes when distorting shapes for a better overall effect.

The Descending Bounce

With the entire bounce complete you should flip all the drawings to see if all is working and flowing well. The complete first part of the action should look like the following figure.

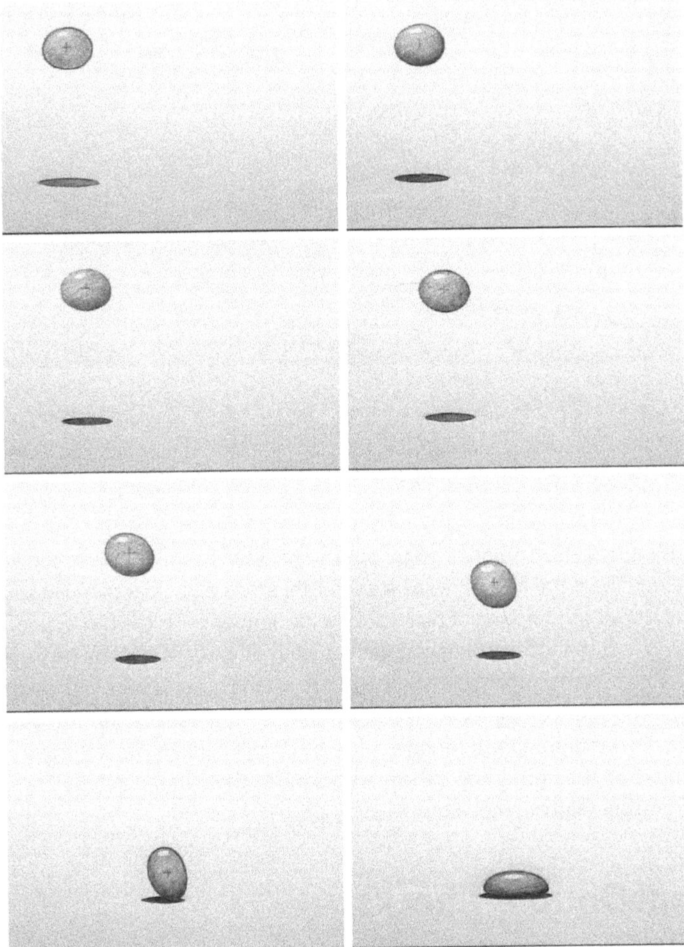

Note how the added shadow really does give a sense of contact when the ball hits the ground.

Flip Your Drawings ... Always!

Now that you have created the initial up and down bounce positions, take all the drawings and flip them as you did earlier (again, lowest number on the bottom, highest on the top). Flipping is an essential aspect of animation as it gives you an immediate idea of how the action is working. NEVER NEGLECT FLIPPING!

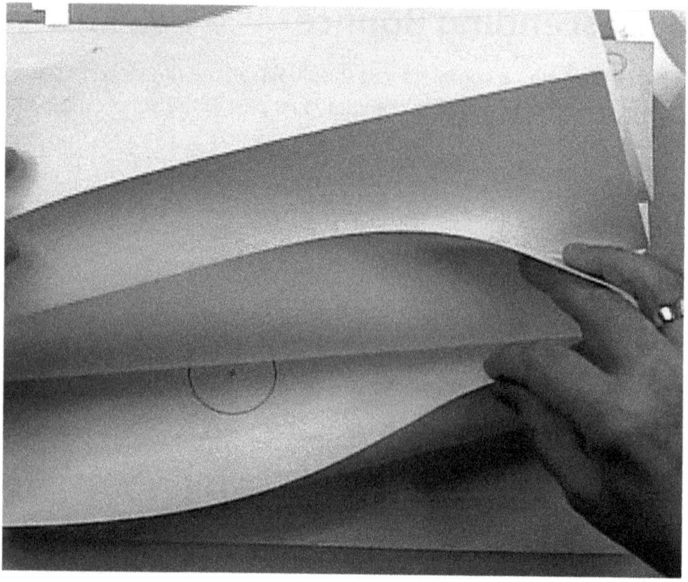

Top pegs flipping (rolling) is something that puts many animators off from using this approach. However, the huge benefits derived from drawing with top pegs more than compensates for the time and effort it takes to perfect the art!

In this particular case, you need to look out for specific things as you flip your drawings. Does the ball follow a nice smooth, arced path of action? Do any of the drawings jump out of place during the sequence? Is the ball action slowing into the top position and then accelerating out of it. It will be hard for you to test the impact of the hit position on the ground until you have another bounce complete, but look out for its effectiveness when you do. However, this flipping test for now, with the drawing you have, will show you if you are on the right track. If there are errors, fix them immediately. If not, then you are ready to move on.

Final Double-Checks

Flipping is extremely useful but it doesn't entirely match the real test, which comes when you see your animation playing in real time on a real screen or monitor. However, before going through all the effort of shooting your work, make a last check on everything on the pegs, to make sure you haven't made any errors that will upset you when you view your first pencil test on the screen. Check that the ball in-betweens become wider apart as they descend and closer together as the ball rises again. This will ensure that the slowing-out/slowing-in approach you have adopted is working.

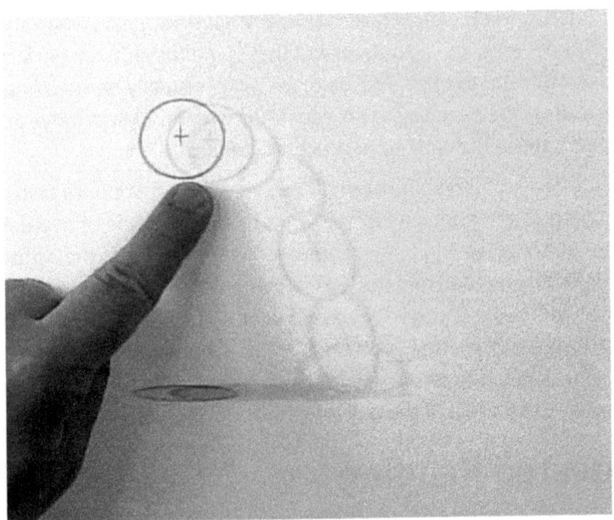

Remember, the closer the drawings, the slower the action. Consequently, this action downward will accelerate as it goes.

Your First Pencil Test

With everything flipping fine, you now should shoot your first pencil test to see how the action works. This will really give you an idea of what your carefully created drawings will look like when they are seen in real time on your computer screen.

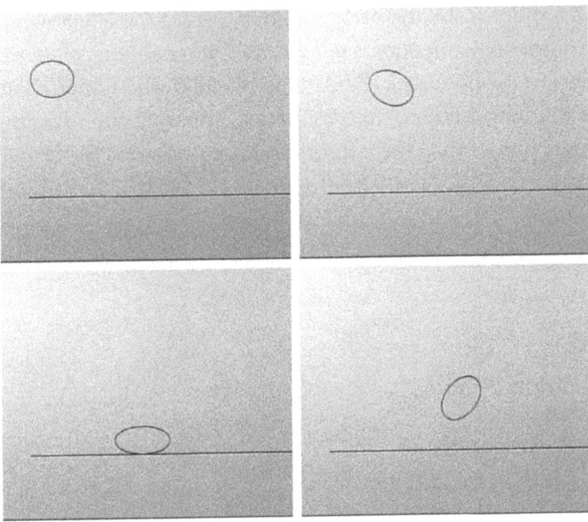

Pencil tests can be really simple or quite complex. These basic outlines are the minimal amount of work that will show the movement you are after.

I think you will be really surprised how fast all those painstakingly created drawings will whisk by before your eyes when you view your first pencil test! My advice to you is to shoot the drawings twice—once on one's (one frame for each drawing) then on two's (two frames for each drawing). This will give you an understanding of how fast or slow the action appears when shot at different frame rates, and also show you that some things work perfectly well on two's as opposed to one's. That said, we will eventually demonstrate to you that one's is the best way to go, especially with fast, large-move actions, although it is twice the work to produce, of course.

Anyway, be honest with yourself when you view your first pencil test. Is it really moving as you anticipated? Is it jerky, or are there one or two drawings that seem out of place and jumpy compared with the rest of the action? If so, you definitely need to go back and fix the problem before moving on. If not—congratulations—you have passed your first test and are ready to go on to the next assignment! (If you can't decide whether or not the action is working fine, show it to an honest-speaking friend, or better still, an animation professional, to ascertain if the ball is really bouncing correctly.)

Suggested Reading

White, T. *The Animator's Workbook*. New York: Watson-Guptill, 1988, pp. 74–75.
White, T. *Animation from Pencils to Pixels: Classical Techniques for Digital Animators*. Boston: Focal Press, 2006, pp. 332–348.

Assignment 2

One of the great Disney intern challenges was for them to create a bouncing flour sack sequence. Essentially, with the background supplied (you have my permission to photocopy the background layout from the following figure or download it from *www.desktopacademy.com*), you need to create a bouncing sequence using the flour sack character in the following figure. (Don't forget to enlarge your photocopy before animating [strongly recommended!] if you're working larger than the background size printed in this book!)

Most young people today have never even heard of a flour sack, let alone seen one! I can imagine their only contact with flour is through the packages found on most supermarket shelves. However, this is where your animator's imagination has to come into play: What does a big, soft canvas sack, filled with fine, yet malleable, powder and tied up at all four corners look and move like?

Treat the flour sack as if it were a bouncing ball and create a sequence that is original and amusing, incorporating that bounce. You can effectively create anything you like but challenge yourself by including a number of bounces and a variation in timing. You may want the flour sack to bounce in from offscreen, bounce off some object in the background, and then fly offscreen at the end. You may want to have the flour sack start off still and then build up to a bouncing sequence within the scene, arriving at an ultimate conclusion. The storyline for your assignment is entirely up to you. You can use the background supplied or create your own, but you do have to draw a bouncing flour sack scene.

This is one of the background layouts that the DigiPen students use for their flour sack assignments. The circular shape in the middle is a trampoline that the sack can bounce on if required. (Source: Student work, courtesy of DigiPen Institute of Technology.)

Assignment Objectives

The key things you are seeking to achieve with this assignment is to produce a believable bouncing sequence using an object that is not a rubber ball. (Although all the squash and stretch, slowing-in and slowing-out principles of movement and timing still apply here, of course!) Remember that the flour sack is a very different kind of object in mass and substance to the rubber ball you have been working with. It is very fluid and flexible externally, being essentially made of soft sacking fabric, but contains an almost full bulk of fluid, powdery flour that will always tend to sink en masse to the bottom due to gravity.

Note how big, round shapes donate weight and indicate the pull of gravity.

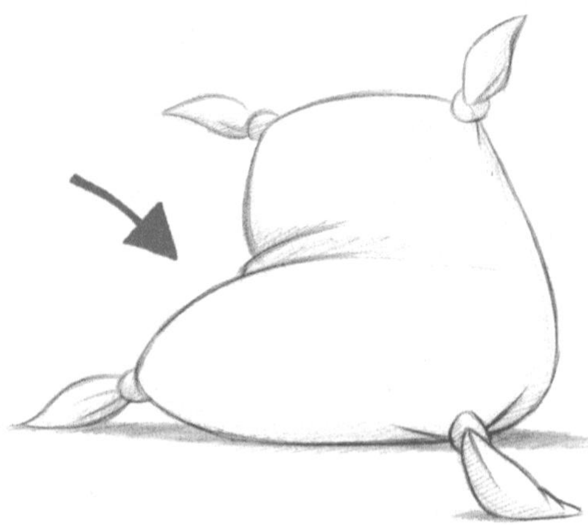

If bent in half, the flour will similarly tend to sink to both ends of the sack, and this tendency and capability should be implied in the flour sack action.

If tipped over, the bulk of the flour inside the sack will find its way to the lowest part, bulging it out in the process. This fluidity and weight element is why the flour sack assignment is such a good one for students.

Speed and Distance

A very important thing to remember is that you are now working in a 3D space (the background, in perspective), so the timing should reflect that. Visually, anything that moves in the distance tends to appear to move slower than anything that is moving close to the camera. Consequently, if the flour sack bounces from the near ground to the distance, you will need to increasingly add in-betweens to the action to give the effect of it getting slower as it moves away.

Note that it takes the large, foreground sack six frames to travel from within the trampoline to the top of the screen, whereas the tiny spec of the distant sack falling through the sky just above the tree branch needs eight frames, indicating a definite difference in speeds between near to far! (Source: Student work, courtesy of DigiPen Institute of Technology.)

Also, because the background is seen in perspective, your character should reflect that perspective by getting smaller the further away it gets.

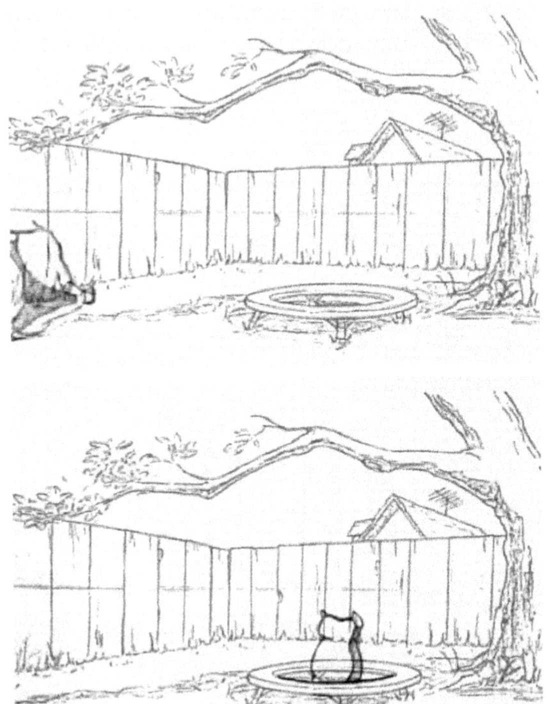

Note the foreground sack gets smaller as it moves away from the camera view. (Source: Student work, courtesy of DigiPen Institute of Technology.)

These are two key areas that you should focus on when attempting this assignment—that is, in addition to applying the bouncing ball principles you have already learned.

Diligent Process

Whether you are attempting an assignment or a scene in a film, you need to apply a diligent process to the approach you will take. We did this in the first lesson of the bouncing ball. First, we drafted the path of action we wanted the ball to take. We then blocked in our key positions. Then we applied distortion to the key drawings we had arrived at. Then we planned and charted how we wanted to time and position our in-between drawings. Next, we produced our in-betweens and flipped the final drawings to ensure that all is well. Finally, we shot the entire sequence and viewed it running in real time on a screen of our choice. This is what a diligent process is, and it is precisely the approach that you should take with this particular assignment. (Indeed, all the assignments you will be faced with!)

So, take the background you have been provided with and tape it to a punched sheet of paper, so that it falls within the field guide area you are using. A 100 percent copy of the background layout provided will most likely not fit in the actual field size you are working with. Consequently, you will have to enlarge it to fit... especially if you are working with a 12 or 16 field.

Remember, you can always use a photocopier to resize the background layout to the field size you want to use. Here, a photocopy of the background is scaled to a 12 field–size guide and taped down for the animator to work with. (Source: Student work, courtesy of DigiPen Institute of Technology.)

Now that you have the background taped into position on a punched sheet of paper sized to your chosen field size, you should place a clean sheet of paper over it and rough out the key positions of the flour sack throughout the sequence you are planning. Don't settle for first thoughts. Rework your ideas until you come up with something quite original and exciting. If you need 20 or 30 sheets of paper to achieve the ideal sequence, don't worry about it. Remember, with anything you do, you only get out of a project as much as you put in. The preplanning is as important as the execution. Therefore, don't just jump in with the first thought you have. It is really important to pay due process to your ideas at this stage. Ultimately, however, you should have something that looks a little like the following figure over the background layout.

The background is placed on one level and the blue pencil drawing of the character is on another. (Source: Student work, courtesy of DigiPen Institute of Technology.)

Once you have the layout and key flour sack positions roughed out on top of it, you can now break down the whole thing into separate key drawings. On the pegs, trace all the key drawings onto separate sheets and then attempt to plan out the in-betweens and number the drawings accordingly.

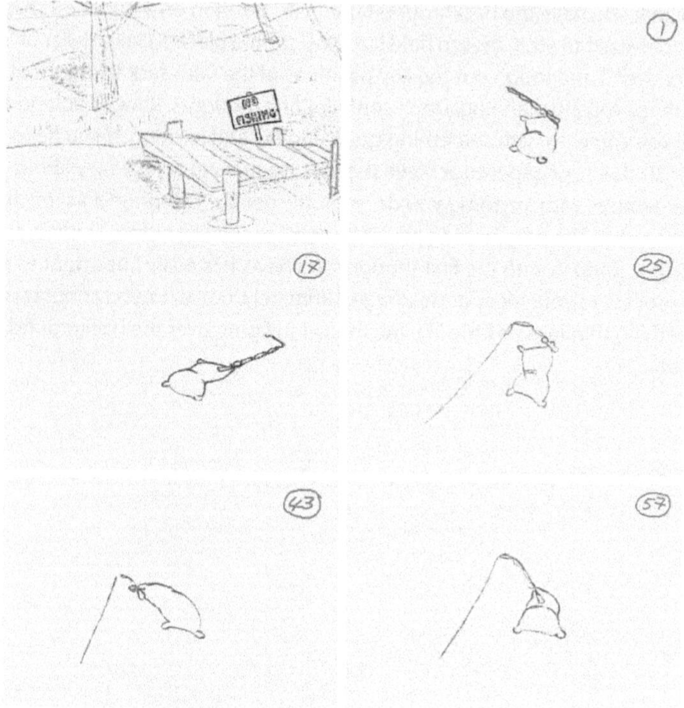

The background is kept on its own level, while each character pose is drawn on a separate level and numbered with the frame number it is planned to be seen on. (Source: Student work, courtesy of DigiPen Institute of Technology.)

Remember to add some pauses in the action and not make all in-betweens evenly paced throughout. Check-out other great animation and see the variations in timing and pace that the best action contains. Build this in as a factor into your own scene as best as you can.

When creating layouts or animatic drawings, it is usual to write your timing ideas on them. (Source: Student work, courtesy of DigiPen Institute of Technology.)

Next, once the key positions are completed and numbered, draw the breakdown drawings on separate sheets of paper, numbering them as you go.

Note

I always number my drawings *before* I actually complete them. This is a good habit to get into. If you don't number the drawings while you are drawing, it can be a challenge to rearrange them later if they get knocked onto the floor or rearranged in any unexpected way. It is better to be safe than sorry and do all the numbering in advance.

Pose Test Your Work

When all the key and breakdown drawings are complete, you should now create a pose test of the drawings. This effectively means shooting the drawings in order, holding them for the number of frames that the subsequent frames will take up. For example, if the first drawing is number 1, the next drawing is 9, the third drawing is 17, and the fourth drawing is 29, you will shoot the first drawing for 8 frames, the second drawing for 8 frames, and the third drawing for 12 frames, etc.

Three frames that show the sequence of action in an animatic. Note that the characters are on one level, while the same background layout is used beneath them. (Source: Student work, courtesy of DigiPen Institute of Technology.)

When played back on your computer screen, this will give you a good idea of the timing, pacing, and posing of the action. Be ruthlessly honest with yourself and critique your work as best as you can: Do you think the flour sack moves credibly across the screen, or is it too fast, or too slow? Do the poses look awkward or too far apart in the sequence? Does the perspective and contact between the character and the background really work? Ask yourself all these things, and more, and fix anything that doesn't look right in this pose test form. Remember, it is far better to go through the extra work of fixing things now, when you have fewer drawings to adjust, rather than in-betweening everything and then having to go back later and change significantly more drawings to put things right!

When you are satisfied that the pose test is working as you want it to, put in the in-betweens as you did with the bouncing ball sequence. Don't forget the value of superimposition and the application of slowing-in and slowing-out with your animation. It is these things that make life easier and movement easier to appreciate.

A climbing character like this is a perfect candidate for a slow-in toward the end, since it is battling with gravity and therefore being made to go slower the higher it moves. (Source: Student work, courtesy of DigiPen Institute of Technology.)

When all the in-betweens are complete, shoot the action on one's and two's to ascertain if everything moves correctly and what timing works best for what action. You will be surprised at the difference both film speeds offer. However, viewing both will begin to give you a sense for how many drawings per second produce a certain speed of movement. Fix or adjust any parts of the test that don't work, even mixing and matching one's versus two's when you shoot your final piece. Don't be afraid to do this—much of the best 2D animation ever produced is a subtle mixer of one's and two's.

Generic Walks

Class objective: To achieve a basic walk sequence that is believable and convincing.
Equipment required: Lightbox, pencil, and paper.
DVD lecture: "Generic Walks."

Those of you who have read my previous books, or have studied with me in class, know that I prefer to approach walks in stages—that is, the bottom half first; then the trunk, arms, and head; then the subtle overlapping actions that can give the walk more fluidity. This section of our book-based animation course is no different. In presenting it here, I can only repeat what I have said before: A good walk is the hardest thing for an animator to master, as it contains pretty much all the principles of animation that any animator needs to know for other things, such as poses, breakdowns, overlapping action, weight, arcs, flowing paths of action, etc. Consequently, I'll guide you through the challenges of creating a generic walk on a stage-by-stage basis, so that you will successfully understand all the principles involved one piece at a time. If I ultimately make you good at creating a good generic walk, then my job in guiding you toward ultimately being an accomplished, capable animator in your own right is well on the way!

The Lower Body

As I noted, I choose to first present only the lower part of the body when teaching walks, because if this part is created correctly, everything else will easily fall into place. Consequently, let us focus only on the leg and lower torso principles for now to ensure that you have a solid grasp of what is involved.

Key Positions

Basically there are two key positions in a walk: one with the right leg forward and the other with the left leg forward. For convenience sake, we'll call these key drawings 1 and 9.

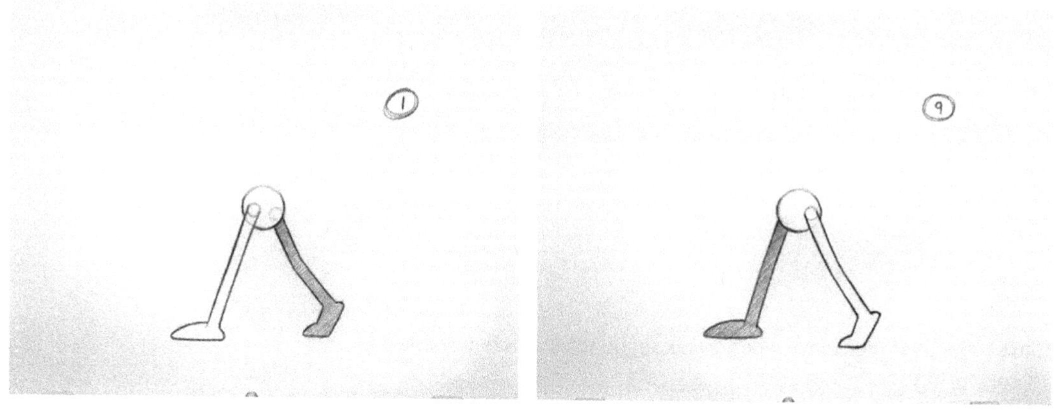

Note that I always shade the far leg (and arm, when appropriate) to give a greater visual clarification of what is going on throughout the action.

Passing Position

Next we need to establish the breakdown position of the first stride. In any walking or running action, a breakdown drawing is actually known as the *passing position*. This is the part of any stride where the free leg is most closely passing by the contact leg, from behind to forward. I often refer to this position as the "number 4 position," as this is the shape that the legs actually make at this point in a stride. For our example, we will number this as drawing 5, which, in keeping with all breakdown drawings, will need to have a parenthesis around it.

The passing (a.k.a. number 4) position.

Note that with a passing position the body area, or in this case the pelvic area, is always raised up higher than its position on the two key "stride" positions. This is because with the straight contact leg below it, the hip is pushed upward.

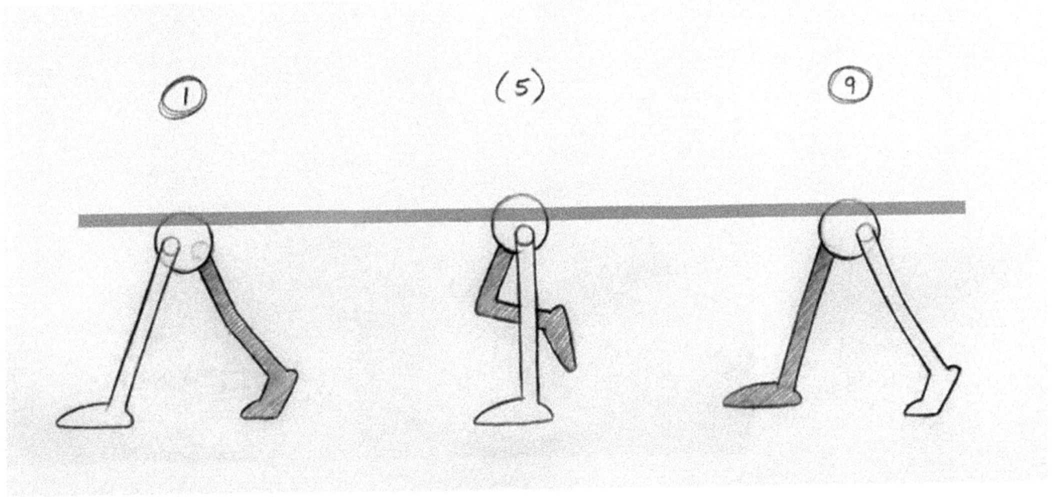

The body of any passing position will always be raised for anything but a specialized, or eccentric, walk.

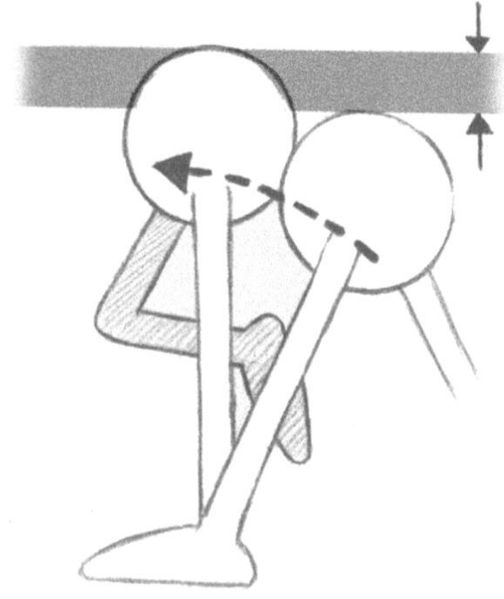

Because the leg will never change its length, unless in a crazy, rubber-hose cartoon way when it is elevated to a vertical position, it will automatically lift the pelvic area, and thus the rest of the body, with it.

Indeed, a simple geometric diagram created with a compass will reveal that the hip joint in either of the key stride positions will be nearer to the ground because of the angle that the contact leg makes with the ground.

With poorly animated walks, the body action on the passing position rarely has this upward movement during the middle of the stride. Indeed, 2D animators will quite often unknowingly make the contact leg on the passing position shorter than in the stride positions on these occasions, so that the body does not rise at all. However, this is entirely wrong and is the major reason why most poorly drawn walks do not work.

I will remind you again that by flipping (rolling) your drawings you will get an immediate idea of what is going on long before you go to the effort of doing all the in-betweens and shoot them!

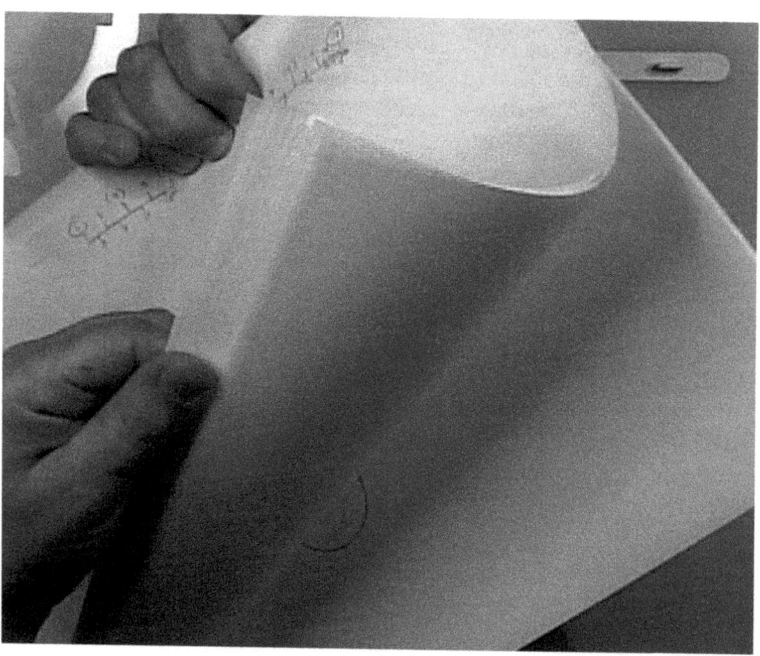

Try to keep your nonflipping hand as steady as possible when reviewing your work, then the subtleties of movement will be easier to see.

In-Between Positions

For the purposes of our basic generic walk exercise, we will assume there are two basic in-betweens that need to go in to complete our first stride—number 3 (between the opening stride position and the passing position) and number 5 (between the passing position and the closing stride position). This will give us a sequence that looks like the following figure.

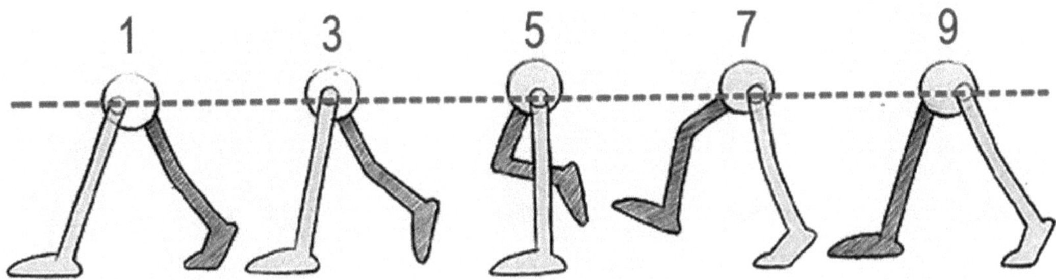

Again, notice that the body rises up as it reaches the passing position.

Note how on drawing 3 the back toe remains in contact with the ground until the last possible moment (giving a more dynamic push to the walk), and drawing 7 has the free foot up and forward before the downward hit position of key drawing 9.

Walking is never a totally mechanical process, so try to have the foot reach out a little before it makes contact with the ground and, at the back of the stride, keep toe contact with the ground as long as possible.

Now, having achieved this first stride we have to complete a full walk cycle by creating the other stride—that is, return the stride back to its original start position. This is effectively done by repeating the entire process we just used, but reversing the legs as we do so. The drawing numbers for this stride can be 9, 11, 13 (the other legs passing position), 15, and 17. (Note that 17 is actually identical to 1 as we need to ensure that at the end of the second step we are back in exactly the same stride position we were at in the beginning.)

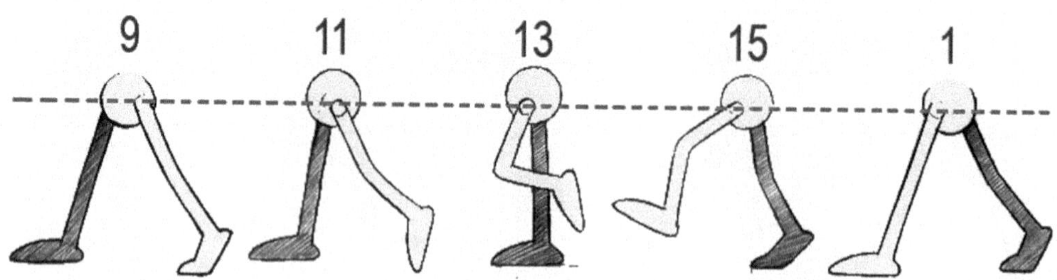

When creating the second stride with the opposite legs, you can pretty much trace the original stride positions, although the foot contact positions of the near and far foot will be different, due to the effects of perspective.

Now we have two complete strides and have completed all the elements we need to create a continuous walk. However, when attempting walks, it is possible to approach the complete walk action in two ways. The first is to create a sequence of drawings that will walk the character from one side of the screen to the other. This essentially means that you will have to draw as many different drawings as necessary to have the character move the required distance across the screen. This is actually far more work than is necessary at this learning stage. A much better way to test and play with the walk action is to do a walk cycle.

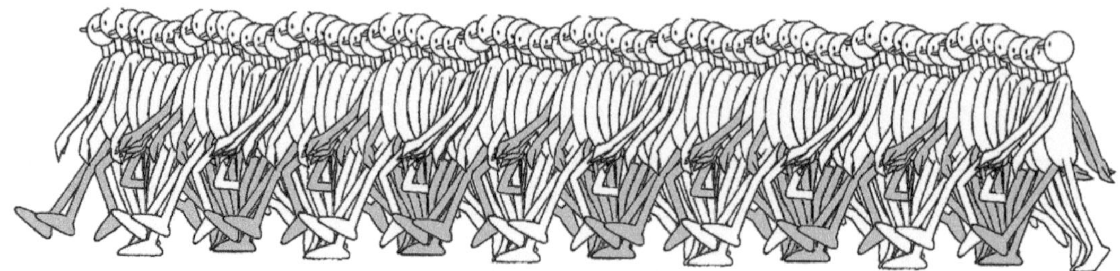

This is the number of drawings you would have to do to create almost 11 strides moving straight ahead!

This is how many drawings you would have to make to have a generic character walk indefinitely using a "cycle" action!

Walk Cycle

A *walk cycle* effectively means that the character will be able to walk over and over again on the same spot (i.e., as if they are on a treadmill) for as long as you need them to. This will require a minimum of drawings. To achieve this you actually only have to produce the two-stride cycle, as we just did and nothing more! Here is the process.

Start by positioning the first key drawing in the center of the animation paper, but leave enough space above it to add the body, arms, and head later.

For this and the following examples I have put the drawing numbers within the shooting area. Remember, however, normally they would be written at the right-hand corner of the paper, next to the peg hole.

Place another clean sheet of paper over the top of this and draw an identical stride to the first, but this time with the legs reversed. Number these drawings 1 and 9, as indicated earlier.

Here I have placed key drawing 9 over key drawing 1 and traced it. I shaded the leg farthest away, so as to differentiate it from the near leg.

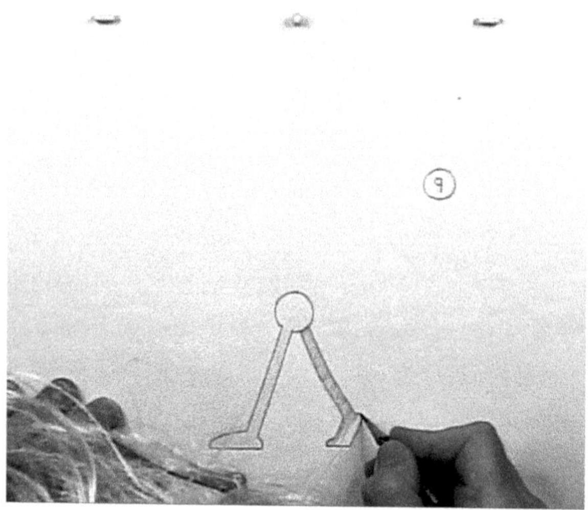

Now place a third sheet of paper over the top of these first two and create the correct passing position on it, numbering it appropriately 5 at the same time. The only thing you need to remember here is that the contact foot on the ground of a walk cycle is actually sliding from the front position to the back and therefore needs to be placed precisely at a midway position between them.

Regularly flip your drawings as you create them, so that you can tell how they are working with each other.

To find the middle position of any walk cycle in-between, I tend to use the sliding-toe position as my main point of reference. When the foot is up on the heel, however, you have to imagine where the toe will be if it is down. That way it will make the midway calculation easier.

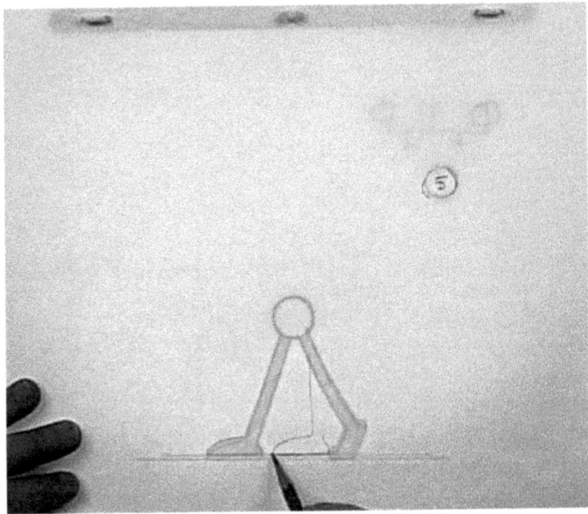

Working with the backward slide on the back (shaded) leg, I have established a midlocation for the proposed passing position, which has the toe halfway between the front and back keys.

Remember though that when doing a walk cycle, it is very important for all the contact feet positions within each stride *to move at an identical distance each time*. So, when you put the other two in-betweens into the cycle, you need to accurately measure the slide distances on them as well. (For a clearer understanding of how to do this, refer to the Introduction to In-Betweening lecture on the accompanying DVD.)

See how the toe of the contact foot for this in-between is also midway between the two toe positions on either side of it.

Now you have completed the drawings of the first stride and the second stride in an identical manner (except for the fact that this time the legs are reversed, of course).

Note that the leg positioning within the second (bottom) set of frames is identical to that of the first (upper) set. It is just the legs that are reversed, made clear by the shaded back leg.

Note that when doing profile walks like this, the far foot should be on a slightly higher path of action for the contact slide than the near foot, due to the perspective involved from this viewpoint.

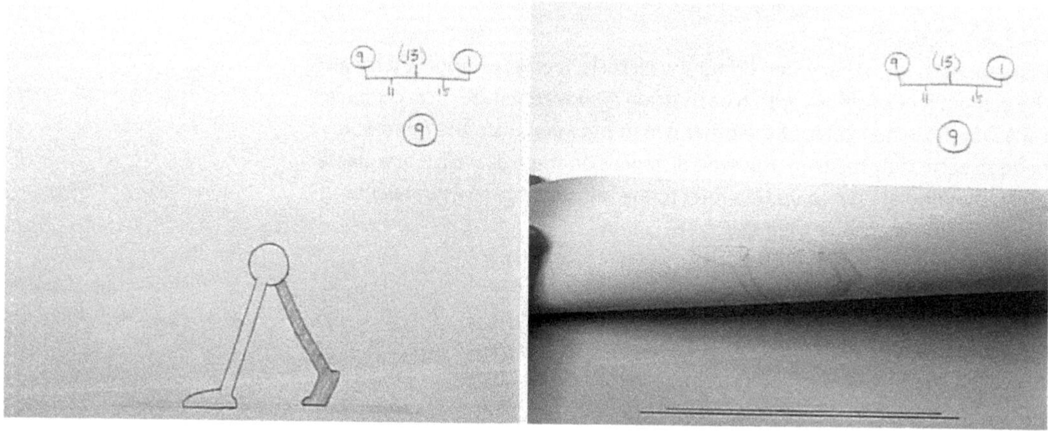

You can make this easier for yourself by adding two lines (paths of action) to an underlying background sheet. Make sure that the far foot always locates to the upper line at all times and the nearer foot to the lower line. This will ensure that you get a correct sense of perspective at all times.

The second stride can be numbered exactly as indicated earlier, except that for the walk cycle you can reuse drawing 1 for drawing 17 (as both these drawings are identical and you don't want to draw it twice). Consequently, if we were drawing the in-between charts for both strides here, they would look like the following figure.

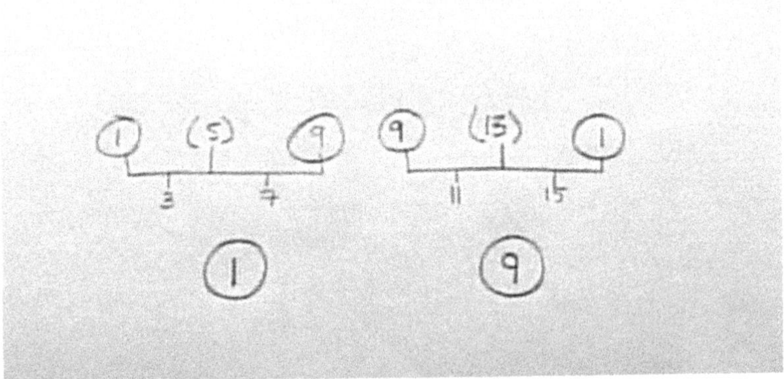

Note that these are even charts with no slowing-in or slowing-out indications suggested.

Shooting a Walk Cycle

Apart from testing the walk cycle by first flipping it, you should shoot it as well. This way you can see how fast it moves in real time on the screen. To get the best effect of the cycle action, shoot the drawings for a minimum of three repeats. This means that you need to shoot them in this order: 1, 3, 5, 7, 9, 11, 13, 15, 1, 3, 5, 7, 9, 11, 13, 15, 1, 3, 5, 7, 9, 11, 13, 15, 1. When animation is numbered with odd numbers, it usually means that it was shot on two's, as opposed to one's. However, to get a sense of the speed of the walk cycle, I would suggest that you shoot these drawings twice, one set on one's and the other on two's. That way, when you play the action back you will be able to better appreciate the difference between the two speed and timing approaches. The first thing you'll immediately notice is that despite all the drawings you will feel you have created, both versions will appear to have the walk moving extremely fast, although the two's version should seem a little more acceptably slow than the one's!

In-Betweening on One's

Having seen how fast (and perhaps a little "jittery") the action can look on one's and two's, you should next do a little experiment to show you what animation animated on one's but shot on two's looks like. So go back to your existing drawings and in-between all the odd-number drawings by including even-number drawings as well—that is, draw 2 between 1 and 3, draw 4 between 3 and 5, draw 6 between 5 and 7, etc.). When you get to drawing 16, however, draw it between 15 and 1 to complete the cycle.

I am superimposing one foot over another to keep size consistency, although on this occasion I am choosing to keep the foot planted firmly down on the ground for the in-between.

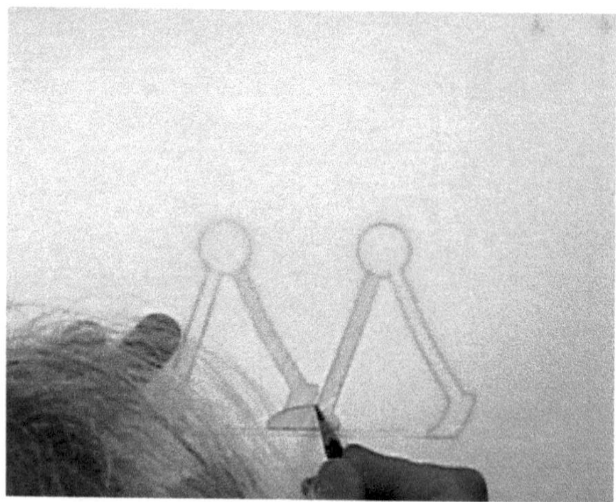

Two important things you need to know about when you do this. First, for drawing 10 make sure you keep the toe down on the back foot before it lifts up and begins to come forward on drawing 11. This will give you a little extra push on the back leg. However, on walk cycles all the slide distances have to be even for every contact foot position on the ground, so you will need to calculate the average foot slide distance back throughout the preceding stride and add it to the drawing 9 position for drawing 10 (see the following figure).

Note how the back leg on the in-between remains in contact with the ground until the last possible moment, with the toe sliding back the same distance as all the other in-between foot slides.

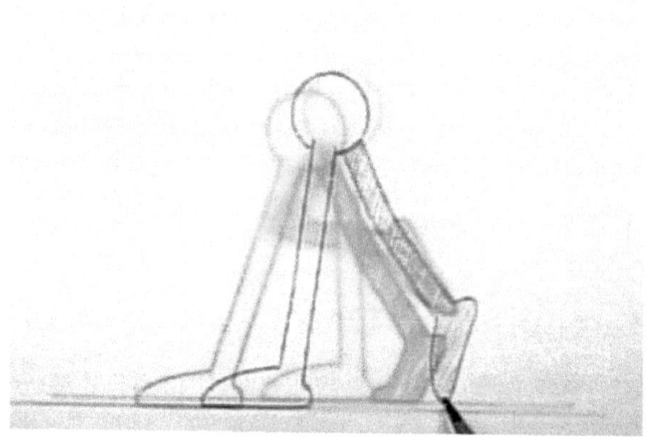

Also, for drawing 16, which links up to drawing 1 again on the cycle, place the heel of the foot just a little higher and forward of the heel on drawing 1. This will give you a forward and back action on the free foot before the heel hits the ground, which is a more natural way of walking that echoes real life.

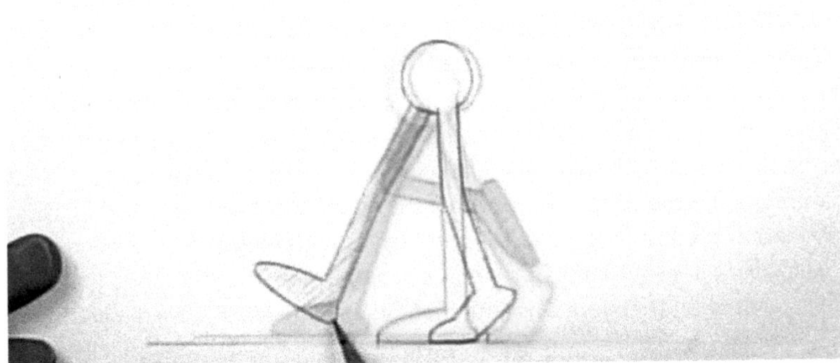

See how the heel of the foot always swings forward and up on the in-between just before it comes down and makes contact with the ground!

TIP

With most characters, and certainly heavy characters, it always helps the walk to put a definite bend on the knee with the drawing after the key contact position. In the following figure you can see the normal lead leg position for drawing 3 and the alternative bent-leg version. This action very much echoes the kind of shock-absorber affect in most cars and bicycles. Very light characters, however, will barely need this, just those with some kind of weight to handle.

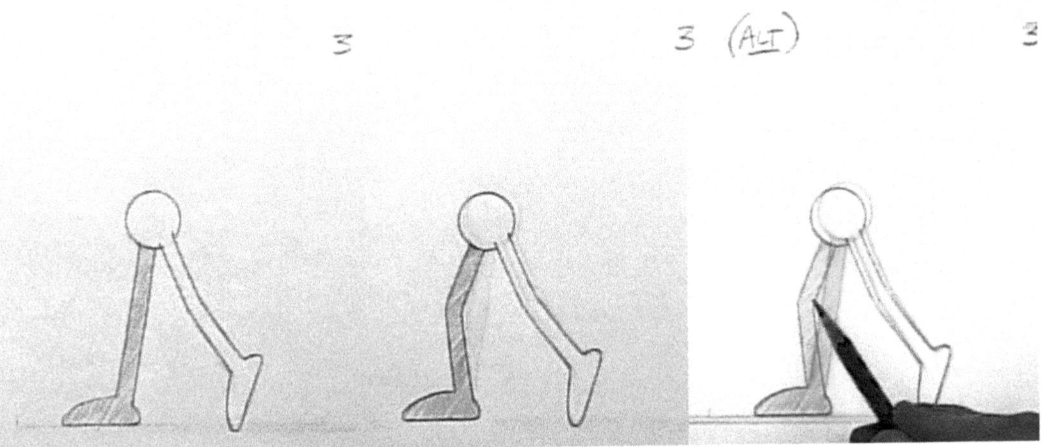

Showing the before and after versions plus the lightbox version of one over the other, which clearly shows the amount of change there is in the lead leg position and the extra dip forward and down there is in the hip area.

Testing the Walk

Now that you have all the in-betweens in, you are ready to test the action again. This time, apart from flipping the action manually, shoot the three cycles of drawings on both one's and two's, so you can see what the speed looks like with this number of drawings being used. Just as animation drawings numbered with odd numbers usually means that the animation is supposed to be shot on two's, even numbers usually symbolize positions for one's. Consequently, the correct way to shoot the new set of drawings would be to shoot the entire cycle on one's. However, by also shooting these drawings on two's, you will see how much slower the action will be if they are shot on two's instead of one's. Therefore, this time shoot your animation cycle a minimum of three times using this new order of drawings: 1, 2, 3, 4, 5, 6, 7, 8, 9, 10, 11, 12, 13, 14, 15, 16, 1, 2, 3, 4, 5, 6, 7, 8, 9, 10, 11, 12, 13, 14, 15, 16, 1, 2, 3, 4, 5, 6, 7, 8, 9, 10, 11, 12, 13, 14, 15, 16, 1. This order will definitely show you how much smoother the new one's sequence of walking will be compared to the original two's version of odd numbers, and it will also show you what the walk will look like when shot twice as slow as before by shooting the one's drawings on two's.

The Upper Body

Now that you have successfully completed the walk action for the bottom half of the body, you can move forward and complete the top half throughout the walk. So, go back to your original stride key positions, 1 and 9, and add the upper body to them.

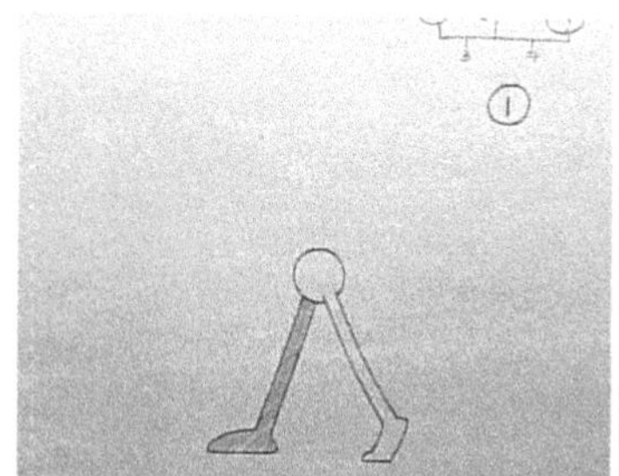

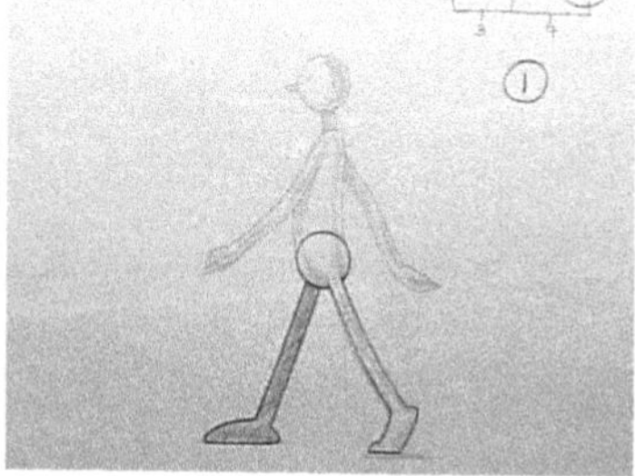

This shows how the body can be built on the existing lower-body version we have been working with.

Note

I have chosen to use the cleaned-up and inked-in version of the full walking character from this point on, as this will illustrate the actions more clearly.)

Note how the torso leans a little forward. This is because for any walk action to look realistic and plausible, a character needs to angle forward somewhat to get momentum. Note how most people in the street walk like that. We take this for granted when we try to walk ourselves, but notice what happens in our own body when we try to walk and don't lean forward or push off from our contact leg first. We just don't move at all. However, if we lean forward slightly we will find that we have to put our free foot forward and down to create the first stride, or we will fall flat on our face! (This is effectively what babies do when learning to walk—they forward lean but don't know yet that they have to quickly put their free leg forward to stop themselves from falling over.)

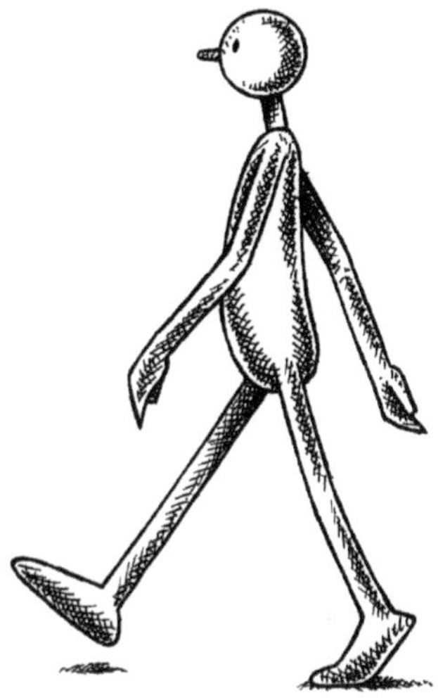

Imagine this character moving forward without having the front leg there to stop his forward momentum. This is what we do when we walk ourselves—we use the contact leg to counteract the forward lean that we use to get ourselves going.

Anyway, because of this, all walks should have a slight forward lean when we draw our key positions, as should all the walk positions we subsequently create (unless we are animating a drunk person destined not to move, or to fall flat on his or her face).

Clearly a figure so far off balance does suggest that he is losing control of his movement. In this particular case, we can imagine the character falling backward unless he throws a leg or an arm out to stop himself!

Again, this is just another reminder that with a generically walking character, the forward and backward arm positions oppose themselves on each key.

Right arm forward/left leg forward, and vice versa.

With the key stride positions in, take the original lower-body passing positions and put the upper body, arms, and head in on those too. Don't forget to keep the slight forward lean to the body here also. You can do this by superimposing one key over the other, and adding the first passing position over the top of that, making sure to line up the pelvic area one with the other and making sure the upward sides of the paper are all parallel with one another. (If they are not, then you will tend to put an unwanted additional angle to the body lean, forward or backward, when you are tracing the character's position.)

Superimposition, an animator's best friend!

Note that the arms in the passing positions are now down by the sides of the body. This is because they are moving from forward to backward at this point, or backward to the forward, depending on what arm you are considering.

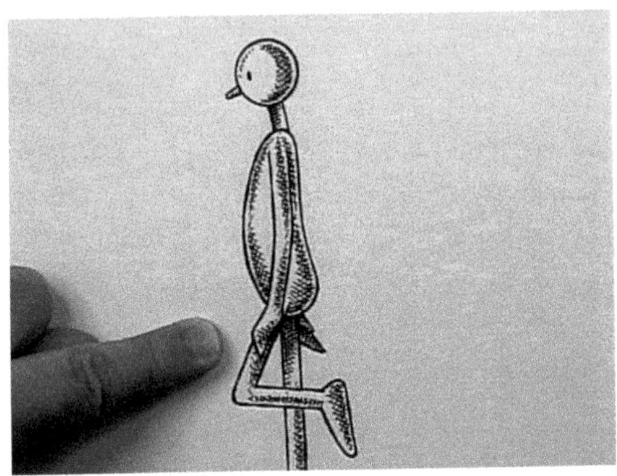

Not only does the free leg pass through on the passing position, but so do the arms. (I will explain why the hands are bent in relation to the arms later.)

With all the keys and passing positions in place and working as you roll the drawings, you can now go ahead and put in the upper bodies on all the other drawings. I would actually only work on the odd-number drawings at first, then test them by flipping and shooting before you put in the in-betweens for the one's drawings.

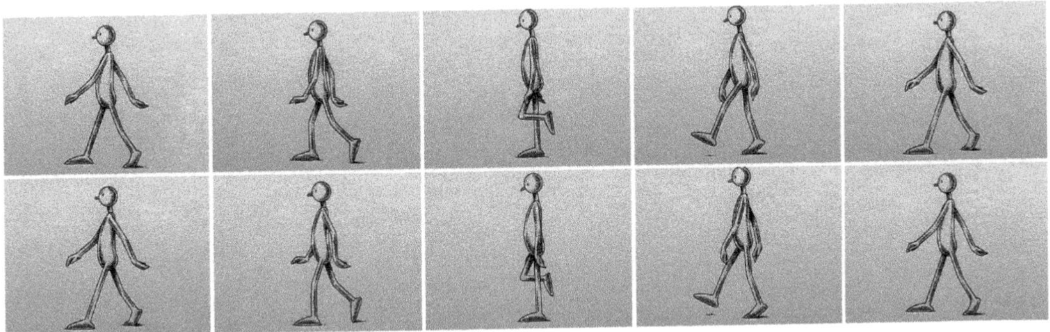

The complete, full-body walk cycle. Note that the position of the arms and the legs are identical on both stride actions, except that they are reversed from one another.

If the two's (odd numbers) work fine, then you can add in the one's (even numbers) in-betweens. Flip and test these. If all is well, you should now have the basic, generic character walking nicely, with a descent up and down movement on the body, and the arms swinging in time with the legs.

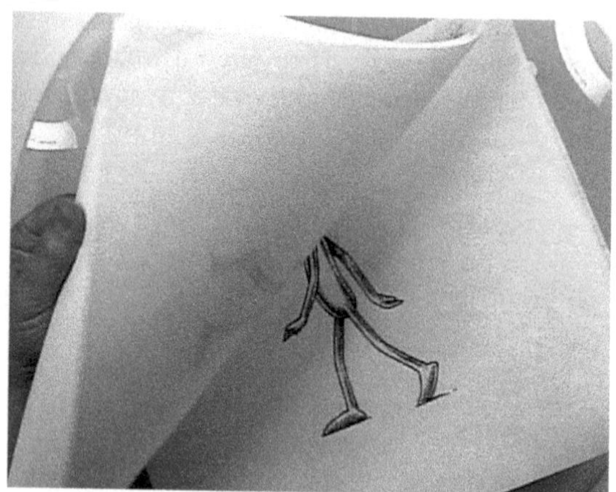

One final reminder that flipping allows you to see a great deal of how your animation is working long before you actually shoot it!

Suggested Reading

White, T. *The Animator's Workbook*. New York: Watson-Guptill, 1988, pp. 46–56.
White, T. *Animation from Pencils to Pixels: Classical Techniques for Digital Animators*. Boston: Focal Press, 2006, pp. 234–244.

Assignment 3

Create a generic walk cycle on one's, as indicated in this chapter lesson.

Personality Walks

Class objective: To evolve the generic walk principles to create more individual character and personality in the walking action.
Equipment required: Lightbox, pencil, and paper.

Now that you have created your first successful generic walk it is time to add a little more subtly and personality to the action—that is, to loosen it up a bit! Although you are probably very happy with your walk already, there are a few things that you now need to do to make it look more natural and give it more character. The first is to give it a more flexible body action.

Hip and Shoulder Rotation

You will notice that when people walk it is not just their arms and legs that move forward from stride to stride, but their hips and shoulders rotate forward and backward too. Carefully watch an arm as it swings forward and you'll notice the shoulder rotating forward too. At the same time, the other arm that is moving backward will cause that shoulder to rotate backward also. Similarly, when the legs move forward and backward, so do the hips. Adding all this together we get a body action on both the strides that looks like the following figures.

Rotations are things that are often forgotten by novice animators, but it is fundamentally important to incorporate them in any convincing action.

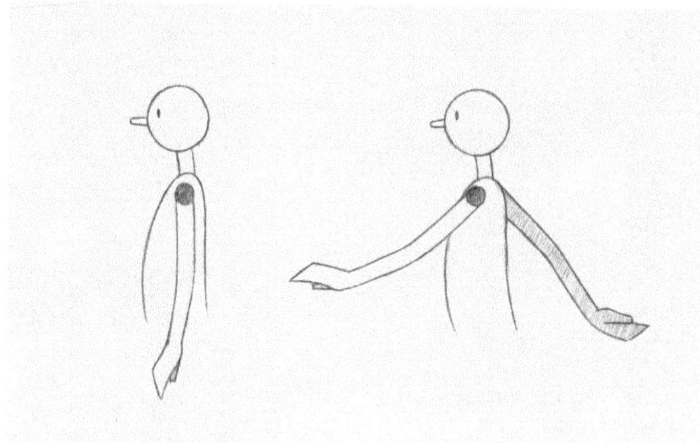

Make an extra study of the up and down action of the hips. This is a factor that can significantly influence the convincing movement of a natural, fluid-looking walk.

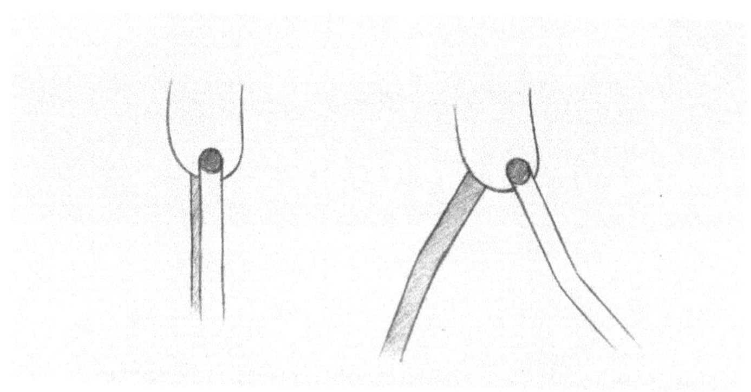

This natural twisting of the torso both ways will bring a more natural fluidity to the entire action.

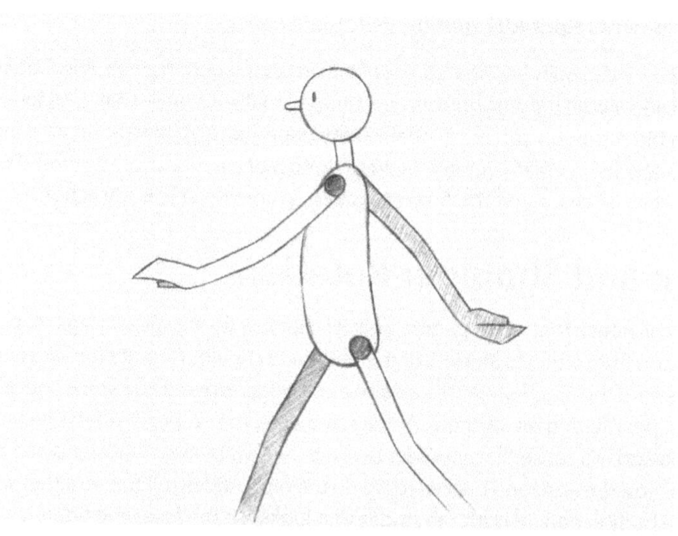

Now you can see that by just putting this rotation into your generic walk alone will make it look that much more fluid and natural. Try it!

Overlapping Action on the Hands

Remember that the human body is not a machine and therefore nothing it does is rigid or mechanical. The arms and hands, for instance, offer an opportunity for demonstrating this. When observing people walking, notice that as their arms move backward and forward, their hands are not entirely moving at quite the same angle. This is not to say they are vastly different, but more that as the arm moves forward, the hand tends to drag back a little, hinged at the wrist. The same can be said for the hand as the arm moves backward. It tends to delay, or drag a little, before it catches up with the arm on its return swing. This is known as *overlapping action* and it should be incorporated in all animation wherever possible, as we'll refer to later in other sections of the course.

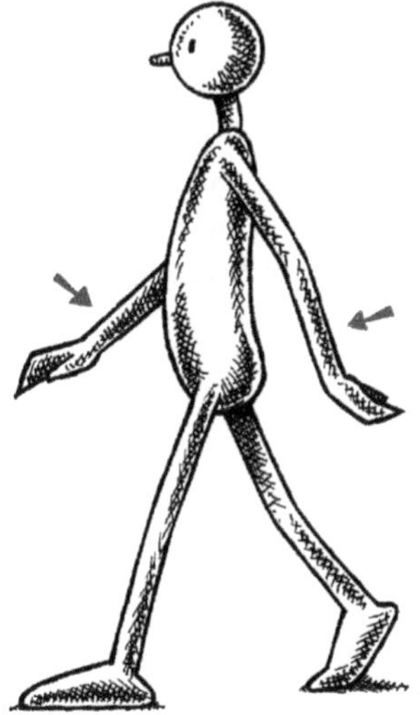

Always add overlapping action to any secondary parts of the body such as hands, hair, or clothing, as this, as well as everything else we have discussed, will offer more flow to the entire action.

A little tip when in-betweening the actual changeover in the hand, from dragging back in one direction to the other: The natural tendency is to in-between the hand's direction in relation to the arm from one angle to the other perfectly, effectively having the hand align in a straight line with the lower part of the arm. However, you'll find that you'll get more snap in the changeover action if you favor one angle or the other for this in-between. For example, the following figure shows what happens when you favor the hand position to the former angle.

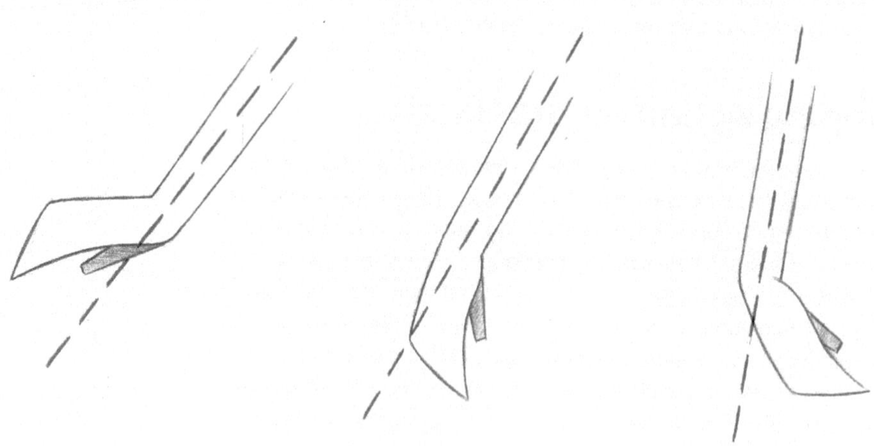

Moving from right to left, the advancing arm creates a drag on the hand until it begins to move back again (far left), where the hand immediately flips over the center line to the other side for the entire arm sweep back.

Alternatively, the next figure shows what it looks like when the swinging arm moves back and then begins to move forward. Either way, it will give you a nice snappy changeover, which a perfectly straight natural in-between position will not.

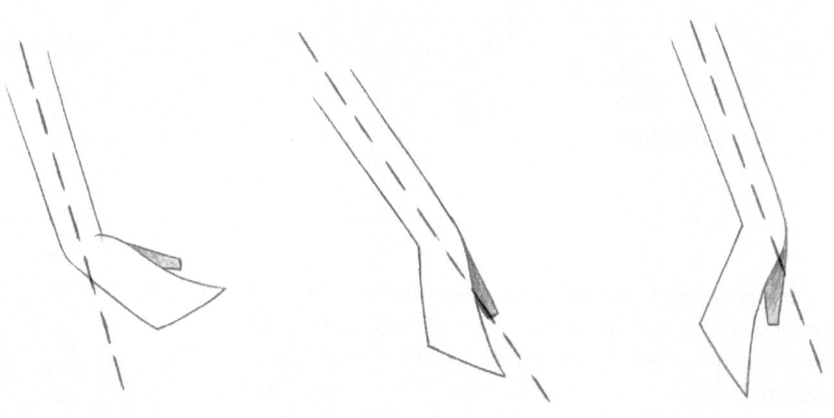

Again reading from right to left, the arm swings back (right), reaches the high point of the back swing (middle), and then accelerates, causing the hand to flip to the other side of the center line (left).

Overlapping Action on the Head

While we're looking at taking our generic walk to the next level, we should look at the head action and see what can be done. Just as the hand overlaps with the arm's action, the head can overlap with the body. This means that as the body rises up on the stride that is the passing position, the head can drag back a little, hinged at the neck or jaw line. Then, as the body drops down toward the key stride position, the head can rise up slightly.

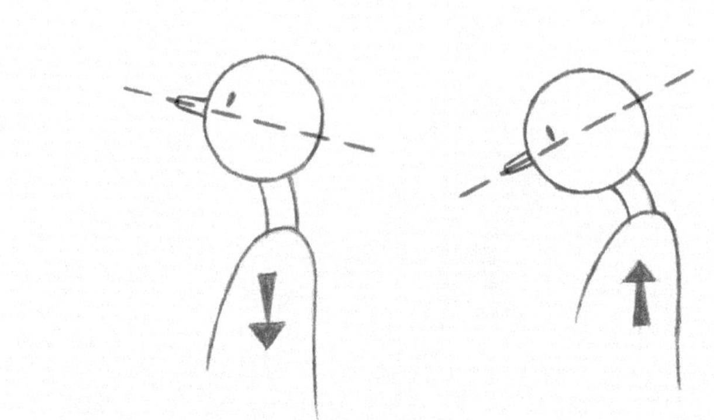

We are talking exaggerated generic principles here, but if you even add something of this countering up and down action on the head, you will bring more flexibility to your walk drawings.

But, when attempting this, please don't overexaggerate the action like this. Otherwise, it will give the head a floppy, rubber look that can detract from the overall walk appearance. (Unless that is what you're after, of course!)

Rotation on the Head

While we're talking about the head, don't forget that it is not perfectly aligned with the body from stride to stride. Consequently, as the shoulders rotate in one direction with one arm coming forward, the head can slightly rotate against it to increase the fluidity and flexibility of the entire action. It can do the same thing too in the opposite direction as the shoulders rotate the other way for the next stride. But again, don't overexaggerate this or else it will look unnatural.

Keeping Good Balance Throughout

Lastly with walks, let me talk here to the 3D-driven animators among you, who need to consider the essential balance in their walks beyond the conventional-profile 2D viewpoint we've been using. Remember that we talked about the body leaning to gain momentum and the legs having to move to stop the character falling flat on his or her face? Well, this is an issue of balance, and this has to be respected at all times in all facets of character animation if the look of the action is to appear plausible. Consequently, when looking at the profile action we have just animated, remember that unless all of our drawn characters respect the natural balance we need, the audience will not feel comfortable with the action they are watching, albeit they may not be consciously aware of it. Therefore, when moving the weight from one leg to another during the stride, the body's center of gravity must always remain in balance over the one or two points of contact the feet provide. So, with both feet on the ground, the bulk of the torso will need to be placed somewhere between the two points of contact.

Red indicates the area that the body's center of gravity can be between the two contact feet.

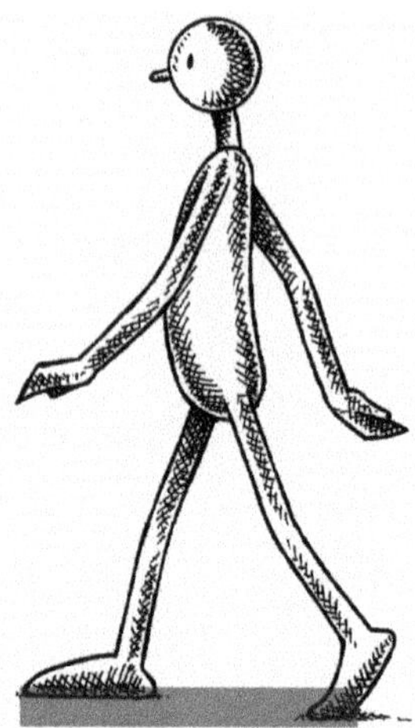

However, once one foot leaves the ground, the center of gravity needs to move above the point of contact the grounded foot makes. Not to do this creates an ugly and uncomfortable pose that implies that the character is falling over, one way or the other.

Here the body's center of gravity needs to be adjusted above the much narrower red area. Keep the lean in the body, however, to maintain a sense of forward momentum.

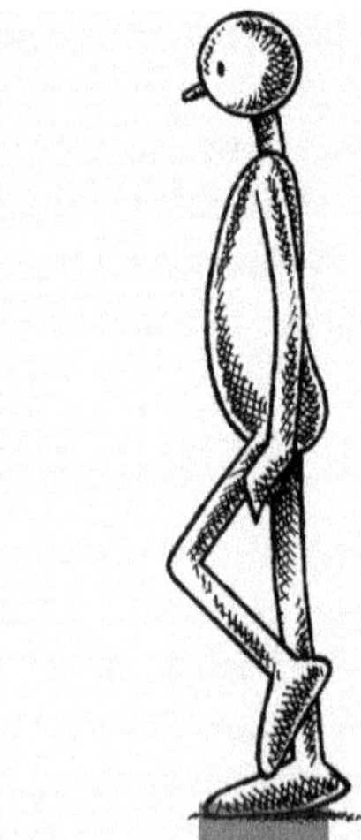

This pose is grossly exaggerated, but it does underline the fact that if a body is outside of the red contact area it will appear to be falling over!

Similarly, when we consider a walk from the front or back view, we have to also shift the center of gravity over whatever foot is in contact with the ground at any particular point in time. Not to do so gives a stilted, false impression of the walk. This is a common error with many animated walks, especially with poorly animated 3D walks where the character's center of gravity tends to be positioned somewhere in between the feet, whether they are both on the ground or not.

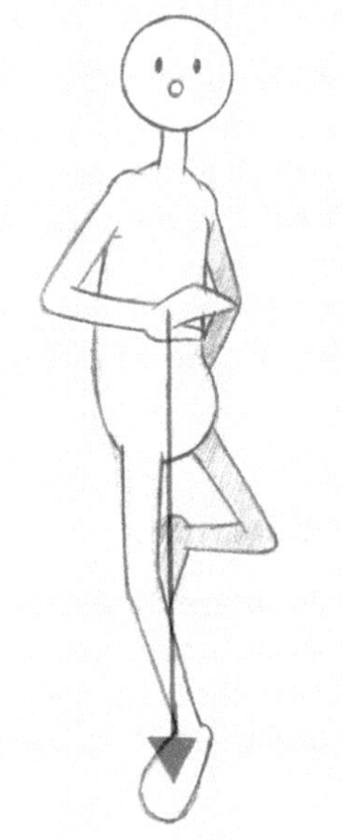

Remember that the contact area is all important, so that any view of the action will require the body to appear over it, unless the character is deliberately out of balance or falling over.

It is clear that if the body is not over the contact area, then the character will most certainly appear off balance.

In-Between Placement and Timing

Now that we have covered all the essential elements of walks, it is time to discuss the way we can give them more individuality and personality. This can be additionally done through both pose and chart modification. As we have seen, the key to a basic generic walk is to place the key stride positions correctly, make sure the passing position is well balanced, and then place the in-between drawings in the correct place. However, by modifying any of these elements, we can give the walk a definite personality.

Dynamic Key Pose Modification

"It is all in the pose." So say all the great old animators who once graced the golden age of traditional animation. For example, in the next figure, look at the two passing position modifications beside our generic one, and you can immediately see that the personality of the walk varies quite considerably from one to the other.

Passing positions can be infinite in their pose arrangement, but even an extremely exaggerated, eccentric one like this should still nevertheless appear plausible and in balance.

Clearly, apart from the generic walk pose, in the figure we have one that is very predictable and quite eccentric. All this is communicated through the pose alone, which is why the pose is everything!

At the same time, you should remember that if you mess around with any of the generic pose positions, you have to keep the character in perfect balance at all times to make him or her perform fully. That is, in a key stride position the center of gravity has to be positioned above the two points of contact at all times. However, the following figure shows the kind of pose I often see students produce, which is incorrect and gives the sense that the character would fall backward if a puff of wind came along.

Another example of a clearly unbalanced character's center of gravity being away from the foot's actual contact point on the ground.

Modifying the Passing Position

Any position can be changed to imply emotion or personality. Just remember to keep the body weight over the contact foot at all times and anything is possible. The next figure is an example of the kind of stride position that you might find with a tired or burdened character. Note how the bent back signifies a huge weight on the shoulders.

Poses can appear awkward when the action is frozen, but work perfectly within the unfolding movement of the action.

In-Between Modifications

Finally, we can consider adjusting the in-betweens to enhance the attitude and personality of the walking character. The following figure is an example of in-betweening follow-through that we might expect for an eccentric, gangly walk.

I put a continuing reversal of the foot's direction on the lead leg, giving a hesitant, shaky feel to the action.

Double-Bounce Walk

Even by changing the elementary positions of the generic walk we can give an entirely different attitude to the character's movement. For example, the old-fashioned Mickey Mouse double-bounce walk is simply created by changing the heights on the relevant stride positions. For example, whereas the standard generic walk poses are as shown in the next figure, the double-bounce action has the body on the key stride positions and the passing position down, whereas on the in-betweens the body is pushed up. This gives a perky, bouncy attitude.

Note

We do this by bending the legs or placing the character's legs at a full extension on the toes. If there is no shortening or lengthening of the lower limbs, this would be an error.

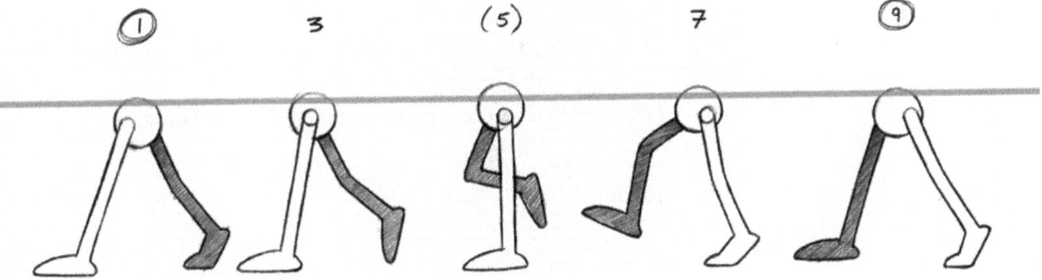

Reminder: With a generic walk the body always rises to and from the passing position.

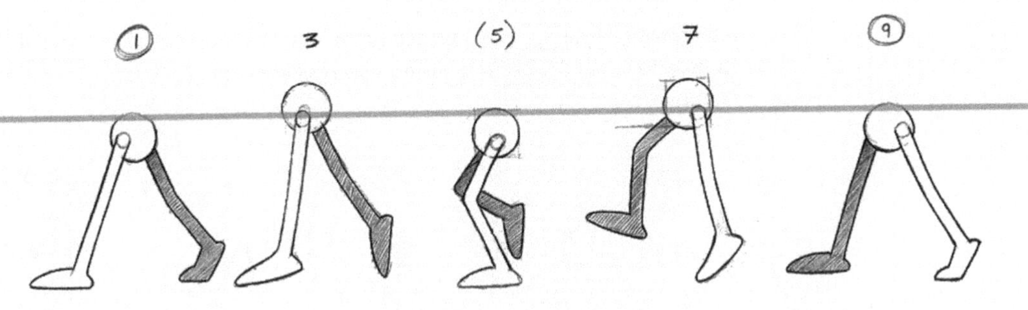

Clearly illustrating the down, up, down, up, down nature of a double-bounce walk.

Chart Timing and Variation

So far we have charted our action with even in-betweens. In other words, our generic walk was created with two keys, one passing position in the middle and one in-between in the middle of these when working on two's. However, to give emphasis to any part of the walk's action and modify its timing, it is possible to add in-betweens to slow it down at certain points. For example, by adding a slow-in to the passing position and to the end of the stride action, you can give an entirely different effect to the walk's attitude, even using the standard, generic walk drawings.

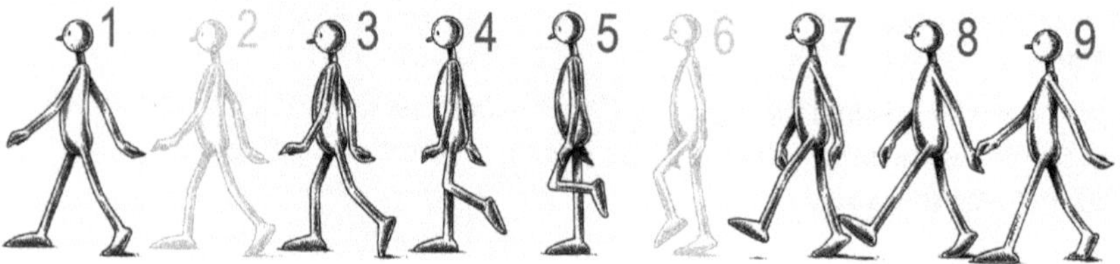

With the breakdown drawings lightened, it is clear to see how the other in-betweens are bunched toward the passing position and then the subsequent hit position, giving a slowing-in effect in both situations.

The charting for this action would look like the following figure.

In terms of in-betweening, you would create the breakdown drawings first, then do the in-betweens linking them to the next key drawing.

Alternatively, if you give the character slow-out drawings from the start of the stride, and out of the passing position, you get an entirely different sense of timing for the walk.

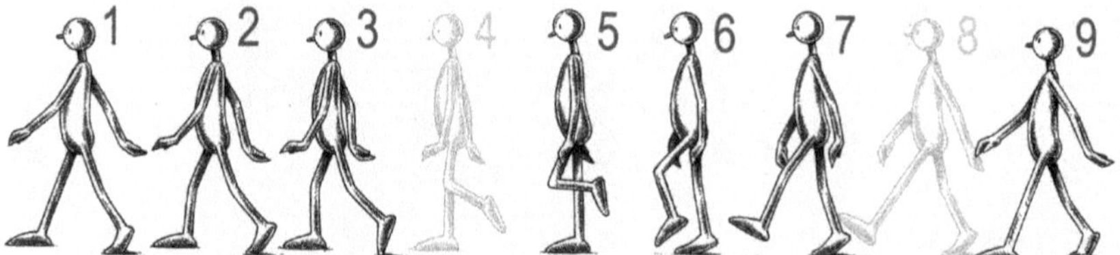

This time, with the breakdown drawings lightened again, it is clear that the extra drawings are slowing-out from the beginning of the action in both instances. The charting on this occasion would look like the next figure.

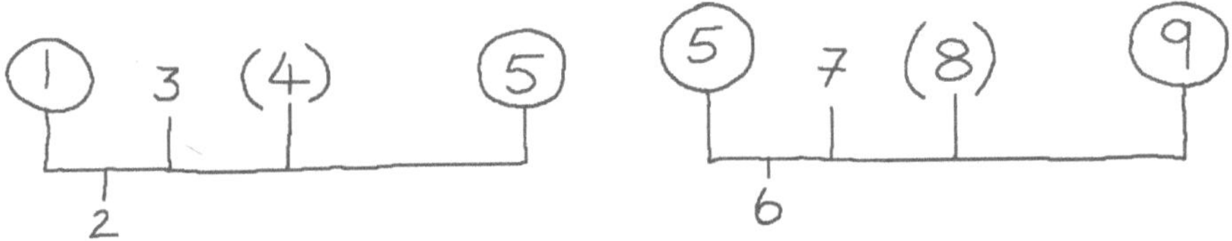

Here the in-betweens are created from the first key drawings via the breakdown drawing to the next key.

Observation and Reference Footage

The reality is that walk action is infinite in its expression. Although every able-bodied person on this planet walks the same way (i.e., by placing one foot in front of the other to gain momentum and direction), there is an infinite range of attitude and personality in the way people walk. Physiological factors play a role too. For example, a big fat, roly-poly person will walk in an entirely different way than a short, skinny, birdlike individual. It is important, therefore, that animators define the basic personality and emotional attitude of their characters before they tackle their walk actions, and adjust characters' pose positions and in-between placement accordingly. There is no better teacher than life itself. So go out into the world and study all the walk actions around you. You'll be amazed at the amazing variations that people offer to instruct and inform you! Take a video camera with you and film the most extreme examples of walking you find. Then study, analyze, and attempt to reproduce the walks you see through your animation keys, passing positions, and in-betweens. Alternatively, if you are trying to create a funny attitude with a generic-style walk, film yourself or a friend performing an extreme, eccentric walk and use that as your point of reference.

The Animator's Survival Kit

No self-respecting animator should be without the ultimate "bible" on all animated walks and runs: *The Animator's Survival Kit* by Richard Williams. Many of the exercises are advanced for this stage of study in your course, but having this book at your disposal, even now, will be an investment for throughout your future career.

Suggested Reading

White, T. *The Animator's Workbook*. New York: Watson-Guptill, 1988, pp. 57–62.

White, T. *Animation from Pencils to Pixels: Classical Techniques for Digital Animators*. Boston: Focal Press, 2006, pp. 234–244.

Williams, R. *The Animator's Survival Kit*. London: Faber and Faber, 2001, pp. 102–175.

DVD lecture: Walking Limp Pencil Test.

Assignment 4

Create a "personality" walk cycle on two's that either expresses pain (perhaps a limp) or excitement (perhaps a skip). Alternatively, your second walk could show a heavy, slow character trying to walk fast or a small, nervous character trying to look big or strong. Actually, as long as your second walk cycle is vastly different from the generic one created for Assignment 3 and your character displays a clear quality, attitude, personality, or emotion in his or her action, you can do pretty much anything you like here to demonstrate your command of the walking action.

Generic Runs

Class objective: To learn and replicate the action of a bipedal running action.
Equipment required: Lightbox, pencil, and paper.

Many people think that a run is just a faster action than a walk. But this is not the case. If you look carefully at a running action in a slow-motion action replay you'll see that whereas a walking character always has one contact foot on the ground at any moment in time, a running figure does actually have both feet off the ground during one point in each stride.

When running, it is necessary that the character is off the ground at some stage during the stride.

Key Generic Run Stages

Consequently, a run is more of a controlled leap than a speeded-up walk. Let's look at the key stages of a generic run, which can be identified in five key poses.

The Drive-Off

Here we start a run stride with the character pushing off from the ground. Note in the following figure the straight contact leg pushing the body up and forward, while the opposite leg bends dramatically upward, with the knee high.

The drive-off position should always be strong and dynamic. Note the strong line throughout the leg and body in this pose, communicating these things.

The Stride

The second position of a generic run action is the stride position. Here the body has already been driven up and forward by the rear leg, so much so that the entire character is now off the ground, up in the air. Now, however, the same trailing leg is overlapping back with the leading foot reaching forward.

As indicated earlier, this position needs to be in the air, with the trailing leg following through the drive-off position and the front foot moving forward in preparation of the reach position.

The Reach

The third position is the reach down, where the leading foot has now made initial contact with the ground. Although there is no such thing as a passing position in a run, this pose is the closest thing to it—the free leg is beginning to come through and the arms are down, close to the body, as each moves from their previous forward/reverse position.

Here the foot hits the ground and the body begins to buckle a little as the impact of height and velocity are being somewhat checked by the ground.

The Contact/Squash

Here the body sinks down into a squash position, caused by the body's weight and momentum putting pressure on the contact leg. The leg, therefore, bends to absorb the shock while the bent free leg is swinging through fast to prepare for its next drive position.

With the body somewhat down through the impact of the landing, the free leg moves through to prepare for the next drive-off position.

The Drive-Off

Now we return to the initial drive-off position, although this time it is with the opposite foot on the ground with the other free leg driving up and forward, thereby completing the first stride sequence and beginning the second.

An identical dynamic drive-off position to the first one, although this time the arms and legs are reversed.

Run Exercise

As suggested, a run is essentially a five-pose sequence that really does not have any in-betweens. So, as an exercise, you should now create your own five poses per the key positions just noted, then complete the second stride in the same way but with the arms and legs reversed. When you have done this, shoot the drawings on both one's and two's. This basic exercise will give you a sense of the speed the run will take when using this number of drawings.

Actually, rather than animate this on a run cycle, just like you did the walk cycle, this time you should draw the character running across the screen, adding enough additional stride positions to extend the distance from one side to the other beyond just two strides. This will give you a greater appreciation of how the number of drawings you have created actually move in speed and velocity. The first two strides of the run, drawn in this way, will look like the sequence shown in the next figure (although your drawings will be each on a separate sheet of numbered animation paper of course).

Note the degree of up and down movement throughout the action. With flatter runs, with perhaps somewhat heavier, weaker characters, this will be less pronounced. With lighter, more energetic and springy characters this movement might be considerably more—that is, where distance of stride may be compromised by the requirements of height. (Note: In your actual animation drawings the contact feet will be overlapping each other in terms of their contact position on the ground, of course. Here I have separated them to show the key body positions involved more clearly.)

Note that each drawing is numbered on two's (even numbers) in this instance. Now that you have created these two strides, you can use them to trace the required number of extra stride positions to take the character further across the screen (remember, all on separate sheets of paper). This will give you a sequence of drawings that look something like the following figure.

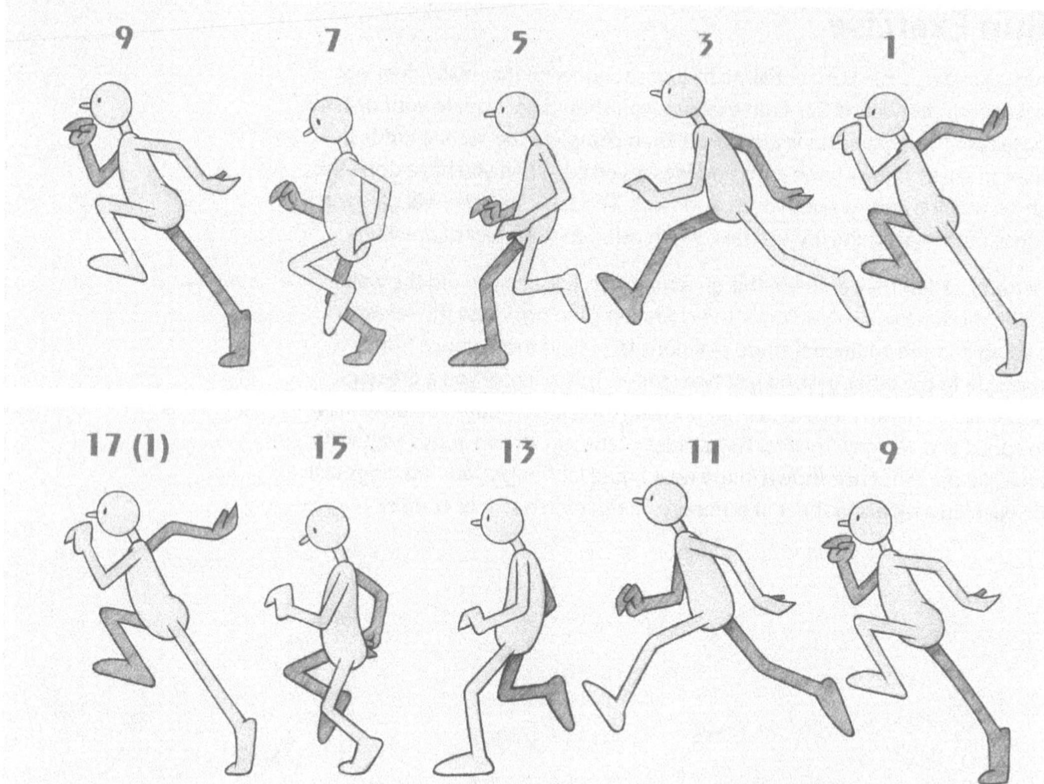

A complete generic run cycle where the front and end positions are identical. (Again, the contact feet positions have been separated here for greater clarification.)

If the run is working fine at this stage, you might choose to further in-between everything, putting in the one's (odd numbers) that are missing. Now film the same sequence one more time, this time shooting on one's and two's for your timing. This will give you greater more appreciation of how fast or smooth this number of drawings will move your character.

Additional Pointers for Runs

The generic run should work fine as a starting point. However, there are additional pointers relating to run animation that you should know. The first is the speed you can animate runs at.

Fastest Run

The fastest run possible is produced using three drawings. This kind of run can be utilized for the kind of really fast, scrabbling look you get in pure cartoon animation. The three drawings possible are as follows in the figure.

Based on a typical "Roadrunner" action, this illustrates the minimal three stride leg positions of a scurrying, scrabbling run.

Slower Runs

Runs, by virtue of their very nature, cannot be too slow, as a character cannot plausibly hang in the air in the stride position forever. However, it is possible to slow a run down, as we did with the previous exercise when putting in the one's and then shooting it all on two's. Clearly this action would be too slow for a sprinting action though unless you are deliberately trying for a slow-motion effect, in which case you will probably have to add significantly more in-betweens to make it work best. A slower marathon runner–type action, for example, has to work at a different speed, as marathon runners cannot afford to burn up the dynamic, explosive energy that a sprinter requires. They also have to adjust their running pose position to assist this process happening economically. Following are some tips regarding the differences between the two.

Body Lean

Unlike a walk that requires just a slight body lean, a run—especially a fast run—will require your character to increase his or her lean forward the faster he or she runs. The following figure shows a comparison between the lean anticipated for a sprinter as opposed to the more energy-conserving action of a longer-distance athlete such as a marathon runner.

The pose defines the energy. The action on the left appears more dynamic and energetic, while the one on the right appears more relaxed and casual.

Arm Action

If you are trying to produce a faster, more dynamic run, you will need to exaggerate the arm action in addition to the body lean. Track and field sprinters are encouraged to pump their arms harder and faster to get the extra speed in their legs that they need. Marathon runners, however, drop their arms in a more relaxed and extended-downward motion to conserve their energy.

Sketches that define three different extreme poses for the arms in a running action.

Stride Length

With the more power that is put into a run, and bearing in mind that the stride position is a process whereby the character propels his or her body more dynamically forward and upward, it stands to reason that the stride length of a run is much longer than that of a walk. Similarly, the height of the torso midstride on a run is much higher than that of the passing position in a walk.

Over and over again these illustrations indicate that the pose defines everything!

Environmental Issues

The terrain and elevation of the ground being covered will significantly affect the way the run positions have to be posed. (Actually, this is equally true for walks too!) For example, if a character is running uphill, his or her body angle and arm/leg action will need to be adjusted to accommodate the necessary additional drive required to push the body through the additional resistance that this situation will create.

It is apparent that when attempting to run up a steep incline a character's body will have to lean into it more, as well as pump the extra-bent arms harder.

Alternatively, if the character is running downhill, his or her body language and positioning will require an entirely different approach.

When running downhill, the lean needs to be backward, with the arms more extended and pumping less.

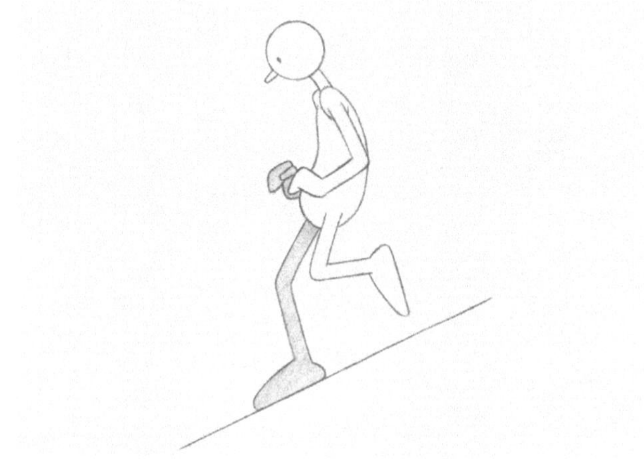

Head-On Runs

Finally, we must consider seeing a run from a different viewpoint. Specifically, from the front, per the following figures. All the main factors of the generic run apply, but the principle of shifting the body mass from side to side, with the weight transferring to a point above the point of contact on the ground, is additionally important.

This was a quick front run that I created for a class demo at DigiPen. Although roughly drawn, and not at all refined within the less than one hour I had to create it, it does nevertheless communicate the dynamics that such a run requires to be convincing.

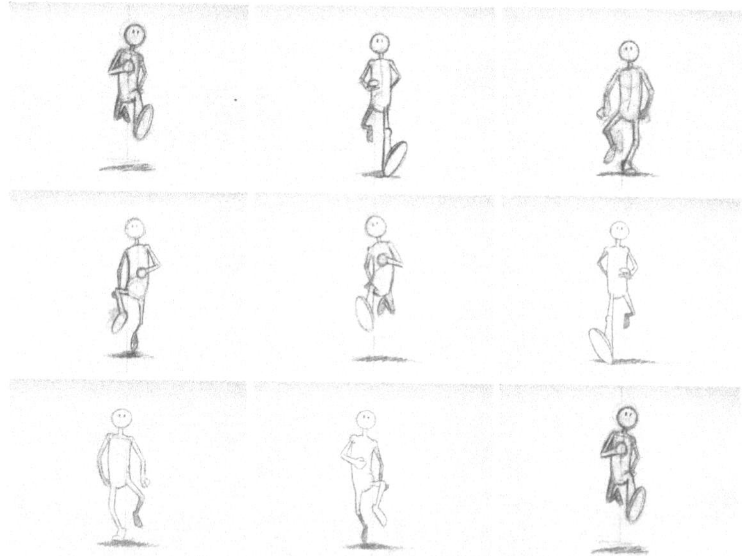

As always, balance is extremely important, with the body's center of gravity needing to be over the foot's point of contact at all times.

Also, don't forget to take advantage of the principles of perspective if you can. Note in the next figure that the parts of the body nearest the camera appear larger, while those far away are much smaller.

Distorted perspective is an approach that can create extremely dynamic action when that action is directed toward the camera. This could have been even more exaggerated than I ultimately created it!

Remember, all these factors have to be considered when approaching the running action, especially when attempting to elevate it from the standard (and often predictable) generic approach.

Suggested Reading

White, T. *The Animator's Workbook*. New York: Watson-Guptill, 1988, pp. 64–70.
White, T. *Animation from Pencils to Pixels: Classical Techniques for Digital Animators*. Boston: Focal Press, 2006, pp. 244–248.
Williams, R. *The Animator's Survival Kit*. London: Faber and Faber, 2001, pp. 176–208.
DVD lecture: "Generic Run—Front" and "Generic Run—Side".

Assignment 5

Now the really hard work begins! For this run assignment, I would like you to take any one of the characters mentioned in this lesson and create a characteristic run for him or her. However, to intensify this challenge (and to examine again your understanding of the principles of a walk action) I want you to take the circular, Stonehenge-style track background supplied (you can photocopy it from the following figure or download it from *www.desktopacademy.com*, enlarging it to the size you are working at) and animate two characters circling the track, one walking and one running. In doing this, I want you to make the action cyclic—that is, both the walk and the run should link from the end of one lap to the beginning of the next so the actions can continue endlessly. For this assignment, however, the walking character should minimally complete three laps of the entire circular track. To achieve this cyclic action, the last drawing of each lap needs to link to its first drawing. That way the same linked drawings can be shot over and over again.

The animator's circular track, where you are tested to the full with this particularly evil assignment! (Note the blue foot positions on the contact area will help when you block out your stride positions.)

By animating a run and a walk together around a circular track, you will be exploring the variance of speed and location each needs, the differences in dynamic posing, and the varying foot location points as both characters circle the track. Therefore, before inflicting such a complex and challenging assignment on you, I think it would only be fair for me to share a few tips with you first.

Speed of Action and Distance of Stride

Clearly the action of the run will be much faster than the speed of the walk, and the distance covered by each stride will be greater too. Consequently, there will be many more drawings required to complete the circuit in the walk than in the run. Additionally, the walk will contain more strides than the run to complete an entire lap.

Body Lean

For this assignment you have to contend with the forward body lean of both the walk and the run, both in themselves being different from one another, as discussed earlier. You will also have to contend with an additional, sideways body lean because of the circular path of action. Let me explain. If you watch motorbike riders as they turn a corner at speed, you will see that they lean in toward the corner as they are turning. This is because if they remained upright, or even more foolishly leant away from the corner, they would be thrown off their bike outward, due to the powerful centrifugal forces involved. Similarly, if a child is sitting on a merry-go-round, he or she will unconsciously and automatically lean inward as the ride accelerates, to stop from being similarly thrown outward by that same force. Consequently, both your walking and running figures will need to lean in toward the center of the circular pathway at all times, due to the slight centrifugal force that they too will be experiencing.

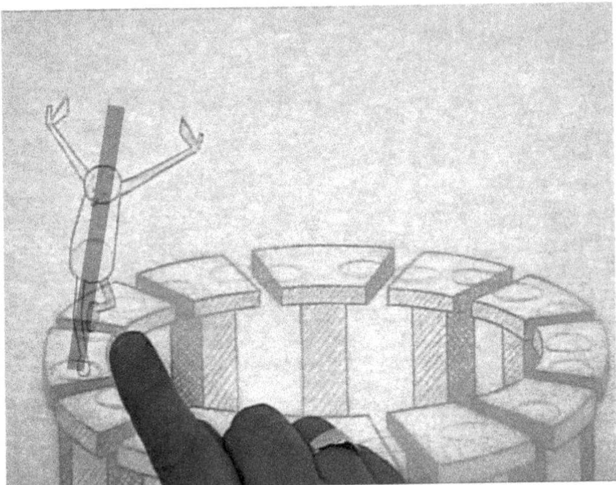

Body lean is something many animators forget, even though characters can be twisting and turning in actions of great speed and maneuverability.

Paths of Action

As the runner will pass the walker several times during the length of the assignment, you will need to plot out the paths of action beforehand, as well as the foot contact points, for each character so that there is room for them to pass one another during the scene. My advice is, therefore, that as the runner will be leaning in toward the center at a more acute angle than the walker (due to the additional speed), I would suggest that you place the runner on an inner track and the walker on an outer one.

First Drawing/Last Drawing

The key to success in this assignment is the smooth takeover point at the end of each lap to the beginning of the next, so you'll need to first carefully block the foot "hit" positions all the way around before you begin to animate either of their actions. Practically, I would suggest that with the background positioned on a pegged sheet of paper, place a fresh sheet of paper over the top (both on the pegs, of course) and sketch both paths of action for the walking and running characters. Then over this, mark all the foot hit positions for both. With these all blocked in, next go around to your hit points, marking each with a right foot or left foot indicator to make sure that you end up with the correct foot position at the end of the lap in comparison to the next foot position at the start of the next lap.

The blue footmarks that help plot the strides all the way around the circular path.

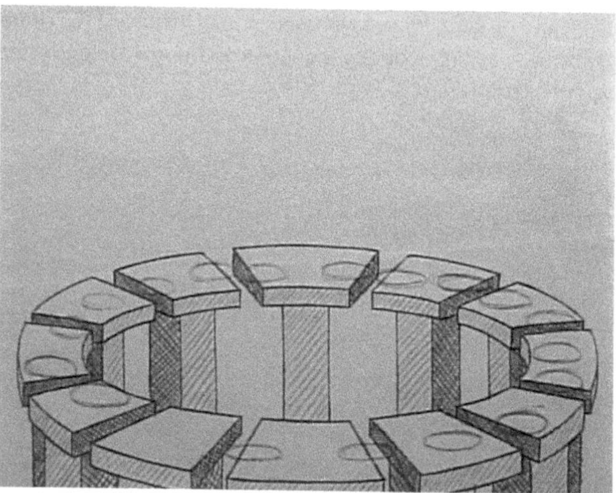

Key Stride Positions

Once you are sure that you've calculated the correct foot pattern in both cases, start to sketch the key stride positions that link to them. This will be easier for the walk than the run, as the walk strides will always have both feet on the ground at the same time.

Note the heel to toe roll on the feet as the character progresses.

However, for the run I suggest you just block in the correct stride positions for now, which will give you adequate points of reference to work with later.

Red marks the run footfalls throughout.

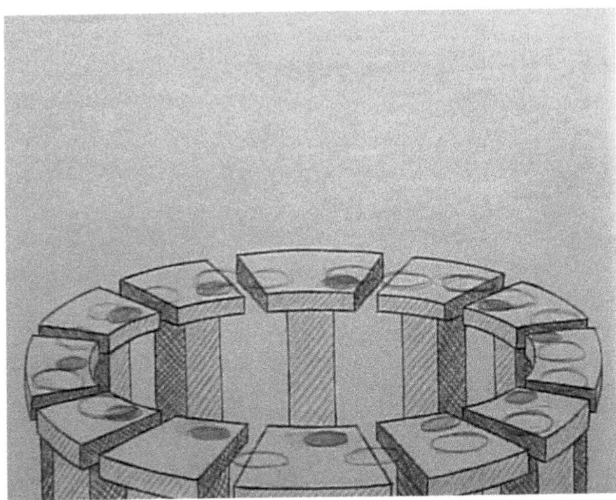

Now, with all the key stride positions in position for both actions (all blocked-in drawings on separate sheets of paper, please) you can number the drawings in each case. I suggest for this basic approach that you use a generic, equal-numbering pattern for the walk. That way the keys will be 1, 9, 17, 25, 33, etc. (i.e., there will be three in-between drawings linking them, numbered on odd-number two's).

Choosing to make the action generic, the numbering I chose for the key positions means that there are three easy in-betweens linking each key with the passing position being the middle of the three numbers, for example, 5, 13, etc. in this case.

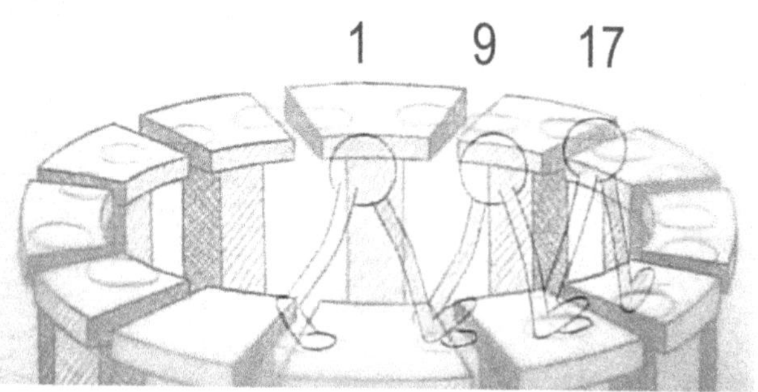

For the run, I would number the keys R-1, R-7, R-13, R-19, R-25, etc. R indicating these are the run drawings containing two pose positions that will link them on two's.

The run stride lengths (red markings) are not as wide as with the previous examples, so the action will need to be modified accordingly. That said, this is more of a generic run drive-off position.

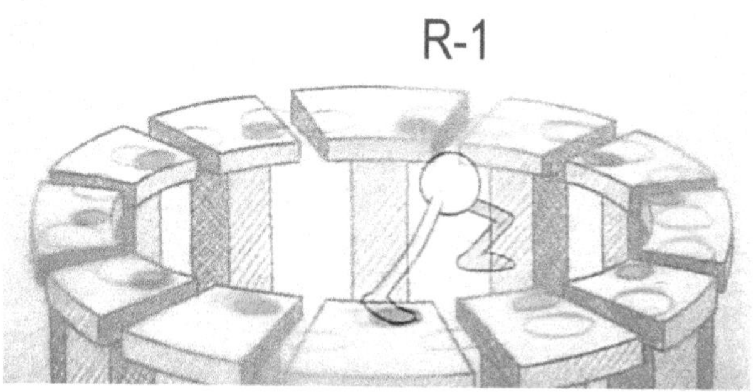

When this is done, shoot the entire sequence as a pose test—that is, hold each key drawing for as many frames as it takes to get to the next key position. That way you will have a very clear idea of how the action will look before the intensive work of putting in all the in-betweens. If you are able to shoot your work as separate passes (i.e., shoot the walk sequence first, then the run sequence, and then combine them both at the same time, such as with DigiCel's Flipbook), then you will be more able to view the overall effect of the two actions working together and their different timings by comparison.

I don't know why I chose to have a birdlike flapping of wings on the arms but in viewing the preceding body animation if felt like the character was trying to take off, thus my adopting this action with the arms.

The big challenge is not to have both actions hit each other at any point within the scene. I tried to separate the foot placements somewhat but it does require some careful preplanning to make it work in the final analysis.

Note

This is a very good time for you to turn to Appendix 6 and study the process of working with animation exposure sheets (dope sheets). Exposure sheets enable animators to keep track of scene and drawing planning, as well as to organize their thinking clearly and precisely. In this case, the exposure sheet planning will enable you to accurately place the drawings with good timings, as well as organize the various layers of action with one another. This can only help you in the challenging assignment you are about to attempt.

If all works well when you pose test the drawings, then you are already on your way to becoming a master animator! If things look wrong, however, go back and correct whatever is necessary. When you have finally completed all the corrections, shoot another pose test. Repeat this process until the pose test works as you intend it to. This is the painstaking process that we all go through to learn, by the way, so don't be daunted if it takes time to get everything right!

Final In-Betweens

Once you have successfully completed the pose test, you are ready to take on the serious task of putting in all the in-betweens. If this seems like a step too far for you, then you are probably not designed to be an animator anyway. However, if you relish the challenge of doing all those drawings, then it sounds like you're made of the right stuff! (It has to be said here ... animation, especially traditional 2D animation, is not for the faint-hearted!)

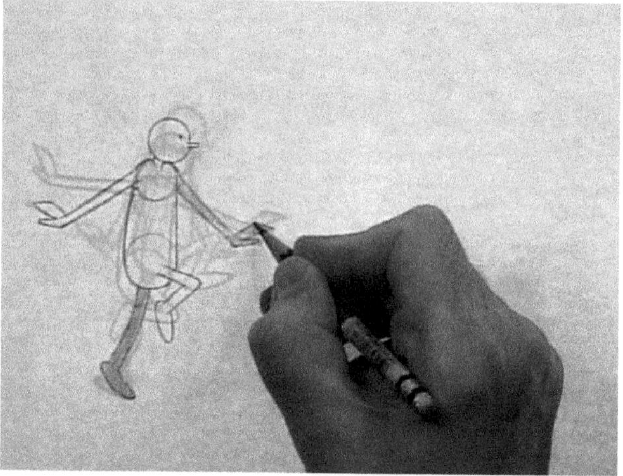

I was in-betweening the action on the pegs because I know the shape and form of this character so well. But for your assignment I do recommend that you use a certain amount of superimposition to assist you in extreme cases wherever possible.

With the in-betweens complete, you can now shoot the entire final scene as a pencil test on two's. When this is done, play back the action and see how it looks. Is it jerky or too fast? Do the characters look to be moving as if they are either walking or running correctly around the path? Are you keeping the characters successfully in proportion as they move around the circular track? These are all questions you must bravely ask yourself as you review your work, unless you have an experienced colleague or teacher who can critique for you.

These are also questions that, if working alone, you *have* to answer honestly if you are really serious about being a great animator. All glitches, mistakes, or distortions of characters should be fixed now and tested again before you are finished with the assignment. As with everything you must do, it has to be right at each stage and you cannot allow yourself to take shortcuts if your ambition is strong. I do believe that the greatest learning ultimately comes from making the greatest mistakes—that is what experience is. So don't despair if you've made one or more mistakes here. It is natural to do so, so just realize that you are not alone. All master animators including myself made horrendous and regular mistakes when we started out, and we still do so now, if the truth must be told!

Quadruped Walks

Class objective: To learn the techniques for animating quadrupeds, both cartoon style and realistic.
Equipment required: Lightbox, pencil, and paper.

In this lesson, we are going to further our understanding of the principles of generic walk animation and explore the challenges (and hopefully solutions) attributed to quadruped animation. We will do this primarily with an eye to cartoon-based quadrupeds, but we will also briefly explore more naturalistic quadruped movement.

Quadrupeds of all kinds are a major challenge to animators, as they effectively double the challenges the more conventional biped walk throws at us. Different quadrupeds have varying modes of walking, as will be seen if you watch any comprehensive documentary on natural history or animal movement. It is, therefore, very difficult for animators to analyze and replicate the enormous and multifaceted ways that individual animals move and, specifically, walk. Consequently, it is hard to formulize this into fundamental principles. However, by tackling a simple cartoon-based quadruped—in this case, a traditional pantomime-style horse—we may just get a glimmer of the process that can be employed when dealing with more ambitious four-legged walks.

You can use your own design, of course, but this one will give you all the elements you need to work through this lesson.

To make our task easier, I am going to break down this character design into clearly defined, more animatable parts (see the following figure). Note that now we have a number of specific elements that can be animated separately and then all brought together into one final piece. We have the front legs as a single biped, and the back legs as a similar, separate biped unit. Next, we have the "tube" that represents the body of the horse that connects both biped units. Then we have the head and neck of the horse at one end, and finally we have the tail element at the other end. Individually, each piece is a significant challenge on its own. But by breaking down the areas of the horse individually, we make the task of animating the entire walking horse much easier. This kind of process can be employed when dealing with more realistic quadrupeds too, as we shall see.

Each color area represents a separate layer of animation.

Front Legs

As indicated, the best way to start our animated horse walk is to separate the various elements and animate them individually, on separate layers. Let's start with the front legs.

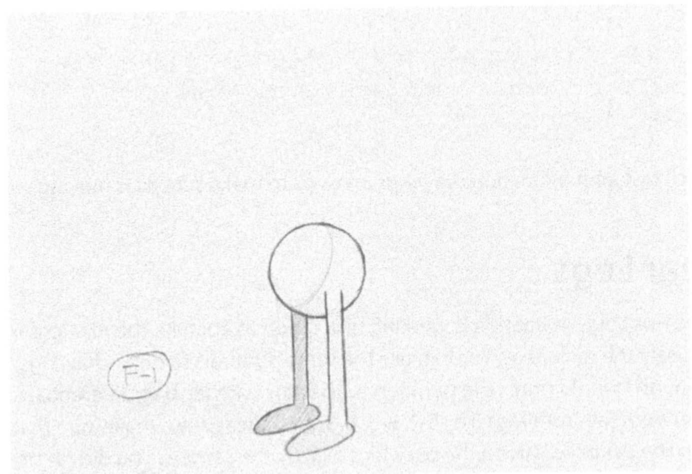

When you create the front legs action, make sure that there is enough space on the screen to include all the other layers of the quadruped's action.

Just as you already animated a generic biped walk in lesson MC 3, you must first create the key positions, passing positions, and in-between drawings of the front legs in an identical way. However, make sure that you size and position the front legs in such a way that there will be enough room for the rest of the animated quadruped when you want to combine the pieces for the overall makeup. Number the keys F-1 and F-9 with the passing positions being F-5 and F-13 and the in-betweens being F-3, F-7, F-11, and F-15. Remember that F-17 can be replaced by F-1 when shooting on cycles.

Note

I've added the prefix letter F before the numbers to represent front legs. It is necessary to distinguish each layer of the quadruped so that each layer does not have the same numbering, which would be extremely confusing. You, of course, can choose your own prefix letter for all level drawings, as long as you do so!

Remember the action I have chosen for this is not generic, it is eccentric. Therefore, if the poses appear unfamiliar, you have to consider them in context with the full moving action, which can be seen on the accompanying DVD.

Pencil test your animation drawings on two's to make sure all is moving well.

Rear Legs

If the front legs animation is working fine, go on to animate the rear legs in precisely the same way. You can use the same numbers for your drawings, although I would prefix the numbers with B (for back legs) to differentiate them from the front legs (i.e., B-1, B-3, B-5, etc.). Please also make sure that you keep the stride length on the back legs exactly the same as you did for the front legs, for reasons we shall go into shortly.

Again, before you animate the back legs, make sure they are positioned correctly, so that they relate to where the front legs are and the rest of the layers of action you have to create.

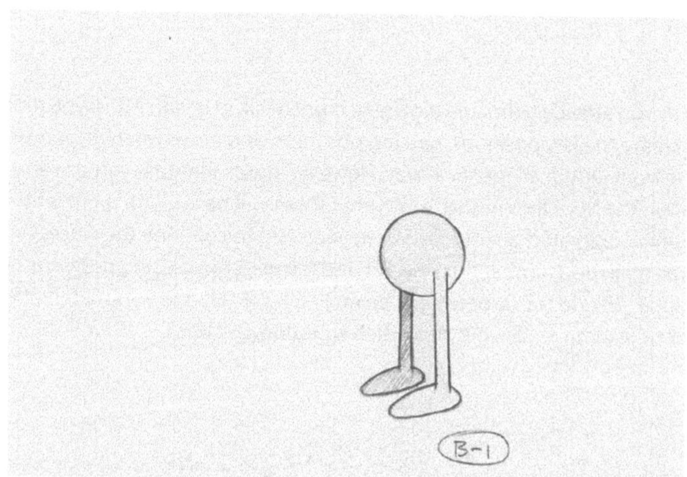

Pencil test the back legs action when you are done to see if all is working. If possible, shoot both the back and front legs together, on separate levels, so that you can double-check that both pairs of legs move at the same speed and timing according to the numbering.

Note that the passing position I have created here is also eccentric. In this case, I wanted the back legs to rotate then move straight through in a regular way, thus the passing position here is high and back, as part of a large, looping arc.

If you want to write this down on an exposure sheet, the following figure shows what this particular doping will look like.

ACTION	DIAL	EXTRA	4	3	2 (FRONT LEGS)	(BACK LEGS)	EXTRA	CAMERA
					F-1	B-1		
					3	3		
					5	5		
					7	7		
					9	9		
					11	11		
					13	13		
					14	14		
					15	15		
					16	16		
					17	17		
					18	18		
					19	19		
					20	20		
					21	21		
					22	22		
					23	23		
					24	24		
					25	25		

Note that I always identify the animation layers by describing them clearly at the top of the exposure sheet. This ensures that I don't get confused once there are several layers being used, something that is quite possible the more intricate and involved the scene can be.

Synching the Legs Together

With the leg animation complete, decide what sync the front legs will have with the back legs. In other words, if you line up all the drawing numbers of the front and back legs in sync as doped on the exposure sheet, you will have both sets of legs moving with identical timing at the front and at the back. However, you might want them moving with different sync timing, so you could, for example, offset the timing of the back legs with those of the front by two, four, or six frames to give a variation in their comparative timing. Any of these suggestions will work, so feel free to choose what you like. (Experiment by shooting them all together if you like, then select your favorite.) The following figure shows what an alternatively timed option will look like on the exposure sheet.

Adjusting the sync between the front and back legs is more a question of try and see at this stage. Shoot several options of their separate timings and decide what the final sync between the two will be. Here the majority of the animation is to be shot on 1's.

ACTION	DIAL	EXTRA	4	3	2	1	EXTRA	CAMERA
					F-19	B-5		
					20			
					21	7		
					22			
					23	9		
					24			
					(25)	11		
					26			
					(27)	(13)		
					28	14		
					29	15		
					30	16		
					31	17		
					32	18		
					(13)	19		
					14	20		
					(15)	21		
					16	22		
					(17)	23		
					18	24		
					19	25		
					20	26		
					(21)	27		
					22	28		
					(23)	29		
					24	30		
					(25)	31		
					26	32		
					(27)	33		
					28	34		
					29	35		
					30	36		
					(31)	37		
					32	38		
					(13)	39		
					14	40		
					(15)	41		
					16	42		
					(17)	43		
					18	44		

When you have decided what sync order you want the two pairs of legs to move in, you should define the numbers on your own exposure sheet so that there can be no confusion later on.

When testing the animation sync, I've found that it is very valuable to see the drawing numbers on the screen at the same time, which is why they are visible here. (Note: Your own animation should not show the head, neck or tail parts of the drawing at this stage!)

Adding the Body

With the front and back legs moving the way you want them to, it is now time to connect them with a body section. Remember, the body design here is effectively a flexible tube shape with a fixed volume. So the more it is squashed and stretched, the more you need to respect the inherent properties it contains. Students and beginners tend to forget this, and when they squash and stretch something it mysteriously changes shape, mass, or volume in the process. It is important, therefore, that you avoid doing this when working with your animation, especially 2D animation.

Position the first two corresponding numbered legs on the pegs and, on a separate sheet of suitably numbered paper (or even on one of the existing leg levels if you prefer to be economic with layers), draw the connecting body lines to each set of legs. For my example I'm using static legs to illustrate the new link (body) drawing.

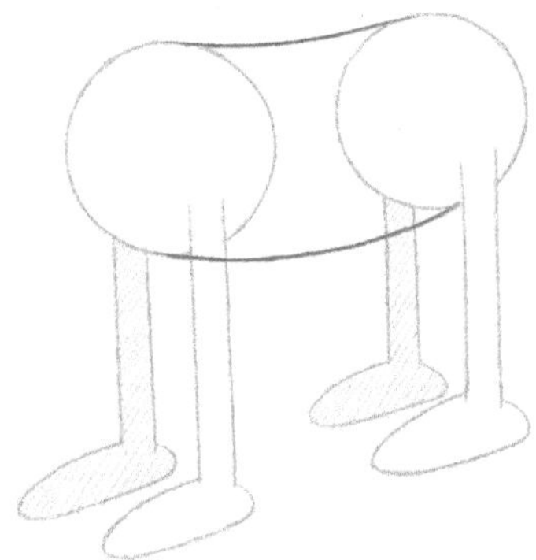

In essence, this level is just two curved lines that join the front and back legs. But it is very important that the shape and volume defined by the two lines entirely gives the impression of the character's body.

Again, I must repeat, always factor in the unchanging volume of the body mass to any distortion that stretching or squashing creates. Remember, too, that this particular body has a natural sag to it and that has to be part of any body drawings you create. For example, in the following figure you will see the shape of the body for the front legs (F-23) and the back legs (T-23).

Sometimes it can be challenging (and strange) to connect two extremely differing layers of animation, as can be seen here. However, the core requirement is that you make sure that the defining lines maintain a similar volume to the body in comparison to previous drawings, no matter how distorted the shapes appear.

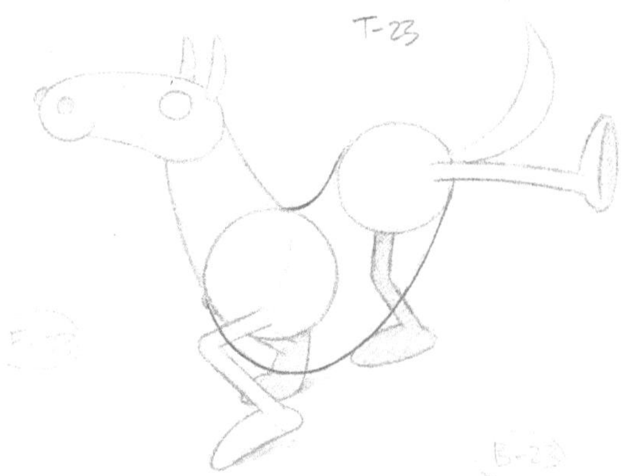

When all the body drawings are attached to all the leg drawings, you should have something resembling the previous figure if you are using the same front/back legs numbering synchronization. If you are not, you will have to work out your own way of numbering them. As it happened in my piece, they did coincide. The next figure shows how it started.

See how all the numbers align in this case on a frame-by-frame basis. However, if you move the sync between the front and back legs, the numbers will not align.

SEQ. (2) SCENE (1) 'QUADRUPED'

ACTION	DIAL	EXTRA	4	3 (BODY)	2 (FRONT LEGS)	1 (BACK LEGS)	EXTRA (B/G)	CAMERA
				X	(F-1)	(1)		
								START!
					(3)	(3)		
					5	5		
					(7)	(7)		
					(9)	9		
					11	(11)		
				B-13	(13)	(13)		
				14	14	14		
				15	(15)	15		
				16	16	16		
				17	(17)	(17)		
				18	18	18		
				19	19	(19)		
				20	20	20		
				21	(21)	(21)		
				22	22	22		
				23	(23)	(23)		
				24	24	24		
				25	(25)	(25)		
				26	26	26		
				27	(27)	(27)		
				28	28	28		

Pencil test the resulting drawing together to make sure that all pieces are linking and moving as you intend them to throughout the cycled action. Shoot the drawing for three continuous repeat cycles as a minimum. If it is not working, then correct the problem. If it is, you can now move on to the neck and head animation.

Neck and Head

Now that you have a moving legs and torso quadruped action complete, you need to review your latest pencil test and imagine how the head and neck action might go. Look at footage of real horses to get a better idea before you proceed.

Remember, for the cartoon horse, the simpler looking you create the various layer elements of the character, the easier it will be to animate them.

At this point, let me remind you of the overlapping action principle we talked about earlier. The principle of overlapping action is that a secondary object, connected to the main one, will move slightly differently, usually delaying behind, the main action. In the case of our horse, the neck will be secondary to the body, but the head will be secondary to the neck. Therefore, when animating the neck section you have to first consider the body's front leg action. The core, generic principle here (which we are working with) is that as the body rises, the neck will delay downward slightly, and then when the body drops, the neck will rise in comparison.

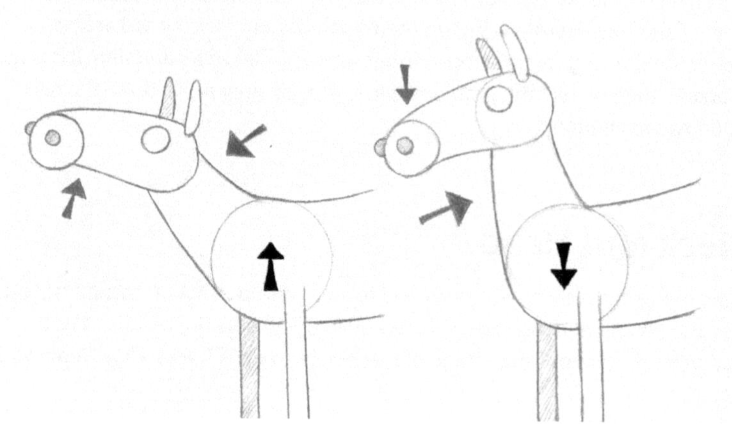

I've drawn this in a very mechanical way to illustrate the point, but in your own action you might want to add side-to-side action on the head or even a slight swaying from side to side to give it more fluidity. Again, trial and error is the best way of knowing what works and what doesn't.

First, the Neck Action

For this exercise, therefore, take just the first "down" front leg drawing and place it on your pegs (this is drawing 1, in my example). Now, with a new and separate sheet of paper on the pegs above this (and numbered N-1, with N standing for neck), draw the neck and jaw position, slightly up in relation to the body (see the following figure).

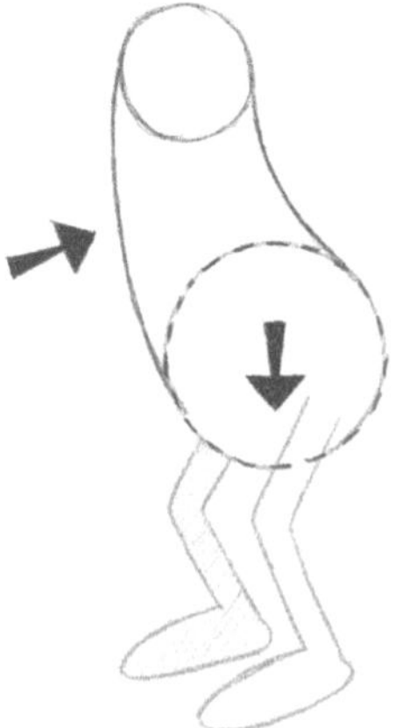

This is a very mechanical approach to get the point across. For more fluidity, you might try a slight twist in the neck as it moves up and down, or maybe a little more flexibility in its shape in general.

This is the most economic and safe way of working here. However, if you are trying to save on the number of levels you need to use, like the body, you can draw this action onto the actual front legs drawing that your are referencing, as I have done. However, if you need to make changes, you will find that the original drawing can get really messy if you repeatedly correct things.

Now take the front legs "up" position (5) and add the neck to a new sheet overlay (N-5) and draw the neck slightly down.

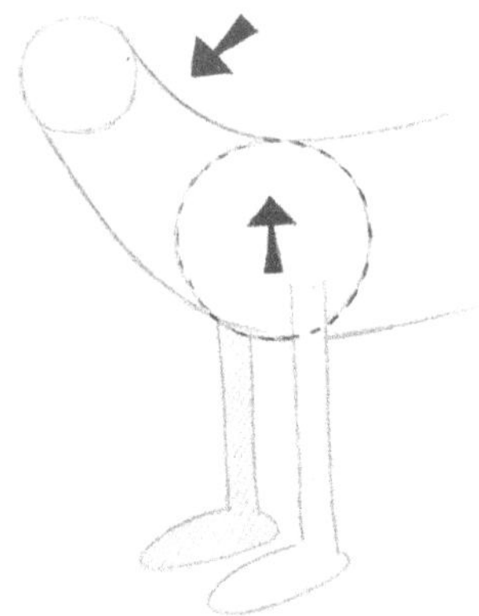

Other factors to reckon with for this kind of action are the placement of the legs and the angle of the shoulders beneath the neck. In this drawing, the legs are straight and vertical, but in your animation you will probably find all kinds of variations to their positioning. Consequently, you will have to balance the neck action in accordance to how the underlying body is supporting it.

Finally, in-between the neck for the other front legs positions and pencil test the result. You should see the neck slightly delaying its movement to the up and down of the front body action.

If you are using separate levels, your exposure sheet should look like the following figure.

NECK / FRONT LEGS

ACTION	DIAL	EXTRA	4	3	2		EXTRA	CAMERA
					N-1	F-1		
					3	3		
					(5)	(5)		
					7	7		
					(9)	(9)		
					7	7		
					(5)	(5)		
					3	3		
					(1)	(1)		

Remember that with all these dope sheet examples I am indicating animation on two's (i.e., one drawing for every two frames). However, if the action is fast and/or very fluid, you should animate it on one's (one drawing per frame).

Adding the Head

With the neck successfully animated, in combination with the body, it is time to work on the head part of this unit. If the neck/body action does not work, however, continue with the corrections until it does. Remember, the best animation is always a process of trial and error, correction, trial and error, correction, and so on until everything is right.

To animate the head on the neck we do not need to work with the legs animation level anymore (if you have them as a separate level). So, with just the individual neck drawings on the pegs, take drawing N-1 and draw in the head. Remember, the neck in N-1 is slightly up in relation to the body, so based on the principles of overlapping action, the head in this case should be somewhat down.

Yet another mechanical-looking illustration to demonstrate the principle. For finer animation you should use side-to-side and rotation movement on the head and neck to give it a more natural and fluid appearance. (Note here too that I've even indicated a separate overlapping on the ears... meaning that when the head turns down the ears will drag back and vice versa.)

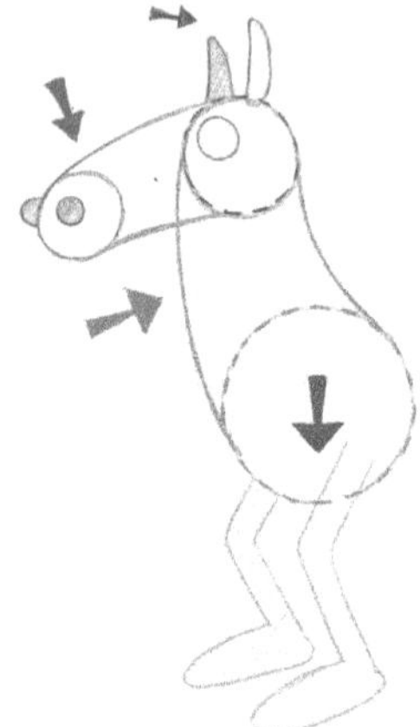

Similarly, the head in drawing N-5 should be slightly up in relation to the neck, which was down in relation to the body, of course.

As indicated in the neck section, a lot of the head-plus-neck action will depend on the way the legs and shoulders support this action. Consequently, you will probably find that the animation with the legs and shoulders in a position to this drawing will require that you position the head and neck slightly different, although the core principles of its movement will remain the same.

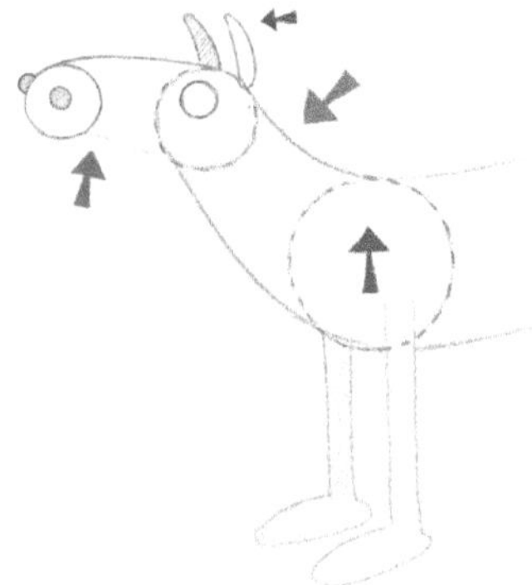

Now in-between the other drawings of the neck to represent the changes the head is making in relation to it. (Don't forget the principles of favoring one side to the other when the secondary animation is changing direction, as we did with the hands on the arms for the generic walk!) When all the in-betweens are complete, pencil test the front legs and the neck and head together to see how it all works. If you have not gone too over the top with the overlapping action, you should now see a gentle, flexible movement of the head and neck in relation to the up and down of the body. The next figure shows what the dope sheet would look like with everything on separate layers.

ACTION	DIAL	EXTRA	4	HEAD	NECK	FRONT LEGS	EXTRA	CAMERA
				(H-1)	(N-1)	(F-1)		
				3	3	3		
				(5)	(5)	(5)		
				7	7	7		
				(9)	(9)	(9)		
				7	7	7		
				(5)	(5)	(5)		
				3	3	3		
				(1)	(1)	(1)		

Remember, again, that I have numbered everything similarly here to make things clearer. In reality, you may find that you need to number each layer slightly different, depending on the less-than-generic action you eventually end up with.

Now is the time for you to approach the final piece in the puzzle—the tail.

Adding the Tail

Compared to all the other more fixed and simple-jointed elements of the horse that we are dealing with, the tail must be approached as being more significantly flexible and fluid. It is still subject to the overlapping action principle, but this time we don't have to treat it with the rigid, jointed effect we have used so far. In fact, the tail can be treated as a fluid and extreme version of the head, but much more floppy—that is, the tail moves as a more curved version of the neck and so its tip is a more extreme and floppy version of the head moving in opposition. If it helps, imagine the inside of the tail being a whole series of closely packed joints, that each delay and overlap with each other as the tail moves.

This is a generic approach to tail design. You will probably want to create your own ideas for what it will look like, but I strongly advise that you look at real tails and base your cartoon version on them. I mostly advise that for this tutorial you create a tail that has some bulk to it and some flexibility.

So, when the back legs of the horse's body move up, the main body of the tail will tend to curve down. However, in overlapping with the downward curve of the tail's body, the tip will tend to curve up at the same time. The opposite is true of the tail when the back legs of the horse move down.

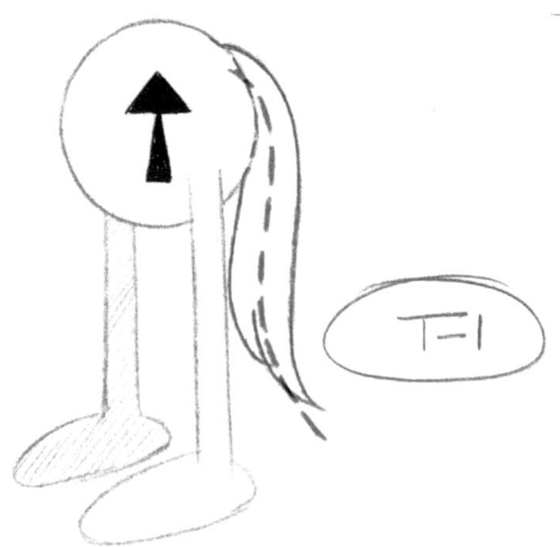

When I refer to the tail moving up, I am referring to the root of the tail where it is attached to the butt of the horse. As you can see from this drawing though, the tip of the tail is still curving from where it came from, not from where the root of the tail is going to.

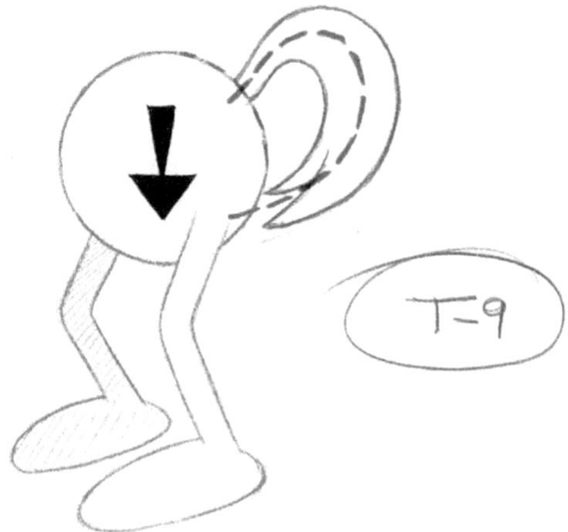

Note that the root of the tail is moving downward, whereas the tip of the tail continues to swing in the upward direction that the rest of the tail was originally going.

The in-between of the tail is also a little more fluid and flexible than the head and neck movement. To get a greater flicking action at the end of the tail, you will significantly need to favor one side or the other when the tail traverses the center line of the body. (i.e. Never use a straight line inbetween linking a convex shape or a concave one… always favor one side or the other of the straight line!)

Note that the tip of the tail doesn't reverse inward until drawing T-9. Prior to that, it maintains the outward curve it started with. By not in-betweening the positions between T-7 and T-9, it gives the action a certain flip that makes it more convincing. Even if this action were to be in-betweened on one's, I would still recommend that there be no in-between from the last frame curving outward (in this case, T-8) and the first frame curving outward (T-9).

Now try to animate the tail yourself. On separate levels of drawings (or on the back legs drawing if you wish to save on levels) create the tail action using the same process you used for the head and neck. Number the tails T-1, T-3, T-5, etc., and when it is all done, pencil test the action. When you are satisfied with the tail animation, reshoot everything together for a final pencil test (i.e., the legs, body, head, neck, and tail). Hopefully it is all working well together. If not, make the necessary corrections to the offending layer (or layers) and repencil test until everything works as you would like it to.

To shoot it all together you'll need some kind of comprehensive image-capture software, such as DigiCel's Flipbook. Alternatively, you can scan every individual level of the drawings and composite and render them together on programs such as Adobe's Photoshop/Premiere or Photoshop/After Effects, or work in a vector environment using ToonBoom Technology's ToonBoom Studio.

The six layers that make up the complete cartoon quadruped action.

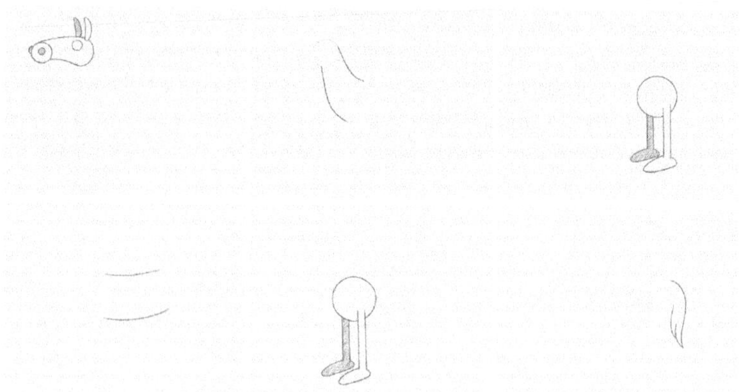

The following figure is what the exposure sheet should look like when everything is finished.

Perhaps here you can see the need for clarity, thus each layer is described at the head of each layer column.

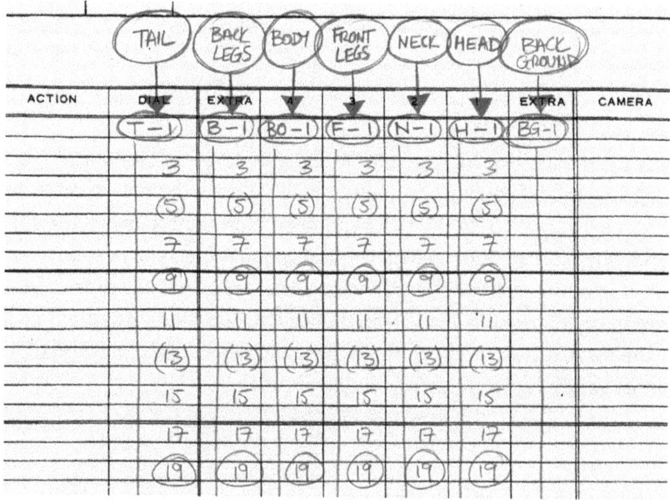

Moving Background

Until now we have not even considered a background with any of our walk assignments. However, here is where all that changes. Remember that when we created the generic walk cycle it was pointed out that every foot-slide distance had to be identical? Here is why.

To get the effect of a character's feet moving along a background surface we have to make sure that the objects depicted in the background move identically in distance to the foot slide. Using the background concept in the following figure as our reference example, you will learn how to make the background move and the foot slides synchronize. (Although you're free to design and use your own background artwork if you so choose, of course.) Because the animation we are using moves on a cycle with the foot sliding a consisting distance from one drawing to the other, the background has to move this identical distance as well. Consequently, all the elements in this simple background structure have been designed as a repeat pattern of movement from left to right, so one section can be in-betweened to the other… creating a repeating action as it moves through the screen.

This is a very simple background with basic coloring to clearly illustrate the principles involved.

In this background the light area to the left is identical to the dark-shaded area to the right, meaning that these are effectively key positions that can easily be in-betweened so that a repeat cycle action can be utilized.

Note that usually the background behind a walk cycle is an extremely long piece of artwork that pans past at precisely the same distance per frame as the character's foot slides. However, for our pencil test examples here, I want you to draw the moves to avoid any unnecessary technical requirements, as well as to help you learn the process of synchronized movement by the more comprehensive hand-drawn process.

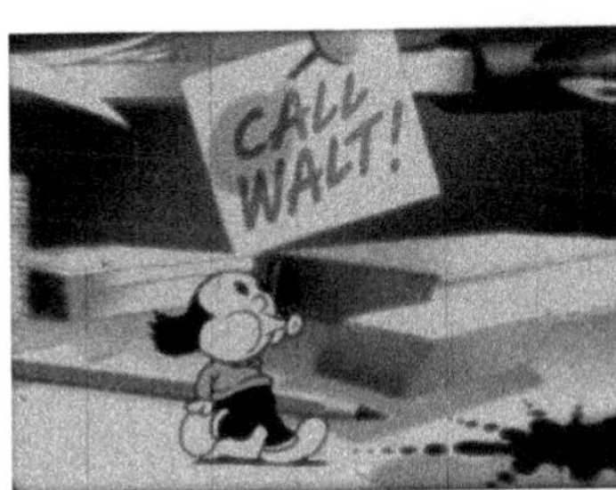

Note that the items on the background move exactly the same distance as the foot slide, frame by frame. If the scene is long, the same cycle animation drawings can be used over and over again throughout. However, the single piece of background art will have to be long enough to pan through for the entire scene without the edges of the artwork appearing in the shot.

The trick here is to design and position the elements in the background (at least those in closest proximity to the feet) in such a way that as you in-between them on their own background cycle animation, the distance they move across the screen is identical to the distance the foot slides. This way the feet will give the clear impression that they are really fixed to a specific point on the ground as the character walks. However, should the background move at a different speed in the area of the foot slide, the feet will appear to slip or skid in relation to it!

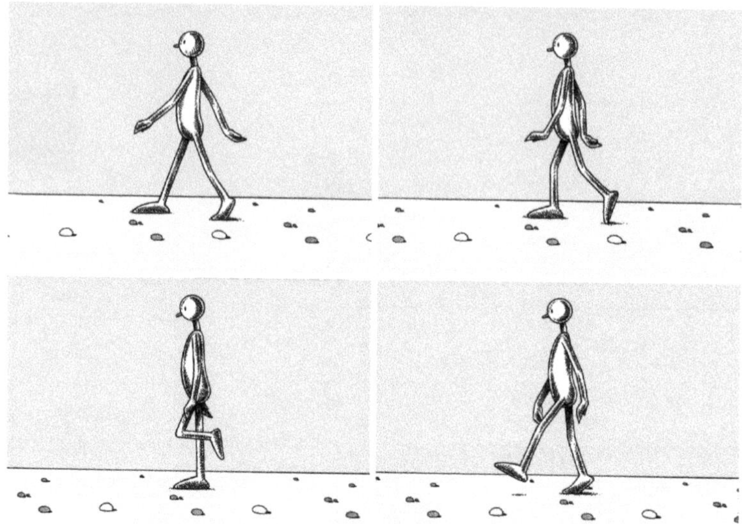

Note how the sliding action on the animated-cycle background animation is identically matched to the sliding foot of the character.

This figure is a unique example of that same matching background slide principle. I created this scene based on a walking bull glass design found in an ancient Egyptian tomb. I wanted to animate the bull on cycle animation. However, to make it convincing, I also had to animate the background pattern beneath the bull. Consequently, although both the bull and the animated background were on separate levels, I had to make sure that they both had the same amount of panning slide movement, linking the background design and the bull's animated foot slide.

Multilayered Backgrounds

The background can be broken up into separate layers if you like, with artwork for the distance, walking area, and foreground on separate layers.

For this scene the various layers would be (1) the far hills and sky (slowest panning speed), (2) the pathway (medium speed), (3) the character (his foot slide matching the pathway speed), and (4) the foreground sign (fastest speed, probably coming in and out of the scene during the entire sequence). Some testing will be required to achieve the most compatible mutual speeds.

Working with the principle that something farther away from us tends to move slower, the panning speeds for the various layers in our background will have to move similarly. Therefore, the distant background layer will move slower than the midground layer, and the foreground background elements will move the fastest.

The various layers.

This kind of parallax action is commonly known as a *multiplane action*, based on the effects that the Walt Disney studio once achieved on their complex multiplane camera. So, if you do decide to have a multiplane effect with your background, make sure that the layer on which the character's feet are in contact with is the one that moves at the same speed as the foot slide.

All that said, it is perfectly fine to have a single layer for the entire background, however, as long as that too moves at the same distance as the foot slide each time. Alternatively, if you use an entirely flat-colored, plain background at the foot contact position, any slight slippage that may occur will probably not be noticeable.

Once you know the distance from toe to toe on a single key stride position, it is easy to divide that distance by the number of frames you have to get the character to the next full stride position. This therefore gives you the amount of slide distance that will be necessary on the contact foot for every frame of the walk cycle.

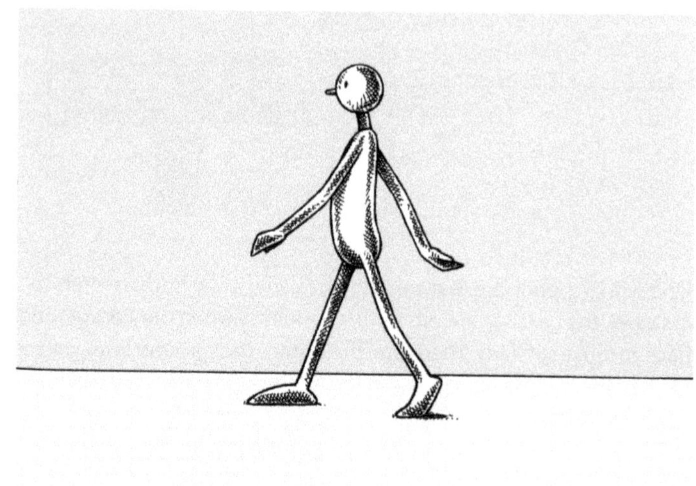

We are talking here of matching the movement on the background with the movement on the feet of the horse, which is currently animated on two's. However, the very best background panning movements are achieved by panning the artwork on one's, particularly with backgrounds that contain strong vertical elements in their design, which tend to strobe (or judder) when moving on two's. If you pan/animate the background on one's, however, and keep the overlying animation on two's, there will be a slide discrepancy every other frame, which might look unacceptable. Consequently, for really top-drawer work, all walk animation in panning scenes really should be in-betweened and then shot on one's to match the optimum background speed. This is not always necessary for the exercises we are working on here, unless otherwise requested.

Although the scene seems dark in appearance, I think it still remains clear that the various layers are moving at different speeds throughout the scene, giving an interesting parallax effect.

Nonwalk Pans

Of course, not all multilevel pans are connected to walking action and foot slides. Quite often stunning visual effects can be achieved by simply having separate layers of background artwork pan at separate speeds to give the illusion of traveling through, or across, scenes that have depth. This is extremely effective with both horizontal and vertical pans.

The three main layers of background artwork that made up the previously illustrated scene.

Realistic Quadrupeds

Of course, animators' work will not always be focused on producing the kind of simple, cartoon-style characters that we have dealt with here. This is especially true in the world of games or movie special effects, where animators are more and more required to replicate lifelike quadruped action through creatures, dinosaurs, or space monsters that cannot be filmed in any other way. Consequently, we need to consider a slightly different approach in this case, although at the heart of it we can apply pretty much the same process of creation.

For this example, I am going to use a walking puma, footage of which I obtained from the wonderful Oxford Scientific Film natural history website (*www.osf.co.uk*) and began to partially animate by way of a class tutorial. At the Oxford Scientific Film site you will find a huge library of still and film imagery of animals and other natural things that you can draw from as a key reference. It is possible to freely view and replay that low-resolution footage as much as you like on the site, but if you want to use that footage in a commercial film for some reason, you will have to pay for it.

Anyway, the sequence I chose was of a puma briefly pacing backward and forward. Clearly there is a lot of complex action here for the animator to take in. However, based on a design of a puma that was created for me by Dr. Charles Woods at the DigiPen Institute of Technology, I was able to break down the shape of the cat into definable, primitive shapes. See the following figures.

The full film sequence shows the puma pacing backward and forward, providing more than enough information to make an educated guess at an acceptable and realistic animated example of how the big cat moves. The only difficulty was that with the long grass it was hard for me to see how the cat placed its feet on the ground, which, of course, is different than a generic human walk.

Note that before animating the scene I created a Xerox copy of the original Dr. Woods' drawing, sized to the dimensions I needed for animation. Then I blocked out (in blue pencil) the foot-slide paths of action, on which I also marked the front and back foot positions.

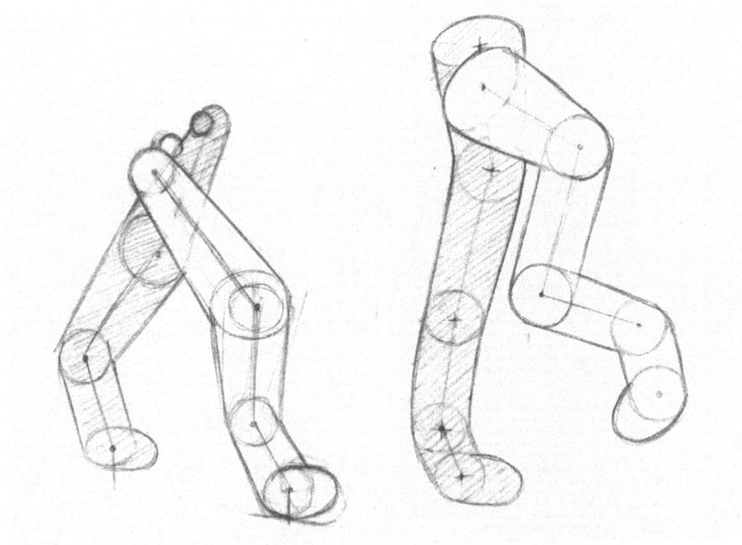

By breaking the body parts of our realistic-looking character to simple primitive shapes, it makes the animating of these body parts so much easier.

From these images, I was much more able to animate each section of the puma independently, essentially in the same way indicated with the cartoon horse. To do this, I studied the footage of the puma over and over again, isolating my attention ultimately on the individual parts that I was animating at any point in the process, placing the individual sections of animation on separate layers so I had control of each of them independently. For example, the following figure is my structural animation for the front legs alone. Then for the back legs, I created a sequence in the same way.

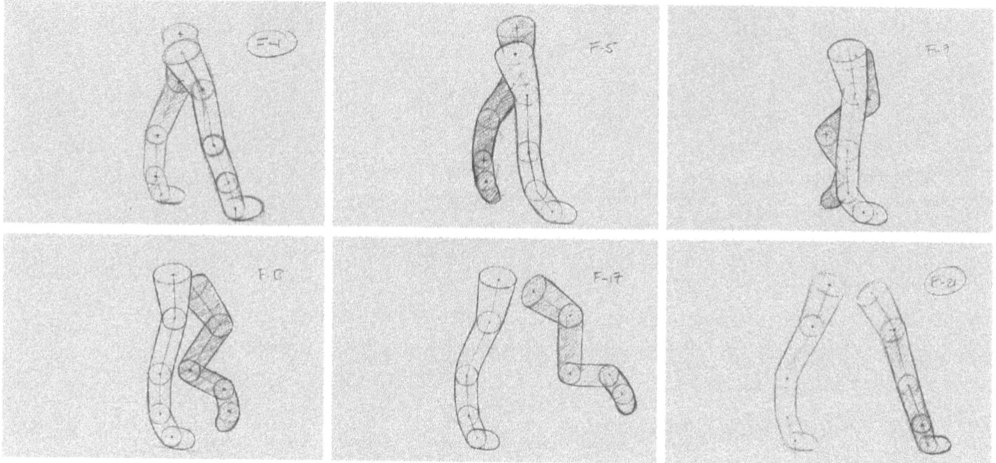

These are not all the leg positions I used in the final animation, but they do show the main positions I created, on four's, to produce one complete step.

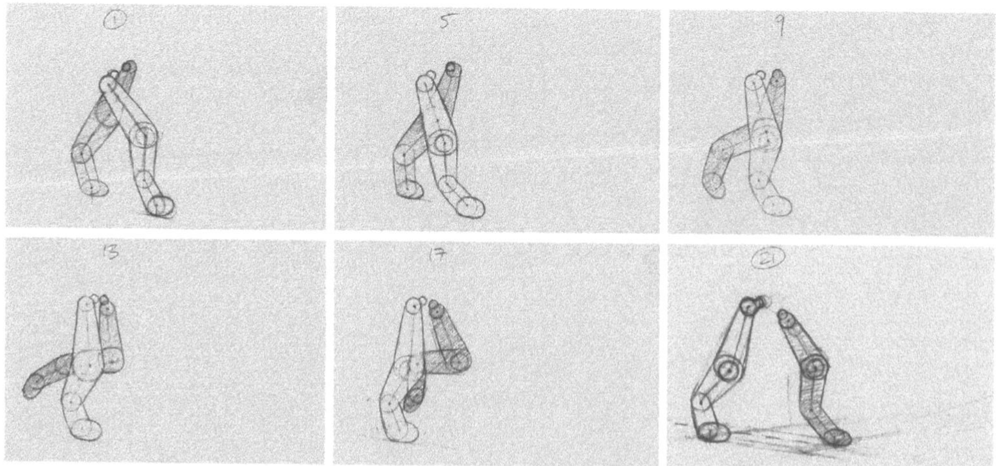

Again, this defines one complete step on four's for the back legs.

Ultimately, you will be able to build up the entire animal in separate, carefully animated layers, after which everything can be cleaned up on one level, then scanned and colored. Remember, all animation is about observation and caricature. Even the most extreme cartoon actions are based on real movement that we find and observe in the world around us. Every animator should train him or herself to study life and analyze the movement that is all around us—from observation comes inspiration.

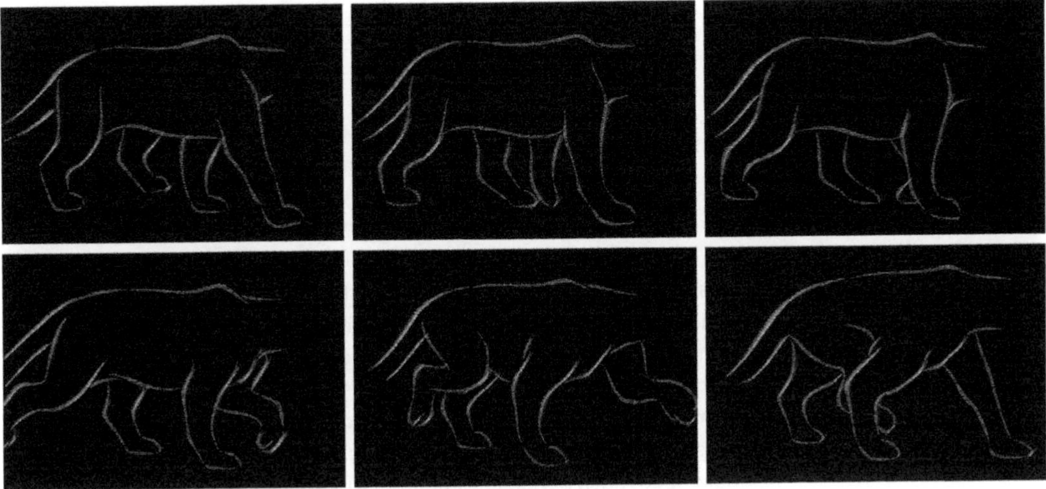

I created this for an animated logo effect—in this case, a moving, white chalk line on a basic classroom blackboard.

Suggested Reading

White, T. *The Animator's Workbook*. New York: Watson-Guptill, 1988, pp. 118–129.
DVD lecture: "Quadruped Walk—Cartoon" and "Quadruped—Natural".

Assignment 6

Taking a three-quarter view of our pantomime horse, create a cycle of it walking eccentrically. That is, none of the walk action should be generic—both the front and rear legs should contain a different kind of walk movement. You can photocopy the version here or download it from *www.desktopacademy.com*.

My original sketch for the cartoon quadruped we analyzed in this chapter lesson. You can create your own character for this, as long as it contains all the layer elements that we have discussed. (Don't forget to enlarge the copy to fit the field size you are using first!)

As just indicated, the front and back legs should also have *different* and highly individualistic walk actions from one another, although the distance that their feet slide on each stride should be identical for moving background purposes. Make sure, too, that the body, neck, head, and tail are all moving in sympathy and support of the main quadruped action of the legs they are connected to, whatever the legs are doing. Animate on two's (although one's would be so much better and smoother for this kind of assignment in reality, if you have the time or inclination) and repeat the filmed cycle five times in the final piece. Lastly, animate the simple kind of background indicated, so that it moves in perfect sync with the horse's foot slide. (This reemphasizes the fact that the stride lengths between both the front and back legs should be identical, and the background movement should perfectly coordinate with the resulting foot slide on both sets of legs, frame by frame.)

Or

Take the reference footage of a quadruped animation of your own choice and create a realistic walk cycle from it that repeats five times.

Note

Both of these assignments need only be taken to the pencil test stage. There is no need to clean them up or color them, as the real purpose of this exercise is to create good pencil-based animation, not finished production animation.

Weight

Class objective: To enhance the quality of animation by executing the action by including the elements of weight and gravity.
Equipment required: Lightbox, pencil, and paper.

One of the biggest failings of poor or inexperienced animators is their inability to create a sense of weight in their work. Weight defines character, personality, and gravity in a scene. Weight is what every one of us on this planet is dealing with at every second of every day, in one way or another. However, poor-quality animation often fails to communicate this. Therefore, this lesson is devoted to the secrets of weight and the ways we can incorporate it into our animation.

However, before we discuss the quality of weight in animation in further detail, I want you to try these three simple examples. We are returning to the bouncing ball principle to do this, but on this occasion I want you to approach it in a much simpler way, using three different kinds of balls: a standard rubber ball, a ping-pong ball, and a bowling ball.

A little over the top, but I think you get the point!

Clearly the size and placement of each ball suggests which is which.

Standard Rubber Ball

Let's start by animating a basic rubber ball, bouncing in place. To make things easy, the ball will bounce straight up and down. However, first you need to create the two key positions, draw the passing position, and add the in-betweens (see the following figures).

Place the second key over the first as you draw it, to get a sense of position and impact.

Remember that the breakdown drawing in this case will be stretched to imply speed.

In this case, there are four in-betweens, slowing-out from the top position.

Pencil test for five bounce cycles, on two's, and save the drawings for future review.

Ping-Pong Ball

Now for the ping-pong ball. Create the two key positions, add the breakdown drawing, and add the in-betweens (see the following figures).

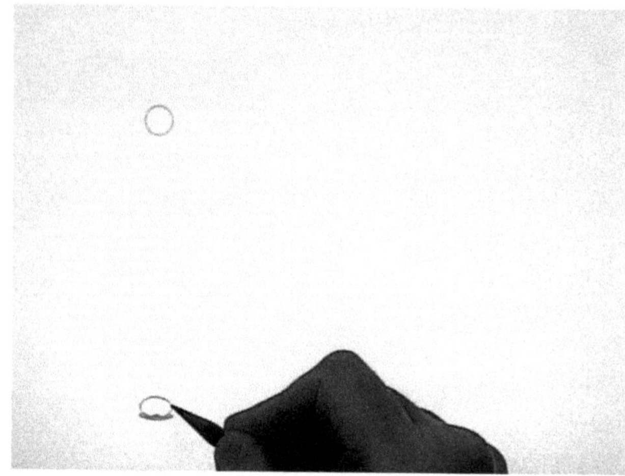

The nature of the ping-pong ball is much different, although there will still be a squash position as it impacts with the ground.

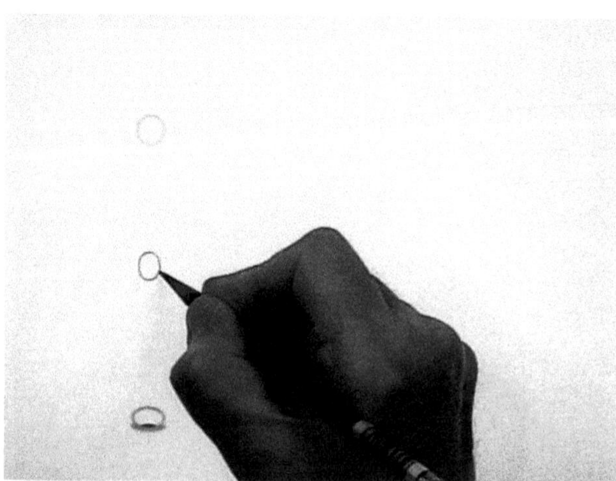

Again there is stretch on the passing position here but not as much as there is for a heavier, rubber ball.

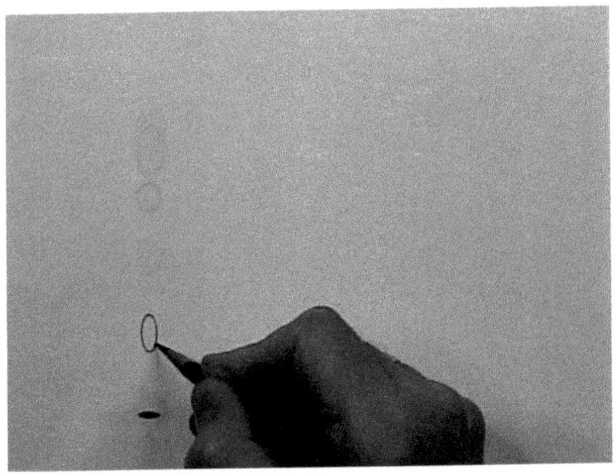

Here I have created seven in-betweens, again slowing-out from the top position. There are more in-betweens here because a ping-pong ball is far lighter than a rubber ball, and so it will move slower. This is simply because there is less mass for gravity to exert an effect on it, and also because it is much lighter, the wind resistance will tend to slow its descent more.

Again, pencil test this version on two's, repeating the bounce five times, and then save the drawings for later.

Bowling Ball

Lastly, create the two key positions, a breakdown drawing, and complete the in-betweens (see the following figures).

Being so much heavier and solid, the bowling ball will barely squash, if at all. It is more likely that the ground beneath it will significantly deform before the ball does!

Being so solid and heavy there is barely any stretch on its descent.

Being so heavy, the bowling ball will drop the quickest, thus less in-betweens.

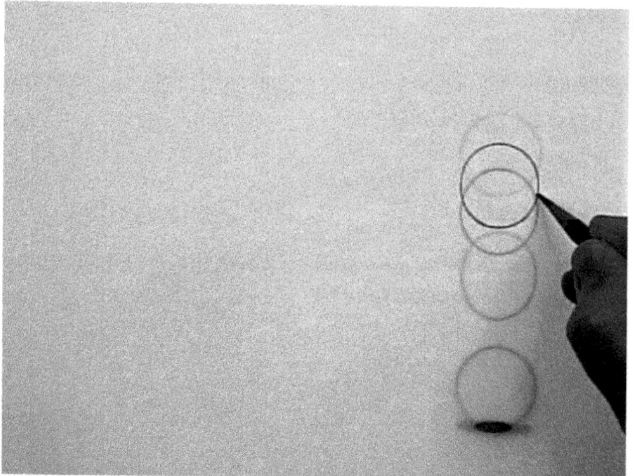

One more time, pencil test this action on two's five times and save the drawings for later.

Comparing the Three Versions

Now compare the three versions of bouncing balls and note which is the bouncier, which is the lighter, and which is the heavier. Ask yourself why this is. Answer the question by viewing the bounce of the rubber ball as the "normal" action, then watch the bounce of the ping-pong ball and note why it is lighter and how it is different. Now compare the bounce of the bowling ball to both the bounces of the rubber ball and the ping-pong ball and work out why the bowling ball is heavier.

A great deal of the differences are in the timing and the nature of the key and breakdown positions. In general, heavier things move slower and have less reaction. Light things have a huge reaction to a surface and are held up in the air longer by air resistance, despite the pull of gravity. If you can see and understand this, you have learned a great deal about weight.

The Pose Is Everything

Now expanding on your knowledge, recognize that the illusion of weight in animation starts with the key poses you give your character. For example, here are two illustrations of a character holding a weight. One pose suggests a heavy weight while the other does not.

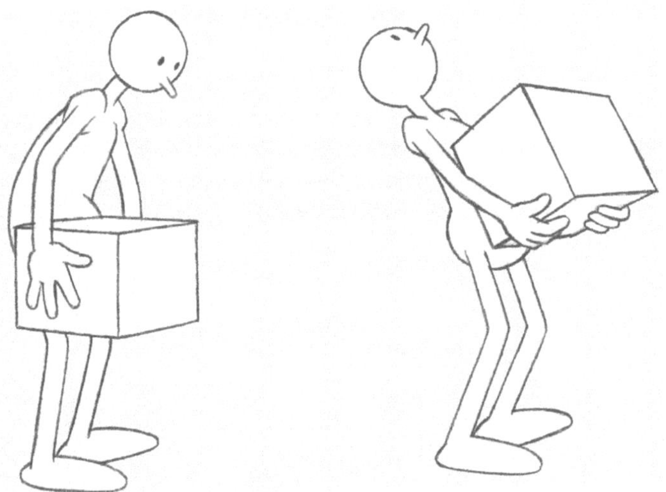

Note that on the heavier pose the character's legs are bent to support the weight better and his hands are under the box, giving him as much support in holding it as possible. He is also leaning backward to counter the additional weight at the front of his body.

The reason the second drawing looks like the character really is carrying a heavy weight is because his pose and posture support it, quite literally. In the above figure, look how the body is adjusted to imply the character is carrying a real weight, as opposed to the other drawing that does not give this impression. Recognize that on the weightier action, the knees are bent to better absorb the downward pressure of the weight and the body is positioned beneath the weight as much as possible to support it. In every way this pose is so much more convincing. Now consider another pose that also implies that a character is really dealing with weight.

This time the character's whole body mass is beneath the weight, implying that it is heavy and needs maximum support to carry it. Again, the knees are bent to take the weight better.

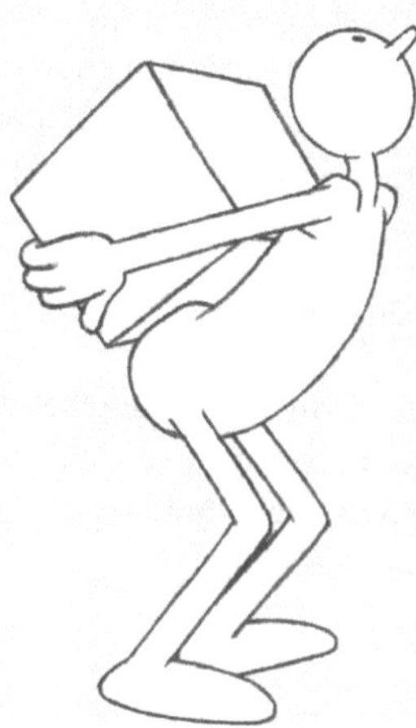

The objective of any animator is to maximize the effect of what is required through dynamic poses, long before the animation is even created. The following poses therefore suggest a believable series of weighty poses that support the illusion that real weight is involved… or do not!

Here the whole of the character's body is directly beneath the weight, suggesting that balance is important. If this balance was not drawn into the pose it would not look like the weight needs to be taken seriously.

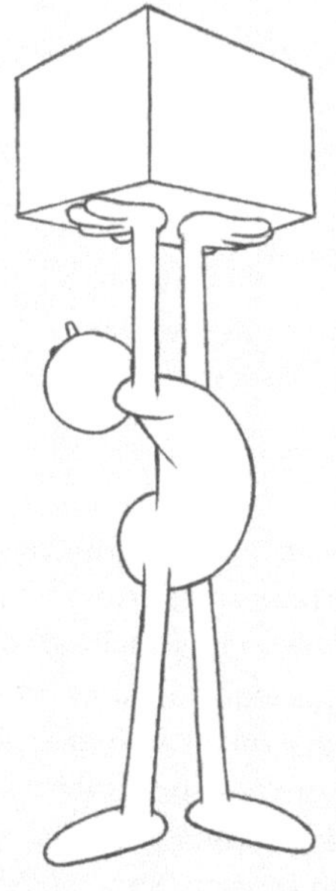

Next, consider another pose, where a similar object is being carried but without the dynamic posture that suggests weight is involved.

Here the box is clearly not heavy because no part of the character's body, except an ineffective hand, is beneath to control it. Note too the legs are straight, suggesting that there is no downward pressure on the body at all.

Consequently, it is extremely important that you, as an accomplished animator, understand your responsibility here—to always maximize the effect that pose and posture communicate to your audience in any animation you present to them (whether this is dealing with the issue of weight or not). That said, there are a number of other things you can do that will create the illusion of weight.

Tips

Here are a few tips that will help you create weight in your animation:

1. When posing a character who is dealing with weight, remember that the strongest parts of the human body are the legs, therefore, they need to bend to cushion the impact of any weight placed on them.

I repeat this image to emphasize the point that the legs must bend when a character is holding something of weight.

2. Where there is an absence of weight, however, or even the opposite of weight—for example, a character with a helium balloon strapped to his or her back—the poses can imply the opposite.

See how an immediate sense of weightlessness is created by having the character dangling listlessly from the balloon. The legs, arms, and feet point downward, suggesting they have no work to do.

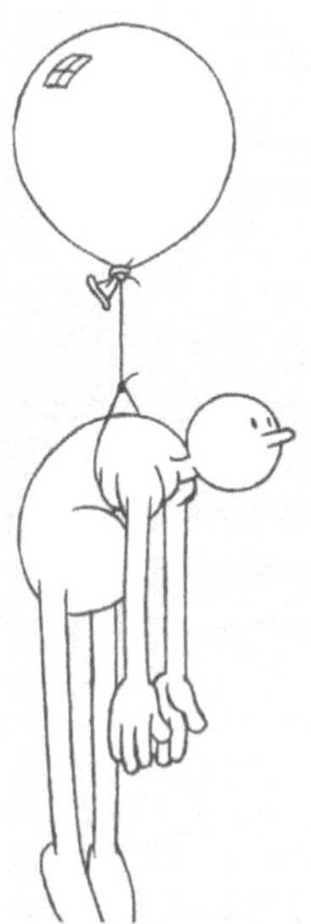

3. The heavier an object is, the slower it moves or can be moved. Therefore, if your character is carrying a great deal of weight, or is very heavily built, then be prepared to slow the action down with extra inbetweens to communicate this fact.

This clearly shows a lumbering character who has no sense of speed or dynamism.

4. Lifting a weight from the ground will initially be difficult for a character to do. Therefore, employ some preparatory action to communicate that the character is finding it hard to achieve the task, then use slowing-out chart timing for the initial raising of the weight so that it slowly accelerates upward until the character can gain leg thrust to achieve the added momentum required for the lift.
5. If a character has a heavy build, or at least has a certain amount of weight around his or her stomach, butt, or breasts, remember to employ some overlapping action on these areas to indicate that there is indeed weight there responding to ups and downs and changing velocity of the overall body.

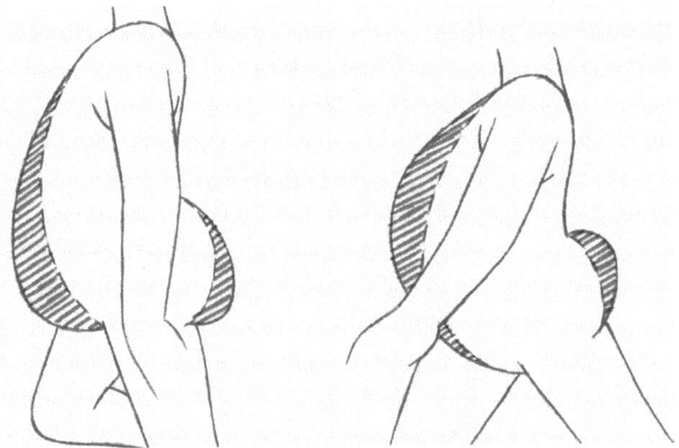

Notice the excess body mass sinks down when the body is up and it is up when the body is down, creating the moving overlap.

6. Because of gravity, weight always tends to drop downward. Consequently, characters carrying weight or characters who have weight in their physical makeup, will always suggest a downward sag to their pose, especially in the flesh of their body.

7. In seeking to lift a heavy weight, a character has a much stronger base to work from if he or she spaces out his or her feet and applies the lift over a greater area for the pulling-up action.

I tried to straddle the feet as far apart on either side of the weight as possible and then keep the character's back straight (as we all should do when lifting a heavy weight!). For the lift, I would animate the character rocking backward on his heels, drawing the weight closer to his body, before finally pushing up on the legs to affect the lift.

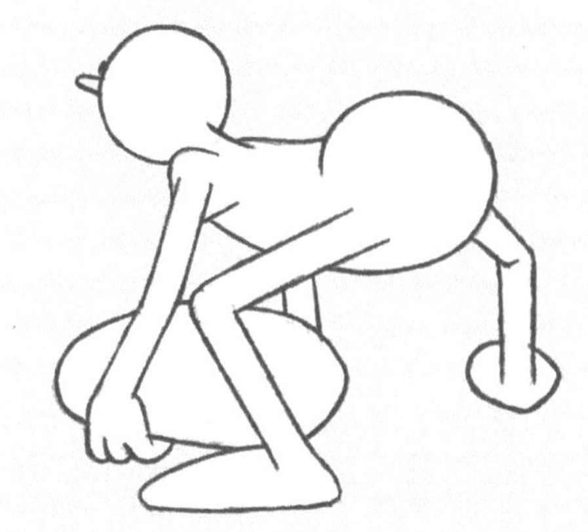

8. When characters walk while carrying a weight, or are very heavily built, their balance and movement will be significantly modified. Also, a character carrying a substantially heavy weight cannot possibly take as large of strides as a character not carrying anything.
9. Very heavy people will not be able to walk the same way as thin people because they have to overcompensate their side-to-side lean on each step to enable them to better move their free leg around the contact leg due to the excessively heavy nature of their thighs.

There are many ways you can achieve this kind of action but basically the body mass will need to shift onto the contact foot more than usual as the free leg arcs around, knee pointing outward.

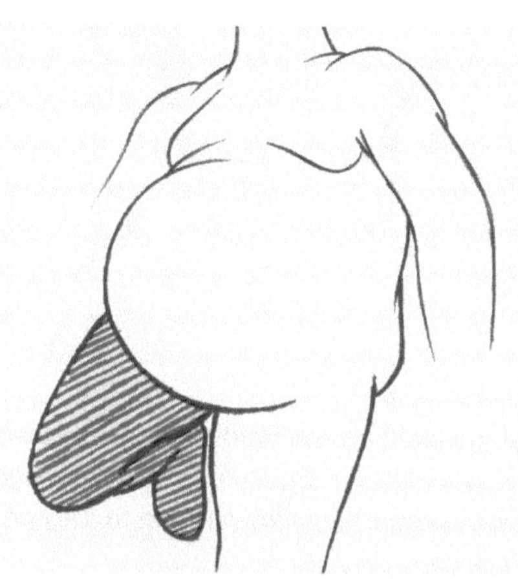

10. In order for a character to move while carrying a very heavy weight, he or she will first have to use a certain amount of a swing in the opposite direction to get some kind of momentum going. For example, as I illustrated in *Animation from Pencils to Pixels*, if a character is attempting to throw a flour sack forward, he or she will find it easier to swing the flour sack back first, then swing it forward to gain extra momentum for the release.

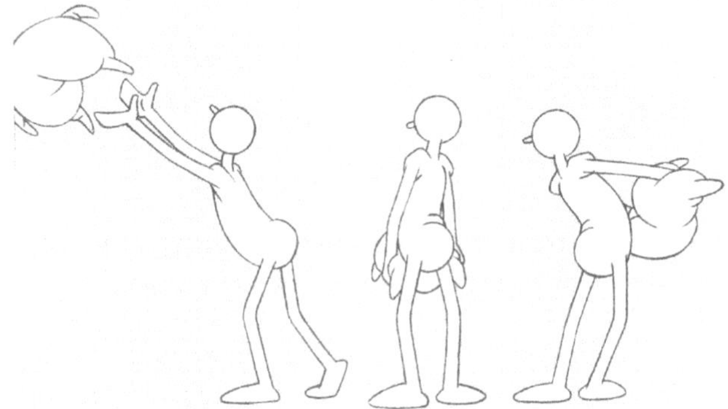

View first the central, static pose. Then the character swings the sack away from the direction of the throw before finally tossing it in that direction.

Note

This is called *anticipation*, but we deal with that specifically in the next lesson.

Suggested Reading

White, T. *The Animator's Workbook*. New York: Watson-Guptill, 1988, pp. 76–79.
White, T. *Animation from Pencils to Pixels: Classical Techniques for Digital Animators*. Boston: Focal Press, 2006, pp. 227–231.

Assignment 7

Taking all this into consideration, demonstrate how you can execute a character action that communicates a greater sense of weight. Let us have our character moving the location of two boxes.

Here the character is closer to the center of the picture. However, for your animation assignment, don't forget to have as much free space to the right of the screen as possible to enable your character to move across the screen and place the boxes down.

From this illustration, create the keys to have the character pick up the first (lighter) box and place it down on the other side of the screen.

This is the kind of arrangement you have to establish on your paper for the scene. The character does not need to walk far from the left to the right side of the screen, perhaps just a few short steps.

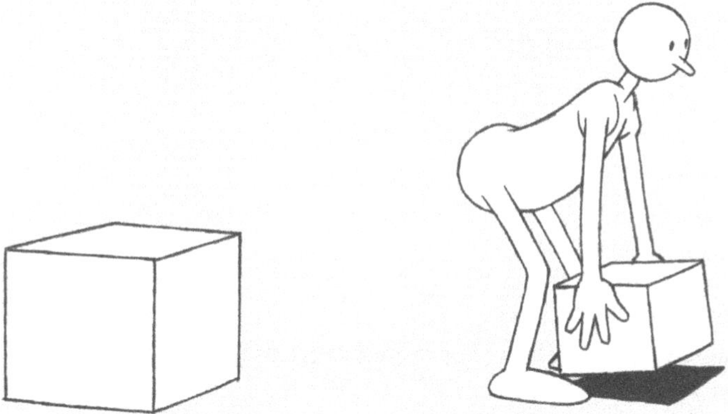

Once you have completed this, animate the character returning to pick up a much heavier box, carry it over to the first, and carefully place it down on top of it, finally stepping back to appreciate the effort.

A few things to work toward:

- The use of good pose and leg drive to assist the lift.
- The use of grip *under* the box (rather than at the sides) to carry the extra weight of the second box.
- A modified walk and pose to imply the character is carrying real weight.
- The use of pose and slow-ins/slow-outs to communicate the character struggling with the weight, especially when carefully picking up and placing down the boxes.

Animate and shoot this scene on two's. If it looks good, then continue to the next lesson. If not, go back and fix what needs to be fixed.

Anticipation

Class objective: To better prepare the audience for a major action and to give more impact with the action being attempted.
Equipment required: Lightbox, pencil, and paper.

Most students know that Newton's third law is that for every action there is an equal and opposite reaction. We might use a little artistic liberty with this and say that animators' first law is "for every action there is a subtle and opposite anticipation." The ancient tradition of Tai Chi also reflects this understanding by suggesting that before any major movement in one direction there is a slight and subtle movement in the opposite direction first.

Simply put, anticipation demands that if you have to animate a character's action in one particular direction, then you should first have a little back movement in the opposite direction to make it more dynamic. We hinted at this in our previous lesson on weight, where the character first swings the flour sack backward before finally swinging and throwing it forward.

The Benefits of Anticipation

Anticipation does not simply apply to the swinging of weights, of course. All actions can benefit from the use of anticipation. Watch a cat prepare to pounce—it will first sink back a little, wiggle its butt, and then jump forward. Watch an early Warner Brothers' cartoon character run off fast in one direction. First the character will wind up slowly in the opposite direction, before eventually releasing him- or herself in the direction of his or her choice and disappear in a cloud of dust the other way. Watch a cowboy go for his gun in a holster. He will first slightly lift his hand up and open his fingers a little, then grab downward for the gun so it can be drawn. (And even then he will be much more effective by pushing the gun down in the holster a little before whipping it out really fast!)

All actions, if they are to be significant actions, need to have a little anticipation employed at their beginning to make the main action have a greater impact. For example, a character throws a punch. It can look reasonably dynamic if we go by the two selected poses alone. But if you first take the hand back from the start position into a backward anticipation position, then throw the punch, the impact will be so much the greater.

The character punches forward aggressively.

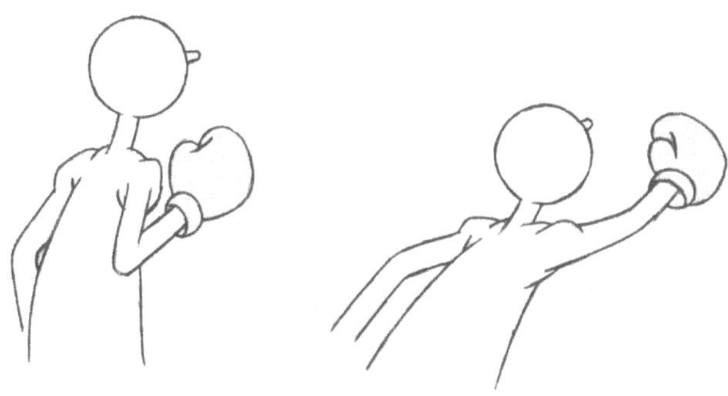

The same punch, but by the character pulling his hand back and rotating his shoulders away from the direction of the punch first, it can be far more dynamic.

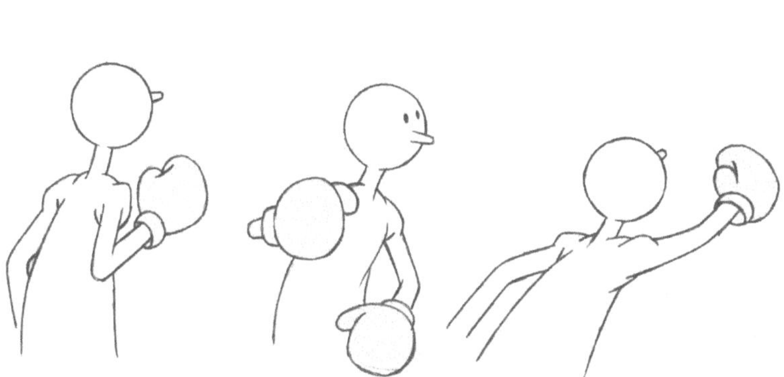

For example, follow along with me to animate a baseball pitcher throwing. The following figure shows the key positions of a poorly animated throwing sequence.

Technically the pose positions are correct, but with little dynamism in the poses the action looks too weak and effortless.

See how flat and undynamic the throw looks. The next figure shows some more dynamic keys with anticipation added, followed by the charts that link those keys.

These much more powerful poses create a far more dramatic throw, achieved by analyzing footage of a real major league pitcher researched on YouTube.

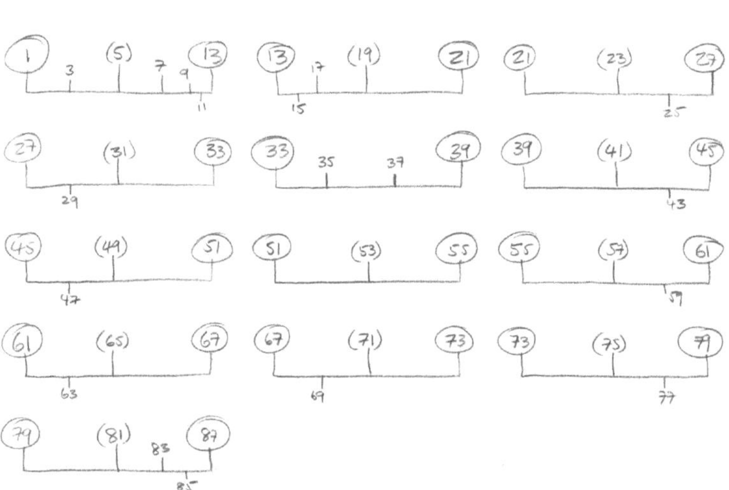

Note the number of keys and charts that make up the complete action, indicating that each aspect of the pitch is intricately posed and carefully timed.

Using these keys and charts, animate your own pitch animation, then shoot everything on two's and save it. The following figure is what the start of an exposure sheet would look like with these drawings doped, as well as some hints for the breakdown drawings.

Remember key drawings are circled and breakdown drawings are placed in parenthesis.

ACTION	DIAL	EXTRA	4	3	2	1	EXTRA	CAMERA
						1 (circled)		
						3		
						(5)		
						7		
						9		
						11		
						13 (circled)		
						15		
						17		
						(19)		
						21 (circled)		
						(23)		
						25		
						27 (circled)		
						29		
						(31)		
						33 (circled)		

Note the changing flexibility of the body and the fluid, whipping action of the throwing arm.

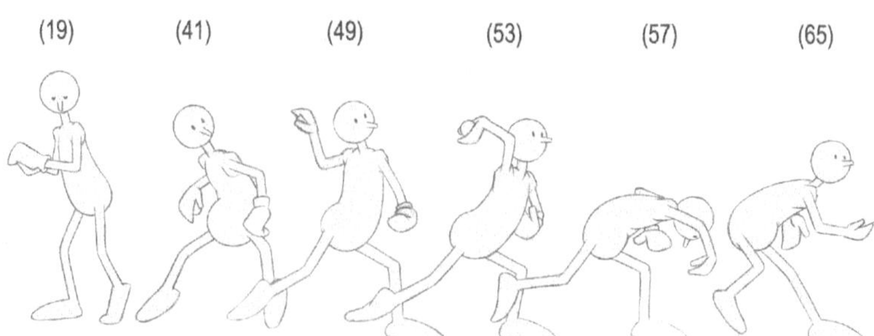

The next set of figures shows what one part of the action looks like, to and from the anticipation, and finally, what part of the completed throw looks like. All this, if nothing else, should show you the value of adding anticipation to all animated movement. Hopefully you will never forget to do this, whatever you are animating!

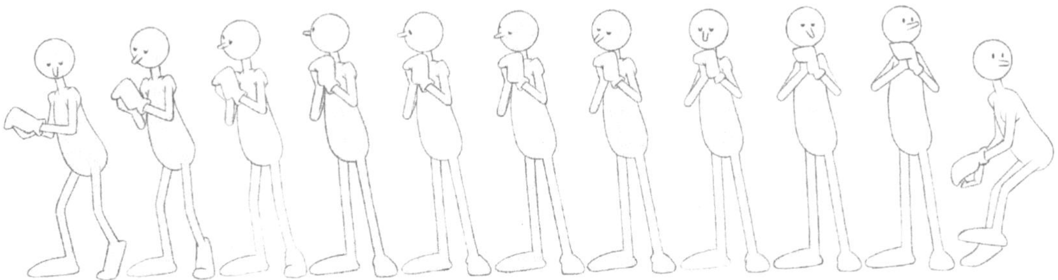

Moving from left to right, the character's head turns away from the direction of the throw before returning to the front to make the pitch.

Note how the body leads the action throughout and the pitching arm then whips through at the last moment, changing direction on the last frame of the throw.

Anticipations Are for Everything

Remember too that anticipations can be used in the smallest of movements, not just for the major ones. The slight change of look with the eyes to a side direction will best benefit from a little eye adjustment in the other direction before the main look. I have even found that by shutting the eyes on the anticipation drawing, you get far more impact on "the look" when the eyes are open and looking in the final direction you want them to.

A simple head turn, but the turn-away anticipation in the middle of the action gives the final look (right) more impact.

Consider a character standing up from a sitting position. Instead of just having the character stand up mechanically, have the character rock backward first, before standing up. This makes the entire sequence so much more natural and believable.

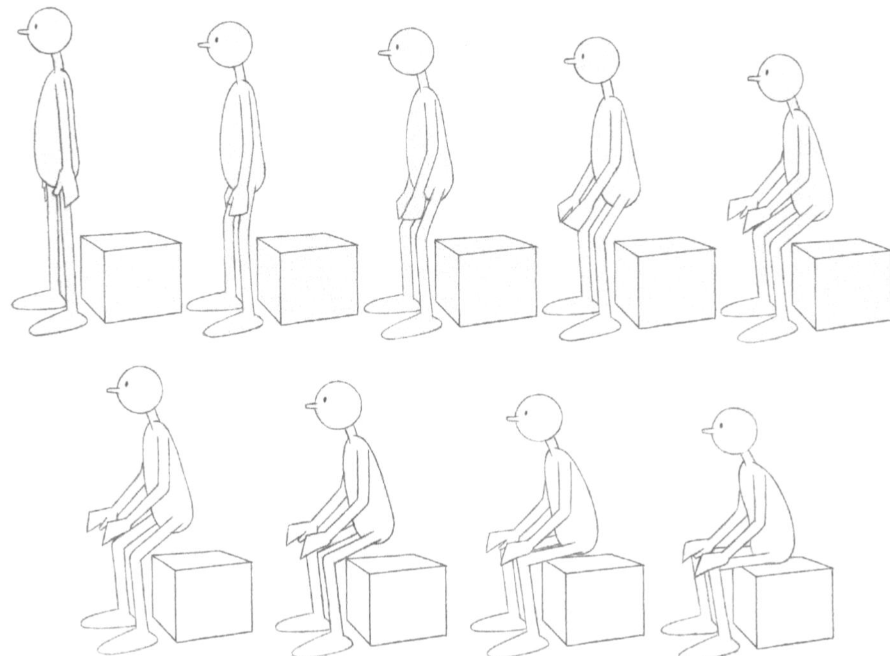

This sequence literally in-betweens the character's movement, from sitting down (bottom right) to standing up (top left). Note how unconvincing and mechanical it looks, with the body mass remaining implausibly behind both contact positions of the feet.

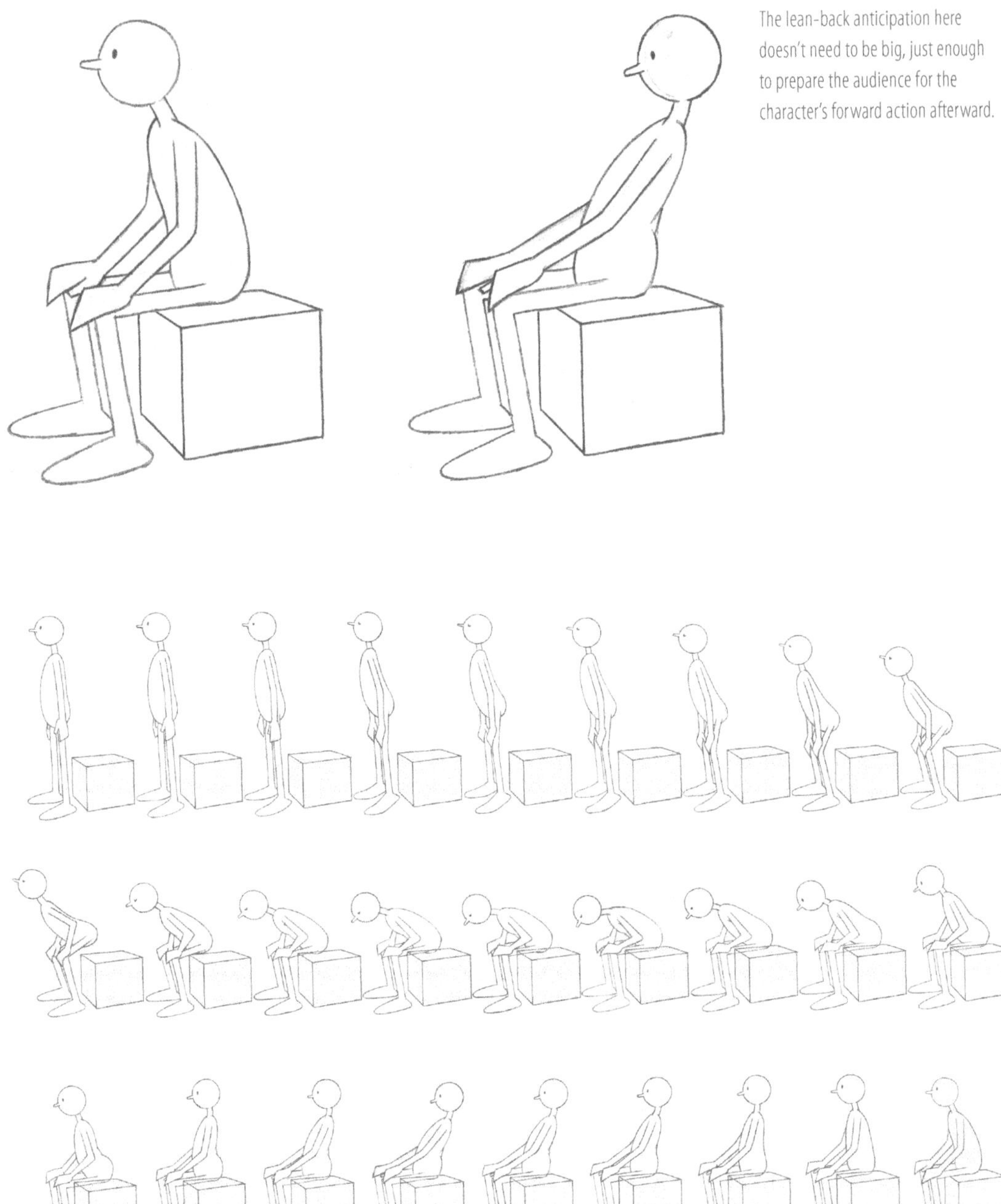

The lean-back anticipation here doesn't need to be big, just enough to prepare the audience for the character's forward action afterward.

Once more reading the action from the bottom right to the top left, note that after the backward anticipation, the character moves his weight forward over the feet before using the strength of the legs to lift his body upward.

Finally, consider the impactful animation of our character throwing a punch at the camera instead of in profile, filling the screen with his fist at the end. The punch starts way back, comes hurtling forward, then stops as it hits the screen. But, if you actually take the fist further away from the camera before it comes forward, then you will give the whole punch toward us far more energy.

The distorted perspective effect of a punch being thrown directly at the camera can be quite dramatic.

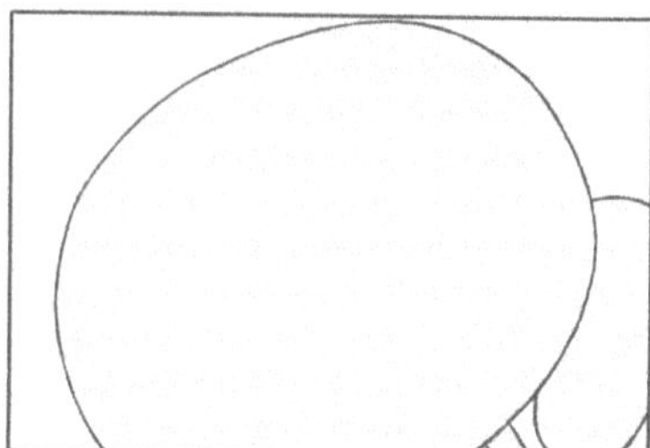

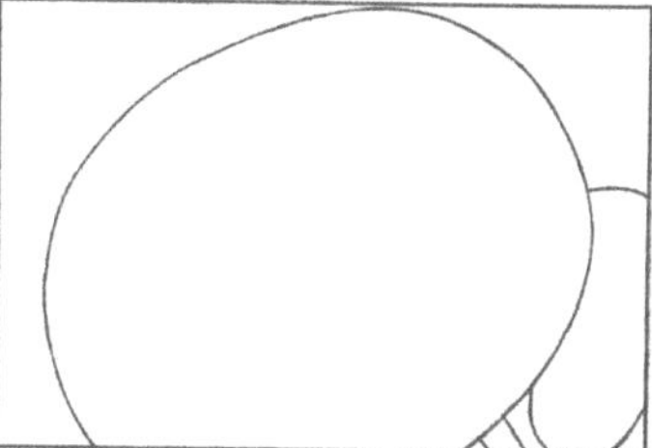

By pulling the arm back before the fist comes forward, you can enhance the effect of the punch being thrown.

Actually, if you do a kind of "reverse" anticipation at the end too, you will enhance the action further. This is achieved by actually bringing the fist further forward than you ultimately want it to be at the end, then sink it back a little toward where you actually want it at the end. This really doubles the impact of the entire action.

Bring the fist closer to the camera than the position you want it to end in.

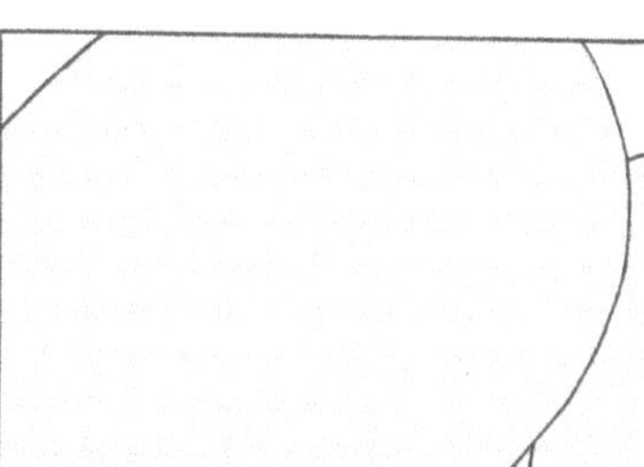

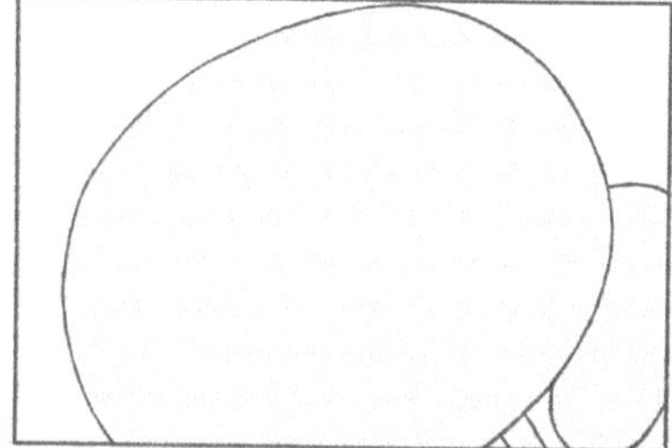

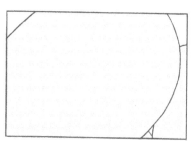

Remember that you can be as subtle with the anticipations as you can be with the main actions on occasion. The simple blink of an eye can be occasionally emphasized by the eye widening for a fraction a split-second before it closes. A closed hand opening can look stronger if you just tighten the closed position first. A child being swung on a swing can be started more effectively by pulling him or her a little further back before being pushed forward. There is no end to the innovative ways a good anticipation can be applied. The only way you can ever really go wrong is NOT to use anticipation at all!

Suggested Reading

White, T. *The Animator's Workbook*. New York: Watson-Guptill, 1988, pp. 70–71, 79.

White, T. *Animation from Pencils to Pixels: Classical Techniques for Digital Animators*. Boston: Focal Press, 2006, pp. 226–227.

DVD lecture: "DEMO—Jump" and "DEMO—Pitcher".

Assignment 8

With a character of your own design, animate a basketball player taking a penalty shot. From the player in a static position, holding the ball and facing the hoop, have him or her make the shot, score the point, then jump up and down in triumph afterward, while the ball bounces to a stop. For this, use all the techniques we have discussed so far, but most of all, find ways to use well-timed anticipations as much as you can throughout.

Dialog

Class objective: To create a really convincing character talking, utilizing good body language and facial expressions, and accurately syncing mouth movements.

Equipment required: Lightbox, pencil, and paper, and an audio track, broken down.

The first thing to be recognized in dialog animation is that it is not just about making the lips move in perfect synchronization with the audio track! It is important to do this, of course, but really great dialog animation is all about emotion and expression, mood and posture. Most of these things come from the systematic action the animator first places in the body language of a character as it relates to the attitudes underlying the dialog.

Secondly, the facial expression reflects in the emotional and mood content that is built into a character's actions. Finally, the lip synching should be the cherry on the cake, where the mouth finally opens and closes, and distorts recognizably, in time with the spoken words. Consequently, we will approach our dialog exercises in these three stages.

Note

Before any dialog animation can be attempted, the audio track has to be recorded and a track breakdown achieved, which is the frame-by-frame analysis of the phonetic sounds being made throughout the entire piece. A more comprehensive explanation of this process can be found in my book, *Animation from Pencils to Pixels*, pp. 153–154 and 298–299. (A prerecorded track and breakdown information can be obtained at *www.desktopacademy.com*.)

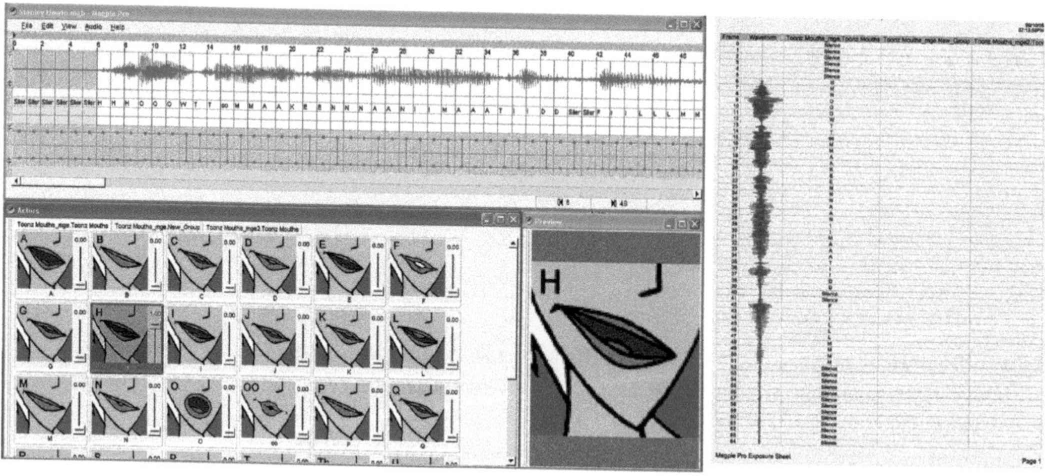

A program like Magpie Pro can assist you in easily breaking down the audio track, then printing out a ready-made dope sheet of the breakdown for you to work with.

Body Language

To make sure the key expressions of the dialog sequence are reflected in the body language of the character, we will start by identifying and creating the key poses of the action. First download the audio track and breakdown material from *www.desktopacademy.com*.

ACTION	DIAL	EXTRA	4	3	2	1	EXTRA
001							
002							
003							
004							
005							
006	H						
007							
008							
009	O						
010							
011							
012	W						
013	T						
014							
015	OO						
016	M						
017							
018	A						
019							
020	K						
021	E						
022							
023	N						
024							
025							
026	A						
027							
028	N						
029	I						
030							
031	M						
032	A						
033							
034							
035	T						
036	I						
037							
038	D						
039							
040							

The standard dope sheet, with breakdown material transferred to the audio track column.

With a ready-made audio track and breakdown, you will now be able to work with the exposure sheet to emphasize the emphasis points in the track. In the following figure I have indicated this on my exposure sheet to establish what I would use as my own key expression points.

ACTION	DIAL	EXTRA	4	3	2	1	EXTRA	CAMERA
001								
HAT OFF!!! 002								
003								
004								
005								
006	H							
007			1					
008								
009	O							
010								
011								
012	W							
013	T							
014								
015	OO		3					
LOOK 016	M							
TO 017								
AUDIENCE 018	A		2					
019								
020	K							
021	E							
022								
023	N							
024			2					
TURN 025								
026	A							
027								
028	N							
029	I							
030								
031	M							
032	A							
033								
034								
035	T							
036	I							
037								
038	D							
039								
040								

I've scribbled into the notepad column my thoughts in terms of the action with the sound and then circled the areas where I think the pose emphasis must be. To the right of the audio column, I've indicated the strength of the emphasis point, with 1 being the strongest.

Now, by writing in the required drawing numbers in the animation column on two's, I have circled the numbers that coincide with my key expression points, indicating that I intend these to be key drawings. With the key drawings marked I can proceed with drawing my key poses, stressing and exaggerating the required emotion and expression the character needs for each key point.

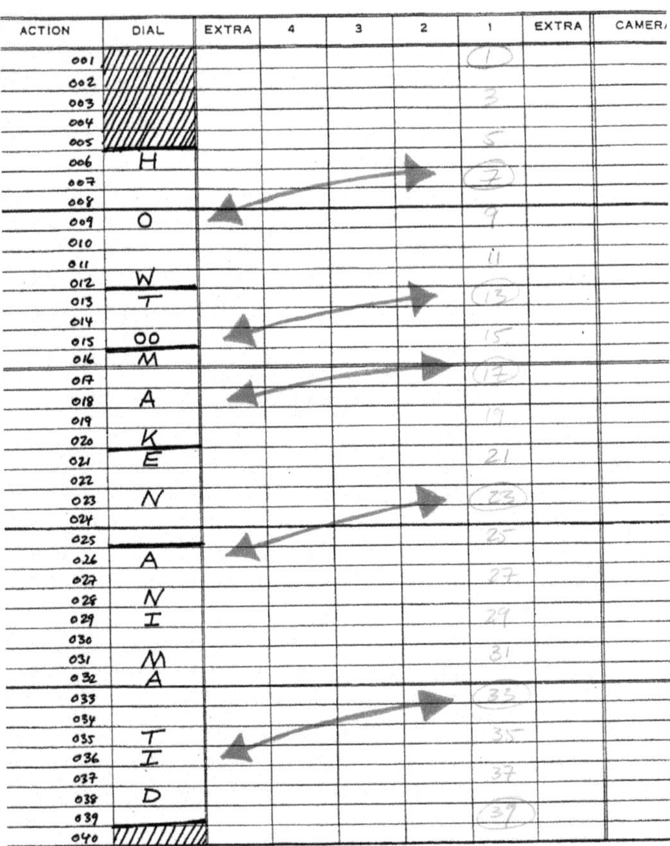

ACTION	DIAL	EXTRA	4	3	2	1	EXTRA	CAMER
001						1		
002								
003						3		
004								
005						5		
006	H							
007						7		
008								
009	O					9		
010								
011						11		
012	W							
013	T					13		
014								
015	OO					15		
016	M							
017						17		
018	A							
019						19		
020	K							
021	E					21		
022								
023	N					23		
024								
025						25		
026	A							
027						27		
028	N							
029	I					29		
030								
031	M					31		
032	A							
033						33		
034								
035	T					35		
036	I							
037						37		
038	D							
039						39		
040								

I start the scene by assuming the animation will be on two's (although it's invariably not like that in the end). The red arrows indicate how advanced the actual emphasis points of my key drawings will be.

Key poses are similar to animatic frames, although being key animation frames they are more expressive of the tighter animation action. Note that I write onto my key pose drawings the part of the track I am emphasizing.

This is the point when you have to create your own key drawings. Replicating everything I just indicated on your own exposure sheet, shoot the drawings as a pose test, holding each one on the screen for as many frames as necessary before the next drawing kicks in.

Note

Here is where a program like Digicel's Flipbook comes in handy. With Flipbook, for example, you can load in the audio track from the first frame and play back the pose test and soundtrack at the same time.

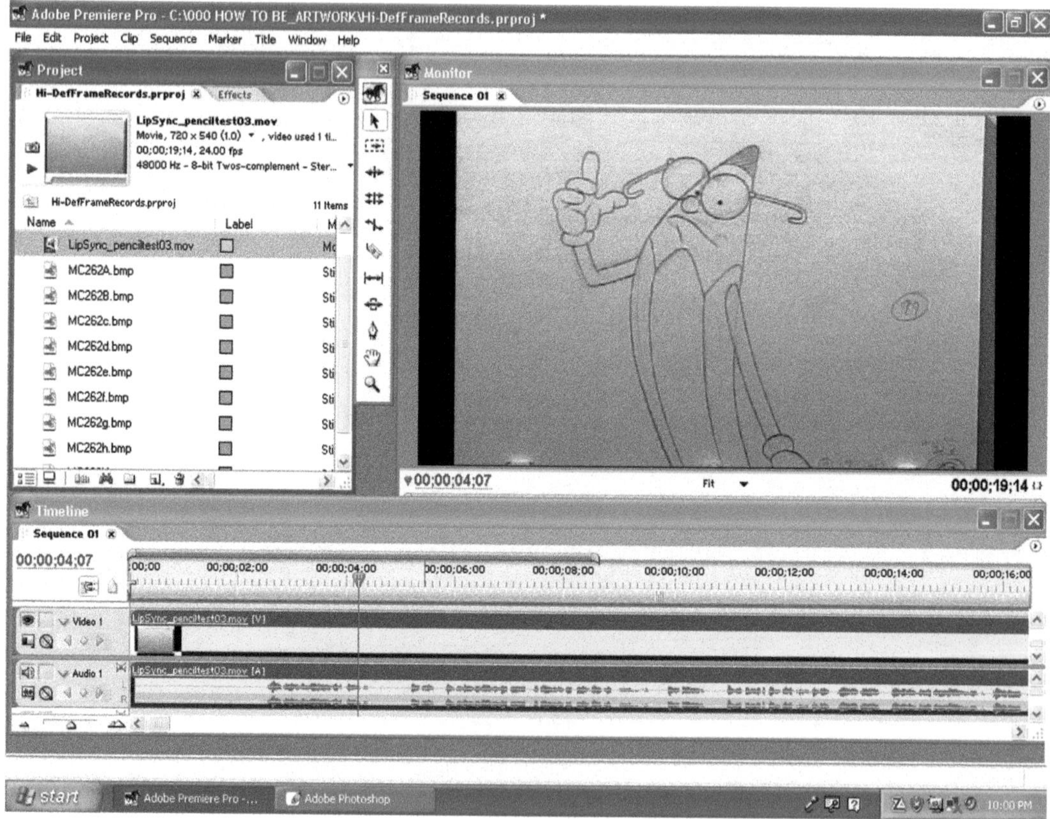

Adobe's Premiere Pro is a valuable movie-editing program that is ideal for creating animatics. Final Cut Pro is a similar one for Macintosh users.

Check if the overall sync of the action and the sounds work together as anticipated. If not, adjust the timing, or the drawings, then reshoot over and over again until it moves with the soundtrack as you want it to.

Note that there is a case for positioning a key pose several frames ahead of the actual sound it is attempting to hit. By anticipating in this way, there is an added emphasis, because placing the image exactly on the same frame as where the sound occurs can give the impression that the impact is late. This is very much true of synching open-mouth positions when working on the lip sync, but more on that shortly.

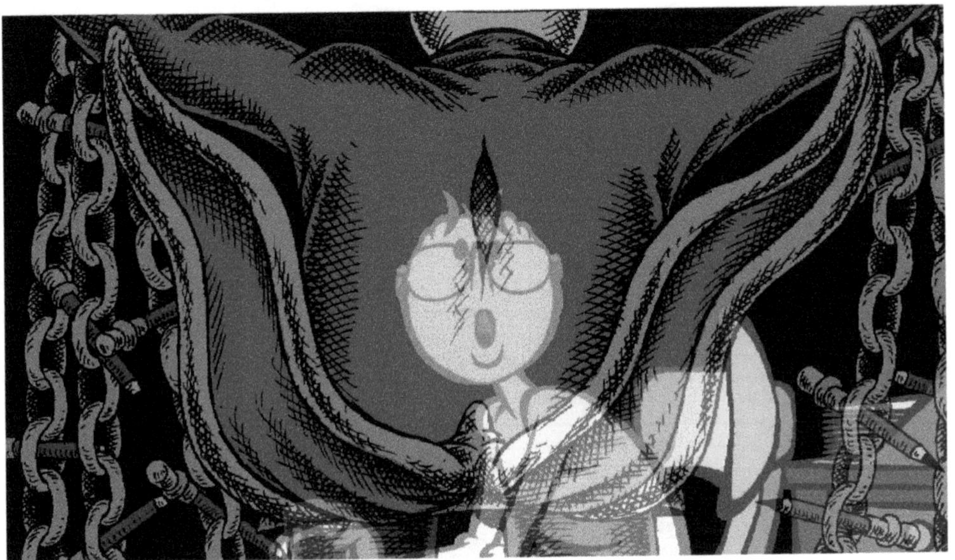

Mouth shapes are so expressive of emotion, whether the character is speaking or not!

With all the key pose positions located visually, you should now adapt your exposure sheet accordingly. In these kinds of situations, the visual editing of the picture against the audio track is the preferred way of tightening up the sync between them both. However, when you have done that to your full satisfaction, go back to the exposure sheet and check where the drawings have shifted in relation to your original doping of them. Renumber the drawings to match their new frame numbers if necessary until your exposure sheet reflects exactly what your visual editing arrived at.

Again, when positioning key drawings in a pose test animatic, you should always anticipate by several frames the emphasis point you are highlighting on the soundtrack, with bigger anticipations going with the bigger sounds.

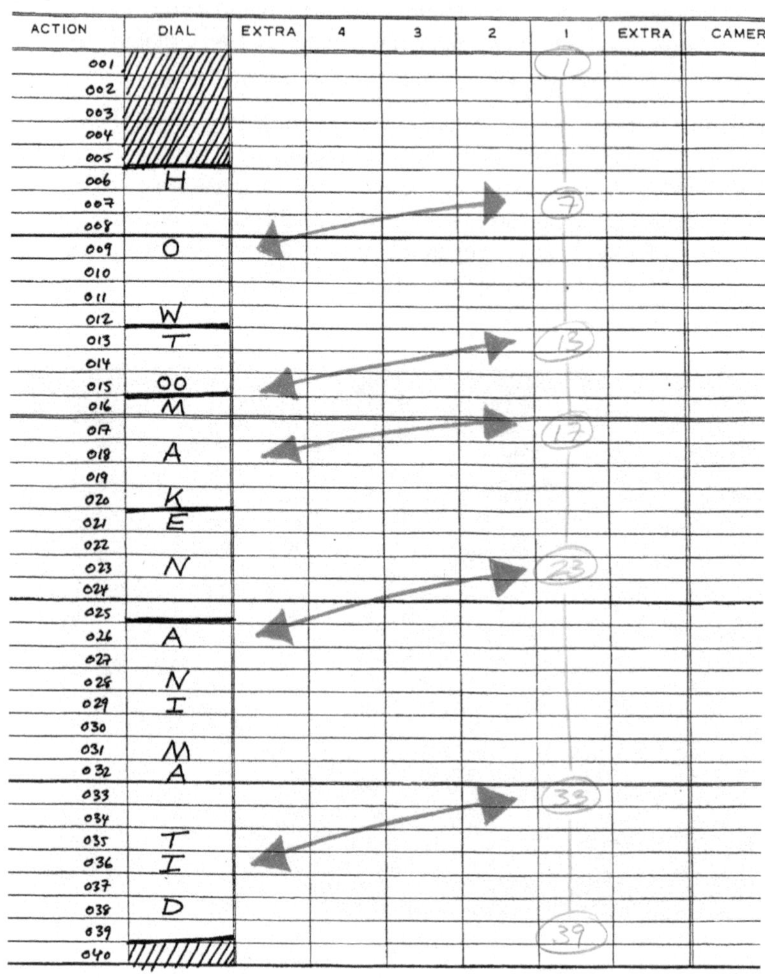

Note

If you intend to animate on two's and the new sync position of a key drawing falls on an even number (i.e., a frame normally reserved for a one's drawing), then always move the number one frame *forward* to match the preceding two's number, never back. For example, if after reediting, a key pose drawing was originally on frame 17 and is now on frame 16, make it frame 15 instead, since to anticipate it "ahead" of the sound is better than placing it "behind" the sound. If you are animating on one's, however, it will be fine to number the new position for the key as 16.

ACTION	DIAL	EXTRA	4	3	2	1	EXTRA	CAMER
001	/////					(1)		
002	/////							
003	/////					3		
004	/////							
005	/////					5		
006	H							
007						(7)		
008								
009	O					9		
010								
011						11		
012	W							
013	T					13		
014						(14)		
015	OO					15		
016	M					(16)		
017						17		
018	A							
019						19		
020	K							
021	E					21		
022								
023	N					23		
024						(24)		
025						25		
026	A							
027						27		
028	N					30		
029	I					29		
030						30		
031	M					(31)		
032	A							
033						33		
034								
035	T					35		
036	I							
037						37		
038	D							
039						(39)		
040	/////							

Sometimes with the mouth moving fast it is necessary to add one's into the action, so that the more rapidly changing mouth shapes can be accommodated.

ACTION	DIAL	EXTRA	4	3	2	1	EXTRA	CAMER
001						1		
002						2		
003						3		
004						4		
005						5		
006	H					6		
007						7		
008						8		
009	O					9		
010						10		
011						11		
012	W					12		
013	T					13		
014						14		
015	OO					15		
016	M					16		
017						17		
018	A					18		
019						19		
020	K					20		
021	E					21		
022						22		
023	N					23		
024						24		
025						25		
026	A					26		
027						27		
028	N					28		
029	I					29		
030						30		
031	M					31		
032	A					32		
033						33		
034						34		
035	T					35		
036	I					36		
037						37		
038	D					38		
039						39		
040						40		

With fast-talking dialog or action that is moving fast with the character speaking, you might as well bite the bullet and do everything on one's!

In-between all the body positions, charted via the key frame renderings, but just indicate the head shapes without the mouths… or even the faces… actually being drawn in.

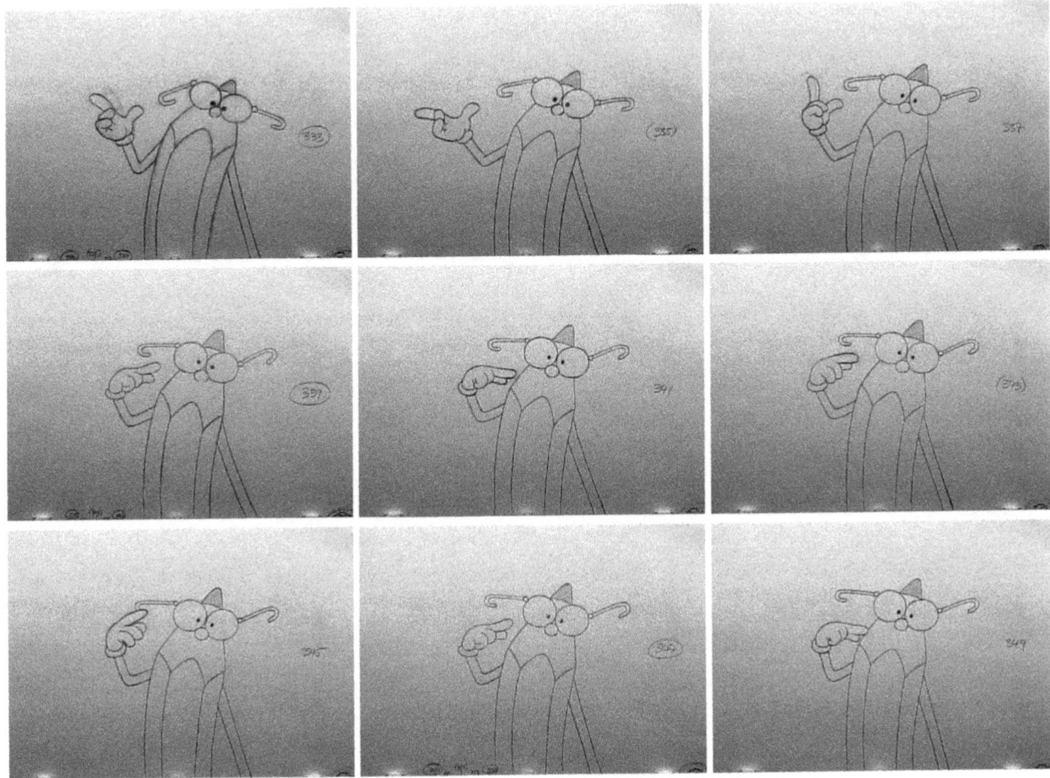

Always remember that the mouth is the last consideration when successfully animating dialog. Good animation should ideally express the emotion, motive, or meaning of the words through pose and attitude, without the need to see the mouth moving at all.

Shoot a pencil test of the body animation and test it with the soundtrack as before. You may find that you still have to adjust the timings, as there is a big difference between a pose test action and a fully in-betweened pencil test sequence. Adjust as necessary. If things are not quite as impactful as you would like, consider using slow-ins or slow-outs to maximize the timing and pose selection, thereby emphasizing a particular pose in the sequence.

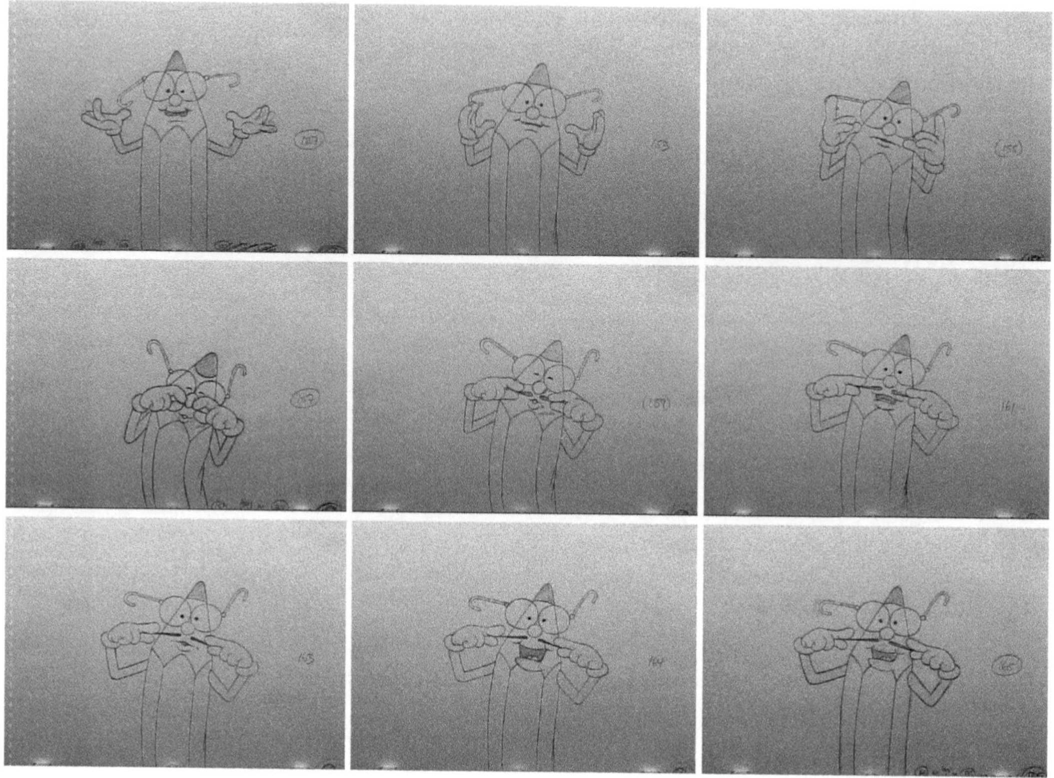

Timing and the subtlety of mouth movement should complete the action in a plausible and convincing way.

This is something not easily communicated with the written word, however. It is much more a process of trial and error until you get it the way you want it to work most effectively.

Facial Animation

Now that you have created the correct body language of the piece through your correct drawing and timing of the key poses, you need to concentrate on the facial expressions of the character to better define the mood or emotion of the piece.

The pose and facial expression says everything!

First, to loosen you up a bit, I would suggest that you put aside the dialog sequence for now and work on a quick new assignment—a bite and chew test.

Bite and Chew

Draw a medium close-up of your character, holding a candy bar in his or her hand.

The start point of the bite and chew exercise. (Source: DigiPen student art by Laura Franke.)

Now animate the character bringing the candy bar to his or her mouth, biting off a piece of it and broadly and enthusiastically chewing it. Finally, have the character swallow the chewed piece.

Be sure to study yourself in a mirror chewing, to see how the mouth and jaw work. It is not just an up and down movement of the chin, as is often portrayed. Especially build a special snap action into the movement, as having pulled at the bar with the teeth, it suddenly comes away, ready for the chewing action.

Remember to get as much tension on the pullback as possible, with anticipation forward before the backward movement. (Source: DigiPen student art by Laura Franke.)

Look at the nature of the circular rotation of the jaw in relation to the head and get the sense of grinding that the teeth need to breakdown the candy in the mouth.

Get as full and round an action as possible with the chew. (Source: DigiPen student art by Laura Franke.)

Finally, have the character swallow and smile with enjoyment at the piece of candy he or she has just eaten!

The gulp should always be a convincing swallowing action before the character returns to a normal position. (Source: DigiPen student art by Laura Franke.)

Now you'll know a lot more about facial distortion and using the anatomy of the face and head to achieve certain expressions and deformations.

Working with the Face

Clearly, the main reason for producing the bite and chew animation is to give you a sense of how much the face distorts and how extended positioning of the jaw can affect the features of the face. This is an extreme of most dialog positioning, of course, but it is an invaluable way for you to experience the speed, positioning, and timing involved in producing a major piece of facial animation.

Anyway, with the bite and chew successfully created, you are now ready to return to the dialog challenge.

Study Real Facial Emotion

Watch a great actor on the screen deliver a line of powerful dialog and you will see a vast range of emotion communicated in quite small and subtle ways. Consider the look in the eyes, the nature and timing of a blink, a hint and duration of a smile (or scorn), and the general presence of happiness, sadness, anger, and humiliation in the expression. All these things communicate the mood or emotion underpinning the words that are being spoken.

This is the heart of being a great dialog animator and why it is not just the mouth opening and closing in perfect sync with the soundtrack. It is also what makes the challenge of working with spoken dialog so exciting for the serious animator.

Returning to the audio track, play it over and over again and listen to the subtle inflections contained in the words. You have painted the important key poses with your broadest brush so far, but now you have to work finer and finer to emphasize the more subtle qualities of what is being spoken. Listen behind the actual words for the shades and tones of emotion.

The subtlety of this 3D-created talking Dale Chihuly action for the film *Fire Gods* reveals a surprising amount of subtlety of expression. (Source: Courtesy of Royal Winchester.)

If you feel a word or phrase has a happy quality to it, then that is the facial expression you need to begin to work with. If you feel a hint of displeasure, disdain, or sarcasm is being expressed, then the facial expression for that word or phrase has to hint at this also. Whatever emotion that drives the dialog at any moment has to be captured in the face, and especially the eyes, which are the "windows of the soul" and what the audience will basically be looking at for the majority of the time.

Even the most simplistic of animation can demand attention and have impact on the audience if the dialog is animated well. (Source: Courtesy of Monte Michaelis.)

It is not easy to capture subtle expression in the face or eyes in animation, but you must try to do so because that is what constitutes great animated dialog, as opposed to just making the lips move. Check out the fabulous dialog work by Frank Thomas, Ollie Johnson, or another of the nine "old men" of Disney animation such as Milt Kahl to see what this is all about. Again, I urge you to study the expressions of great actors as they deliver their lines, or even everyday people as they are emotionally driven. Quite often actors can communicate huge emotion with a minimum of expression. But a regular person, fired with anger or excitement, happiness or sorrow, can present expressions of emotion that are quite surprising at times. (Stop any video of a person speaking, midword or midsentence, and you will see what I am talking about!) It is truly the selection and replication of these powerful facial expressions that will take the emotion communicated through the dialog animation to the next level.

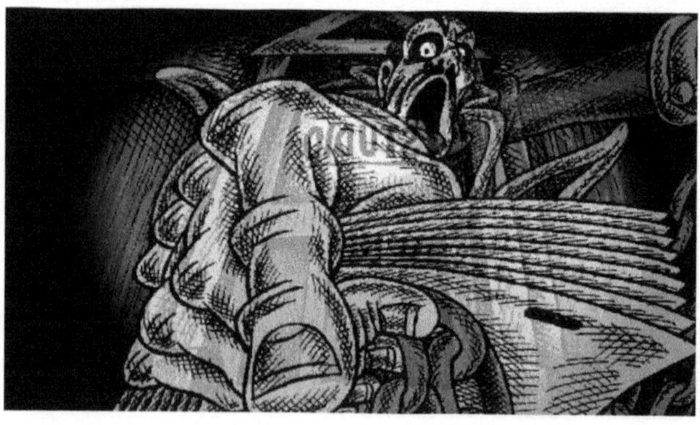

This dark and disturbing ghost from my film, *Endangered Species*, reveals the power of animated imagery outside of the more conventional cartoon genre.

The Process of Facial Expression

Technically, you should approach facial expression just as you approached the body language poses. Take from your mind the existence of the keys you have already selected for the key positions of the body. Here you are identifying expression keys that will have timings and numberings entirely of their own. The facial action will be connected to the pose key numbering in some way, of course, but quite often the face will express itself independently of what the body is doing. This should, therefore, be reflected in the facial animation and key numbering selection.

SEQUENCE | SCENE ① | "ACTOR" | SHEET ①

Action	Dialog	5	4	3	2	1	BG	CAMERA INSTRUCTIONS
						1		
LOOKS TO	T					3		START
AUDIENCE	OO					5		
						7		
	D					9		
"BLINK"	EE					11		
IN						13		
ANTICIPATION,	O					15		
	R					17		
HEAD & *	N					19		
ARM UP	O					21		
*	T					23		
HOLD						25		
	T OO					27		
						29		
LOOKS BACK TO *	D EE					31		
AUDIENCE.						33		
						35		
						37		
						39		

As before, I always start by writing my action intentions in the left column, beside the audio breakdown column, and write in the two's animation numbers, ready for the key positions to be marked.

So, listen to the audio track over and over again, as you did before with the body pose selection, and indicate on the exposure sheet where you feel the facial keys for the key expressions might lie. You can circle them with a different color pencil if it helps.

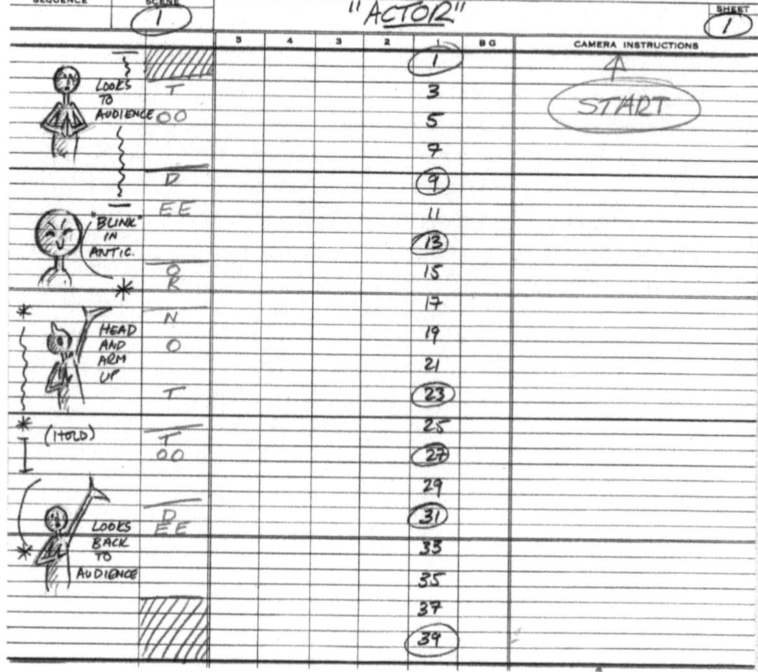

Little thumbnail sketches beside the breakdown column on the dope sheet assist in defining the numbering of the keys.

I can only repeat again that these should be entirely different frame numbers than the key body positions. So, be brave and astute in your selections, although it might be that you're happy to use the existing body keys regardless.

Make sure the key drawings express the strong emotion indicated in the track.

Note

Three-dimensional animators will actually find this approach much easier than their 2D colleagues. Often model rigs for the body will be quite separate than facial rigs, and so it is far easier for 3D animators to work with both of these in isolation, especially when trying and retrying options between the two. Two-dimensional animators unfortunately have to redraw entirely everything they do, unless they draw the face on a separate level.

Lip Synching

Finally, now that all the visually explorative and expressive work is complete, the actual lip synching can at last be attempted. I think you will now appreciate that dialog animation is just not a question of simply opening and closing the mouth on a frame-by-frame basis in relation to the sounds being heard. This noted, it is now time to do just that!

I used this illustration in *Animation from Pencils to Pixels* to emphasize the range of choice an animator has in selecting even the most basic and generic of mouth shapes.

Much thinking has to now go toward the shape of the mouth, the size of the mouth's opening, and its overall relationship to the expression and shape maintained by the face at any moment in time. Consequently, consider these things very carefully as you draw the mouth positions.

Following are a few golden rules you should be aware of when attempting the lip sync interpretation.

Vowel Sounds

Vowel sounds are the peg on which all other dialog lip synching hangs. If you successfully hit all the vowel sounds on sync, then whatever you do for the consonants will pretty much work fine. Vowel sounds—a, e, i, o, and u sounds—are the ones that *have* to have open-mouthed positions of some kind to emphasize them precisely.

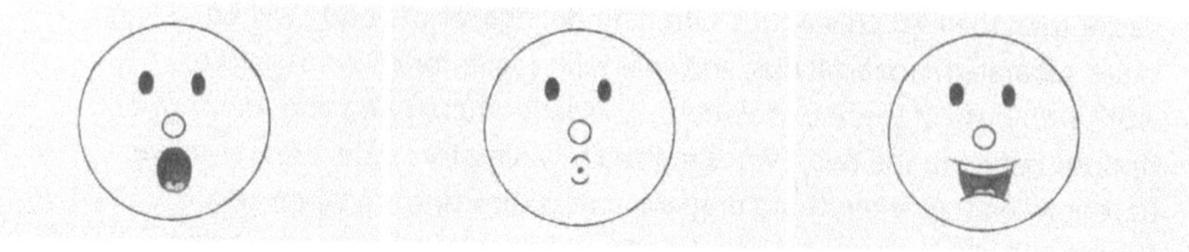

The outer, open-mouth positions will be the most powerful tool animators have in emphasizing the major impact points of any dialog.

The figure shows just generic shapes, of course, to give you an idea of the broad differences between them. However, the final (and more correct) shape of the open mouth on the vowel sounds will vary from sound to sound, emotion to emotion, mood to mood, and delivery to delivery, all totally dependent on the nature of the words being expressed. Mouth shapes will also be very dependent on the anatomical nature of the character design you are working with!

Two contrasting mouth shapes that communicate two entirely different emotions.

TIP

Animators of dialog cannot work without a mirror to guide them. Consequently, place a mirror in front of your desk, mouth the words as closely to the expression contained in the audio track as you can, observe the shapes that your own mouth makes, then adapt these shapes in your drawings to reflect the design of the character you are working with.

A dialog mirror only needs to be large enough to show the mouth shapes you used when mimicking a particular audio track. Full-length mirrors, however, are necessary for observing full-body poses and postures.

Frame Anticipation

As we have already discussed, anticipating major audio emphasis points on a frame-by-frame basis gives much more punch and authority to the action. Therefore, in highlighting especially the vowel sounds of the dialog track, you will make the lip sync all the more convincing. Again trial and error will enable you to arrive at the perfect solution for your style of animation, but I usually work two to four frames ahead of the actual sound sync point and get good results.

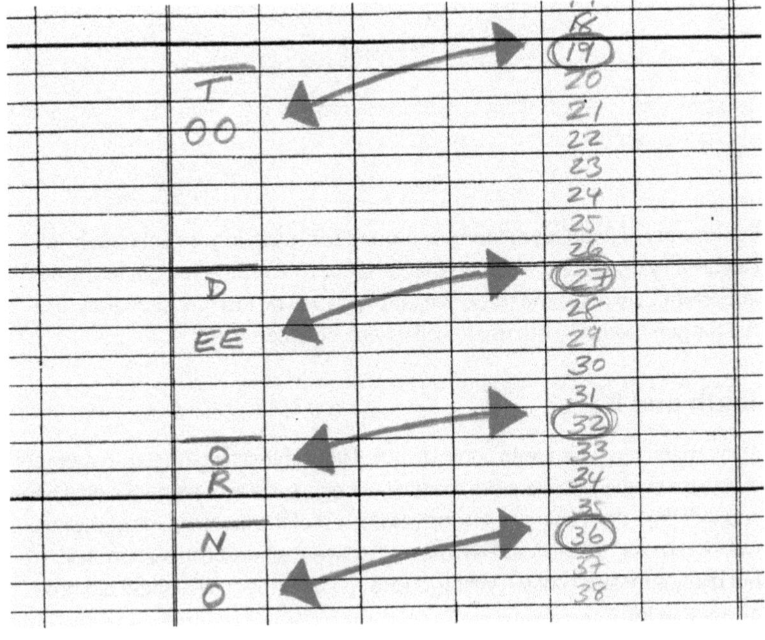

Illustrating the need for key poses and even open-mouth positions to anticipate the actual vowel sounds being expressed.

With major sound sync points, such as coughs, sneezes, and explosive laughter, I have known animators who anticipate the major impact points by anything from 8 to 14 frames. Then again, you will have to arrive at your own perfect anticipation formula by trying and seeing what works best for you.

Tongue Action

Don't forget the valuable addition that selective tongue animation can offer to the dialog. Watch yourself in the mirror and see what your tongue does, especially when there is an L in the words being spoken.

Just flap the tongue up into the roof of the mouth from a previous down position to communicate the L sound whenever it is required.

But be wary of flapping the tongue around too much in your animation. It can be very distracting if you do that because by the time you get to the all-important L points in the track, the emphasis will be lost. Consequently, use the tongue sparingly, but use it well wherever necessary.

Teeth and Bones

Many characters have teeth. Some do not. If your character has teeth, remember that teeth on the whole are like the skull—they are made of solid, inflexible bone and therefore don't animate as much as the rest of the fleshier parts of the face will. That is okay for the Max Fleischer or Tex Avery school of animation style, but rarely advisable today. (Unless you are spoofing the style of these old-time greats, that is!)

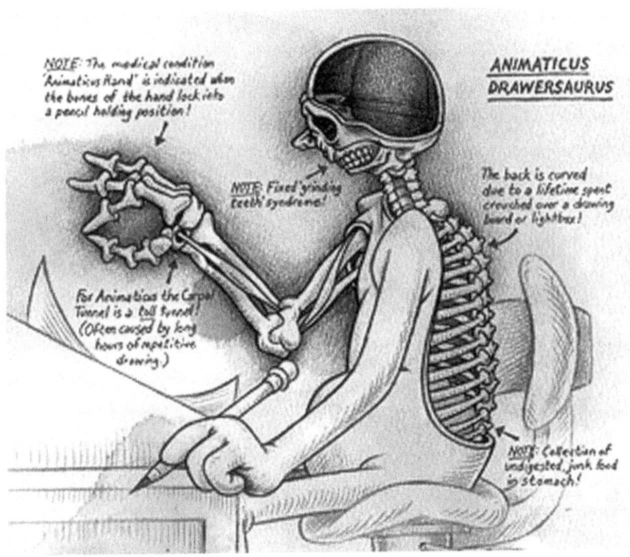

All animated characters, cartoon or otherwise, can be visualized with an internal skeleton supporting them. Consequently, unless you are deliberately animating an old Max Fleischer style, you should make sure the volumes and length of limbs should remain consistent at all times. (Source: From *Endangered Species*.)

Quite often animators move the teeth as if they are as fluid and flexible as the lips. But this is not so. The lips, cheeks, and jaw move around the teeth, which in most cases are rigid and attached to the skull. So, utilize this fact when you animate.

That said, unless your character has definite buck teeth, don't emphasize the teeth too much either. They are set in the mouth, yes, but they should not protrude or have too much undue emphasis. It will be distracting. Keep them natural looking and let the lips and other parts of the face work around them wherever necessary, as happens in real life.

The Practical Approach to Lip Synching

Practically, work lightly with the mouth as you are beginning to fill in the lip sync. Test often, because the only way you will really know what is happening is by seeing it on the screen.

Before I commit to my final mouth positions, I draw them in very lightly at first, then test them to make sure all works well before strengthening the mouth lines.

Some animators are natural dialog people. Others are not. Some find it quite natural to hit the right blend of movement and expression from the get-go. Others (like myself) have to work really hard to get it right! So don't settle for your first effort and think it is fine. There can always be improvements. As I say, it is not just about opening and closing the mouth in perfect synchronization with the audio track, although much animation today usually doesn't demand much more than that.

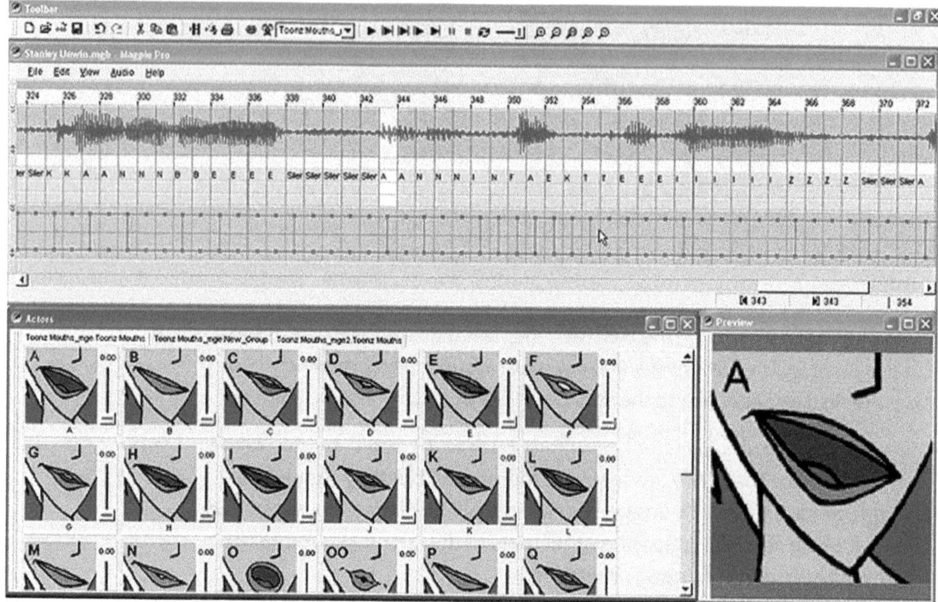

Using your own imported mouth sets, in addition to the moving preview window (on the right) in the Magpie Pro, actually enables you to test the lip-sync timing before even drawing it!

The secret to being a great animator is practice, practice, practice. The more you try (and maybe even fail) the more you will begin to learn the subtleties that work for you and separate you from the herd. Dialog is a very subtle art in many ways and so it does take a lot of effort to pull it off if you're not naturally inclined to it in the first place. But try, and keep trying. We all do get there in the end, no matter how long it may take!

Two-Character Dialog

Not much is ever written about two-character (or more) dialog. So we will briefly touch on it. Just as with single-character dialog, two-character dialog is not just opposing characters looking at each other and opening or closing their mouths in relation to what is being said. Usually a dialog between two people involves a degree of emotion of some kind—indeed, probably more so than with single-character dialog.

Timing of delivery can make even the most minimal of TV-style animation work in the right circumstances!

Two characters can be happy together, unhappy together, angry at one another, consoling each other, or just one telling the other a joke. But whatever is occurring between them, what needs to be communicated is much more than the actual words being said. So pay great attention to their body language and to the expressions they share one to another.

Always look to the composition you choose to highlight the kind of mood you are looking for with the scene and the relationship between the two talking characters.

Also, remember that with two-character animation a great deal can be communicated to the audience by the listener, not just the one who is speaking. The character hearing what is being said, however it is being said to him or her, has to have some responsive appearance on his or her face, not just a placid, static expression.

The pose and body language of a character speaks almost as loudly as his or her words!

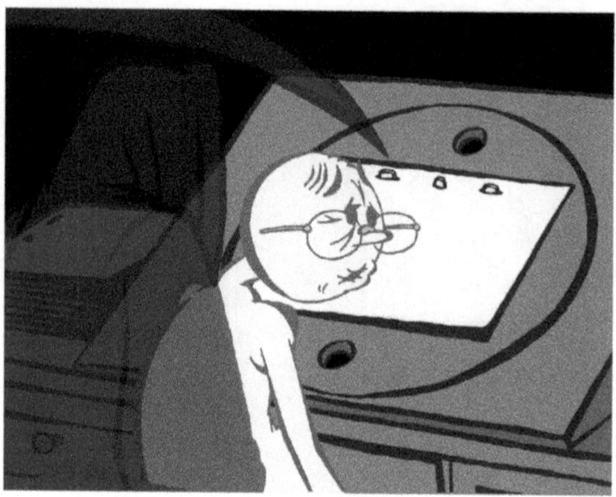

Is the recipient involved angry, amused, sad, impatient, whatever? All these are part of the recipient's dialog attitude, even though he or she may not be speaking a word throughout! Remember, the best dialog animation communicates what is being said *within* the character, not just the words that are coming out of his or her mouth. So with two-character dialog especially, you need to pay a great deal of attention to the mood, emotion, and motivations that are underlying everything.

Neither character is actually speaking, but their body language conveys so much!

The Process of Two-Character Dialog

The process of creating two-character dialog should be the same as with the single-character approach indicated earlier. First, identify the impact points of the audio and create body language poses to underpin them. Pose test these and view in sync with the soundtrack.

Again staging, composition, and body language say so much!

Next, work on the facial expressions to and from each character. Then once again test the action with the soundtrack.

A pose without the mouth can express so much to the audience.

Finally, add the lip sync to both, even if the passive character is listening. Subtle changes in the passive character's mouth shape can communicate so much on what he or she is "saying" to the active character, even though words may never pass from his or her lips!

Even a passively positioned mouth says so much, even though the character isn't actually speaking.

Again: Test, correct, test, correct, etc. until everything is working well, as you would want it.

Staging

Staging is the filmic process of setting the scene and framing the shots to get the maximum impact or communication from the action. If you have two people speaking, you want to identify all of what we have just discussed in this chapter, plus the way you want the audience to best see what is going on. Consequently, before you do anything, you might want to create a simple thumbnail storyboard of how you intend to stage the dialog sequence. This can better define how you approach your animation and how much you put into it at any particular stage.

For example, if two people are arguing with one another, you might start with a wide "establishing" shot, showing them both together and highlighting the particular body language that is being displayed. Note in the following figures that the silhouetted body shapes alone define the nature of their relationship.

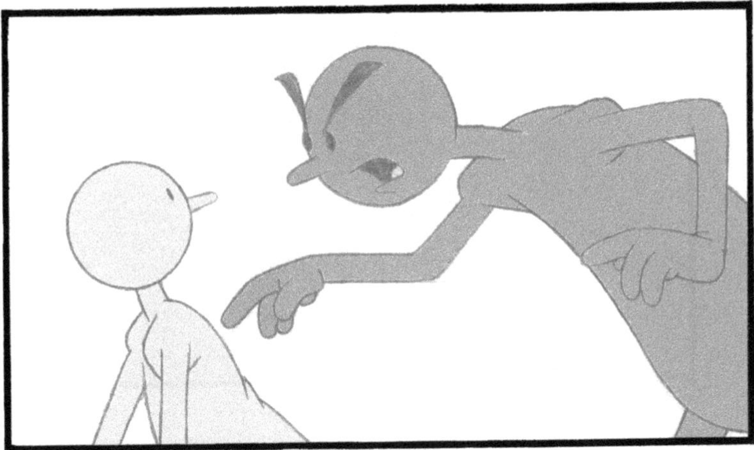

The size and position of the two characters in the frame clearly suggests the nature of their personalities and their relationship.

Always check the silhouetting in any animation, not just dialog animation. As long as the audience can clearly see what you want them to see, you will have succeeded in the staging and composition.

Remember always: Every animator needs to silhouette their animation well. This means that they need to create clearly defined outlines to their poses. If all the elements of the body overlap or obscure each other, then the action is not so clear. Take the following poses and silhouette them and the problem is apparent.

See how much more confusing and less communicative the same character poses from a less-appropriate angle appear.

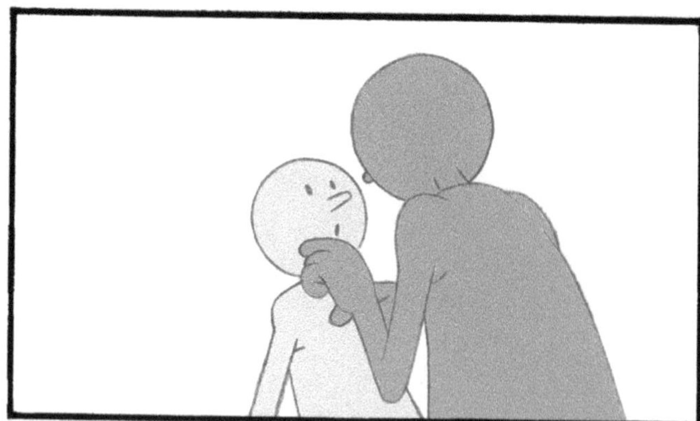

The silhouette version of the last figure shows this even more starkly.

Anyway, in terms of our staging, returning to our establishing shot we can immediately see who is the aggressor and who is the recipient of the aggression.

Again, note how the body language and scene staging tells the story... even without words!

Next we might want to focus in more on the aggressor, see him close up and hear specifically what he is saying. Clearly his expressions will carry a great deal of the weight here, so this is an opportunity for the animator to place a great deal of detailed facial and lip-sync work into the action. The recipient is not even in this shot, so we don't see him at all (which saves a great deal of work for the 2D animator at least).

A close-up, well-composed image can appear very powerful in the context of the scene storyline.

Next, we might actually want to share with the audience the mood and reaction of the recipient. So we can cut to him while the aggressor is still speaking. Clearly, he is looking intimidated and even a little nervous. This tells the audience a great deal, although this character is hardly moving, and certainly not talking.

Even passive poses can suggest so much!

Lastly, we might return to our wide two-shot to reveal the conclusion of the scene, which in this case we have to actually handle in two storyboard shots. Again, this silhouettes through body language and full-figure action the culmination of our story. Being a wide shot we don't necessarily have to focus specifically on subtle and complex facial work, but we do have to make sure our full-body action is well animated.

If you establish your scene well earlier on, the final payoff can utilize that same shot to underline that element of surprise.

Further References

This gives a quick overview on how two-character dialog can be approached. However, I refer you to my book, *Animation from Pencils to Pixels* (pp. 91–135), for a fuller and more in-depth explanation of staging, continuity, camera work, and many other aspects of filmic storytelling. This way you will be better informed for when you need to attempt future character/dialog work. Also, I always urge students (of all ages) to study film and TV work as core reference material to see how all aspects of filmmaking and acting are delivered because there is so much that can be learned from respected work by great actors and directors in these related fields. This is *especially* relevant with two-character (or more) dialog pieces.

Although animation will probably never be able to replicate the subtlety and sensitivity of great stage or film actors, it should never stop animators from studying their techniques and applying them to their animation work to raise the game of animation's capabilities.

It has often been said that an animator is a frustrated actor at heart, and thus it should always be!

Similarly, animators should at all times be encouraged to act out dialog sequences on their own, either in front of a mirror or on camera, so that the recorded delivery can be played back and studied ad infinitum. Animation is always a caricature of real life, and therefore animators have to keep their eyes open to the realities of what is all around them, whether on stage, on the screen, in their own living rooms, or in the streets they journey down every day.

Suggested Reading

White, T. *The Animator's Workbook*. New York: Watson-Guptill, 1988, pp. 130–141.

White, T. *Animation from Pencils to Pixels: Classical Techniques for Digital Animators*. Boston: Focal Press, 2006, pp. 249–256, 455–457 and 404–405.

DVD lecture: "DEMO—Lip Sync".

Assignment 9

With a portable audio machine, go out into the community and record any two-character dialog interaction that is taking place. (Note that Aardman's *Creature Comforts* films are a perfect example of what this approach can offer the imaginative animator!) Select a suitable section of this recorded dialog (I would advise it lasting no longer than 30 seconds if possible), and animate two characters of your own design speaking the dialog to one another. Make sure you emphasize the dynamics, emotions, and expressions between them, as well as making the lips move in perfect synchronization with the soundtrack, of course!

Final Project

Class objective: To take everything learned so far and demonstrate your competence to bring it all together in one coherent and well-thought-out sequence.
Equipment required: Lightbox, pencil, and paper.

Well here we are, almost at the end of the road for the 10-stage foundation course on animation techniques. By now you should be a reasonably competent rookie animator, armed with enough principles of movement to tackle pretty much anything that the world throws at you. You need to be, because now is the time of reckoning—your final project.

So far, you have learned the secrets of key positions and in-betweens, charting and timing. You have learned the differences and complexities contained in walks and runs, and you have discovered what weight, anticipation, and overlapping action mean to the improvement of your characters' movements. Lastly, you demonstrated your knowledge of making a character talk, and hopefully how to make that character speak well with personality and emotion. Now, the final piece of the puzzle is to bring it all together in a way that demonstrates your skills as a fully competent animator. However, before you do that, I just want to give you an additional potpourri of techniques and reminders that will give you additional skills for the challenge ahead.

I bet your pencil can hardly remain still with the excitement… time for a "stagger"!

Staggers

Skill in animation is about having a broad bag of tricks you can draw from to achieve certain objectives with storytelling and movement. A sound knowledge of staggers, for example, is an important trick of the trade you should know about. For example, have you ever seen an arrow hit a target and shudder as it finally comes to a halt? That is what a stagger is. Have you also seen a cartoon character run into a solid object and judder around the scene in a state of agitated shock? That is also what a stagger is.

A stagger is a fast and effective way to underpin impact in an action. I have talked about this before, but let us again take the generic and standard example of the arrow hitting the target, and explain how it is done. In fact, it is more a process of doping and shooting than it is an assignment of complex animation drawing.

For example, a character plucks a string. To animate a staggered vibration of the taut string you essentially need three key positions. The first frame we need to work with is key drawing 1. We will animate this (as a four-drawing slow-in, on odd numbers) to the static key (11). We will then take the other extreme key, 2, and in-between it (on even numbers) with a slow-in to the same static key (11). With the in-betweens done, you need to dope and shoot your drawings (on one's) in their correct numeric order.

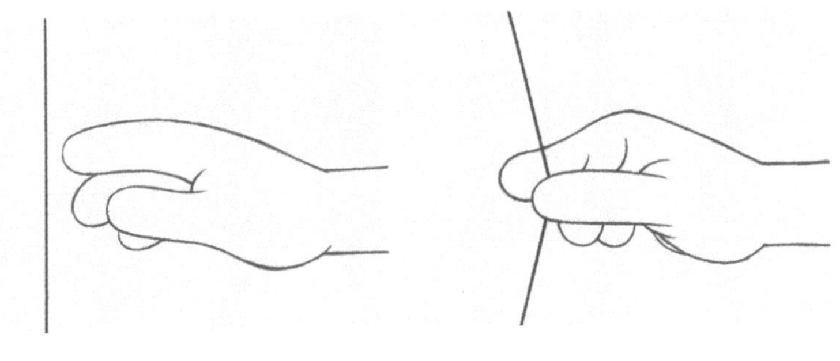

A simple hand moves in and pulls a taut string before letting it go.

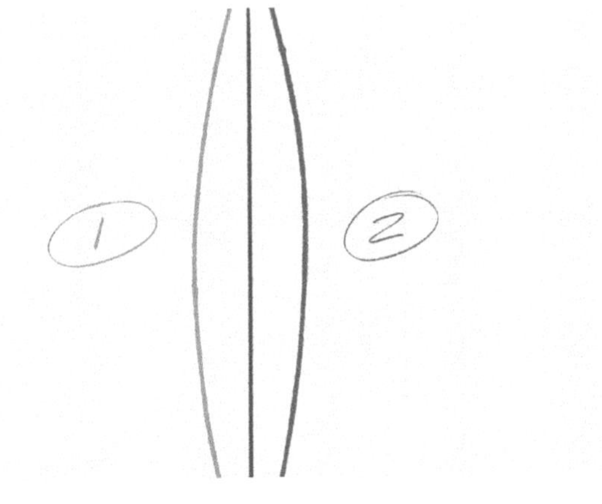

The string flies to the far left (1), rebounds to the far right (2), and eventually returns to its original static, taut position (11).

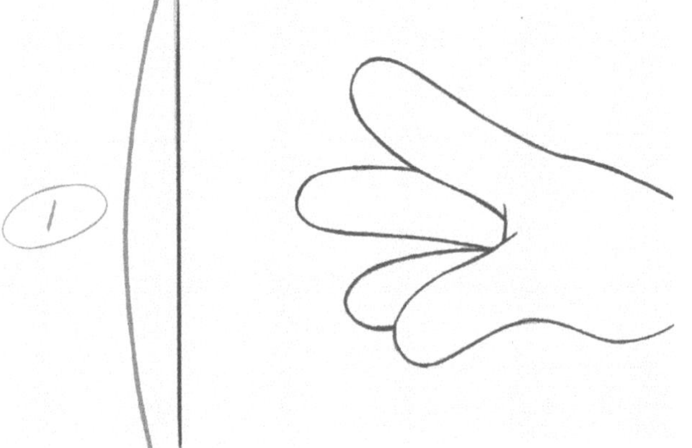

The amount of extreme you put into the extreme positions of the string will dictate how violent and agitated you want the stagger action.

Here I have chosen four slowing-in in-betweens, from 1 to 11 on odd numbers, but you can make as many in-betweens as you like. The less you use, the more violent and sudden the action will appear, and the more you use, the longer and more cushioned the action will become.

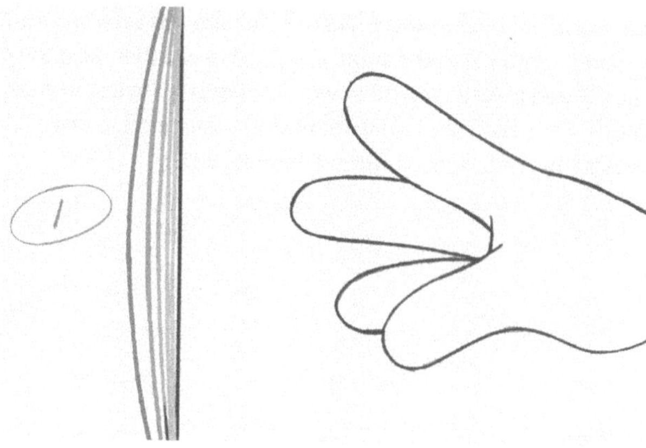

The same comments here apply to the last figure, but just remember to make the same number of in-between drawings in both directions.

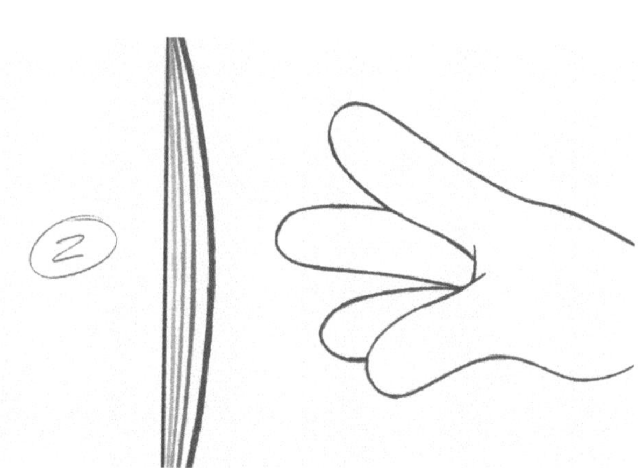

Note that when filmed, the drawings interweave, giving a left, right, left, right, etc. action.

ACTION	DIAL	EXTRA	4	3	2	1	EXTRA	CAMERA
						11		
						1		
						2		
						3		
						4		
						5		
						6		
						7		
						8		
						9		
						10		
						11		

This will effectively give you a string that staggers from side to side in ever-decreasing amounts until it comes to rest. When seen on the screen, this will provide a powerful, short-lived stagger action that depicts a plucked string coming to a halt.

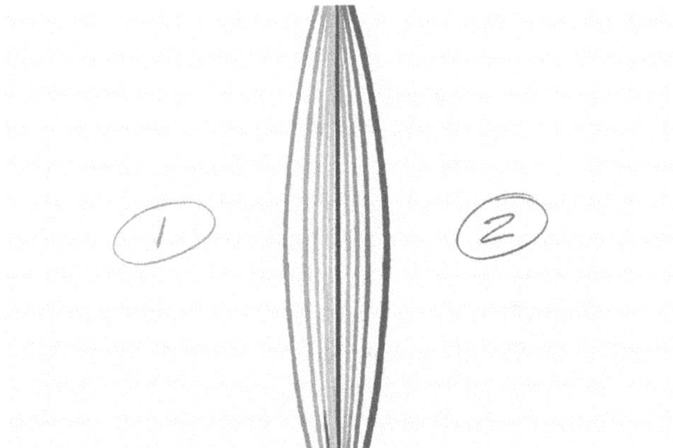

The complete action in one shot.

Staggers can be applied to all aspects in animation, including a stagger on the background when a heavy weight or character crashes down onto it or into it. This is traditionally known as a *camera shake*.

Successive Breakouts of Joints

It is always important that your animation, specifically action animation, is smooth, natural, and as realistic as possible. This requires a certain understanding of the mechanics of anatomy to some degree, especially if your character is a humanesque biped. With this understanding, you will be better off utilizing the qualities of your character's inherent anatomy, especially in relation to his or her joints and the range of movement in these joints.

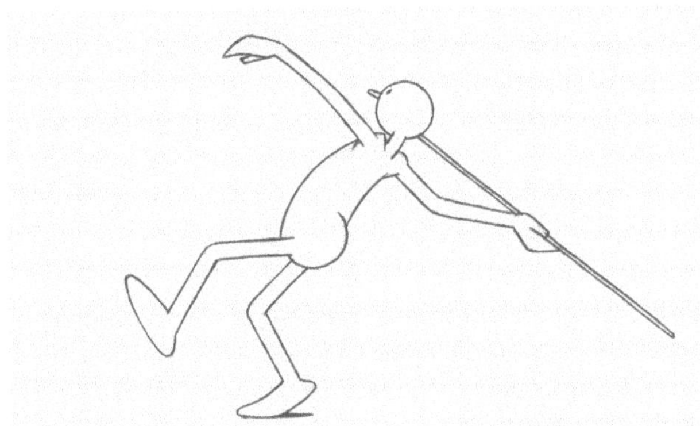

I always find that describing a character throwing a spear underlines a perfect example of the "successive breaking of joints" principle in action.

Joints "break" (move) in a specific way and usually in a specific order. The great old animators of the golden past used to talk about the "successive breaking of joints" when animating full-body action with their characters. What this means is that if a character is throwing a spear, for example, he or she doesn't just randomly hold the spear and toss it from a rear position to a front position in a straight and direct line.

The two essential positions of any throw, from the back position to the front position. However, it is what goes between and after that makes it a good throw in animation!

What really happens in life is that to get maximum speed and distance from the throw, an intricate, split-second sequence of events takes place in the body, taking advantage of its natural catapult capabilities.

Notice how the two key drawings are not just connected by straight in-betweens, but a series of complex key positions link them, even beyond the actual release moment of the spear.

In a nutshell, the biggest joint triggers the firing of the next largest joint, which triggers the next, which triggers the next, and so on down the chain. This controls all the periphery actions of the body. Let's look again at our spear thrower in the following figure.

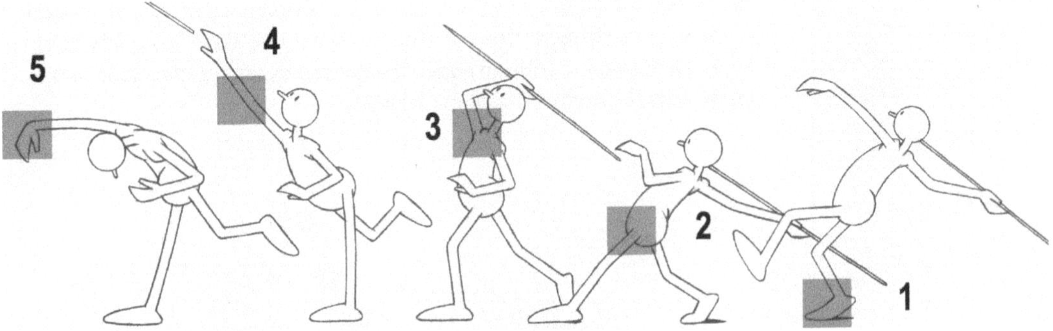

Note that first the hip, then the shoulder, then the elbow, then the wrist, then the knuckles, and finally the finger joints contribute to the throw before the release. In other words, a successive breaking of joints.

Similarly, if a character is pushing a doorbell, don't just mechanically put the character's arm out and have the finger push the button. Instead, aesthetically unfold the joints of the shoulder, arm, and hand so that there is a more fluid and elegant approach to the push.

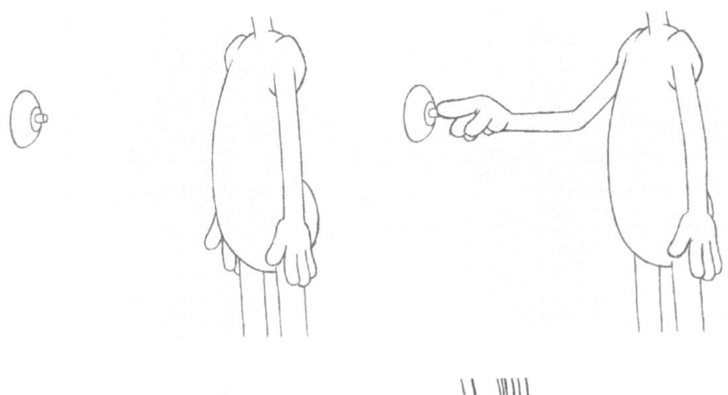

Again, the two key positions of the action.

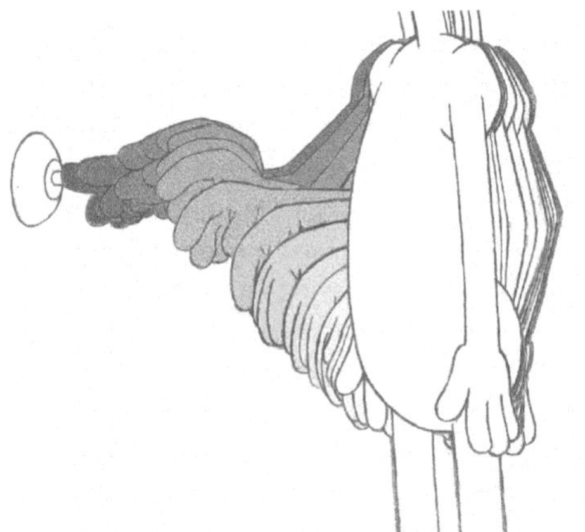

See how with this version of the bell push the hand rises on a curved arc, rises a little higher than the bell push, and then stabs forward at it with the finger. Notice the variations of time based on the placement of each position. Not visible in this illustration is the fact that, at the end, the finger touches the bell on the penultimate position then pushes a little harder on the last one, causing the finger to bend a little.

Even when the button is pushed it is not just a straight, mechanical pullback to the original character position. This movement needs to be equally fluid, logical, and elegant. This can again be achieved by taking advantage of the joints, muscles, and arc of action involved.

See that the hand again rises higher on a concave arc (higher than on the first sequence, in effect) then drops down to the character's side on a reverse arc, with the fingers slightly delaying behind the arm until the very end.

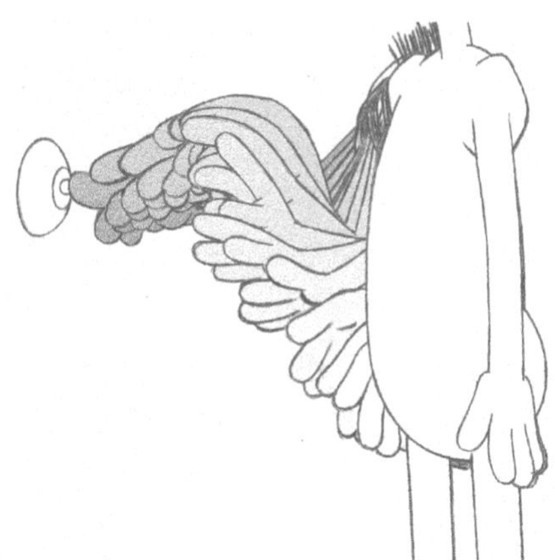

Everything that a character does can be complimented by using a successive breaking of joints in some way or another, unless just one or two joints are involved in the movement, of course. The most fluid animation possible takes advantage of this process and you should therefore utilize it whenever you can.

Eye Blinks

Eye blinks are such a small item in the greater scheme of things, but it pays the resourceful animator to focus on them a little more than you would think. A simple blink on a static character keeps the character alive and can communicate so much. I remind you again that when an audience watches a character's face on the screen, specifically as a close-up such as in a dialog one-shot/close-up for example, they will predominantly look at the eyes, not so much the mouth. Therefore, in paying attention to the eyes, you are adding to the box of tricks you can work with to get the maximum effect out of your animation. An eye blink is such a simple thing. But timed or placed correctly within an action or a speech, it can be pivotal in the message that you want the audience to receive. An eye blink can be a punctuation mark in a long sentence, a gesture of defiance, a sign of boredom, or repetitively used, an indication of some embarrassment or insincerity.

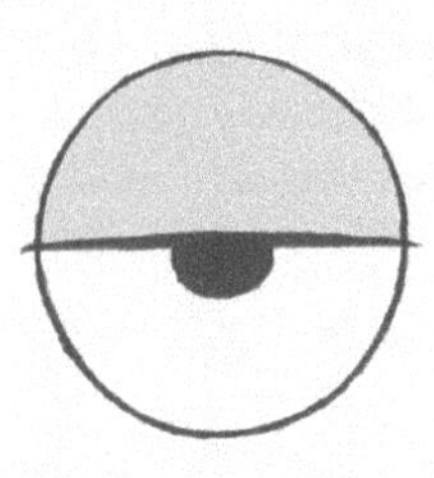

The eyes communicate more than any other part of facial expression, therefore they are a valuable resource in communicating mood and emotion to an audience.

In reality, there is not too much to be taught about eye blinks, but what there is can be useful.

The Generic Blink

Essentially there are three positions involved in an eye blink. The outside two are key positions. If you shot the sequence as eyes closed, half closed, shut, half closed, open, you will get a basic blink that is okay but not particularly exciting or unique.

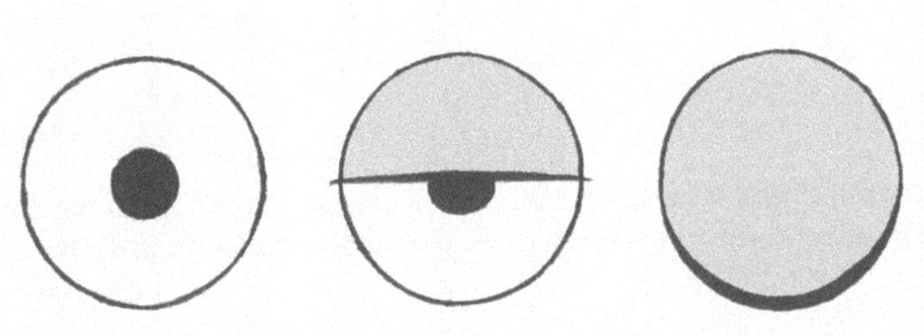

The core to all blinks are an eyes open position, eyes closed position, and one or more in-betweens.

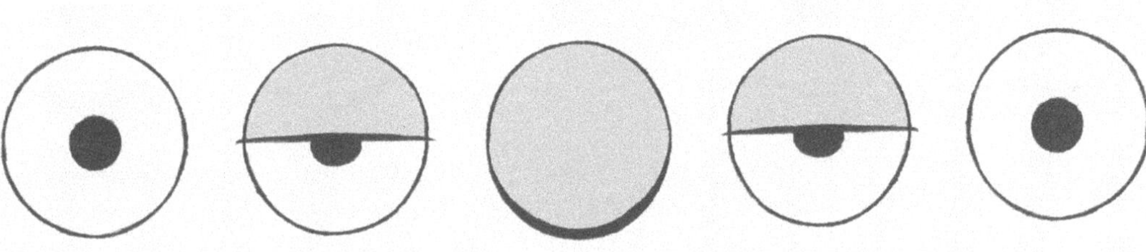

The generic sequence of an eye blink.

However, if you create some in-betweens and modify the sequence, you can get a great deal more expression with the blink. For example, if you add more slowing-out in-betweens to the downward close and then reverse these same positions for the open position, you get a very lazy blink.

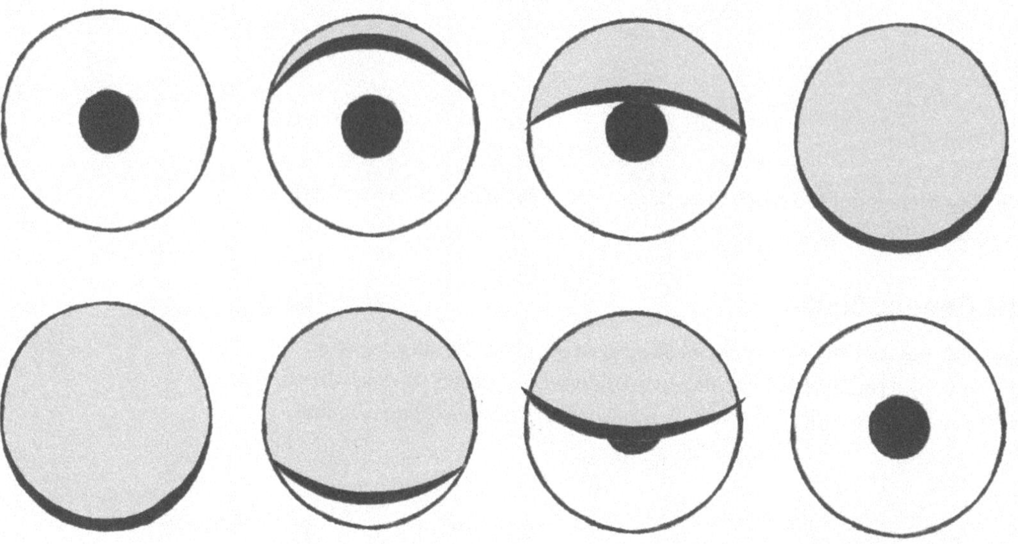

Just one of the many possible timing combinations you can use to make an eye blink less than generic.

On the other hand, if you use just a couple of downward positions for the closing and no in-betweens for the opening you get a different effect from the norm.

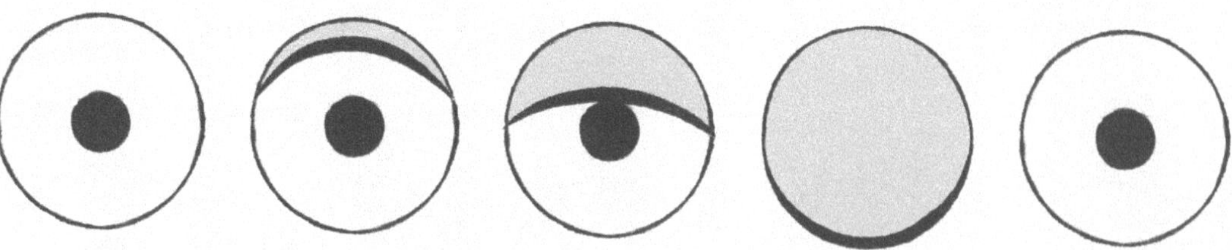

The sudden opening of an eye suggests shock or energy in the minds of the audience, so if you are looking for this reaction, you could add even more closing in-betweens or a long closed position to set up more impact.

If you want the character to look from one direction to the other, you will find it so much more effective if you put a blink in the middle of the action.

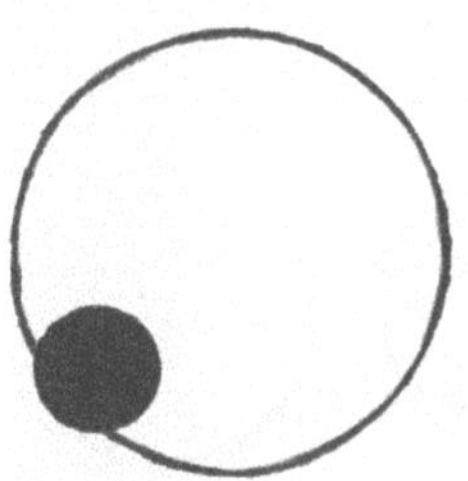
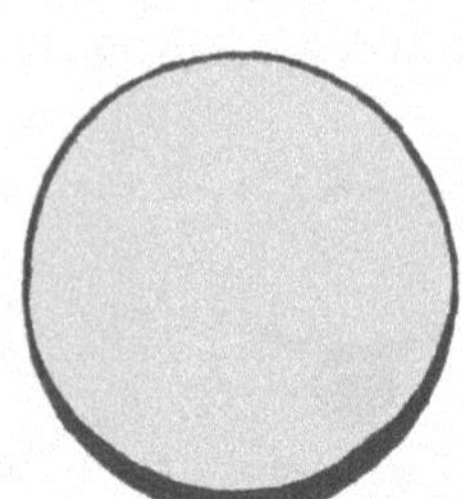
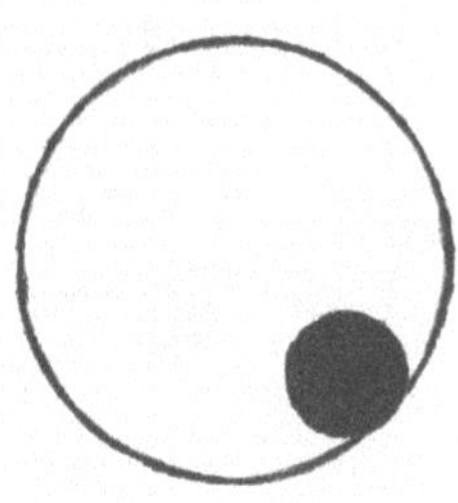

There is no movement in the pupil from left to right. However, depending on how many in-betweens you use to close and then open the eye, you might want to put a little drift in the eye from one direction to the other.

Better still, if you put a lazy close and an active open into the eye movement, you will get a much more impactful gesture of looking.

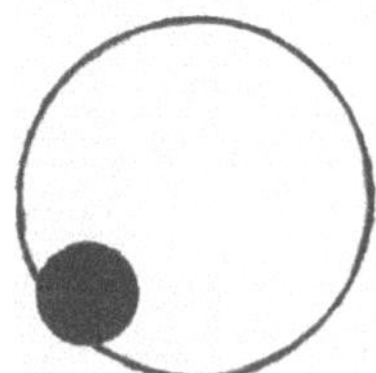
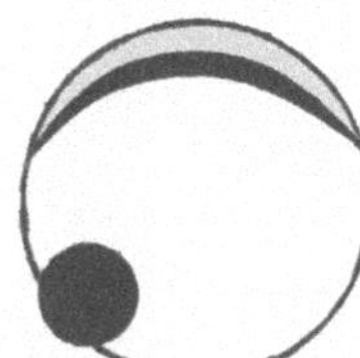
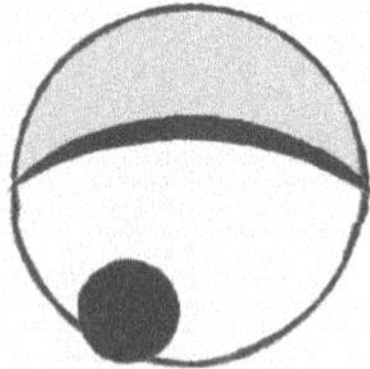
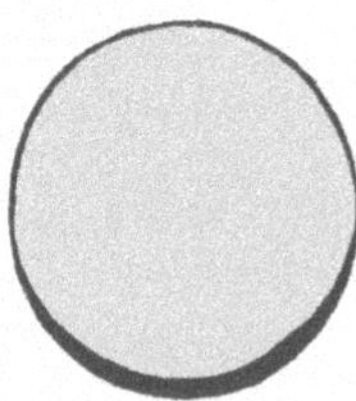
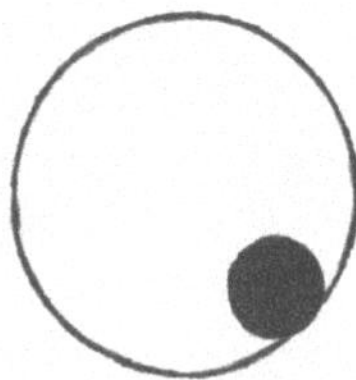

I began to creep the pupil across a little as the eyelid closed, but then I popped the eye open with the pupil in its end position.

TIP

If you are changing the direction of the look from one side to the other but do not want to use a blink to do it—that is, the character's eyes are staring at something or someone who is passing by—do not move the pupil across on a straight path of action. The eyeball is a sphere, so anything moving across the surface of that sphere will move on an arc, such as the pupil.

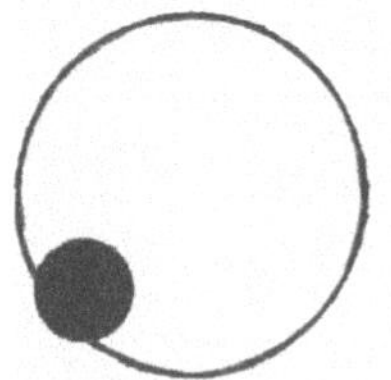
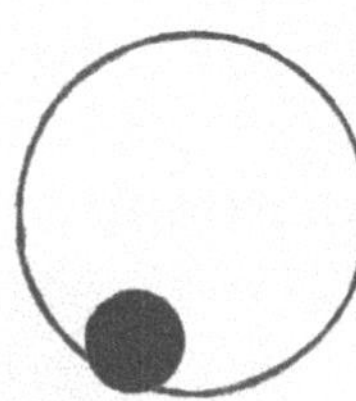
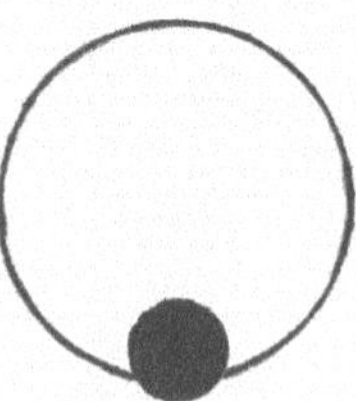
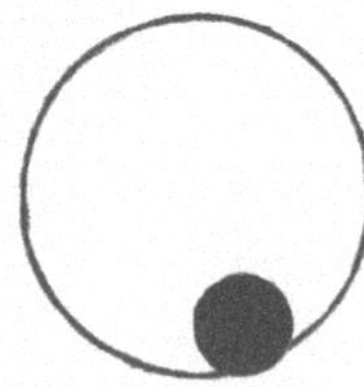
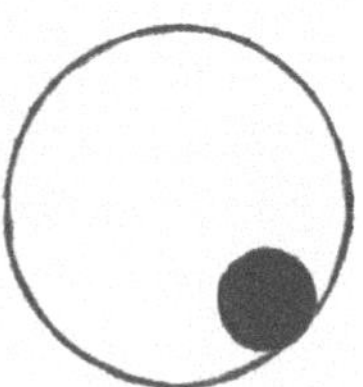

Note that the pupil does not cross from left to right in a straight line because the eyeball is a sphere and therefore the pupil will move around it on an arc. Note, too, that the pupil is positioned just overlapping the circle of the eye, which is an indication it is on the eyeball's surface, not arbitrarily stuck inside it.

If you use a standard blink but take the pupil of the eye down and up with the eyelid, you tend to get a lazy or dull look to the character.

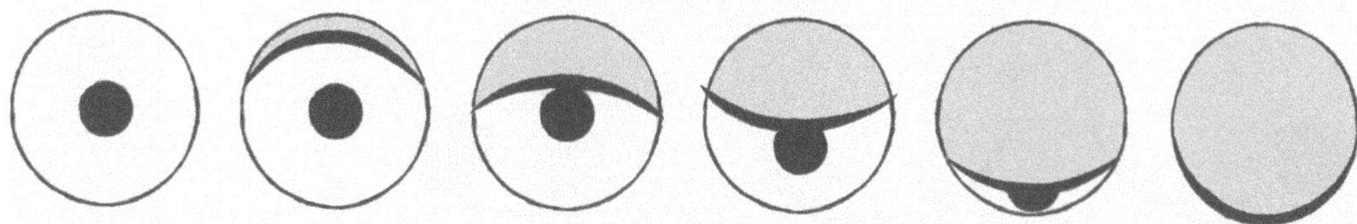

Make sure that the eyelid overlaps the top of the pupil to some degree, otherwise it will look like the pupil is stuck to the outside of it, not connected to the eyeball beneath it.

Finally, if you want a character who just has a dot for an eye blink, then drawing a half dot, then no dot, then a full dot will create an effective blink.

Popping the full eyeballs on the next frame after this approach will give a really alert feel to the character too!

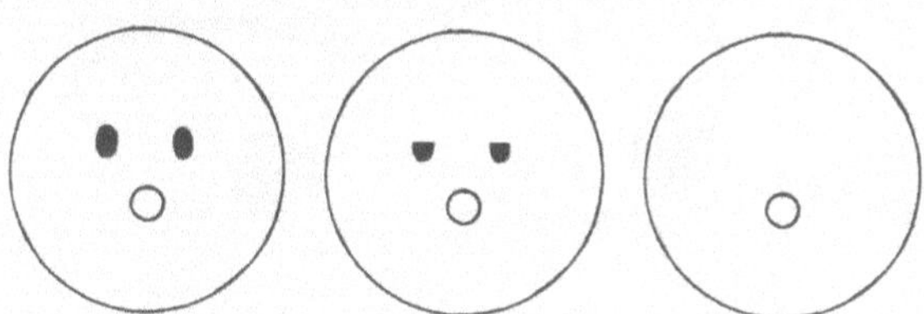

In this case, you could even remove the half dot from the sequence and you will still ensure a strong, if not more powerful, blink with this kind of design.

Pupil Dilation

Finally, don't forget to use dilation of the pupil if you want to suggest attentiveness of an "in love" look from one character to another. Similarly, if a character emerges from a dark place to a light one, the dilated pupil of the eye will narrow to a fine point as he or she adjusts to the light.

Pupil dilation is not often exploited in animation, but it can be really effective in communicating interest or attraction (widen pupils) or boredom of disbelief (narrow pupils).

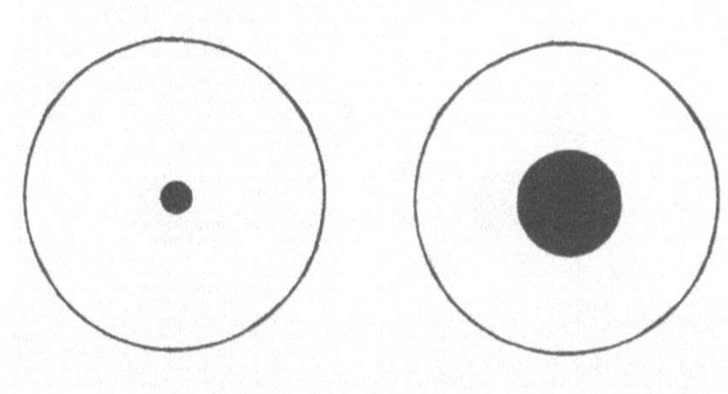

Eyebrows

While we are on the subject of eyes, don't forget the powerful effect that moving the eyebrows above them creates in terms of invoking emotion or personality. For example, the following figure might be the standard eyebrow position for the character we are using.

Neutral eyebrows are balanced and symmetrical above the eyes.

However, if we want to make the character look angrier (without even moving the eyes or anything else), we can simply pull the eyebrows down in the middle. Similarly, by changing the shape of eyebrows, we can invoke a sense of wonder in the character's expression, create a sense of doubt or confusion on the face of the character, or give the character a look of quizzical wonder. See the following figures for examples.

By drawing the attention downward toward the center of the eyes, a definite sense of anger or aggression can be achieved. Placing a single or V-shaped crease in the center of the eyebrows can emphasize this further.

Note the difference between the angles of these eyebrows and those from the previous drawing, and the definite change in personality they invoke (even though the rest of the face has not been altered in any way).

Again a change in the curvature, but not the angle, of the eyebrows offers a very different emotion than the previous one.

By mixing and matching different eyebrow positions, you can get a varied assortment of facial expressions without even moving another part of the face.

Always Gravity!

Remember that even in an animated environment, gravity will always exert an influence. For example, a character prepares to jump into the air in the next figure.

When animating a jumping character don't forget to leave enough space within the framing for the character to jump up into!

To create a believable sense of push from the ground there needs to be an anticipation. Following the anticipation downward, the character now has to strongly push off from the ground, with the feet remaining in contact with it for as long as possible. Then, at the top of the jump, there needs to be a definite slow-in (as we did with the bouncing ball). On the way down from the upper part of the jump, there has to be a slow-out as gravity increasingly begins to exert an influence on the character. Finally, on the landing, the character's legs bend to absorb the impact of the body's weight as it hits the ground. Lastly, a return to normality. See the following figures for the sequence.

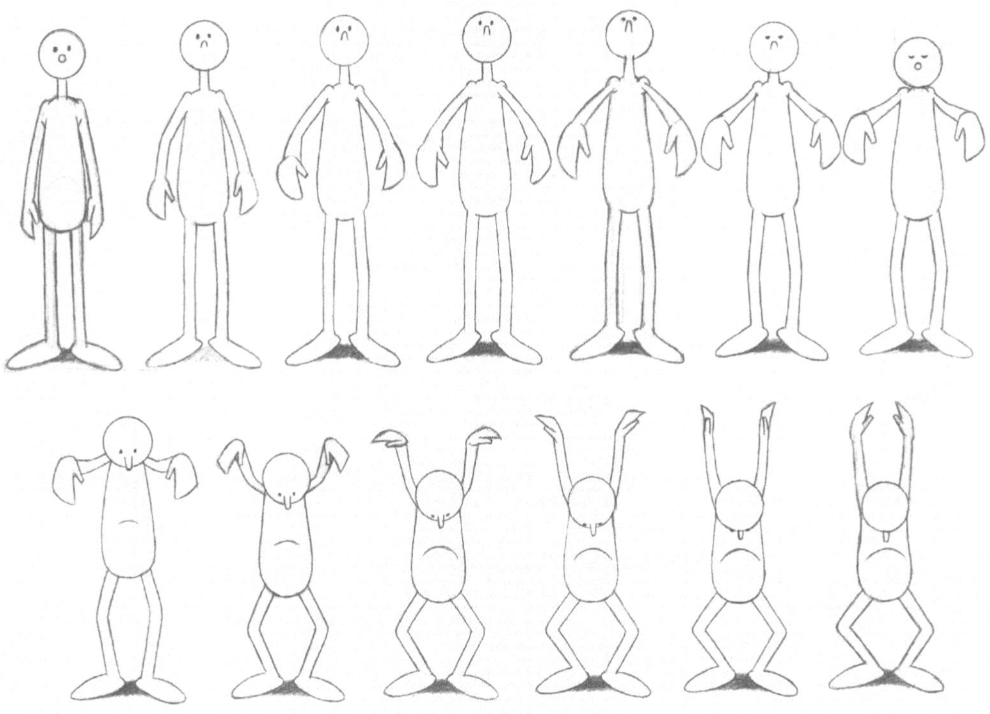

The movement is downward, anticipating the jump upward. However, even for the anticipation, I created a little anticipation upward first, where the character raises up on his toes before dropping downward.

When pushing vertically it helps to use the arms to assist the drive up.

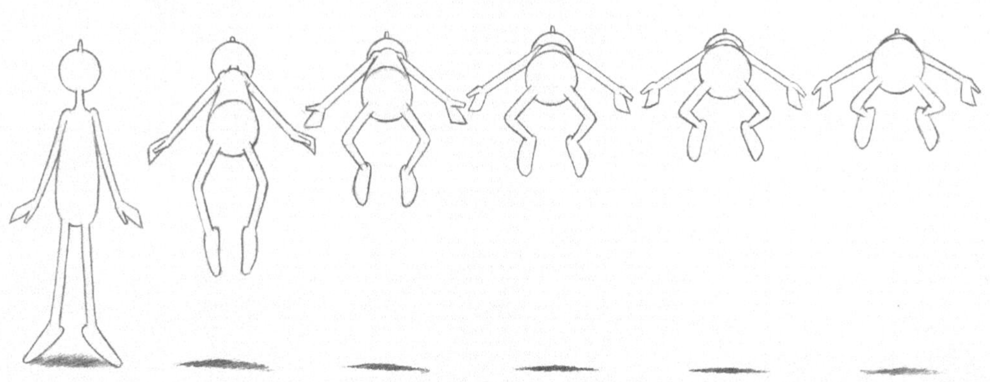

The more you slow-in to the upper motion, the better you will anticipate the accelerating downward action.

During the enhanced slow-in I actually temporarily lifted the feet up higher as the body began to move downward, as a piece of overlapping action, prior to accelerating them down quickly to touch the ground ahead of the body.

Again, I use the arms to balance the landing as the character adjusts to his new contact with the ground.

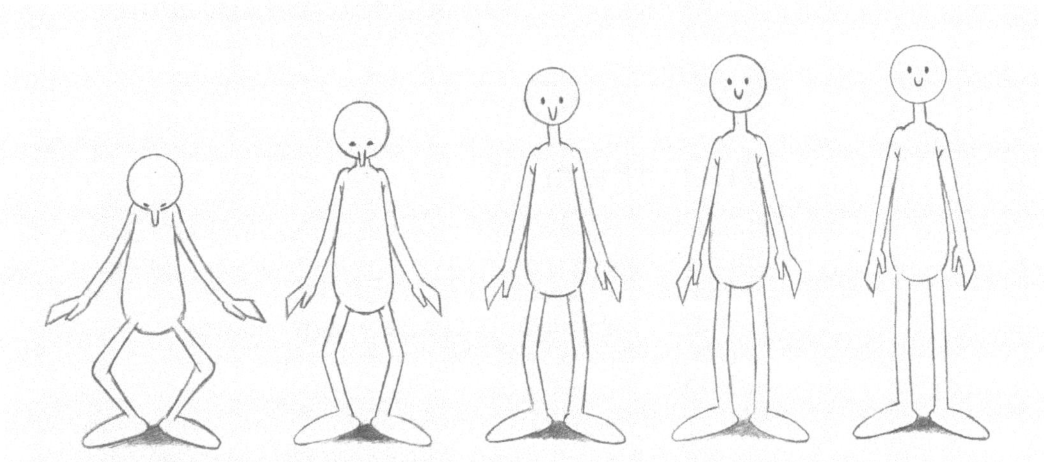

Another slow-in to the final position.

All this thinking needs to go into a simple jumping action if you want your audience to believe that your character is plausible, as well as the world he or she is acting in. If you can achieve all this, then you are more than on your way to being an animator!

Conclusion

Remember that in life no two human characters are the same, therefore in animation no two animated characters will move in exactly the same way. It is incumbent on you as a potential master animator to really get under the skin of your character's personality before you begin to animate, and have your character pose and move in accordance with that inherent way of being. Even then, the same character will have a number of different emotional states that he or she will be going through from moment to moment, so you have to use your bag of tricks to effect accordingly the character's normal way of moving. That is what animation, the infusing of believable life to the inanimate, is all about. That is why you need to know, and perfect, your bag of tricks to make the animated experience for the audience all the more real, plausible, and, of course, entertaining.

Suggested Reading

White, T. *The Animator's Workbook*. New York: Watson-Guptill, 1988, pp. 38–43, 80–84, 106–109 and 112–117.

White, T. *Animation from Pencils to Pixels: Classical Techniques for Digital Animators*. Boston: Focal Press, 2006, pp. 232–234 and 259–264.

Williams, R. *The Animator's Survival Kit*. London: Faber and Faber, 2001, pp. 297–302.

DVD lecture: "DEMO—Jump".

Assignment 10

For the final assignment for Part 1 you need to take a minimum of four of the styles you have learned from all the preceding lessons and add them together with a walk to tell a single, simple story. (For example, you can combine a sample of weight, anticipation, stagger, and a bouncing ball action together with the walk, or even add more if you so wish.) Your story should involve one character, a minimum of one prop that the character works with, and one environment that all the action takes place in. There has to be an establishing/setup shot, an interaction with the prop, and then a satisfactory conclusion. Throughout this process the character needs to have a change in emotion or personality—that is, go from happy to sad, angry to appeased, nervous to confident, etc. The scene can be animated on two's but use one's where necessary. Sound can be a factor, but it is not mandatory. Overall, I would suggest that your sequence be 20–40 seconds long.

Note

You are invited to submit your final assignment to *www.desktopacademy.com*, as those worthy of inclusion will be screened in the student gallery section of the web site.

PART 2

How to Make an Animated Film

The chapters in this part are a comprehensive course in animated filmmaking for the student-level animator. I have almost exclusively used the work of the junior and senior project students at the DigiPen Institute of Technology to illustrate the text. I have done this because I believe their work definitely stands up to the test, and also in a spirit of "the proof of the pudding is in the eating." Consequently, and based on my extensive experience in teaching animation students in the production process, I strongly advise *against* any readers of this book working on the material contained in this part until they have a full grasp of all 10 lessons from Part 1 under their belt. In other words, don't run before you can do the walks!

Production Challenge

By now you should have a solid grasp of all the principles that constitute animation and you should be ready to prove this knowledge by producing a short animated film for yourself. Through the following 22 tutorial chapters you will learn how to take everything you know and apply it through the process of animated filmmaking. The expression of an animated film is infinite, but the process of creating a movie is pretty much common to all kinds of animated filmmaking, whether they be two or three dimensional, for theatrical release, for the Web, or as cinematics and moving assets for games.

What follows is a process that has been tried and tested by master animators through the past 100 years or so of collective experience. This long tried-and-tested process, therefore, should make the challenge of creating your own animated film much less of an ordeal than it might otherwise be. If games animation is your ultimate passion, then recognize that most of the processes contained here also apply identically to games—you just have to modify them to the slightly varying production terminology and proprietary refinements that games studios adopt.

Students should also know that additional illustrated DVD lectures of this production process will be available from *www.desktopacademy.com* as part of the Pencils to Pixels Lecture Series.

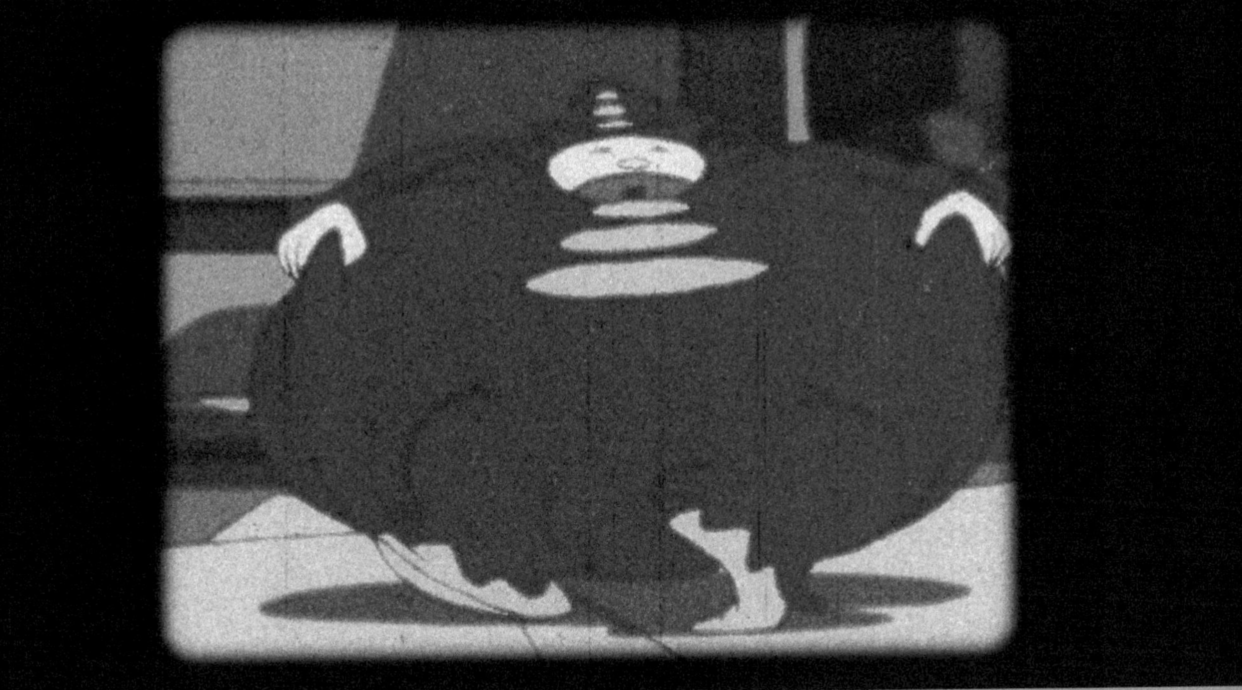

Exploring Ideas, Storytelling, and Scriptwriting

It goes without saying that before you can make a film you have to come up with a good idea and then an even better script! It's amazing how many animators spend inordinate amounts of time working on their projects but fail to entertain or inform their audience because the idea or storyline is so dreadful. Sometimes the reverse is true, of course—the idea is wonderful but the execution is awful, and that is more tolerable for the audience. However, hopefully you can rise above and succeed in both—story and execution!

The greatest exponent of animated storytelling in the past was Walt Disney, who combined storytelling excellence with the highest and most innovative production values imaginable at the time. Sadly, that innovative Disney magic died with him, I'm afraid to say!

There is no secret to what constitutes a great story. Indeed, the potential for animation to tell a good story is infinite. My much repeated advice is, "If you can imagine it you can draw it, and if you can draw it you can animate it!" Long ago Alfred Hitchcock, one of the great all-time directors of superb suspense movies, said that there are three things that make a good film: the script, the script, and the script! There is certainly no denying that a good story is crucial to a good film. So filmmakers will only be rewarded by spending significant time working on this aspect of its creation, even though I know you must be so eager to just jump in there and start animating.

Animation should never bite the hand that feeds it—that is, the story, wrapped in artistic imagination!

This really is a natural temptation, now that you have all the principles of movement under your belt and you desperately want to show what you can do with them. However, I do urge you to resist jumping straight in there, as so many projects are scuppered by too much wild enthusiasm, blinding the animator to the practical and creative realities that have to be dealt with first. I've found over and over again that you only get out of a project in direct proportion to what you put in at the beginning. If you work really hard at the preproduction stage (including idea, script, storyboards, design, Bacher boards, layout, final animatics, and the necessary production planning paperwork that goes along with these things), you'll be fully liberated to create the exciting part that you should already be fully competent at—the animation. It has worked for all the great Disney and Pixar animators, so why not for you?

There is nothing more reassuring than having the whole project worked out and "pinned down" before you begin the fun work, which is the animation. To do otherwise means that you'll be constantly distracted by doubts about the project's length, ending, construction, continuity, staging, and design. It is better to tie all this down from the get-go, so that all you need to do for the production stage is to bring your characters and ideas to life through movement and performance. Therefore, please *do not* neglect any of these earlier stages of preproduction for your project, as close attention to everything now will pay you handsomely later, when you are doing what you probably will enjoy most.

You only get out of a project in direct proportion to what you put into a project, especially at the beginning!

So, where do we start when looking for an idea? Well the world is full of ideas and inspirations just waiting to be brought to our attention. But before you consider anything, let's be really practical for a minute and decide just what parameters you need to work under for this, probably your first film. Being your first film, you probably need to limit the range of your ambition. This doesn't necessarily mean that you will limit your creativity or your impact on the world. Just establish for yourself some genuinely obtainable boundaries to work within. There is nothing worse than being overambitious and finding that after weeks, months, or even years you throw everything you have done in the trashcan because you overestimated what you could achieve with the resources you have. It is better to be cautious and wise and restrict yourself to an achievable objective.

My suggestion would be that you aim for a film that is between 30 seconds and 2 minutes long. I know that this sounds minimal in comparison to the movies you see in the cinema, or the programs that you see on TV, or even the short films that you have seen in many film festivals. But it is at least realistic and obtainable, and you can still make a heck of a good project with a film of this length, especially if you have a great idea and have worked hard on the preproduction stages to express it to its fullest potential.

Carry your ideas "out of the box" and try to explore previously unexplored areas. (Source: Scene from *Fire Gods*, animated by Saille Schumacher.)

Also, limit yourself to a very simple storyline concept at this stage. The core requirements on the final assignment for Part 1 would still work well here: a single character, a minimum of one prop, an interaction between the two, and a final payoff resolution. This has all the satisfying qualities that audiences usually look for, plus it will give you a platform to really express yourself as an animator. Such a simple storyline does not limit your expression or limit the dimensions within your film. You can set the whole thing on a journey through space, a voyage across an ocean, an adventure in the jungle, or a simple moment in time as you get out of bed in the morning. It doesn't matter as long as it is entertaining and gives you full scope to apply all the principles of animation you have learned so far.

The concept art for the opening title sequence of the student-based film, *Fire Gods*. (Source: Produced by the Animaticus Foundation for the Museum of Glass in Tacoma, WA. Artwork by the author.)

In terms of the core idea, anything is possible. Just walk through your town's main street, read today's newspaper, explore the Internet, or flip TV channels for an hour or so. Something, somewhere will give you an idea. Remember, the world of animation, and specifically your imagination, is infinite. Therefore, all is fair game for the subject of your first film. Just remember too that the real purpose of making a film in the first place is to communicate your idea to others. (Otherwise, why don't you just relate the story to yourself in your own head without doing a single drawing and be done with it?) Working for an audience requires that you conceive and plan your idea to the best of your ability, via the best filmic techniques you can muster. Do not neglect an appeal to the universal emotions we all share. If you can skillfully tap into these you will surely capture your audience.

This is why preproduction is so important. It is one thing to have a great idea, but if you can't communicate that idea to an audience—to entertain, inspire, elevate, frighten, amuse, or whatever—you have failed as a filmmaker. Audiences usually like a solid beginning, a middle, and an end to their entertainment, although great films do sometimes work outside these traditional guidelines. Although a great many more films that are "outside the box" fail rather than succeed, ensuring that audiences tune the film out or even leave before it ends! (I say this as someone who hosts an animation festival each year and consequently sees a lot of films that we would not, for one second, allow audiences to see or be bored by!)

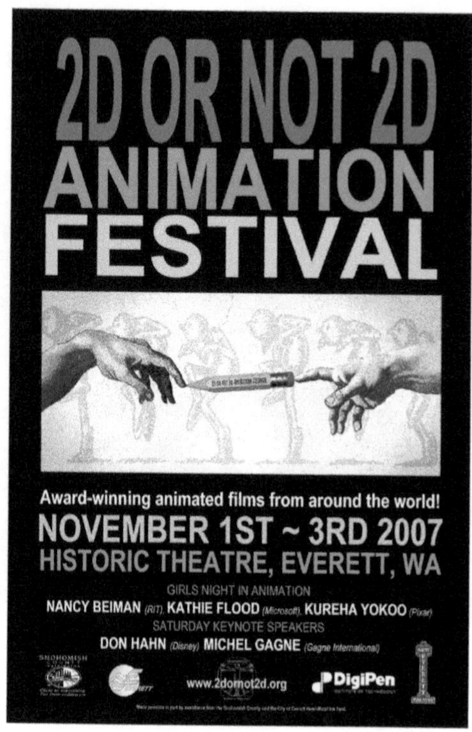

The 2007 poster for my 2D Or Not 2D Animation Festival, where we seek to promote and support animated innovation of all kinds.

Anyway, find first your idea, then work with it. Write it down onto a piece of paper and then, as one way of approaching it, write down all kinds of other associated keywords that come into your head based on this original idea. Play with them, add to them, walk away for an hour or two from them, and later return to them. Whatever it takes to get your mind totally focused on your concept, do it to expand its potential. Eventually, a really strong story theme will emerge that you can build on and develop.

My best ideas come to me early in the day, before I've actually gotten out of bed. That is when I'm in that nonsleep world, but not entirely awake either. This twilight world is a perfect place for coming up with clear and original ideas. (Although, unless you write them down immediately, they don't stay clear for long, and you usually forget them when you're up and about!) I find that keeping an ideas book next to my bed can work well for these circumstances. You can just scrawl your thoughts down in a few words, keeping your eyes closed if you like, so that you get enough of the thoughts and impressions down before full consciousness eventually obliterates them. I use that technique for problem solving too. Sometimes I've worked and worried about a challenge all day, only to go to bed having not resolved it. However, almost miraculously, when going to bed with an expectation of the solution or idea being with me in the morning, it more often than not is, and so I am able to write it down and work with the solution throughout the following day!

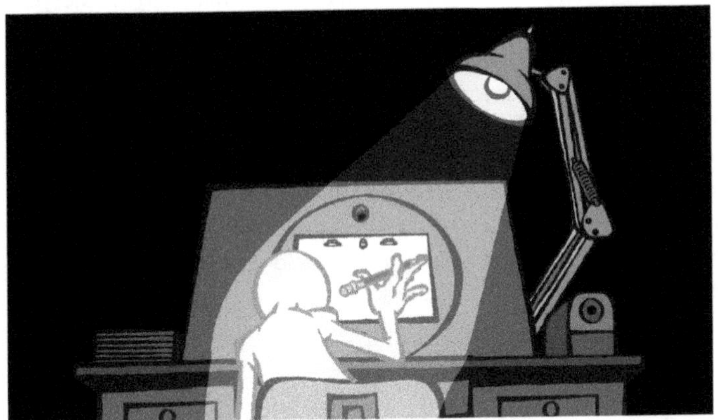

It is not often that an animator falls asleep at the wheel, but it can happen with the long hours that animated filmmaking requires at times! (Source: Screen capture from *Endangered Species*.)

Whatever method you arrive at, you will eventually discover a solid idea and be content with it. When that moment arrives, imagine over and over again in your mind how you want to present that idea. Again, write down concept ideas or do thumbnail sketches of the kinds of worlds and ideas you envision within your core idea and build up a stockpile of material that fully explores all the aspects of your initial concept.

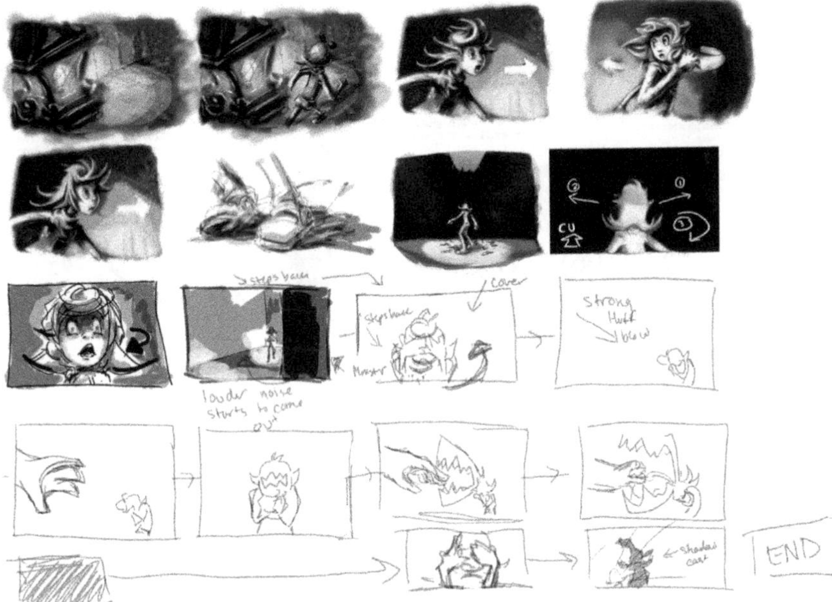

An initial thumbnail storyboarded idea for a short film project. (Source: DigiPen student art by Jenna Smith.)

Eventually, you should have more material than you can possibly use. So, begin to whittle down your thoughts to just the strongest ones, or the ones that hang together best in a sequence of events, culminating in a storyline conclusion that resolves everything. Remember that (conventionally, at least) the audience will expect a setup/establishing sequence that presents the normal world of your central character. Next, one or more things will change or go wrong in that world. Next, the character will have to find ways of resolving or overcoming the changes that he or she are threatened or challenged by. Then, the character will reach an ultimate conclusion that will provide a resolution in his or her world, as well as in the minds of the audience. If you can achieve all this with your idea, then you are set to go, at least to the next stage, which is the script.

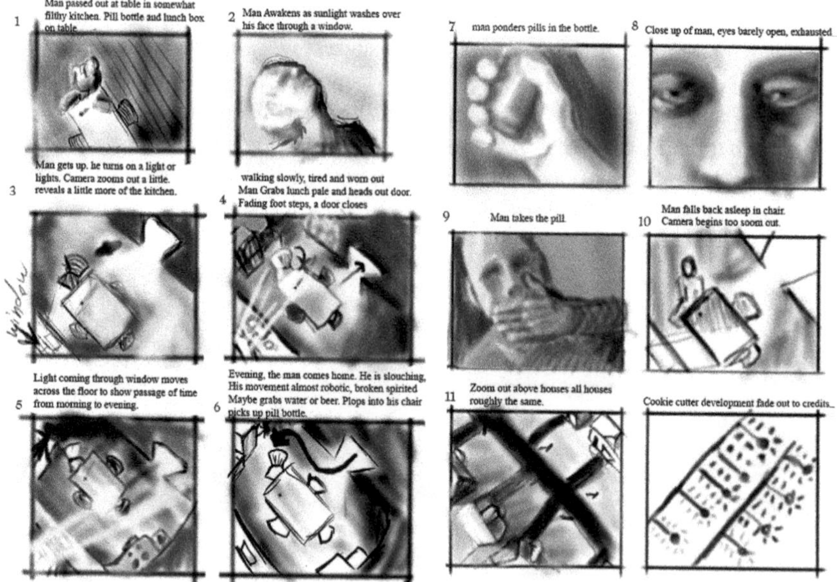

More resolved ideas in an early thumbnail storyboard format. (Source: DigiPen student art by Greg Attick.)

There are no magical secrets to the technical aspects of scriptwriting. Essentially, a scripted story is broken down into definable sections: a new scene slug line, its action content, any character dialog and narration that the scene may contain, and then the mode of transition that the scene requires to take it to the next scene. The following figure shows a typical example of a scripted scene.

```
horizon for sign of the Bag-bird and little Peter.  Seeing
none, he determinedly places his hat on his head again and
enters the house... to think up another ingenious way of
saving his precious little Peter.

                                            FADE TO BLACK.

                    CAPTION:
          SECOND ADVENTURE: THE SEA-SERPENT

                                                  FADE TO:

INSIDE OF LUBIN'S WORKSHOP.

The place is a veritable Alladdin's Cave of quirky
inventions, failed ideas and gadgets. Amidst the chaos is
Uncle Lubin, who is putting the finishing touches to an
amazingly bizarre boat.

                    HEATH ROBINSON
          Poor Uncle Lubin soon got over his
          disappointments and made up his mind to
          look for little Peter in the depths of
          the sea.

Lubin begins to push the boat out of the door and towards a
nearby river.
```

Sample script from a future film development.

In the figure, see how everything conceived is written briefly and succinctly. There is no need for elaborate prose here, except for the actual spoken dialog (or narration, if that occurs instead). Ultimately, you will be expressing the whole of your storyline visually through storyboards and animatics. Therefore, as a "picture is worth a thousand words" (and if so, what is an animated picture worth?), you don't need to elaborate too much on the action at this written script stage. All you need to essentially establish at this stage is the number of scenes that you think it should have, what order those scenes take place in, what happens in those scenes, what is said in those scenes, and finally how one scene transitions to another. Once you are able to put this all down in writing, in the format suggested in the last figure, you have completed your first script. Congratulations! (It wasn't really that painful now, was it?)

'FIRE GODS'

~ A History of Glass ~

The screen fades-up to see an animated glass blower enacting the process of blowing glass.

> **Narrator**: "The art of glassmaking has been with us pretty much since the birth of Man."

The camera follows the end of the glassmaker's blowpipe towards to the round, open entrance to a furnace.

> **Narrator**: "Today we take glass for granted but few of us realize so much has gone into its creation since those days when it was first discovered."

The end of the blowpipe enters into the furnace and the camera follows it right on into the flames.

> **Narrator**: "The one thing that has linked all those centuries of discovery and development for glass is fire…"

Dialog script for *Fire Gods*, indicating that script ideas do not always need to comply with the standard screenplay format.

Of course, by completing your script, it doesn't necessarily mean that it is the final script. We can get so close to our ideas that we often don't see the flaws or missed opportunities that are there. My advice, therefore, is for you to show your finished script to a trusted friend or colleague, or even more than one if possible, for honest critique. It is hard to hear any criticism of one's work, but (trust me!) it is much better to hear it at this stage than right at the end, after you have down so much backbreaking work! Of course, everyone's opinion and taste are different, so ultimately you will have to make up your own mind as to whether their criticism is valid or not. That said though, I would suggest that if the consensus of opinion among all of your confidants throws up a theme or a particular item that they all have negative comments about, then there is probably cause to pay attention to it and adjust your thinking as necessary. Again, the final responsibility and judgment lies with you. But as you are presumably making your film with an audience in mind, and as the feedback of a number of people will probably be representative of the reactions of your audience later, I think you should respect that advice and work with it a little more.

Meaning and WTF?

It always pays to question and challenge everything you do to ensure it is the best that you can do . . . and the sooner the better!

We have an interesting challenge at DigiPen when students are presenting their initial project ideas. We utter a simple question: "WTF?" WTF or "What's that for?" confronts the filmmaker with a challenge. The question may acknowledge that the initial concept is a good one, but it does then ask for a deeper meaning to the idea. Ideas can be so exciting and crystal clear to the creator but the meaning to the audience is often overlooked.

Thumbnail sketches and storyboards can mean a great deal to the person who drew them but absolutely nothing to those who view them each time. Consequently, the WTF question challenges the students' precepts of what they are producing and what they are pitching for acceptance for their project.

Every facet of a student's pitch has to be explained. A character does something, but why does he or she do that? Why does the character need to do that? What happens if he or she doesn't do that? All these are WTF questions. Even if the idea storyline is solid, the images or designs associated with it are questioned too. Why that establishing shot? Why that camera angle? Why that action? Everything is scrutinized until the full meaning of every idea, shot, or camera view is understood and defended. This scrutiny produces more powerful films with greater meaning.

Meaning is what it is all about. Without meaning for the filmmaker, and therefore for the audience, there is no purpose. It is meaning that an audience picks up on when watching a film. If the film doesn't have meaning, it doesn't resonate within us, and therefore we cannot identify with the characters, story, or action that is unfolding before us. As filmmakers, we need to provide the audience our eyes and ears to perceive what we want them to perceive. If they do not have eyes to see or ears to hear, than all our work is wasted and ineffective, for that which is not seen or heard does not exist, and for filmmakers, this is the kiss of death for their creative work. So regardless of how good you think your idea is, or how good you think your visuals are, ask yourself the WTF question on everything you do. Challenge yourself and you cannot fail to improve your idea and your film, for again, a film without meaning is not film at all!

Assignment

Complete a finished script that you feel is worthy of all the hard work you will be required to put in on your film from this moment on!

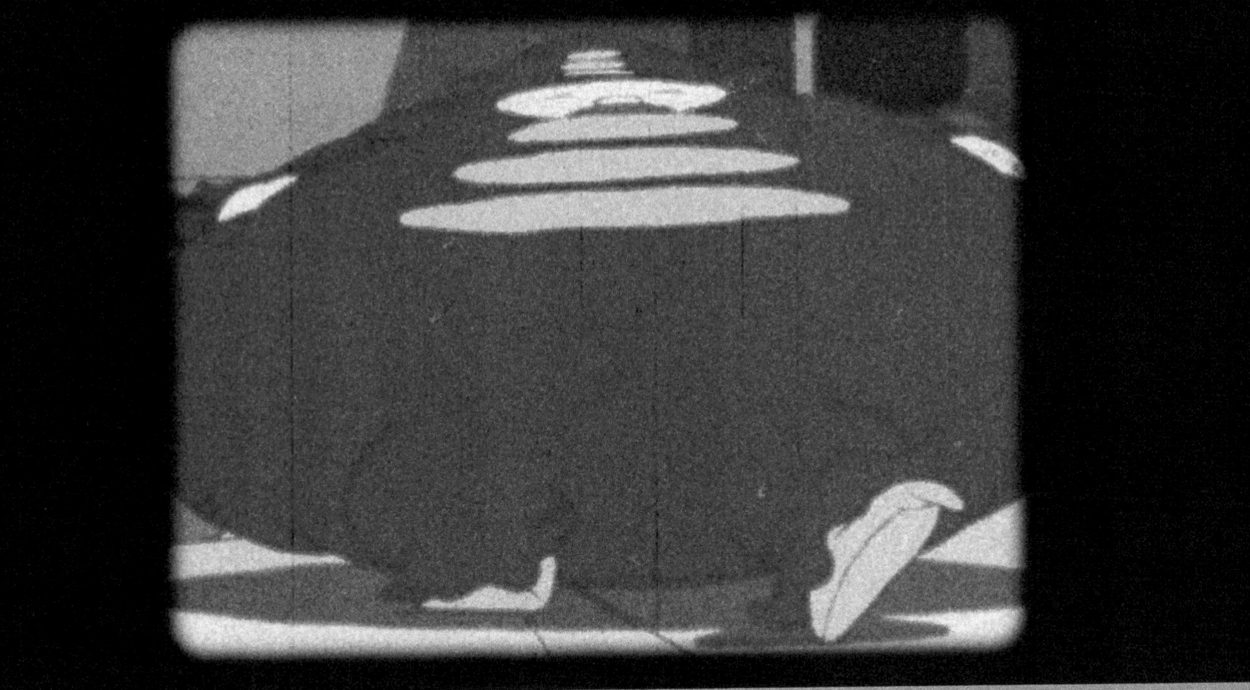

Concept Art, *Viz Dev*, and Camera Maps

Concept Art

As a creative person you should be able to understand the value of concept art, or *viz dev* (visual development), in your preproduction development efforts. With the story idea defined clearly by way of script it is now important that you begin to come to terms with what your film is going to look like. We are not talking about finished designs, but rather more initial concepts that sum up the look and the mood of where your story is going. Concept art for Disney or Pixar productions is often "high art," creative work that is the equal, or better, of some of the best creative work ever produced. But for your film it is good to lower your sites on more attainable objectives.

Creating a film poster for your film at the outset will encourage you to establish a great deal of the 'look and feel' of your film, as well as focus in your own mind the key elements that you want to communicate to your audience. (Source: DigiPen team student art.)

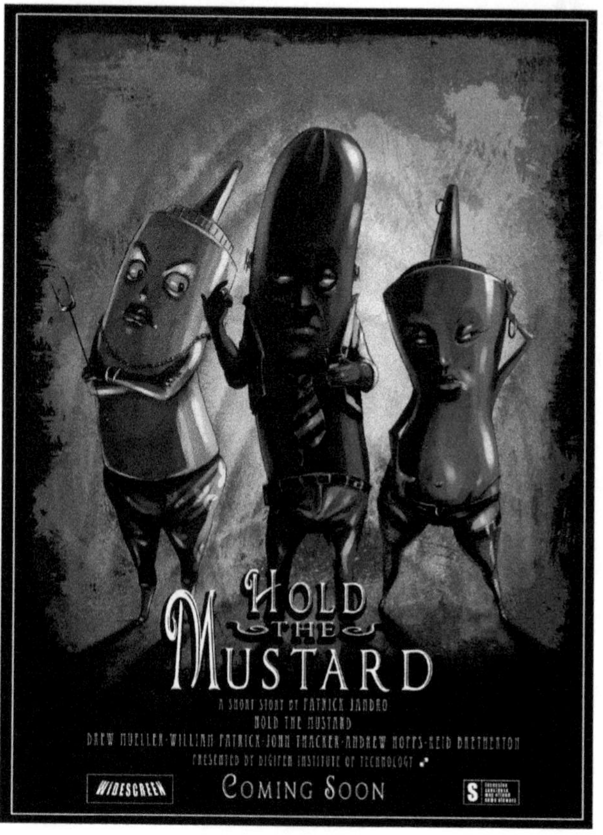

Some of the many color concept designs created before reaching a final conclusion with this 3D-generated but 2D-look film. (Source: DigiPen student art by Jeff Weber.)

As long as your concept art takes in the look of the character(s), prop(s), and environment(s), you will be on the right track. Color and style will define mood and emotion. You may find that you prefer someone else to do the visual work for you at this stage. Not all animators are great character designers or environment painters. Why should they be? Their skill is usually in the art of movement, not the art of static images. Character design artists or background artists do not necessarily make good animators either, so don't feel defeated if you prefer to have someone else tackle your concept art. Indeed, I would respect you better as an animator/filmmaker if you can recognize your limitations and seek outside help at this production stage. I would not accept someone else doing your assignments in our DigiPen-related courses, but here in the realm of home-based/independent film production it is sensible to have a specialist artist brought in to tackle an important aspect of your film's development—that is, the look and feel of it. Of course, you might be a master designer and painter, as well as capable animator, and that is great too. Just recognize what your best skills are and focus on them for this production challenge.

Early environmental design line drawings for a short film project. (Source: DigiPen student art by Nick Wiley.)

It is hard to say how many pieces of concept art you will require for your film. You could choose to use one scene (or environment) throughout or there could be many. There could be many facets or moods to your story, or only a few. Suffice it to say, the concept art should represent and visually define each major event in your film, whether it is a major change of scene, time, location, or action. Normally, it would not be entirely necessary to produce concept art for an intensely personal production like this one, but as we need to explore every phase of the production process that you will need to work through on a professional-level production, I am asking you to do so now, so that you will be fully prepared when your first major career break happens.

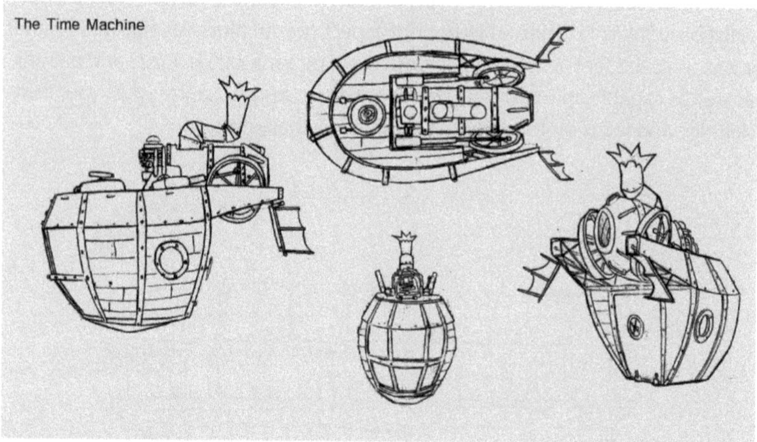

Line drawing concept art for a short 3D film project. (Source: DigiPen student art by Eric Wiley.)

Camera Map

One of the key elements at this stage of your project development is the creation of a camera map. A *camera map* is a standard part of the live-action process. A scene is written and a set design is conceived. However, by creating a rough top-down view of the proposed set, the director can set his or her camera positions so that the rest of the team can understand what parts of the set will be featured in-shot at any point in time. This, therefore, allows everyone to know the facets of the set that they need to focus on more than any others. (Indeed, some parts of the set may not be visible at all, so nothing at all needs to be done for these areas!)

This approach is a very valuable one in animation, especially 3D animation, where the environments need to be painstakingly modeled, textured, and lit. If there can be any savings in this part of the animation process, then a significant amount of time and effort can be saved, leaving the filmmaker freer to concentrate on other more relevant things. Consequently, when you have worked out the location or environment, create a top-down sketch of the entire scene and indicate where you want the cameras to be positioned (see *Animation from Pencils to Pixels*, pp. 92–135, before doing this or the following storyboarding stage). With this planned out in your head, as well as on paper, you can then easily decide what environment material needs to be illustrated or modeled (depending on whether your film is a hand-drawn 2D film, a computer-created 3D film, or even a 3D claymation or cut-out animation film) and which does not.

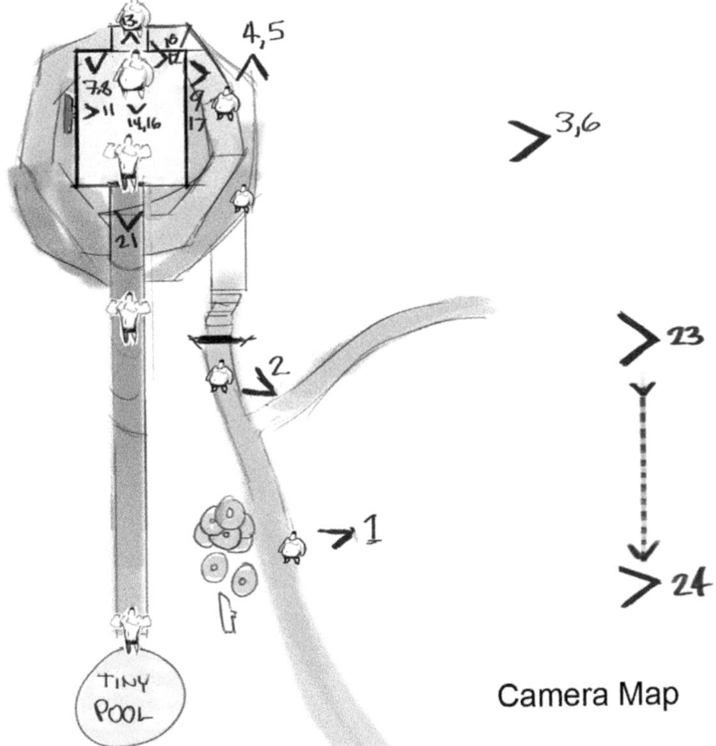

Camera map showing camera positions and shooting sequence for a film set around a giant water slide in a theme part. (Source: DigiPen student art by Drew Gamble.)

Assignment

Create three or four pieces of concept art that define the main shots and/or sequences in your film, in addition to all the relevant camera maps you will require for each location within your film.

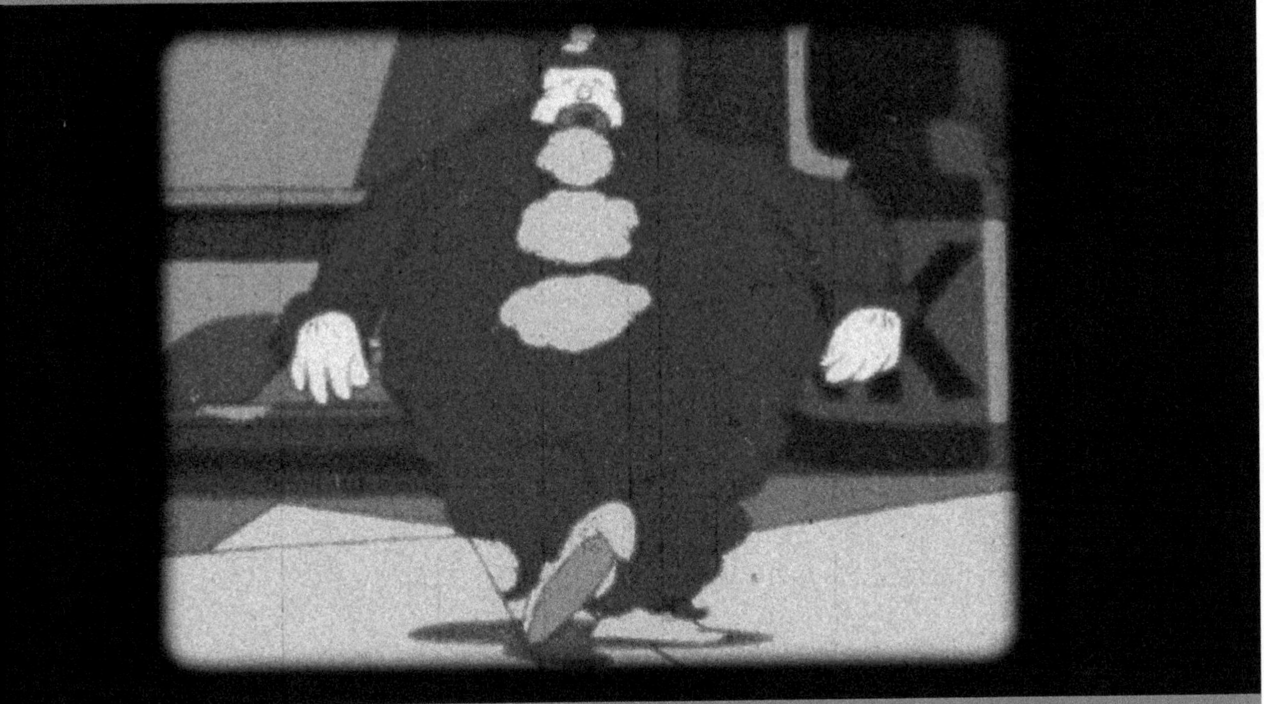

Character Design

Character design is another specialist area in itself. I believe that you either have the ability for it or you do not. That said, so as not to frighten anyone away, you can easily be a fine character animator without being capable of drawing original and well-structured character designs! Here are a few guidelines that can make you design better characters, whether you're naturally good at it or not.

Concept art of two film characters. (Source: DigiPen student art by Mark Barrett.)

Style

The first thing you need to consider is style. With your concept art you should already have defined this to some extent but now it is time to hone in on the precise look you want to go for in design and animation. Style is infinite in its conception. Do you want your film in its approach to be stylistically illustrative, traditional cartoon, wild and wacky contemporary cartoon, photorealistic, etc.? All these things have to be thought through at this point.

A highly stylized character sheet. At DigiPen character design students are required to create a character design from one popular genre in the style of another. Here Lucius Malfoy is designed in a style after Samurai Jack. (Source: DigiPen student art by Cody Flynn.)

The one thing you most likely don't want to do is have a character design style that is very dissimilar from your background or environment style. Or do you? (Perhaps your film will totally contain that kind of off-beat novelty.) Chances are, though, that you'll want a compatible style throughout. But then again animation is capable of anything, so don't entirely close off all your options at this stage. Don't forget, too, that using a rounded, curvilinear style of line approach will give you a softer, cuter style of character. Angular, rectilinear line and form will give a more aggressive, hard-cut style of character. Similarly, with the colors you use, generically pastel shades imply a softer, cuter style, whereas pure primary colors suggest a more "out there," wacky kind of personality.

Designs in a harsh and hard rectilinear style and others in a soft and gentle curvilinear style. (Source: DigiPen student art by Mike Mazza and Jarod Erwin.)

Just remember than when you ultimately make your decision, be conscious about *why* you have made it and why it works best that way in the first place. Don't just stumble through, thinking it will all look good in the end. It won't. You have to have a reason for doing everything in animation. Everything you do needs to be planned with eyes wide open.

This set of rhino designs is both aesthetically pleasing and solidly structured from all angles. (Source: DigiPen student art by Eric Wiley.)

Personality

Next, think about the kind of personality your character will have. Is he or she friendly, aggressive, dumb, bright, laid back, uptight, attractive, ugly, whatever? So much of the personality of a character defines the design style. The hero type would not normally be drawn to look like a wimp. Similarly, a rocket scientist would not look like a country and western singer. Therefore, think carefully about the shape and the style that you give your character, as the form and nature of the drawing will very much determine how the audience will perceive him or her.

An inanimate object challenge—how to give a telephone personality and character. (Source: DigiPen student art by John Thacker.)

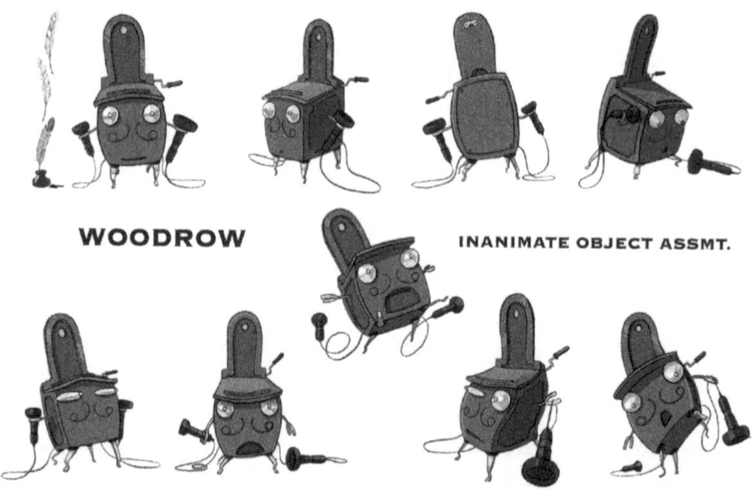

Attitude

Attitude is another aspect of your character's design that you need to visually communicate to your audience. The pose or stance of the character will very much define his or her attitude. If your character is a kind of "wimpy coward" type of guy, you don't want to draw him with an aggressive, fighting stance. Similarly, a big, clumsy-looking oaf will just not cut it as a sensitive brain surgeon. Look at styling in other films and analyze what the attitude their best characters exude and why they work so well for the parts they play.

How to take a flower character design and give it presence and attitude. (Source: DigiPen student art by Mark Barrett.)

Proportion

The proportion of your character says so much about him or her. The short character with a big head is much more likely to convince us that he or she is bright and intelligent, than the big, pinhead, lummox of a guy with knuckles scraping the ground. Alternatively, the big broad-shouldered hunk with a square jaw better defines a person of action and courage than it normally would a mathematician or an accountant. (But then again, there are always exceptions to the rule, if you can pull them off.)

Two extremes for characters: the narrow-hipped, wide-shouldered, strong type, and the wide-waisted, heavy-weighted opposite. (Source: DigiPen student art by Brian Bassir.)

Head Heights

One very important aspect of character design is being aware of head heights. Head heights define just how tall your character is and what size the character's head is in relation to his or her body. The more cartoonish your character design style, the less head height he or she is likely to contain. Typically, the head height of a character is calculated by the number of times his or her head divides into the overall height. Human head height measurement is usually defined as seven, meaning that the size of the head makes up one-seventh of the overall body size. With Manga characters it can be as much as nine, but in the simplest of cartoon characters (such as the PowerPuff Girls, for example) it can be as low as two. The head height of a character will therefore define how realistic or cartoonish he or she appears to be.

Students are often asked not to measure their characters in head heights but by a common currency related to that character. Here, an approximately two-and-a-half head height (excluding the hat) magician character is measured by 14 spell books! (Source: DigiPen student art by Andrion Becker.)

Silhouette

Nothing more immediately defines the nature of a character than his or her silhouette. Take a number of your favorite characters and create solid-black silhouetted versions of them. Place all these silhouettes side by side and see why they are clearly silhouetted differently from one another and how those silhouettes define the characters' inherent personalities. Recognize how important a silhouetted shape is in "branding" a particular character too. This is something you very much need to keep in mind when designing your own original character.

A fine designer lamp character is echoed by its silhouetted double below, defining clearly its shape and readability. (Source: DigiPen student art by Andrion Becker.)

Detail

Remember, especially if you are a 2D animator, that every line that you put into a character design has to be redrawn 24 times a second (or 12 if you are animating on two's)! Consequently, you want to make sure that you keep your inner detail to an absolute minimum if possible. Imagine creating a character with a plaid shirt and then having to draw it every time for every animation drawing!

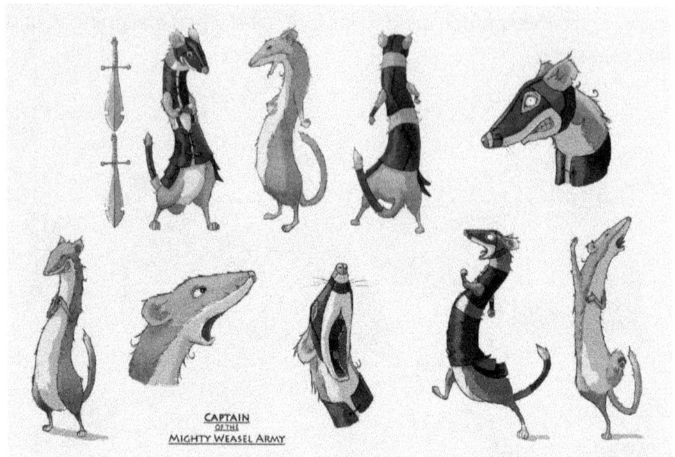

A beautiful animated weasel design, but far too complicated for something like a TV show where characters need to be simpler and faster to draw! (Source: DigiPen student art by John Thacker.)

Minimalism has a lot going for it, especially when you are designing a 2D animation character. So try to create your character with the least amount of detail and texture that you can get away with. You will most definitely thank yourself for doing this when you reach the animation stage later on!

The opposite of the previous design. This one is so much simpler and minimalist in "pencil mileage," and therefore perfect for TV or Flash-syle animation! (Source: DigiPen student art by Drew Gamble.)

Process

With all these thoughts in mind, it is time to start your character design. Clearly, the very first thing to do when approaching your initial design is to rough draw your thoughts as quick thumbnail sketches. Get as many ideas and approaches down as you can, and as quickly as you can.

Preliminary sketches of the girl character seen at the start of this chapter. (Source: DigiPen student art by Mark Barrett.)

As suggested before, definitely look at your favorite character designs to guide you, to help you decide what area you want to concentrate your design thinking toward. Don't copy them though—that could lead to a world of legal hurt—just use them for inspiration and direction only. Narrow it down to exactly what things you like and what things you don't like about your character ideas.

The final sketched girl character. (Source: DigiPen student art by Mark Barrett.)

Even show your initial sketches to others for feedback. Ask them to look at your designs and tell you what they think the inherent personalities and attitudes your characters have. Better still, first show them the silhouette versions of your characters and ask them the same questions before showing them your development sketches.

Silhouette versions of the girl and boy characters featured at the start of this chapter, delineating that both their outlines are clearly different and therefore they will be easily definable in a scene that doesn't have strong light or color values. (Source: DigiPen student art by Mark Barrett.)

Once you have established the broad characteristics of your character, begin to focus down by better defining his or her key essentials. Does the bigger nose really make him or her better? Would the character work better thinner, fatter, or more buff? Ask yourself these questions about all aspects of your character. Feet too big? Too small? Are the arms more effective longer or shorter? And so on.

The same girl character, now more comprehensively defined in two dimensions with consistent proportion lines defining scale, placement, and proportion. (Source: DigiPen student art by Mark Barrett.)

Here is where style comes in too. If you have a favorite cartoon or illustration style that you like (e.g., *Triplets of Belleville*, *Ratatouille*, *Lion King*, *South Park*, etc.), begin to redraw your character roughs in that style. As previously suggested, don't copy the original characters; just use them for their style approach. Try to analyze the way they are drawn and their inherent simplicity or otherwise, and try to emulate that with what you are trying to create with your own ideas.

The Queen of Hearts is also designed in a Samurai Jack style. (Source: DigiPen student art by Drew Gamble.)

Warm-Up Exercise

One great character design exercise at DigiPen is to have students create a new character from one popular production and style it with the look of another production or artist. Therefore, as a similar warm-up exercise for you, create a new *Incredibles* character, but drawn in the style of the *Yellow Submarine*, or a new *Spirited Away* character drawn in the style of *Spongebob Squarepants*. The options for experiment are endless and fun to do. You can actually choose your own categories to work with if you like. Just try a few and it will definitely enlarge your visual design vocabulary in terms of character form, personality, style, and technique.

Another mixed-genre design, this time Draco Malfoy in the style of Gorillaz. (Source: DigiPen student art by Crystal Quimby.)

With your character's personality, style, and shape accomplished, create a model sheet of your character.

This essentially means that on one sheet of paper you draw your character from a number of angles and possibly in a number of poses, all with the character having a similar height and identical proportions throughout. You might also want to throw in an indication of head height too. Indeed, you can include anything that indicates what your character looks like from all angles (and even how your character compares in scale and height to other characters you might have him or her animated with in certain productions).

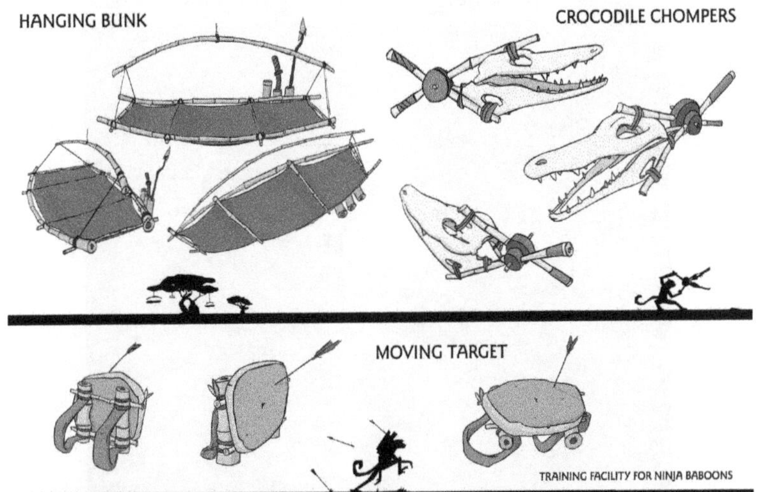

Often character sheets are created for animation props too. Here, a design sheet depicts instruments from a crocodile chomper to a training facility for ninja baboons! (Source: DigiPen student art by Eric Wiley.)

Another wacky head height measurement, this time Harry Potter as a *Simpsons*-style character, measured at "5 blinkys tall." (Source: DigiPen student art by John Thacker.)

Remember, it is comparatively easy to create one knockout drawing of your new character, but quite another thing defining what that character looks like from every conceivable angle. Therefore, draw the character from the front, side, rear, and perhaps a three-quarter front and rear view. A comprehensively planned and drawn model sheet will solve all these problems for you long before you begin the real challenge of animating the character. Also, if you are designing a character who will be modeled in three dimensions later, you will most likely need to design your character in the classical arms up, "crucifix" mode.

A typical 3D "crucifix" character pose. (Source: DigiPen student art by Chelsea Thurman.)

The really accomplished among you might even move on to creating a *machete* of your character. This is a small but detailed sculpture of your character, created in fired clay or Sculpy™. A well-constructed machete will allow you to view and define what your character looks like from every particular angle, a great asset when you finally animate him or her for real.

Is this a clay-based machete or a 3D-generated model? Sometimes it's hard to define the difference. (Source: DigiPen student art by Zach Mckee.)

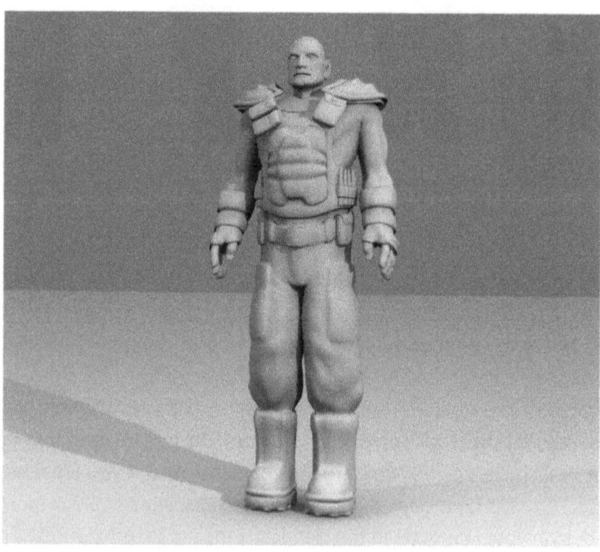

Lastly, in order to solve all the issues related to your final character design, you will now need to color your model sheet so that you know exactly how many, and what, colors your design needs to contain. Again, you will need to make sure that the colors selected work well with the color schemes and painting techniques depicted in your background or environment art style, as envisioned in your concept art.

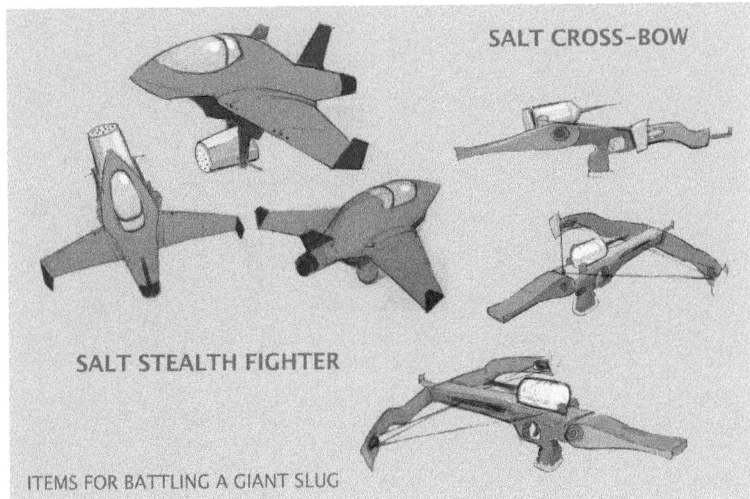

A model concept sheet of object designs to battle giant slugs, featuring a salt crossbow and a salt stealth fighter. (Source: DigiPen student art by Drew Gamble.)

Assignment

Before you move on further in your production, make sure you have a detail model sheet of your main character, seen from all angles and including a head height diagram.

Thumbnails

With the script written and the major concept and character design work done, it is now time to seriously think about your filmic approach, without tying you down too much to a rigid structure that may limit your creative imagination at this state. This is where thumbnails come in.

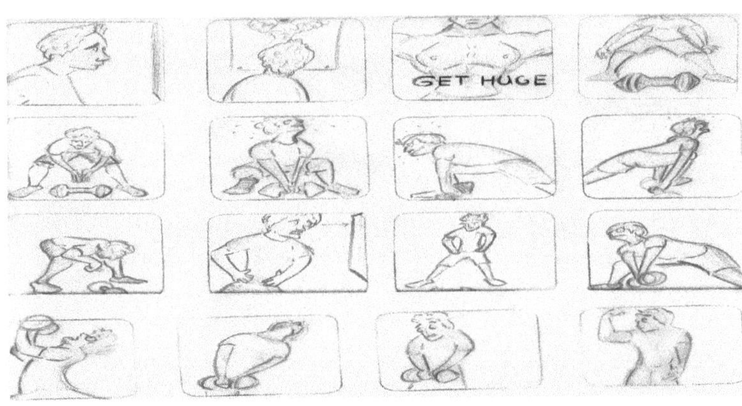

A full thumbnail storyboard sequence outlines the entire storyline. (Source: DigiPen student art by Aaron Lamb.)

Thumbnails to a filmmaker are what five-finger exercises are to a pianist or a-b-c is to a writer. Thumbnails are small, expressive sketches that enable filmmakers to quickly get down what occurs to them through their inner, imaginative vision. They need not be sequential images at this stage, although they can be. They are more initial, doodled impressions of how the film unfolds, or how a particular scene plays out. As I say, this doesn't have to be literal to the story sequence, or even filmicly solid progressions at this stage. They are just "first thoughts" that you have as an animator or director.

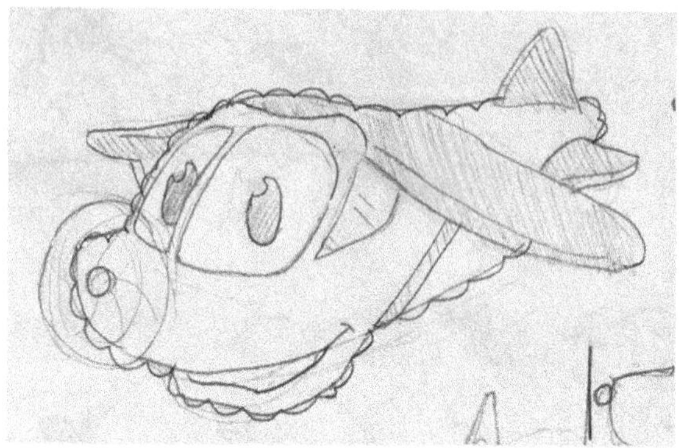

The first thumbnail sketch can strongly dictate how a film and its central character will look. (Source: DigiPen student art by Nick Vigna.)

Thumbnails can be created anywhere at any time—in bed, in the bath, on the bus when you are traveling somewhere. If you take a small notebook and pen with you wherever you go or wherever you are, there is no excuse for not capturing the magical ideas that come to you in the most unexpected ways or at the most unanticipated times!

These thumbnails started life on a page of a regular sketchbook. (Source: DigiPen student art by Jeff Weber.)

In terms of actual process, it is just a method of reading the script, mulling over the design concepts in your mind, and seeing what they suggest to you in any particular part of the story. You can work sequentially or just pick out moments in your storyline that pop into your head at any time. You don't even have to do them all at one particular sitting. Indeed, it is best done over a period of time if you can be patient enough to wait that long. Just cover all the ground and options. Don't even stick to your first thoughts, as new and alternative ideas will come that might be better than what you initially thought was good.

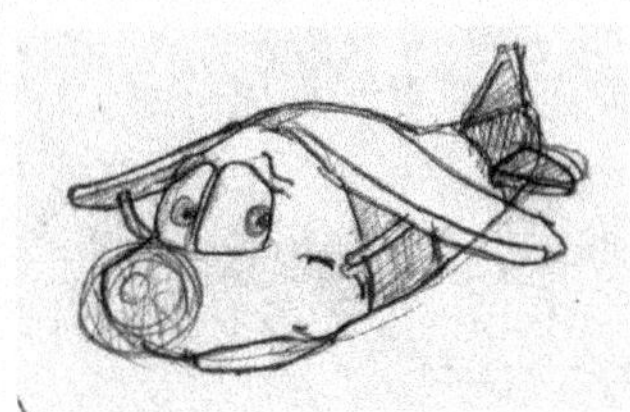

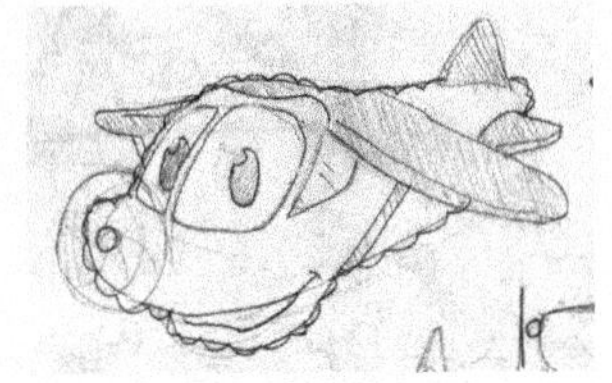

Character morphs and transition ideas should be worked out at the thumbnail stage. (Source: DigiPen student art by Nick Vigna.)

Ultimately, you will ideally have a number of thumbnails for each scene and story moment in your film. Sift through and decide which among them are the best approaches for each filmic moment. Don't worry about animation at this stage, or even color. (Although, if you have a fabulous idea for a color or lighting effect, scribble it down as notes, or if you have colored pens and pencils with you, sketch what you are thinking of!) Just select the ideas that most grab you, and when you have them, paste the thumbnails in order of the script or storyline you are developing. Eventually you will end up with a final thumbnail storyboard, and you will be ready to move on to the next production stage, solidifying and defining in greater detail what the thumbnails suggest.

A full storyboard, drawn in thumbnail style. (Source: DigiPen student art by Nadine McKee.)

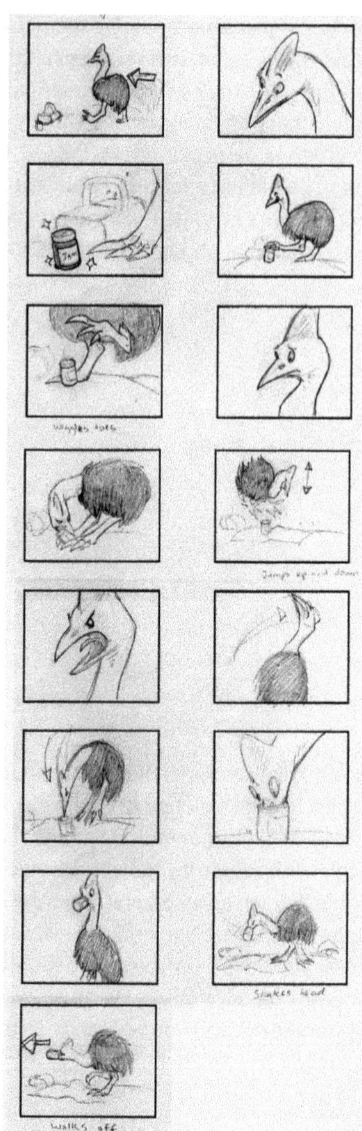

Assignment

Create a thumbnail storyboard of your script. Again, don't just make the sketches from the first things that come into your head. Work at it. Create alternative ideas along the way, and then select the ones you like best and paste them into a sequence that best defines your entire film idea.

Storyboards

Having committed your sequential thoughts to some kind of thumbnail idea, it is time to consolidate these thoughts into a more tangible, structured approach. A storyboard is such a structured device for representing script and story ideas visually. Storyboards can be either created within a standardized page format (with three or four storyboard frames per page) or they can be constructed with larger drawings (one drawing per page), which gives a much more detailed visual explanation of the story idea.

For personal films you can stick with your original thumbnail board at this stage. However, that is not really the best way of finalizing your creative ideas, and inexperienced filmmakers really do need to take their ideas to the next stage through storyboarding. Usually, the multiframe, one-page approach is enough for anything from a personal film, game concept, TV commercial, to even a 30-minute TV show. However, for bigger projects, such as TV special or theatrical movies, larger-size frames are best. These are usually pinned up in sequence onto a large corkboard (or many large corkboards!) so that the invariably large production team can easily view, rearrange, and redraw them to suit as required. (Many changes are usually required on a large-scale production such as a movie, meaning the more people involved, the more opinions there are that have to be contended with!)

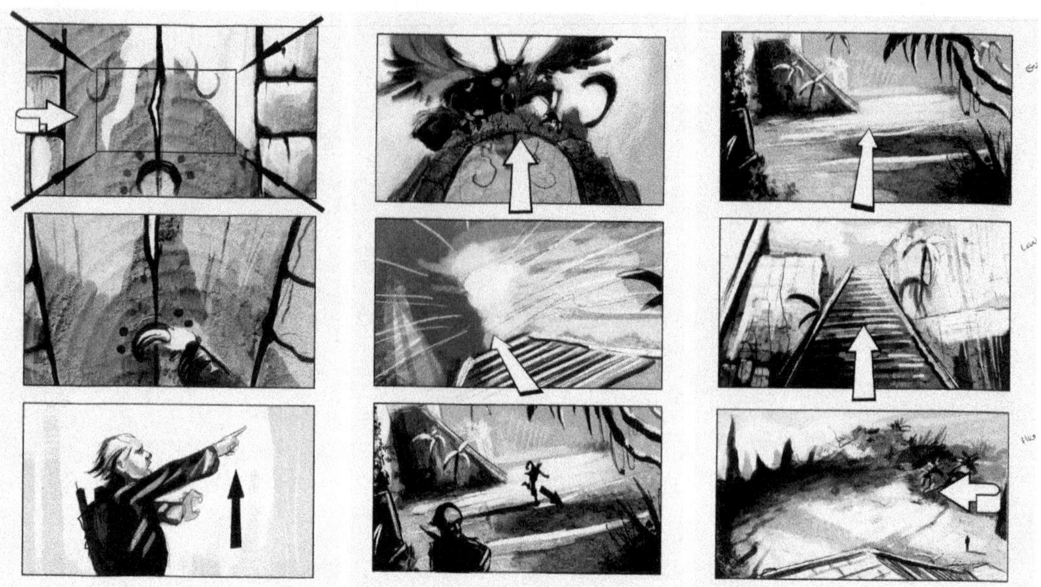

A storyboard for a student project pitch. (Source: DigiPen student art by John Thacker.)

A storyboard for a 2D animation sophomore project. (Source: DigiPen faculty art by Dan Daly.)

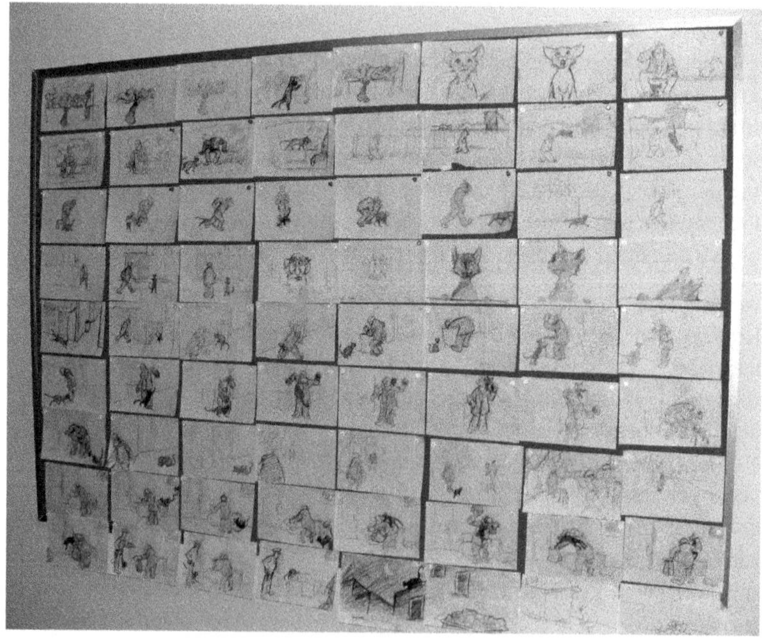

Whatever format your storyboard takes, it needs to contain a specific amount of information. First and foremost it needs to show the drawn frame that represents the scene or that action in a scene that you're seeking to define. It will also need provision for a scene number and/or frame number, any descriptive text that goes with the scene, and also any dialog or narration that accompanies that particular frame (or frames, if more than one frame is required to depict the changing action within a scene).

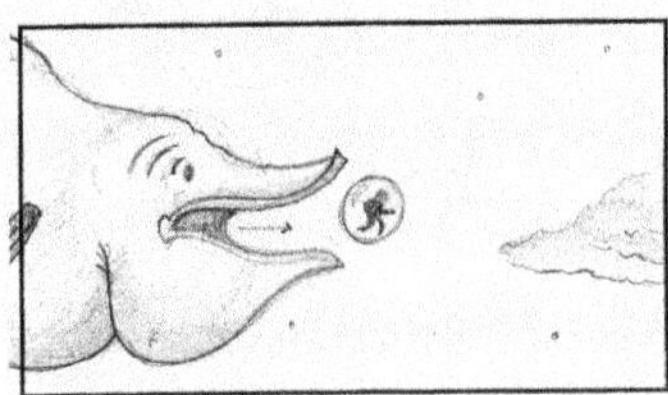
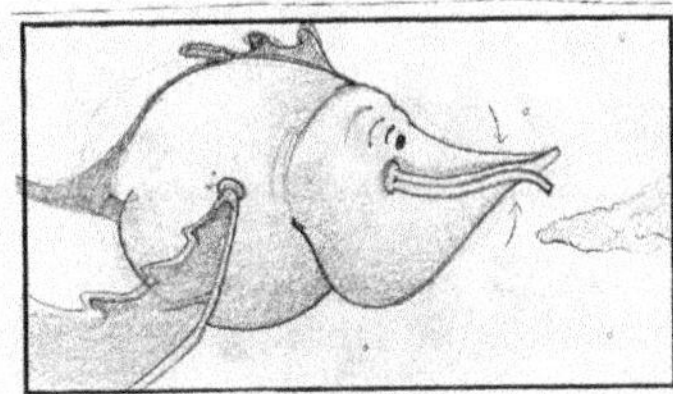

Unfolding-action storyboard frames for student project pitch. (Source: DigiPen student art by Mark Barrett.)

Additional information that is common to an entire whole production (normally found at the top of the storyboard sheet) is the name of the production, the sequence number within the production that any particular sheet refers to, the scene number the sheet refers to, and the page number of that particular sheet.

Episode No:	Page No:

Additional cutaways.....

Shooting Requirements:

B/Screen	Anim.	Symbolics

Episode No:	Page No:

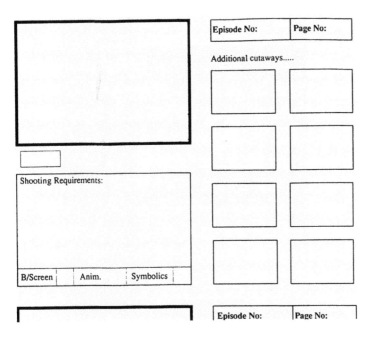

My most comprehensive storyboard sheet template, which allows for complete production information and alternative shot options to the right.

Armed with preprinted sheets per the figure, and with your thumbnail board to guide you, draw your film's scenes in greater detail—that is, from the original thumbnail idea sketch to a close-to-finished storyboard image that the scene will represent.

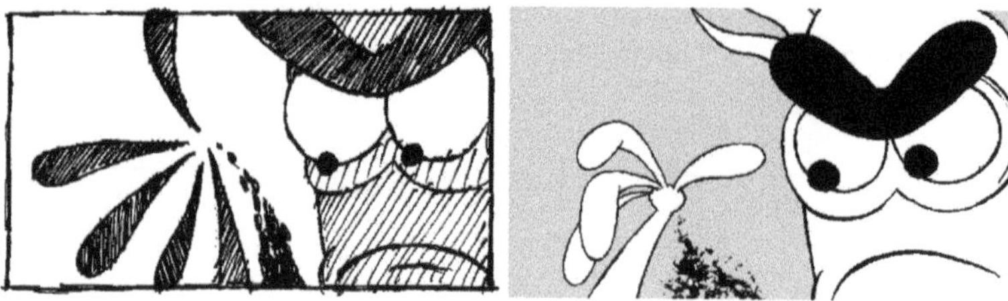

Initial rough storyboard frame and first-draft animatic frame. (Source: *Fire Gods*.)

You will invariably find that some scenes contain action that cannot be defined in one single drawing. In these cases, you should create enough storyboard frames for each scene that do cover all the action anticipated. I tend to draw the first position, middle position, and end position of each scene action when I'm storyboarding a film.

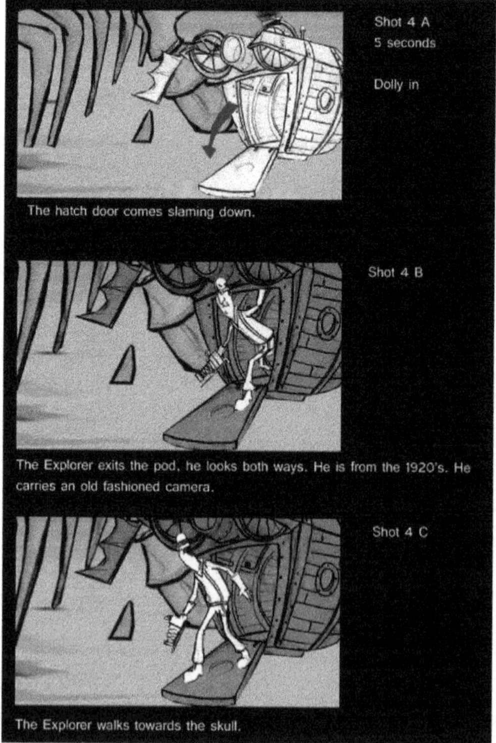

Shot 4 A
5 seconds
Dolly in
The hatch door comes slaming down.
Shot 4 B
The Explorer exits the pod, he looks both ways. He is from the 1920's. He carries an old fashioned camera.
Shot 4 C
The Explorer walks towards the skull.

Sequential storyboard frames showing the beginning, middle, and end action. (Source: DigiPen student art by Eric Wiley.)

Alternatively, a complex action can be worked out with one drawing, and then camera frames added to indicate the separate shots.

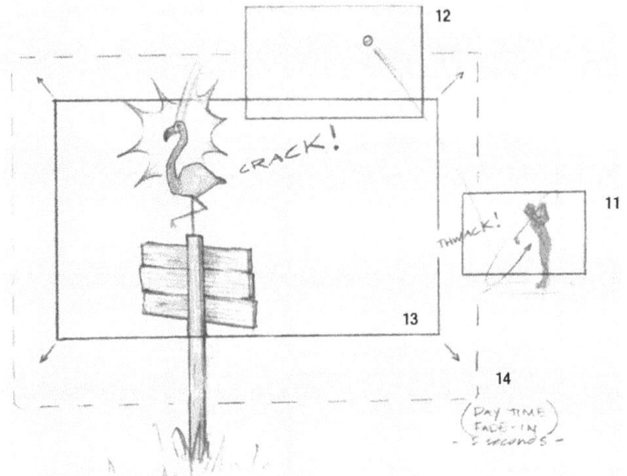

A golf ball sequence defined in one drawing with camera staging frames indicated. (Source: DigiPen student art by Jarod Erwin.)

Before you finalize your own storyboard, however, I strongly advise you to read the next lesson (FP 6, Filmmaking Techniques) before you begin drawing. If you already have an understanding of the rules of filmmaking, then this is not necessary. However, it is surprising how many animation directors or animators, especially current professional directors and animators working on films or TV shows, who seem to not understand the core principles of filmmaking. It took me a considerable amount of time to learn the essentials, and I only did so when I was commissioned to direct a live-action/animation/computer graphics interface (CGI) drama series for television. The director of photography (DP) was a veteran of over 30 years in the movie business. He took me under his wing on the first day of shooting and proceeded to teach me the essential rules as we went along. It mattered nothing to him that I had won countless awards for my animation and ran my own respected animation studio at the time. The fact that I was supervising the entire cast and crew (as well as him!) and clearly didn't know the core principles of staging, continuity, and action was far more important to him. However, his kind and generous advice resulted in us completing the production on budget and a day ahead of schedule, and far more important, with no callbacks or reshoots at all. I will be forever grateful to him for providing me with that priceless knowledge that will serve me well for the rest of my career. That is why I have dedicated a whole lesson to it in the next chapter, effectively short cutting the process for you, and why I strongly advise you to study the material and take it seriously.

Process

When starting a storyboard I tend to read and reread the script many times. I try to picture all the action in my head (which effectively you have done already with your thumbnail board) and then mark up the script, indicating where each scene, or shot, begins and ends.

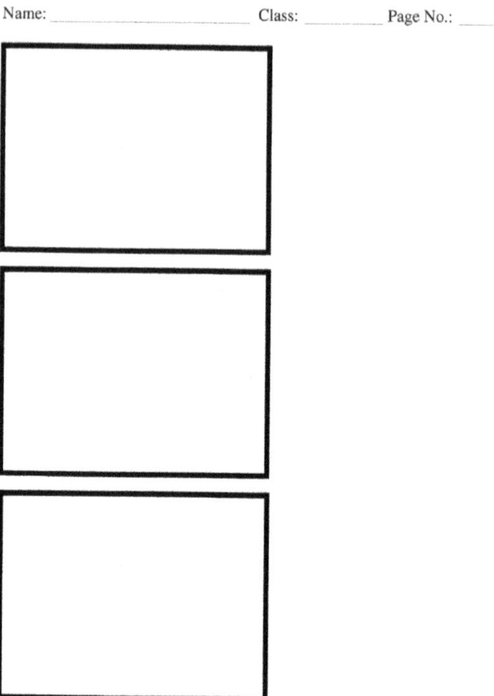

There is nothing more exciting, or frightening, than a blank storyboard frame. Imagine what worlds of magic are waiting to be created here!

With the script marked up in this way, I write in the scene numbers I want to establish and then base my drawing numbers on these scene numbers. For example, if scene 7 has three frames defining its action, I will indicate this on the board (see the following figure).

Rough storyboard frames. (Source: *Fire Gods*.)

Before doing final drawings for each frame, however, I will first research my subject matter as much as I can. This is much more important when you get to the layout and background stages of your production. But even at the storyboarding stage it really pays off when you do your homework. For example, if I were creating a storyboard for a film set in a forest, I would visit a forest location or two, make numerous sketches and shoot a large number of photographs and use them as my visual reference when drawing my storyboards or layouts.

Assorted photographic shots of a real forest location, providing infinite inspiration for the kind of imagery I can draw on my storyboard.

Occasionally reference material inspires framing and layout too, as sometimes you can use your camera to find a more interesting angle that you might normally imagine without location reference.

Finally, *never* rely just on Google images for your references, especially when creating your final layout designs. Photography flattens perspective, color, and lighting. Therefore, it is essential that you go out and draw from life wherever possible. There is no substitute for the infinite inspiration that observation from life offers, as has been demonstrated by great artists throughout the ages. It is not different now that we are in the digital age, despite the temptations and easy access that the Internet alone offers!

Quick shots from my local Starbucks, indicating the different kinds of visual dynamics that can be achieved using varying camera angles even from a single point of view.

Sketchbook images from my visit to the San Diego zoo.

It will not always be possible for you to find a stereotypical Victorian mansion, for example, in your own locality of course. But if you do have one, definitely go out and sketch it, preferably from the angles you wish to establish in your film storyboard. It's amazing how much extra information you get from actually studying the real thing. Disney would send out their designers on road trips, so they could view and draw locations and props that were not found in the Los Angeles vicinity. Photographs are invaluable in the absence of anything else, of course, but the really great storyboard artists/illustrators always have their own library of reference images, invariably derived from drawing or color sketches that they have created from real life.

A color sketch from nature for a student assignment. A wonderful reference that can be retained and reused later if required. (Source: DigiPen student art by Cody Flynn.)

Practically, storyboards are best roughed out with blue pencil and then perhaps completed in ink and color later, if required.

More storyboard frames from a student project pitch. (Source: DigiPen student art by Jarod Irwin.)

Inking in frames is more often done for professional work. For your personal student project it is probably not necessary, as long as you can clearly define what you want, scene by scene, when you start your production in earnest. Inked-in and colored frames, however, have finality and a definition that helps lock you into a final style.

Early color frames for a student film project, including swatches to indicate the kind of color palette being used. (Source: DigiPen student art by David Bolton.)

Coloring storyboard frames is not always entirely necessary either. If I were working on a TV commercial or a film for clients, however, it would be automatic. But for your own student or personal project, I would say that it is not at all necessary, although the color script discussed later (see FP10) will most definitely be, in my opinion!

Before and after storyboard frames for a student project. (Source: DigiPen student art by Jesse Havens.)

Final Check

When your entire board is complete, check through it one more time to see if it all makes sense and the story works in visual continuity. Don't assume it will. Quite often, as you develop themes and ideas, you will lose sight of your original vision, so it is always wise to go back and check. Don't be afraid to add or delete frames if you think you need to. Remember, this is the most important structuring moment for your film and changes here are nowhere near as drastic (or even catastrophic) as later when all the animation is done and something is suddenly found to not work!

It is always best to keep your storyboard "down and dirty" while you're still finalizing the action. Too much fine and time-consuming work may be wasted if you produce beautiful storyboard drawings then have to make one (or more) changes after everything has been tested at the animatic stage. (Source: *Fire Gods*.)

A good litmus test for your work is to shoot a rough animatic (see FP 8) of your storyboard and view your ideas played back on a full-sized screen in real time. I learned to do this when I was working with advertising clients. Initially, I used to pitch my storyboard ideas to them in paper form. I would lay my frames out on a boardroom table and talk them through the action. I would carefully explain how long each shot was on the screen for and what was going on in each scene. This usually met with approval at the time, and so I would happily have my studio team start the animation in earnest. However, after it was all done and the client viewed our final pencil test, they would sometimes complain how short the shots were and that they didn't understand it during my storyboard presentation. Although they would accept their responsibility and pay for subsequent changes (if they insisted that changes were necessary), I hated doing changes and therefore thought the whole thing through. I hadn't recognized the fact that by presenting my drawings on a boardroom table, often for up to 30 minutes or more, the clients had all the time in the world to look at the shots and understand them at leisure. However, when they eventually saw the images flashing by on the screen in their 30-second commercial (and scenes *do* very much flash by in 30-second commercials), there is no mistaking how fast everything has to be!

Consequently, I arrived at a process where I would actually shoot my storyboards as an animatic and show that to the clients at the pitch stage, rather than using the paper-based storyboard drawing approach. Then there was absolutely no confusion about what was seen on the screen and how long it would be on the screen for. After that, there were never any misunderstandings, and I didn't have to do any of my animation work again!

Two pink highlighted moving frames, here showing one with the leg up and the other with the leg down, will give a little more energy to your animatic than a single drawing would. (Source: *Fire Gods.*)

Consequently, if you really want to get a sense of how your storyboard is working out, and personally appreciate what each shot and action means in real time on the screen, then film your storyboard frames and time them out as you imagine they need to be. When playing your rough animatic back to yourself like this, you will begin to appreciate film timing, which is a really valuable thing for any new animator/director to get a handle on as soon as possible. Then, if still in doubt, show your rough storyboard to colleagues who have not seen any of your project until that moment. If they fully understand what is going on, then all is well and good. If not, then you will definitely need to make changes before you go any further!

Finished young Miyazaki animatic drawing. (Source: *Endangered Species.*)

Assignment

Read the next chapter on filmmaking techniques, then draw a final storyboard from your original thumbnails and shoot it as a rough animatic.

Filmmaking Techniques

Filmmakers who wish to get a full explanation of filmmaking techniques should read the material in my book, *Animation from Pencils to Pixels*, pp. 92–135. However, this chapter lesson is a lighter version of the core information you will need to make your course film more effective and have more impact. Film is a subtle language of communication. We see so much of it these days that we take for granted the techniques filmmakers use to express themselves most effectively. The correct or incorrect use of film language can make or break a production. Therefore, an awareness of the core principles of good filmmaking is invaluable for animators embarking on their first film.

Framing

When designing a shot it is important to remember the major framing options available to you—in other words, what the camera sees of the scene and what it does not.

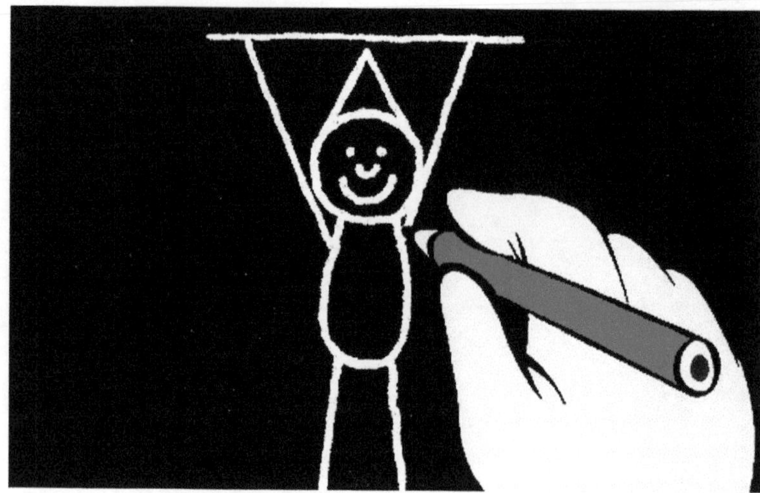

Wide Shot

The wide shot is where the camera not only sees the full-figure character, but it also sees a large amount of the background environment.

Considering the stop sign as a figure, this is a typical location wide shot.

Midshot

Midshot framing usually features the top half of the character, from around the waist upward, and therefore significantly less of the background environment.

Close-Up

The close-up shot focuses mainly on the character's face, usually from the neck to just above the top of his or her head.

There art two other framing options you might consider: the ultrawide and the extreme close-up shots.

Ultrawide Shot

The ultrawide shot minimizes the presence of a character (if the character is there at all) in a wide, expansive background environment. This is typical of the large-scale, epic kind of movie because it is wonderful for depicting wide expanses of landscape or big-city shots.

Extreme Close-Up

The extreme close-up shot frames very tightly on a detail from the shot the director especially wants the audience to focus on, such as the face of a wristwatch, a drip coming from a tap, a fly crawling across food, etc.

Using these five key framing shots you can represent pretty much any element within your film's storyline. However, there are a few camera movements that will help set the scene or pace of the film too.

Locked-Off Shot

The locked-off shot is the basic shot where the camera is in a fixed position for the selected framing setup with no movement in or out.

Track-In/Track-Out Shot

Often described as a zoom-in/zoom-out shot in live-action filming, the track-in/track-out shot is where the camera moves in or out within a particular framed action. For example, a scene could start with a wide shot and end with a midshot.

Pan

A pan is a shot where the camera moves along a background and reveals more of that background as it travels either horizontally or vertically. An example would be where a camera follows a character along a street, maintaining the same framing shot all the way.

Frames left to right represent a pan away from the forest path.

Track/Pan

The track/pan is similar to the pan shot, but the camera moves in and out of its framing position as it moves along. It is sometimes described as a *dolly shot* in live-action filming.

From left to right, the camera starts wide and moves in to a close-up shot of the boats.

Dolly (Crane) Shot

The dolly (crane) shot is where the camera rotates around a 360-degrees arc, wholly or in part, to reveal more of the character that would be apparent otherwise.

Alternatively, the camera can "crane around" the character or object to reveal more of the background environment that would normally be possible with a more static shot.

This is a far simpler shot to achieve in live-action, 3D, or stop-frame animation. In 2D animation the shot has to be drawn, frame by frame, for the entire duration of the crane shot of both the character and the background, which is something I chose to do to open my award-winning film, *Hokusai: An Animated Sketchbook*.

Zip Pan or Zoom

The zip pan or zoom shot is effectively a super-fast-moving shot, where the camera covers the same amount of ground as it does in a conventional panning shot, but does so in very few frames. Quite often it works better if there is a speed blur added to the image throughout the move.

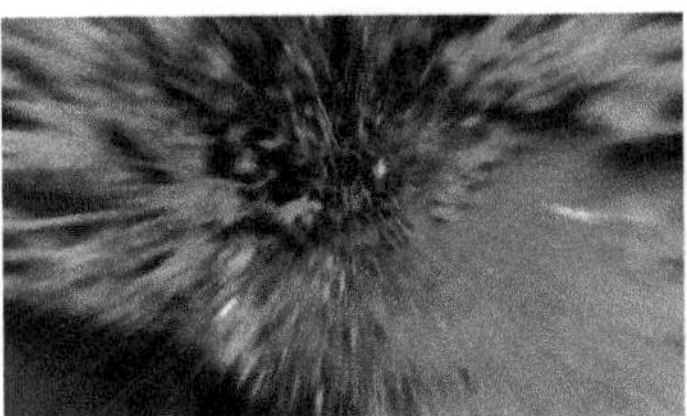

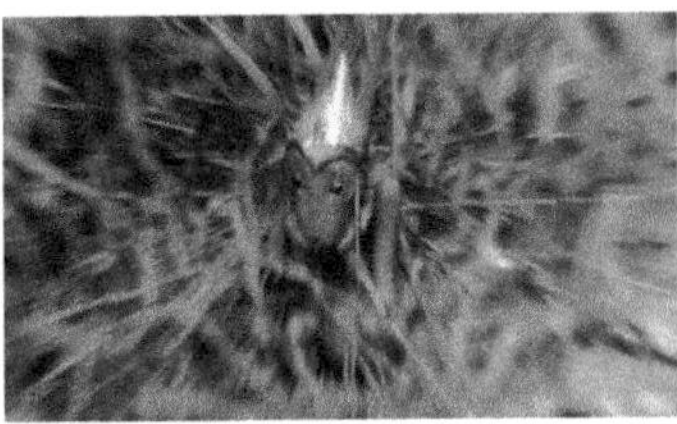

The zip pan or zoom shot moves so fast that an exaggerated motion blur will always help.

Framing Example

All these framing options are very important when planning your film at the storyboard stage. For example, 99 percent of the time you will want to start a particular film or sequence with a wide shot. This will be your establishing shot, where you enable the audience to understand the location, the featured characters, and the relationship between those characters and their environment. Establishing shots are the norm for filmmaking, but they need not be so if suspense or intrigue is being sought at the beginning of a film or sequence.

Once the establishing shot has been made, you might want to draw the audience into your character with a midshot to give them a little bit more information about your character or what your character is doing.

Next, you might want to go to a close-up or even an extreme close-up shot to provide the audience with detailed information about what is going on at any crucial plot moment.

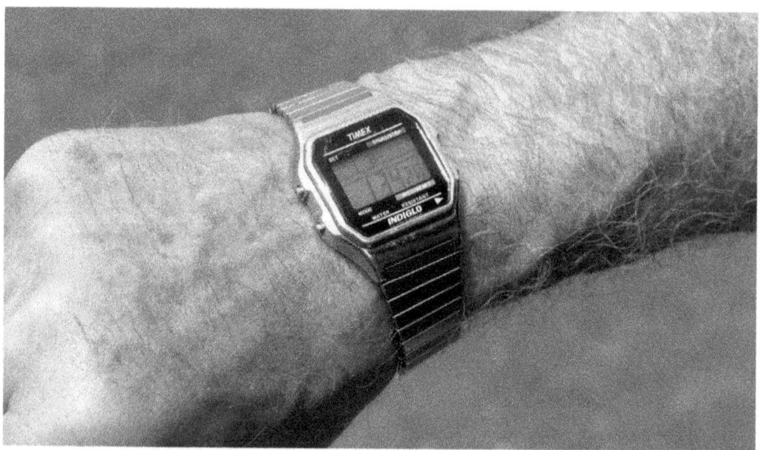

Finally, you might want to return to a wide shot or perhaps two related shots that show a conclusion to the action.

The creation and sequential storytelling of your film storyline has to be thought through as carefully as possible, as each scene or event will need to be framed in a manner suitable to what that storyline demands.

Transitions

In addition to the framing options that better tell your story, you will also have alternative transitions from scene to scene. Transitions have a pace and mood about them, and therefore they can be very subtle, yet valuable, ways of communicating specific things to the audience.

Cut

A cut is where there is an immediate transition from one scene to another in one frame. The cut is what you predominantly see when watching most films. It is the shot used more than any other by filmmakers. Cuts usually give a sense of alertness, suddenness, or pace to the action, being that the audience is confronted with an entirely new setup with each new scene.

Make sure that on all cuts you remember the continuity of action. For example, here the character on the desk is revealed when he walks from behind the desk from left to right. In the next midshot, the character continues to move and look from left to right.

Fade-Up/Fade-Down

A fade-up is where you use a number of frames at the start of a scene to slowly bring in the image, or a number of frames at the end of the scene to take it out. Essentially, a fade is a change of exposure from frame to frame. For example, a ten-frame fade-up (or fade-in) is where your first frame at the beginning of a scene is exposed 0 percent and it increases in exposure frame by frame until it reaches 100 percent on frame 10.

A fade-up from black.

A fade-down (or fade-out), on the other hand, is found at the end of a scene, where the exposure starts at 100 percent and goes down to 0 percent.

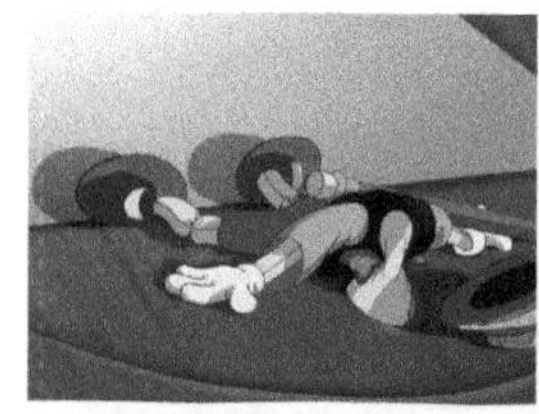

A fade-down to white.

Fades can be to or from black or white in the majority of cases, although any other colored frame will work, dependent on the style and mood of the film you are creating, of course.

Fades are used to give a slower more emotive transition from one scene to another. For example, a fade-up gives the audience a slower or more intriguing introduction to a new scene. A fade-down gives a more reflective moment at the end of the scene so the audience has a moment to digest what they have just seen. A fade-down from one scene and then a fade-up to the next can indicate a passage of time or place.

Dissolve

Dissolves (or mixes) are where two scenes overlap—that is, one is fading down and the other is fading up over the same amount of frames.

The scene on the left is fading out and the scene on the right is fading in.

Like fades, dissolves give a sense of transition in time and space and yet provide the audience with additional information in a more subtle way than a cut. At the same time, this will also keep the pace of your action up more than a fade-down/fade-up might.

Wipe

Not so popular with filmmakers today as it once was, a wipe is still a significant transition effect. A simple horizontal wipe would have an imaginary vertical line traveling from one side of the screen to the other, showing the old scene on one side of it and the newly arriving scene on the other.

The middle frame shows the scene on the right beginning to reveal itself as the diagonal wipe moves from right to left.

Wipes come in all styles: horizontal, vertical, diagonal, spiral, clockwise, and counterclockwise. Stylistically, they can be very valuable in film-noire styles of filmmaking, but otherwise they can be distracting or overly dramatic in regular films.

Staging

The next tool in the filmmaker's bag of tricks is staging. It will probably be quite boring if you just show a single character (or more than one character) in the same shot setup throughout the entire film. For example, if the characters were falling in love, fighting to the death, or secretly passing something from one to the other, you would tend to frame and stage the action differently as a director. Let us take a look at some of the most common staging approaches you might take with two characters talking to one another.

Two-Shot

A good establishing shot with two characters would be a two-shot, where both characters are seen together in a wide shot against their background location. This way the audience will understand that the characters are talking and have some kind of relationship together.

Note

If there are more than two characters, it would be called a three-shot, four-shot, five-shot, etc., depending on how many characters are in the shot at the same time.

One-Shot

Establishing our conversation in a two-shot, you might now want to focus more intently on one of the speaking characters. Therefore, you will need to move your camera and feature only the one you want to see in a one-shot.

Alternatively, you may want the audience to keep some contact with the listening character too, so you will need to choose an over-the-shoulder one-shot, where part of the back view of the listening character can be seen beside the full view of the talking character.

There can be many positions of the camera for all these different shots, of course. This just happens to be from a low camera angle.

Similarly, you might actually want to focus on the listening character to feature his or her reactions to what is being said, so you can again choose to use an over-the-shoulder one-shot to feature that character instead.

Again, this shot could be from a high or low camera angle, closer or further away.

You have so many options in framing these kinds of shots that they don't need to seem predictable or boring.

In addition to this, you might consider the elevation of the camera when framing your shots. For example, the speaking character might need to be seen as dominant, heroic, or a bully. In this case, you can set your camera low and literally look up to him or her, emphasizing that character's dominant role. Alternatively, if the listening character is fearful, distasteful, or supplicatory, you can set the camera up high and literally look down on him or her.

Perhaps a little better framing of this shot would have the character's head just a little to the left of center so that he is looking more into a space before him.

The slightly higher camera position tends to diminish the subject matter.

In each of these framings you are effectively painting a picture with your camera as well as with your staging, so think every shot through and communicate it to your audience in the most significant way possible.

Continuity

Lastly, we must discuss continuity, for without it, many films are ruined by erratic framing or action. Remember that you have to coax your audience along with your storyline and its portrayal, so make it as easy as possible for them to follow what is going on. For example, if a character is walking from left to right in one scene, then appears running from right to left in the next, the audience will be momentarily confused, especially if the entire running sequence is fast cutting. It is, therefore, better that you have your character running in the same direction in both shots. That way the audience will follow the action much better.

See how awkward shot three looks with the same character suddenly moving in the opposite direction to the rest.

If you do need to change the direction of the action for any reason, think up a device for making it easier for the audience to understand. For example, in a running sequence, cause the character to turn a corner at some point and then as he or she disappears from sight, he or she begins to start moving from right to left.

Crossing the Line

Finally, when staging a shot or sequence requiring two characters, never forget that there is an imaginary "line" between them.

The markings on the ground of the parking lot make a very convenient line between the characters!

If you cross that line with your camera from one shot to another you will most definitely confuse your audience. For example, if you show our original two talking characters and then suddenly throw in a shot from the other side of the line, it will not look comfortable from the audience's perspective.

The confusion that occurs when crossing the line is clearly seen in the middle frame!

See in the last figure how the characters in one shot suddenly seem to be oriented in the opposite direction to what the audience is familiar with. Even if the audience is not consciously thinking about this, they will unconsciously be trying to work out what has just happened on the screen: Are these different characters? Are these the same characters in a different scene? Has time passed and this is a new sequence? This effectively runs the significant risk that your audience possibly will not pick up on the most important line of dialog, at the most significant point in your plot, and that could be disastrous!

The Line Is Not Limiting

Remember, once you have established the line between your characters, you still have 180 degrees of options to set your camera, such as high or low, in a one-shot or two-shot, tracking-in or tracking-out, etc.

Some of the many possible camera positions that can be established on just one side of the line.

There is no end to the creative staging you can draw upon before resorting to something dramatic (and confusing), like seeing the shot from a different angle and thereby crossing the line. For example, in the following figure, by establishing a cut-away shot to the clock (frame E), you can safely return to seeing the characters on the other side of the line if you so choose!

The cut-away to frame E allows shot F to cross the line with no confusion to the audience.

There is absolutely no reason why your action ever needs to be boring or predictable, once you recognize good framing, staging, transitions, and camera work. As another example, have one of the character's walk past the other and away, thereby creating a new line position between them.

Ultimately, it is your skill as a director and a filmmaker that will win your audience over to your side, or not!

Assignment

Complete the storyboard as requested in the previous lesson (FP 5), taking extra care that you are observing the film techniques you have just learned in this chapter lesson.

Audio Record

It is now necessary to have a working audio track to work with. The next stage of the program will be to create a fully timed-out animatic as the basic foundation of your film. Consequently, the timing and action judgments necessary will best be made by using the timings of your audio track. It isn't always necessary to have the final track to work with—to be honest, a guide track will often do. However, some kind of track, even if it is a piece of music with no dialog at all, is far more useful for working out scene cuts and animation timings than with using nothing at all.

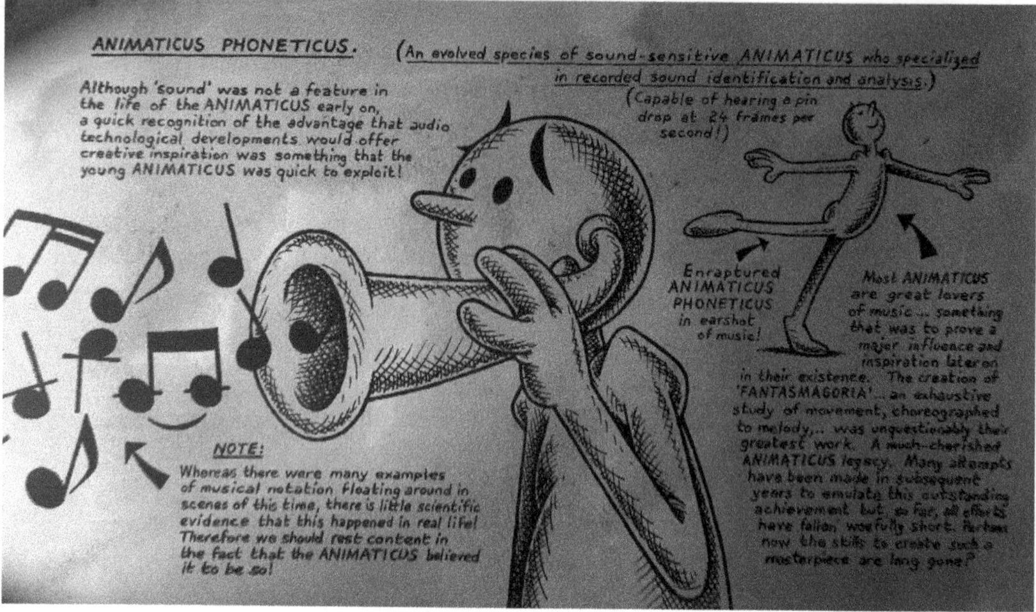

The advent of sound in animation was very crude compared to today's technology!
Source: "Endangered Species".

Guide Track

If precise lip synching is not a priority with your film, then it is perfectly okay to use a guide track at this stage. If precise dialog *is* required, however, you will definitely need to create a final track, with final actors and final sync sound effects included. However, based on the notion that you *can* use a guide track for now, which is perfectly acceptable for narrative and non lip-synching approaches, you should have no problems recording what you need. With your script to read from, it is perfectly acceptable to use the built-in microphone that most computers have these days. Your own voice, recorded in the way you want the final actor's voice to perform the lines, will certainly give you timing cues that you can use to structure the images in your animatic and beyond. It is even better if you have a webcam attached to your machine because it will allow you to both record your track and see yourself performing the lines, which eventually could be a valuable visual reference for when you go to animate a character's performance! Therefore, you should try as hard as possible to put the same kind of timing and delivery that you will require the actor or actors to use when you do the final recording with them.

The better your recording is, the more expression you will be able to get out of your animation! (Source: DigiPen student art by Sirio Brozzi.)

The thing that you particularly must pay attention to is the fact that if you read the lines fast, when you get the actor to re-record them in accordance with the timing of your animatic (which will be edited to the timings of your own guide track, of course), he or she may not have enough time flexibility to speak the lines in his or her own style, especially if he or she tends to speak slower and with more subtlety of expression than you do. So, if anything, err on the side of slowness when recording your guide track. That way it will be much easy for the chosen actor to speak the lines in the time given, and of course, make it far easier for you to make time cuts in your animatic or animation at a later date.

Although Hollywood continually uses "star" actors for the voices of animated characters in movies, I have personally found that many celebrities are pretty flat in their delivery and that many unknown character actors are far better! (Source: DigiPen student art by Andrion Becker.)

Also, make sure that you save your audio track (whether it is a guide track or a final track) in a file format that is compatible with the software you will be using to break down and edit it with the animation! The most popular is the WAV format, but others can work too.

Always try to cast an actor who looks somewhat like the character they are recording the voice for. More often than not, it sounds much more natural! (Source: DigiPen student art by John Thacker.)

Final Track

For your final track it most definitely will be desirable for you to record everything with a professional actor on professional equipment. To do anything less will entirely undermine your film project, unless you are trying to give it a "home movie" look and feel. This is where the real expenses for filmmaking start to bite into your budget. You may have a friend who is a great voice actor, and another friend who has his or her own professional-level recording studio. But if not, you will just have to bite the bullet and pay for the professional-level services you require.

I am assuming that you will be using professional actors and a professional studio to record your final track. If so, you will have the benefit of a professional recording engineer too, who will advise you on the best ways to achieve your recorded results and will supply you with a final edited file in the format of your choice. If you are not able to do this, however, here are a couple of tips that you should bear in mind when recording your track:

1. Make sure the sound quality of your recording is high and, as mentioned earlier, you save your audio file in a format that can be used later. If nothing else, ensure that the microphone you use is of good quality.

2. Make sure your voice artist does not get too close to the microphone during the recording. Otherwise you will get loud and unwanted "pops" on the track as he or she breathes or speaks certain words forcefully.
3. Make sure your actor is fully conversant with the script before you start. Better still, have the actor read through the script with you before you ever get to the studio. This way you can actually use the read-through as an audition, which will help you decide if you even want that actor to record your track in the first place.
4. Don't try to have the actor attempt to read the entire script in one sitting. Work at sections and only move on when he or she gets the first section correct. Show the actor your storyboard and explain what is going to visually happen for the section he or she is going to record. That way the actor can focus his or her performance on just one section at a time and almost certainly give you a better reading as a result.
5. Never accept the first thing your actor records. Sometimes, but very, very occasionally, the first "take" (recording) is the best. But more often you and the actor will have to work on the delivery until you get what you want. As the actor records each take, number the take and mark against the number how much you like that particular delivery, on a scale of 1–10. If you get a 10 for each section, you are in good shape. However, settle for less if after a significant series of attempts your actor is beginning to sound jaded through an overfamiliarity with what he or she is saying.
6. Don't have the voice artist read through the script too many times. After a number of attempts, even the very best actors tend to sound jaded and you want to avoid this at all costs. If possible, take a break if the actor doesn't get it right in the short term. Get him or her to have a tea or coffee outside the recording booth for a short while, and then return later. That way it will preserve any spontaneity or expression that may occur otherwise.
7. If you have more than one actor working on your script, try to get them all to attend the recording session at the same place at the same time. (This is always the preferred way with comedy especially, as they each feed off one another, often resulting in a level of humor that you hadn't even anticipated when you originally wrote the lines!) If, due to their schedules and other commitments, you can't get all your actors together at the same place and time, record the major part with one actor and then play that track back to the second actor, with suitably long silent gaps between the recorded lines where the new words will go. That way the second actor will, to some degree, be able to feed off the previous recording and have enough space to drop in his or her lines within the silent sections. I have even done this by reading the lines of the second actor from the engineer's section of the studio, where the actor can hear my voice in the headphones but, of course, without my voice actually being heard on mic. You can even sit in the recording booth with the actor. However, you

have to be super careful that your feed lines don't "crash" with the actor's lines—that is, your voice doesn't overlap the actor's voice. This would make it impossible to separate the two voices later, when you bring in another actor to read the required second character lines.

8. Once you have your "perfect" reading from the actor, ask him or her to do some wild deliveries. This means invite the actor to push his or her performance beyond the guidelines that you have provided. Allow him or her to also use his or her own words instead of yours if he or she has any ideas. You'll be amazed how the more "improv" style of actors can come up with something you may never have thought of in the first place, which will work much better for your film than what you originally wrote. You don't have to use it, but at least it's in the recording to give you the option to do so if you choose.
9. Sometimes actors will stutter, cough, or even sneeze during a take. Don't stop them. Sometimes the unscripted or unexpected will bring greater presence or believability to the lines, as well as give you a "hook" to animate to, which could bring more personality to the speaking character at the same time. Naturally, if the "fluff" sounds bad though, you should not use it!

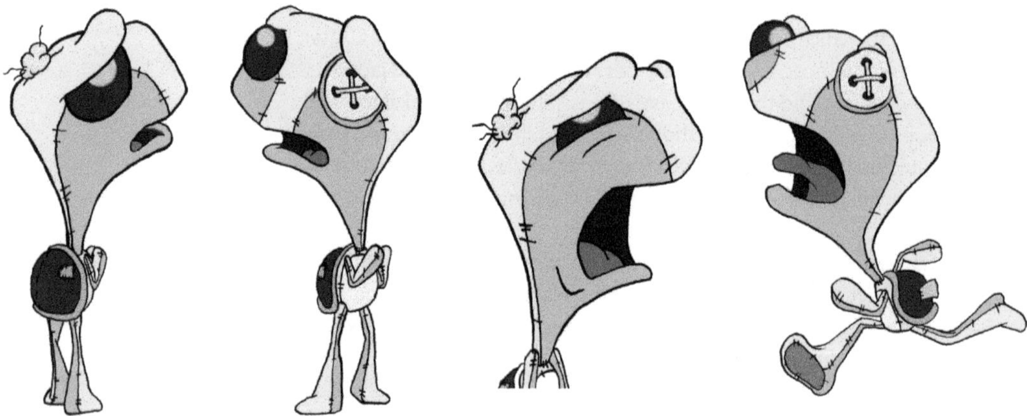

Slow-thinking characters require slow-speaking deliveries by the actor. However, sometimes that adds significant production time to your film, and therefore your budget! (Source: DigiPen student art by Pat Jandro.)

With your final takes complete, you now need to edit them all together to create your final track. A software program like Sound Forge will not only give you the capability to easily do this, but will also give you sound effects options to add to your recording, such as echo, megaphone, stadium speaker, radio speaker, etc.

Technological magic can round everything off perfectly! (Source: DigiPen student art by Drew Gamble.)

Eventually you will have your completed track edited and timed to the length that you want it. This will now become the foundation of the challenge to come—the creation of your animatic.

Assignment

Record and edit your audio track as indicated in this chapter lesson.

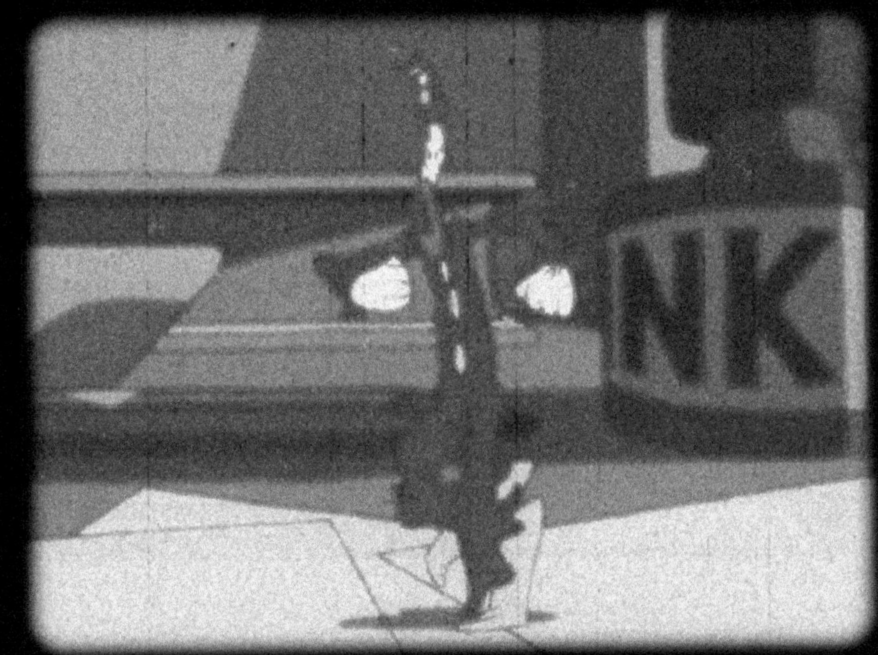

Animatic and Bacher Boards

An *animatic* is quite simply the filming of the finished storyboard in synchronization with the final soundtrack. Technically, it is a very easy process, but creatively it is very challenging, as the animatic is the foundation on which everything else in your film will be built. Consequently, the animatic stage of a production must *never* be underestimated by the conscientious filmmaker.

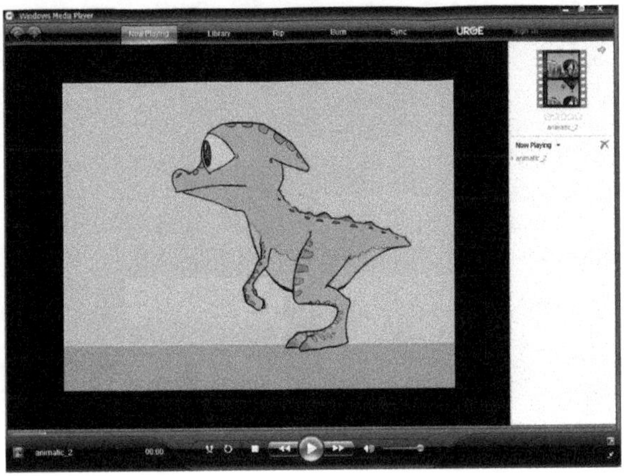

This is the great moment where we begin to see things appear on the screen! (Source: DigiPen student art by Eric Wiley.)

However, before we explore the world of Animatics we should first briefly examine a relatively new aspect to film production... a process I prefer to call "Bacher Boards."

Bacher Boards

Less is more! (Source: DigiPen student art by Nicholas Rubatino.)

I first coined the term "Bacher Boards" while supervising project classes at DigiPen in the fall term of 2008. Hans Bacher had just released his excellent book, *Dream Worlds*. (Focal Press, 2007) which, among other things, instructs designers on the use of minimal value designs in creating solutions to major shots in a film. (See pages 136–137.) The idea is that if the filmmaker reduces the visual content of each major scene to simple light to dark values (specifically three grays in this case, with perhaps black and white thrown in if you really need it) prior to defining key visual requirements such as staging, lighting and composition.

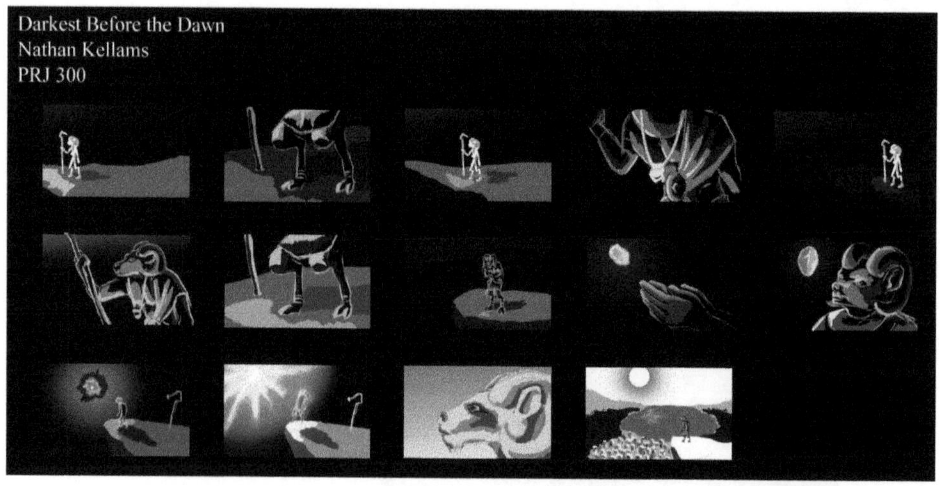

The judicious use of even quite limited values can still create an amazingly dramatic visual sequence. (Source: DigiPen student art by Nathan Kellams.)

Hans Bacher is one of the outstanding art directors and concept artists that have come through the Disney studio in recent years and I strongly recommend his book to everyone who wishes to approach any filmmaking from a mood, impact, emotional, and aesthetic direction. He recounts how just by using a few values like this you can attempt to replicate the general themes of nature and define various options available to you in your visual scene-setting palette.

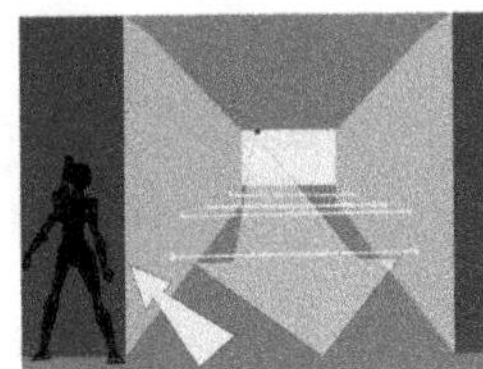

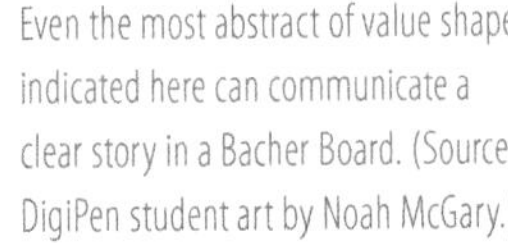

Even the most abstract of value shapes indicated here can communicate a clear story in a Bacher Board. (Source: DigiPen student art by Noah McGary.)

By exercising certain tried and tested rules of visual perception and layout … i.e. light over dark/dark over light, etc. the filmmaker can really mold and define the actual impact of each shot on their audience. Consequently, part of my own (and therefore my students') production process is now to adopt "Bacher Boards" in the pre-production stage of creation. Indeed, the process of "Bacher Boards" will serve any filmmaker or artist well if the technique is applied to any aspect of presentation, layout, and design for any media project.

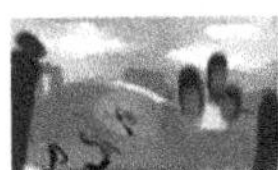

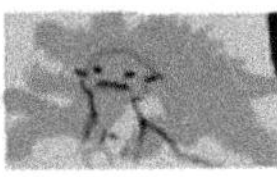

Even a charming little piece about a colorful chameleon-like creature can be well represented through just a few gray value shapes. (Source: DigiPen student art by Sarah Markley.)

Bacher Boards can be created at any time in the pre-production stages of a film of course but usually they will be best applied somewhere between the Animatic stage and the Color Script/Background painting stage. Indeed, even color storyboards can begin as simple, low value, Bacher Boards initially, to establish underlying visual needs for each shot, before color is applied to create mood, emotion, and dramatic intention.

But now to the process of creating animatics …

Animatic Process

Take each storyboard drawing and scan it individually. Most scanners have the ability to frame a specific area on a sheet of paper, so make sure that when you scan, you only scan the frame you want.

Animatic images can be monochrome or color scans, or even drawn straight into the computer if you have the facilities to do this. (Source: DigiPen student art by Greg Attick.)

Number your frames in accordance with the scene number and their respective drawing number within the entire scene. For example, let us say that scene 3 has five drawings, culminating in a black screen. You will need to number the drawings 3_1, 3_2, 3_3, 3_4, and 3_5.

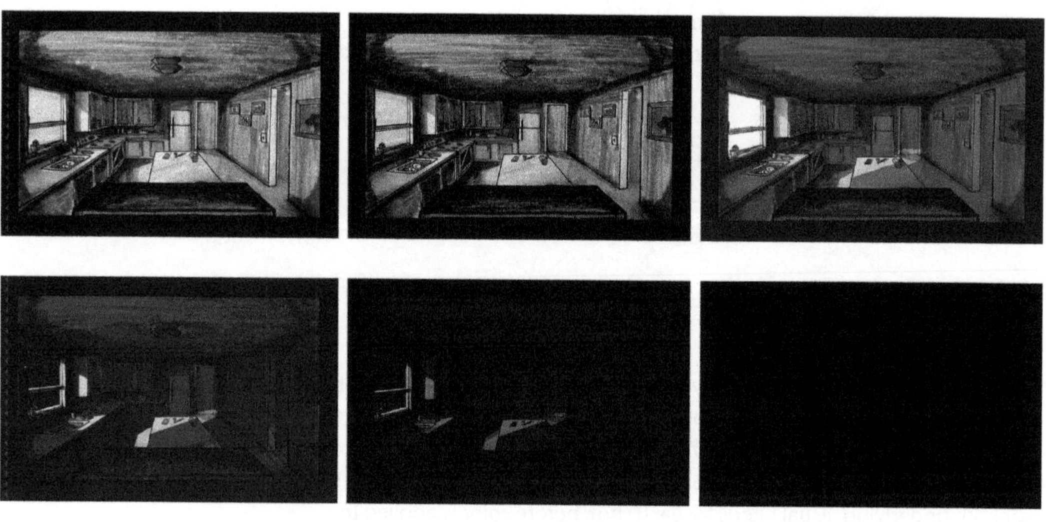

Five animatic frames indicate a slow change in time of day in a kitchen, finally arriving at a black screen. (Source: DigiPen student art by Greg Attick.)

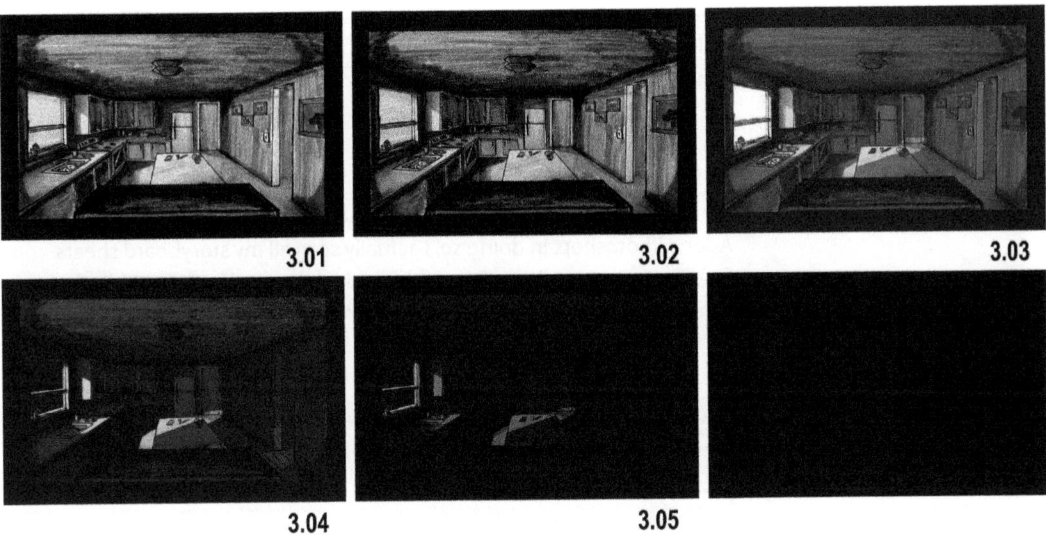

Initially, each drawing should be numbered outside of the image, until it is certain that each image will appear in the final animatic. (Source: DigiPen student art by Greg Attick.)

Make sure that you do this for your entire film storyboard without leaving out any scenes or drawing numbers in the process. I find that it helps to have the scene/frame number visible in the corner of the screen, so that when you watch the final movie of your animation, you can see what scene and frame you're at during any point in its viewing.

When you are sure that each image is going to feature in the final animatic it is important to number each frame in accordance with what scene it is in and what order it appears in the screen. (Source: DigiPen student art by Greg Attick.)

Actually, you can write these numbers in when you create the storyboard drawings in the first place, or else you can add them later using the film-editing software that you will compile the animatic with.

Note

When scanning storyboard frames, I tend to scan my drawings with Adobe Photoshop. In doing so, I actually scan all my storyboard sheets first. Then I crop and number the individual drawing frames within the program until I have them all as numbered separate frame files.

I use Adobe Premiere Pro for creating my animatics. (Source: *Fire Gods*.)

With all your storyboard drawings separate and numbered according to scene and frame order within the scene, import them into a film-editing program such as Adobe Premiere Pro or Apple's Final Cut. Also import your final track.

Then, with the track positioned from frame 1, proceed to add your storyboard images to it, adjusting them to the timed length you wish them to be seen as you go. Eventually, it will be possible for you to view your entire storyboard drawing collection in synchronization with your final audio track. You have created your first animatic!

It is only when you play back your animatic and see your ideas and drawings running in real time on the screen that you know if they have a chance of working. (Source: *Fire Gods*.)

In reality, you will probably have to fiddle a lot with the lengths of each frame image until you get the timing and sync just how you want it. This is normal. Don't forget, too, that by advancing the picture a few frames ahead of the audio sync point (as you did for your dialog animation), you will tend to make that cut/sync point stronger than if it were edited with level sync.

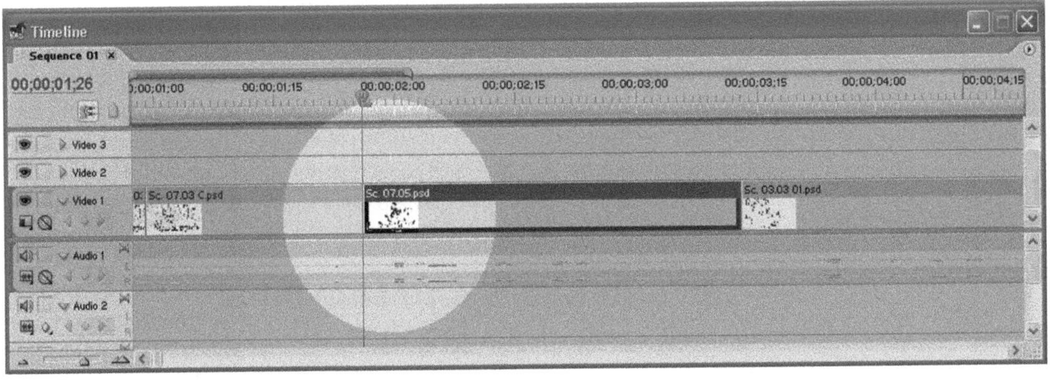

The highlighted area indicates the beginning of the scene drawings on the timeline and the shaded pulses of the audio track positioned a little behind the start of it. (Source: *Fire Gods*.)

Also, you will almost certainly find that although you thought your storyboard was perfect when you first drew it, when it is in sync with the track and played back on the monitor in the animatic, you could well find that you have missed something. This will, therefore, be an opportunity for a new shot to be added or a frame to be taken out if you have done too much to describe the action in a scene. Therefore, don't be afraid to cut out drawings to make the sequence work better on the screen. Likewise, don't be afraid to add new, quickly sketched frames if you think the action needs them.

I often scribble out a new frame to include in the first-pass animatic if I feel the animatic needs it to keep the story flow going. (Source: *Fire Gods*.)

Anyone who owns the fantastic *Spirited Away* movie on DVD will note that as an extra feature there is effectively the entire film animatic that was created before the animation was begun. As you watch it, you will notice that the director, the wonderful Hayou Miyazaki, has dropped in quickly scribbled sketches in addition to his original storyboard drawings to emphasize or add action where he had missed it before. This is all part of the process of creating a good animatic for your film, and consequently you should never go with your first thoughts from the storyboard point of view when creating it.

The Animatic Is Your Film Bible

Ultimately, you will arrive at your final animatic, upon which all the action sequences and scene cuts will be based. This will be your "bible" that everything else will be based on. Therefore, if you have edited your animatic well, there should be no reason to change or edit your film later, once the animation is done. All the creative decisions are made and established, leaving you with just the creative challenge of making the movement wonderful within each shot.

Check Your Scene Timings

Sometimes you'll find that you don't have enough time for a particular sequence of animation to occur within the time you allocated for it within the animatic. This is a common error with student or novice animators. (It is also true of professional animators on occasion!) In time, experience will give you a sense of how much a particular action takes to be animated well within a scene. However, for the time being, always err on the side of adding time if you are in doubt. It will always be easier to cut down the length of a scene later than it will be to add footage if your animatic judgment has underestimated the time required. That said, try to be as accurate in everything as you can at the animatic stage, favoring longer rather than shorter if in doubt. Ultimately though, it is far better never to have to make any changes in a film when it's in full production!

Note

If you have underestimated the length of a scene and have to add frames or actions to it, don't be afraid to extend the audio track during silent sections. This will make them longer than they were originally and will enable you to accommodate the extra animated action you need to add.

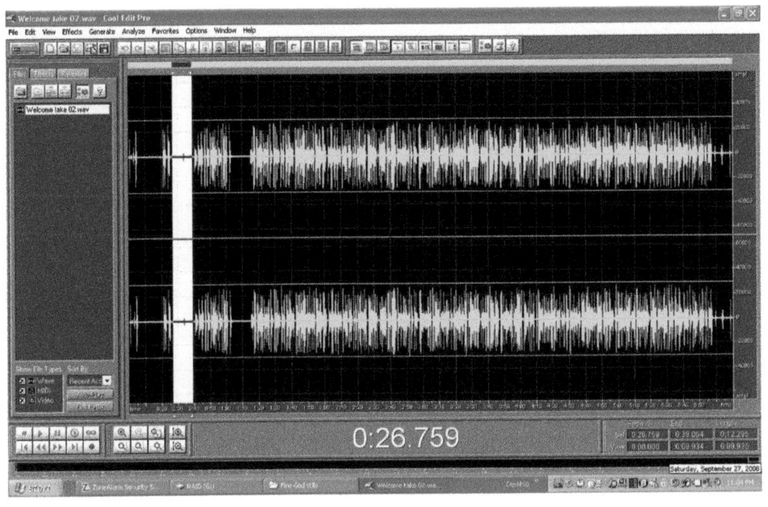

The white vertical band on the audio timeline in Cool Edit Pro highlights the area of silence that can be edited out if the track needs to be shortened. (Source: *Fire Gods*.)

Remember, the animatic is the most important establishing moment for timing and action within your film, so it is really important that you get everything locked down and fully established at this stage. It cannot be stressed enough that to make changes later will be far more costly and time consuming to you as a filmmaker, not to mention demoralizing! So, it pays to focus long and hard on your animatic at this stage to make sure that you are covering all the bases before the really intensive work begins!

Assignment

Finalize your animatic with your final track and original storyboard, adding or deleting material as you feel fit. When the animatic is complete, render out the entire animatic as a movie, so you can easily and repeatedly play it back for your final checks.

Note

This animatic movie will ultimately be the template for all your future edits when completing pose tests, pencil tests, and final footage later.

Background and Environment Layouts

You are now almost ready to begin animation at last … but not quite!

The scene is ready to go in terms of the colored background but the animation has yet to move beyond the animation layout stage. (Source: *Fire Gods*, by Saille Schumacher.)

The next things that need to be attended to before your produce your animation are the film backgrounds and layouts. In 2D animation it is impossible to start to animate without first knowing where the elements that move and those don't move are going to appear on the screen within each scene. Consequently, the layouts need to be created to delineate this. A background or environment layout defines all that does not move in a scene, whereas an animation layout defines all that does move.

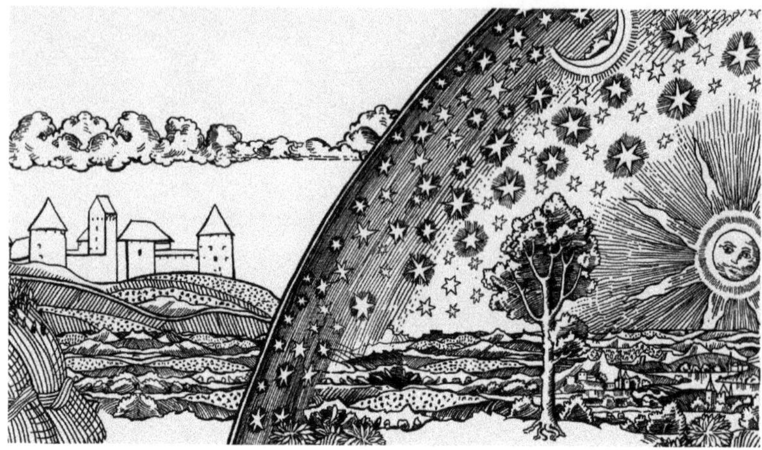

The original background layout of the scene from the prevous figure. (Source: *Fire Gods*, by Saille Schumacher.)

The animation layout drawing for the same scene. (Source: *Fire Gods*, by Saille Schumacher.)

However, before describing the actual process of creating layouts, we should first look at some of the rules of layout design that will affect their creation. The following are just a few pointers that apply to pretty much all visual art imagery. But they are particularly pertinent to creating background and layout design in animation.

Distance and Perspective

Most scenes look best when they depict the qualities of distance and perspective. In other words, many of the most powerful and attractive pictures contain a clear foreground, midground, and distant view.

This demonstrates an excellent use of perspective, as well as the composition use of foreground, midground, and distance. (Source: DigiPen student art by Brian Lawver.)

The layout artist should remember that these levels of distance and perspective will bring a great vision and depth to a shot, whether an internal environment or external landscape.

An excellent use of perspective and planes of foreground, midground, and distance to bring a dynamic look to the composition. (Source: DigiPen student art by Mark Barrett.)

Focus of Attention

Most scenes require that the animation be the focus of attention. There are exceptions to this, of course, but this is normally the way of animation. Consequently, when designing your background layout, make sure that as many lines and objects that define the background converge on the point where you want the main action to be seen. This is most easily achieved with perspective lines, but not always.

See how your eye is drawn into the central point of interest through the use of both perspective and light. (Source: DigiPen student art by John Thacker.)

Here, the absence of perspective still does not detract from the focus of attention in the center of the shot, due to the stark use of light and graphic shapes. (Source: DigiPen student art by Maryeli Rodriges.)

Silhouetted Action

The most effective animation is clearly framed and silhouetted. Therefore, when you work on your layouts, make sure the area that the animation is to appear in is uncluttered and enables the action to be clearly silhouetted.

This exceptional and impressive layout never detracts from the intended point of focus. (Source: DigiPen student art by Cody Flynn.)

Not doing so will clearly diminish the impact of your character's effectiveness within the scene, invariably obscuring his or her action. The next figure shows another good use of skillful silhouetting, followed by more illustrations of excellent composition in painting.

A dramatic shot, contrasting both sharp profile and perspective. (Source: DigiPen student art by Jarod Erwin.)

Note the dramatic use of light and shadow in each case. (Source: DigiPen student art by John Thacker.)

Process

With some golden rules defined, we can now turn to the actual process of creating layouts. Remember, we are eventually going to separate these layouts into two types: those that define things that don't move in the scene (background layouts) and those that define things that will move (animation layouts). However, to begin with, you should first establish what field size your film is going to be animated within—that is, 10 field, 12 field, or 16 field. On a fresh sheet of animation paper, draw the boundaries of your chosen field size using thick black ink, and utilize this as a field guide template that will go under all your subsequent layout drawings.

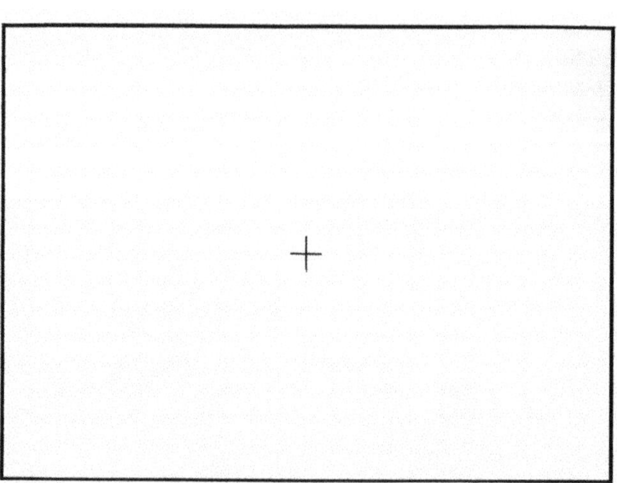

A 10 field–size layout guide with the screen center position marked.

Now, with a fresh sheet of paper laid over the top of the field guide, rough out your first thoughts for the shot, based on the storyboard frame you've already created. If you have a clear and detailed storyboard drawing already that pretty much represents what you want for the scene, plus a photocopying machine that enlarges images, you might even copy/enlarge your storyboard frame to the final layout size you've chosen and tape it onto the animation paper to become your rough layout.

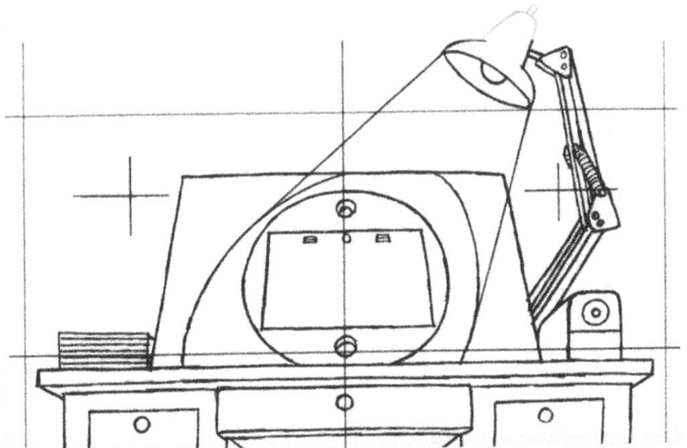

A copy of the original layout design allows you to enlarge and reduce this image frame by frame to create a camera move-in or move-out. (Source: *Endangered Species*.)

Remember, whatever way you do it, this is still only a "rough" layout design at this stage. So, like most other things we have discussed, don't be tempted to jump in and accept the first thing you do. Work at it. Maybe ask yourself:

- Is this rough layout giving me the depth, dimension, drama, and dynamics I am looking for in the scene?
- Does this layout showcase the necessary animation in the best way possible?
- Did I get the perspective and scale right?
- Will the continuity in this scene match that of the preceding and subsequent scenes?
- Is this quality of drawing the best I can do?
- Is the character in correct proportion and position to everything else?

When you have asked yourself these questions (and answered them honestly!), you will most likely want to work more on what you have, perhaps even many more times, until you are really satisfied. Eventually you will come up with your final rough layout and that will be the time to move on to the next stage.

Even this rough background layout is good enough to begin the animation. (Source: *Endangered Species*.)

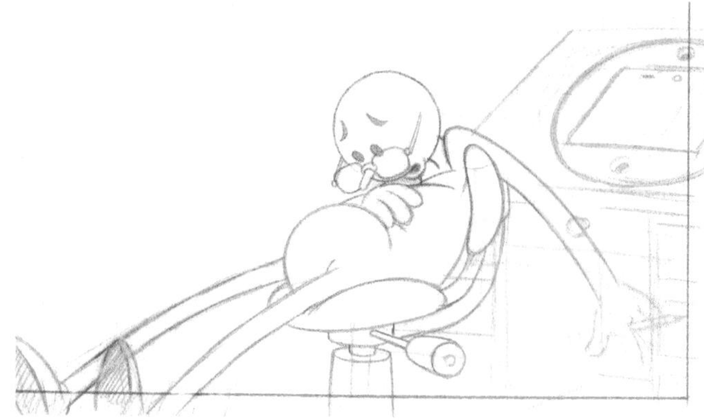

Dividing the Layout

With the final rough layout to guide you, begin separating the two elements that you will ultimately need: the background and animation layouts.

The animation and background layouts seen separately. (Source: *Endangered Species*.)

For the background layout, place a new sheet of paper over your rough layout and begin to carefully and more accurately draw everything in the scene that does not move. Usually, if you work hard enough at getting the rough layout design right in the first instance, this is just a clean-up job, where you literally trace the existing rough design and tidy up the drawing to make it cleaner and smarter. For purposes that will become apparent later, make sure your layout drawing line is dark and strong.

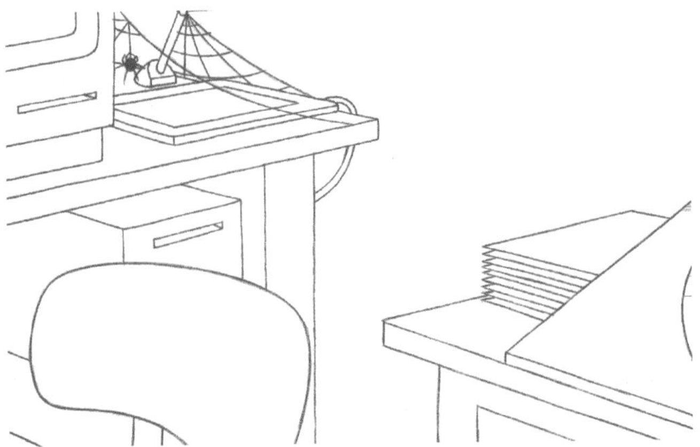

The final background layout with all lines well defined and clear to read. (Source: *Endangered Species*.)

However, for some scenes in your film you may have to do a little more than that if you want to achieve further depth and dimension in the shot. For example, you may decide that a foreground element of the background design will need to go in front of the animation, not behind it. In this case, you will have to draw all those foreground elements onto a separate sheet of paper, so that your entire background material itself has a foreground and a background … with the animation sandwiched between the two.

Returning to the original background design, it was necessary to put the edge of the sky on an overlay so that the animation did not have to be meticulously matched to all the background details when the character passed behind this area of the shot. Consequently, the entire scene is made up of three levels: the background, character, and sky edge overlay. (Source: *Fire Gods*, by Saille Schumacher.)

Note

I have enlarged these layouts slightly so they will be more visible when they are printed in this book. However it is not at all desirable to have a character precisely walking along the bottom of the frame, as indicated here. It is far more aesthetically pleasing and correct to have the character either walk well within the parameters of the screen (as the original does) or have the feet contact to the ground well outside the bottom of the frame.

Whatever the approach to the background layout, you will want to identify the layout drawings in the terms of the scene you are creating. For example, if you have a background layout and a foreground layout for scene 7, you should number the background layout BG 7 and the foreground layout O/L BG 7 (O/L meaning overlay). Remember, all identifying numbering should appear to the right of the pegs, in this case the top pegs. Also, it doesn't hurt to also identify the scene number between the right pegs of the background layouts.

A close-up of the previous figure, this time with the numbering correctly indicated. (Source: *Fire Gods*, by Saille Schumacher.)

With the background layouts now complete, you next need to focus on the animation layout or layouts. I say "or layouts," as it is quite certain that you'll need to draw more than one animation layout design for your character. It is very rare that a character will stand in the shot and do nothing. Usually within any particular scene storyline there is a beginning, middle, and end to the action. Therefore, these definable actions should be represented by separate, individual layout drawings for each.

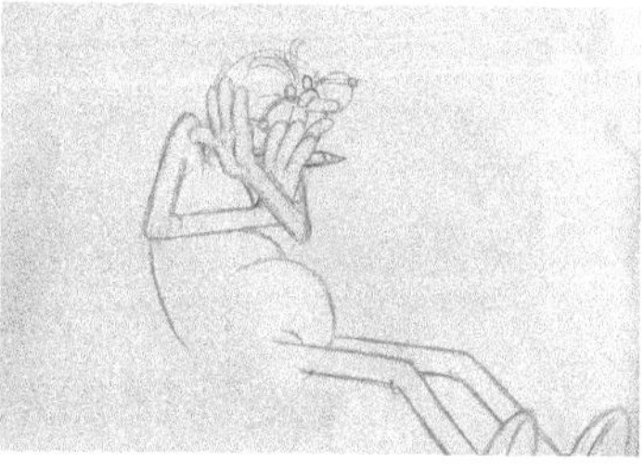

The beginning, middle, and end animation layout drawings of a proposed scene. (Source: *Endangered Species*.)

These animation layout drawings will appear on separate layers and will therefore need to be numbered differently. In this case, I would number the three drawings S-1, S-2, and S-3 (S meaning secondary).

Pose Test Animatic

Finally, once all the layouts in all the scenes are completed in this way, you should go back and reshoot your animatic in a pose test version. This effectively means that you need to replace all the storyboard drawings from your original animatic with the new setups comprising of your timed-out layout drawings.

Now that the layout drawings are on two layers, you can shoot them as such, keeping the background layout on the screen for the entire scene sequence but changing the animation layouts on top of the background when the action requires it. This will give a much clearer indication as to the timing and continuity of your film, as it will pretty much show you what your final film will look like (albeit without color and movement put into it). This can be a very revealing moment for a filmmaker, as more than ever the entire creative intention will be determined before the really intensive work on animation takes place. Essentially, it is a "point of no return" in terms of how the action is to be framed, timed, and designed. So, if you are unhappy with anything at this stage, you have to make the necessary changes while it is not too painful to do so!

A layout sketch for one of the darker moments in the film. (Source: *Endangered Species*.)

Assignment

Draw all the background and animation layouts for your film and shoot them as a pose test animatic.

Color Script

Color script for a junior student's short film project. (Source: DigiPen student art by Sergey Nayal.)

With the color concepts done, character designs complete, animatic established, and layouts finalized, it is time for you to create a color script for your film. Essentially, a *color script* is a small-size, colored-themed strip of each scene (or each lighting/color change in a scene) that your film requires. It doesn't have to be highly finished color artwork, but it does ultimately have to accurately define the colors and/or color or lighting changes that your film will exhibit on a scene-by-scene basis. When complete, your color script will look somewhat like a colored picture strip that represents in linear format all the color, light, and mood changes contained within your film.

The full-length color strip is split into two parts here, so it can be viewed more clearly on the page. (Source: DigiPen student art by Elijah Tate.)

The Right Time to Do the Color Script

It is possible to create a color script at any stage in preproduction. It is even known to occur after the pencil test animation has been completed as well! The equivalent production stage for a pencil test in a 3D production would be the blocked-in key pose stage, or even the completed animation in some cases. However, for a 2D production, this is pretty much the best stage for you to consider doing it because you have everything you need at your fingertips to make the necessary key decisions.

Color concept art of a potential animation scene. (Source: DigiPen student art by Jarod Erwin.)

Process

In terms of actual process, the best approach to take for your color script would be to extract a still frame from each scene of your animatic that depicts the character and the background contained within it, then work over the top of this image in a program like Adobe Photoshop to get the color and/or lighting values you envisage. The same can be done for character coloring, of course.

The classic way of creating any visual art is to work in gray values first, then add the color values once the basic lighting is established. (Source: DigiPen student art by John Thacker.)

A cleaned-up line drawing is colored to great, albeit simplistic, effect. (Source: DigiPen student art by Emiley Flowers.)

Professional Approach

Some production artists create a monochrome-values version of the shot first. This shows all the strongest light and dark values envisaged for the shot, in addition to all the subtle gray/tone changes between them. Then, from this grayscale version, they will work in the color values too, creating the final look and mood they ultimately envisage for any particular shot.

A dark and brooding feel, skillfully created with just a few grayscale values. (Source: DigiPen student art by Ryan Miller.)

Again, minimal color values create a pleasing and effective look. (Source: DigiPen student art by David Bolton.)

Finally, working through each of these images on a scene-by-scene basis, the entire color script for the film is created by joining the individual frames together sequentially to create a long image strip, or even in a colored storyboard format.

A color script doesn't necessarily have to be in a single strip format, although it helps when working in sequences on a major feature-length movie. Here, a storyboard format gives the same information that the strip format would. (Source: DigiPen student art by Keenan Purk.)

Size of Artwork

Remember, the individual frames of a color script do not need to be large or detailed. As long as the broad color shapes of the character and background are indicated (with additional color-value areas to represent the lighting highlights and shadows), you will be fine. Ultimately, it is just a simple process of defining your light sources, shadow areas, and color continuity from scene to scene or moment to moment within a scene. Therefore, each frame size should be between a large postage stamp thumbnail image as a minimum and a postcard size as a maximum.

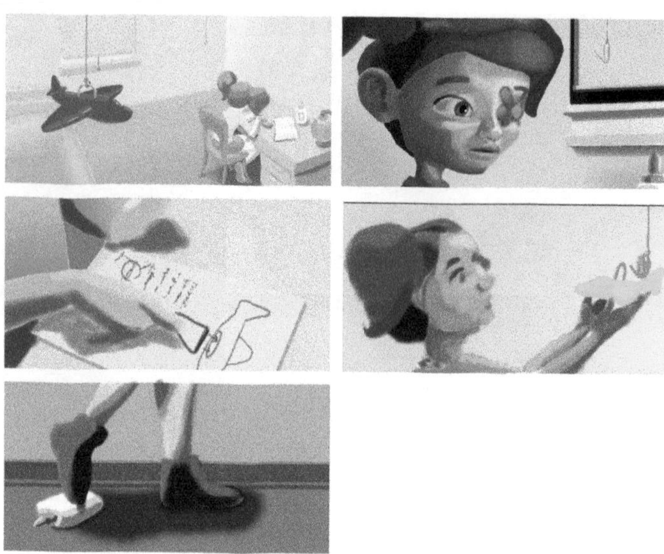

A simple but equally effective color script approach for a short film. (Source: DigiPen student art by Chelsea Thurman.)

The actual image can be created using traditional paints and brushes on paper, or more likely these days by using digital paint programs like Painter or Photoshop.

Don't Ignore the Color Script!

Although you are probably itching to start on the animation already, this is yet one more of those important preproduction stages to ensure that you've covered all the bases before you lose yourself in the animated moment. It ensures above anything else that you have thought through your color and lighting design, which may require you to make adjustments with the animated movement of the character(s) when you finally start anyway, so this is a very valuable stage of production in reality.

A dark and brooding color script for a short film set in the Wild West. (Source: DigiPen student art by Andrew Palfenier.)

Four Valuable Tips

Let me share four valuable tricks with color scripting that will help you enormously:

1. If dealing with distant, perspective shots, delineate your planes with varying color values as much as possible. For example, foreground material could be of the darkest color values; midground would have middle values; and the distant ground would have the lightest color values. This, or the reverse approach, will give a distinct feeling of depth to the shot.

A beautifully evocative piece of work depicting a dark and steamy swamp. (Source: DigiPen student art by Brian Lawver.)

2. The eye is usually drawn to the point of greatest light contrast within a shot. In other words, if you want your animation to stand out, consider giving the area that the character will appear in the most light/dark color values you can.

Note the difference between the first evenly lit environment and the enhanced one that has a starkly lit area featuring the location of where the animated character will be seen. (Source: DigiPen student art by Forrest Sonderlind.)

3. To make your character stand out more, make sure the area of color value behind him or her contrasts strongly with the character's own color values. The rule of thumb is light on dark or dark on light. In other words, if your character is lightly colored overall, place him or her against a darker backdrop. If, however, your character is darkly colored overall, place him or her against a lighter background color.

In homage to a great Disney classic, this scene utilizes backlighting to frame the character that can be seen emerging from it in the shot. (Source: *Endangered Species*.)

4. In all sky-lit scenes, the verticals will tend to appear darker in value, whereas the horizontals will appear to be significantly lighter.

A simple 3D environment that is given structure and form by the lighter ground and the darker verticals. (Source: DigiPen student art by Elijah Tate.)

Assignment

Produce a simple color script of your proposed film using a different color frame for each scene or changes of mood or time within a scene.

Film Production 11

Audio Breakdown

There is one last thing before you can finally animate your film! If you are using dialog, or if your action tightly synchronizes with your audio track, you will need to do an audio breakdown first. Track breakdowns actually can be fun! Although I personally can't wait to get to the animation part of one of my productions, probably just like you, I enjoy analyzing the audio track and working out what sound drops link to what frame I'll be animating on to. The fun can actually start at the recording stage, however!

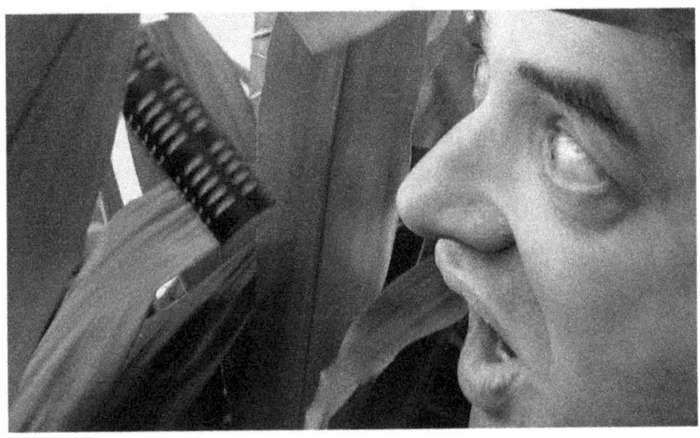

You never know where you'll need to place a microphone to catch the moment!

For my breakdowns I have always stuck with one program that I really like best, although there are many others to choose from. My choice is Third Wish Software's Magpie Pro (*www.thirdwishsoftware.com/magpiepro.html*). Although Third Wish Software has evolved and updated this software over the years, I still prefer to use the earlier, simpler, and 2D-targeted version for my work.

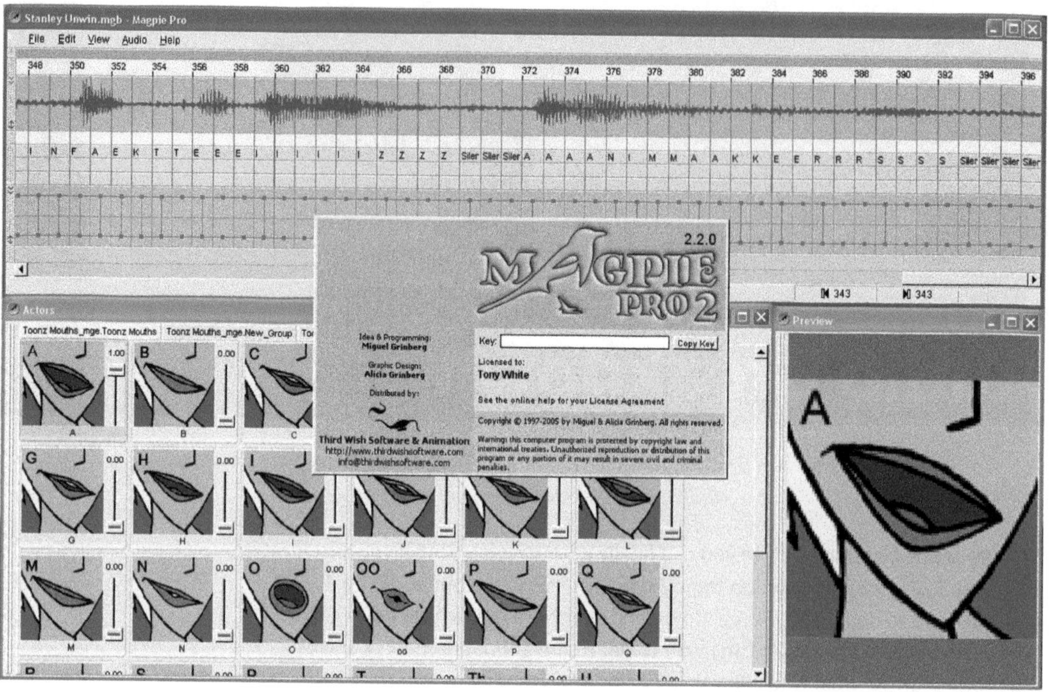

Magpie Pro, version 2.2.0—my old favorite that has never let me down.

To use Magpie Pro is simplicity itself. You just upload your audio track into the program, it arranges the track vertically down an on-screen exposure sheet, then you select shapes from the "mouth set" icons provided to match the sounds you hear during continuous or frame-by-frame audio playback. When selected, these mouth shapes and phonetic sound descriptions appear on the exposure sheet beside the sound on the frame in question.

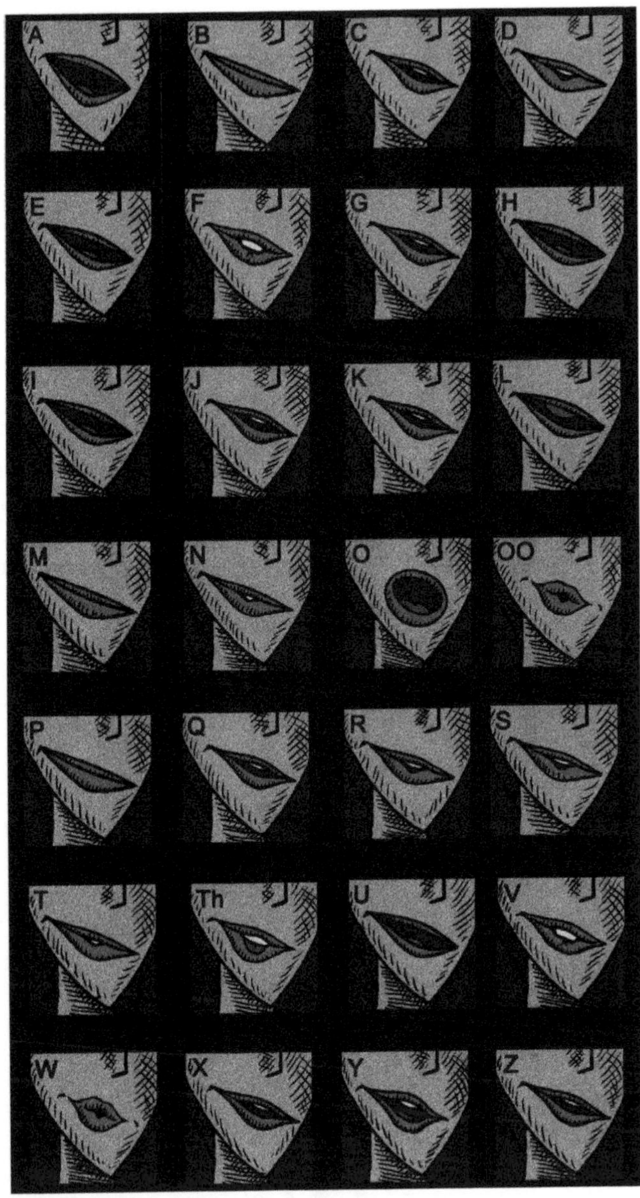

You can create your own mouth sets as you need them in two or three dimensions, and then import them into the program if you like.

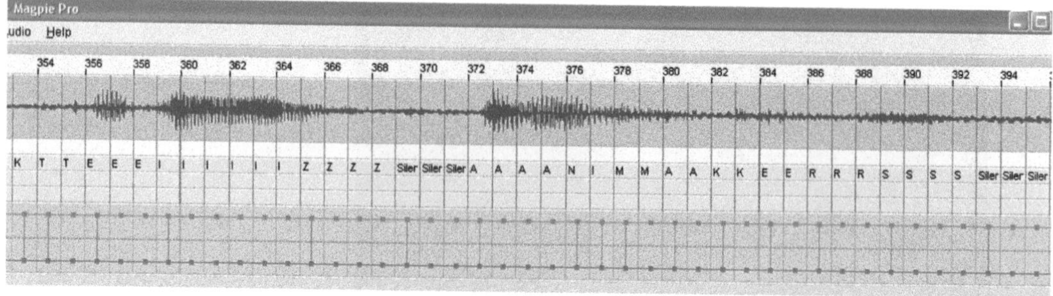

The waveform on the software interface shows you clearly where the emphasis points of the audio are and on what frame they fall.

If you want to test your selections as you go along, you simply hit a play button to see your selections moving in real time. This actually allows you to check your lip sync long before you animate, freeing you up to just focus on the body language of your character when you do actually start to draw. All you then ultimately need to do is make sure that you use the same mouth shape on the animated character that you selected on your Magpie Pro–tested selection and your sync should be perfect every time.

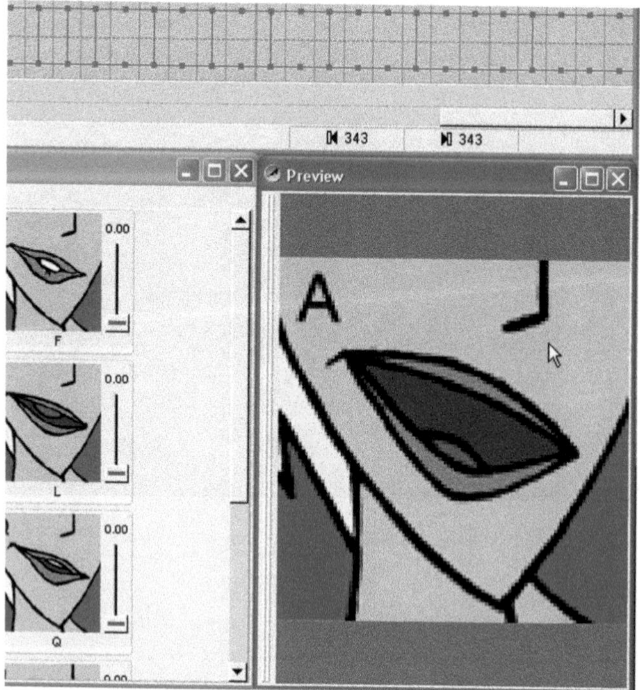

The animated mouth demo in one part of Magpie Pro's interface shows you clearly if your breakdown is working or not before you commit it to your exposure sheet or your animation drawings.

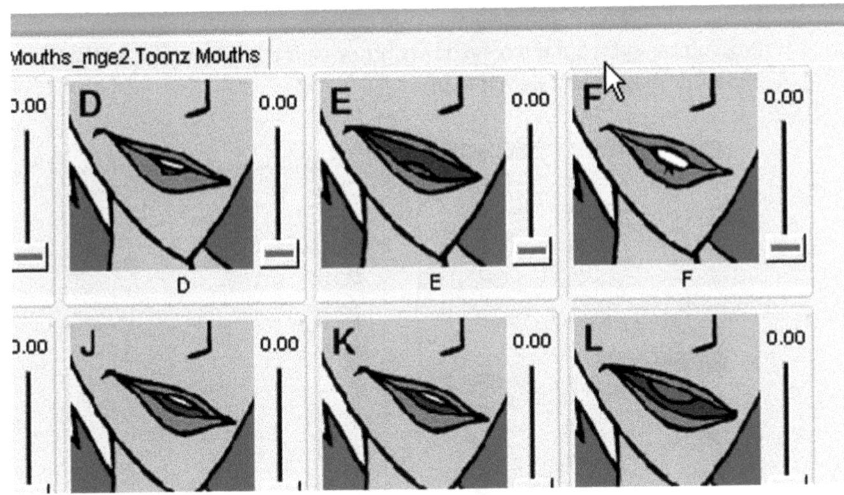

It is so valuable to be able to prechoose mouth shapes before you animate, especially if you create your own mouth set that reflects the design of your character or characters.

Magpie Pro even allows you to draw and import your own mouth set into the program, which is a huge bonus to those of us who prefer to tailor everything about a character's design, especially the mouth shapes, to reflect his or her inherent personality, stature, and anatomy.

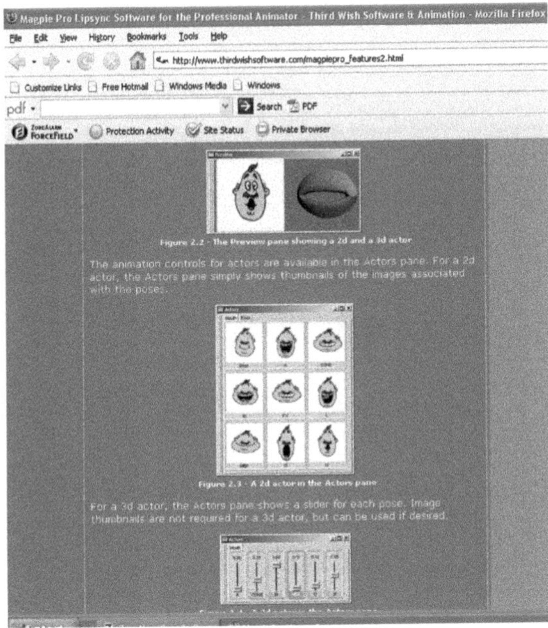

The program does come with its own built-in mouth sets, as displayed on FirstWish Software's own web site (*www.thirdwishsoftware.com*).

Finally, when your mouth selections are made and fully tested in Magpie Pro, you can print out the breakdown into what is effectively your working exposure sheet, if you want it to be.

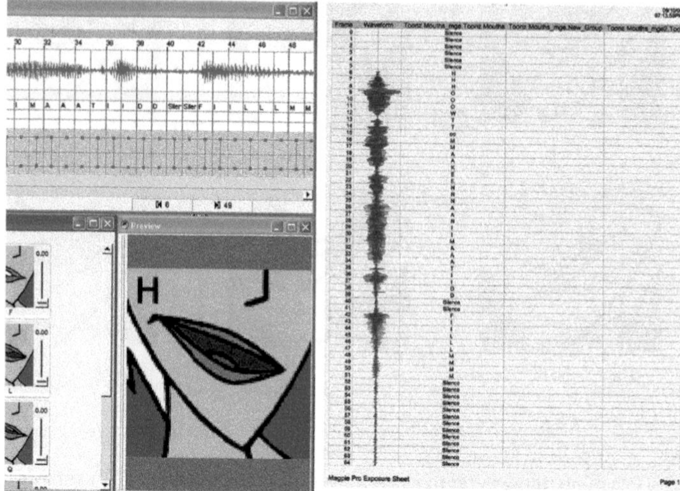

The Magpie Pro interface and the printed exposure sheet you can use for your animation decisions.

If, on the other hand, you want to use your own exposure sheets for your film, then you have to carefully and meticulously transfer the phonetic breakdown from your Magpie Pro frames to your own exposure sheet frames on the audio column.

As an alternative to Magpie Pro's own exposure sheet, you can transfer the entire Magpie Pro–style breakdown details onto a more conventional animator's dope sheet if you wish to.

ACTION	DIAL	EXTRA	4	3	2	1	EXTRA
001							
002							
003							
004							
005							
006	H						
007							
008							
009	O						
010							
011							
012	W						
013	T						
014							
015	OO						
016	M						
017							
018	A						
019							
020	K						
021	E						
022							

If you are a three-dimensional animator, you will also be pleased to know that you can create modeled mouth sets into Magpie Pro in order to test them, and then directly output that mouth animation onto the characters as you animate them in your 3D program of choice.

Hey … at last … you are now ready to start animating. Yee-hah!

Assignment

Break down your entire film's audio track and transfer the phonetic information to your own exposure sheets. You should create a separate sheet (or set of sheets) for each scene the film contains.

Block in Key Poses

At last, after all this time in preproduction you are finally able to begin the animation! What a relief!

Although I work exclusively in a hand-drawn animation environment, most of my teaching these days involves the production of 3D animation. Consequently, I will use many 3D student references (lest it be stated that I am biased). (Source: DigiPen student art by Raymond Ocampo.)

However, I do caution you not to jump right in and start to animate. Even within the animation period there is a preproduction element too. I personally like to block in all my keys first. I will even sketch final thumbnail poses to get into my head the kind of positionings that I want through the scene or scenes. Even if you are a 3D, clay, or cut-out animator, the process of drawing your ideas on an exposure sheet or a sketchpad is extremely important.

Intensive sketchbook studies, prior to attempting a 3D animation assignment. (Source: DigiPen student art by Matt Olch.)

Whatever style of animation is your passion, draw your thoughts for poses throughout the scene you are about to tackle. Do more than one thumbnail sketch per scene if you like. Don Crum, the ex-Disney traditional-style animator who now works at Pixar in three dimensions, demonstrated to my students on a visit his animation process for a scene in *Ratatouille*. He showed his thumbnail sketches and his large-size dynamic pose drawings. He explained that coming from a 2D tradition he learned that to sketch everything first, before even addressing his computer, was the best possible way. As you can see from the accompanying illustrations, this is the core process we impose on students at this stage of their development at DigiPen. Crum even showed takes of footage he took of himself acting out the action, despite his announced embarrassment at doing so. The most interesting thing that he said was that although he had a good idea of what he wanted to do with the scene in the first place, it was only by acting out his ideas on video and then improvising and taking the action further than he had thought to, that he arrived at the great sequence of animation he ultimately created. If he hadn't filmed himself and then pushed himself to do something more, then his scene would be half as good as it is.

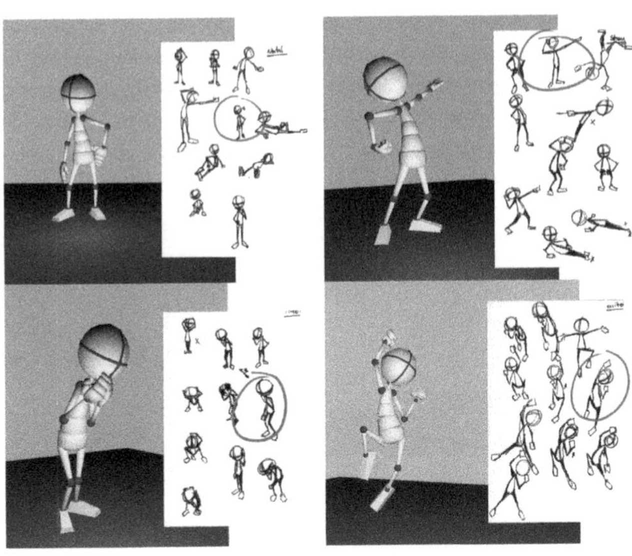

Part of the DigiPen process is to have students create a collection of sketches for each pose, before finally blocking in their most successful one (ringing in red) in three dimensions. (Source: DigiPen student art by James Barwick.)

Consequently, the best approach is not only to block out your key positions but also to act out the action yourself as far as your ability will allow. If you can't do it yourself, direct someone else to do it, and either sketch the key positions or, more practically, capture them on your movie camera. Preferably, sketch the actor in each pose, and then caricature his or her actions to bring a greater dynamic to them. That way you will have the very best reference material to go by and will probably surpass your original ideas for the sequence! If you were able to webcam yourself recording a guide track for the animatic, this is where that footage might come in handy for action reference.

Pages from a sketchbook, depicting drawings taken from life, referencing a baby's action when walking. (Source: DigiPen student art.)

Once you have all of your key thumbnails blocked out either on your exposure sheet or sketchbook, draw the poses to full size on your animation paper or block them in on your computer. Work at these until you really make them strong and dynamic and completely representative of what you are trying to achieve. Remember, these are your "key" poses, so if they're not right, your animation will not be right either. It is *always* in the key poses that great animation is born!

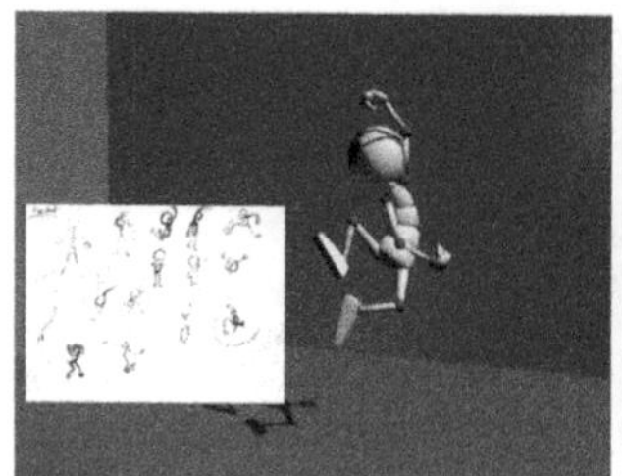

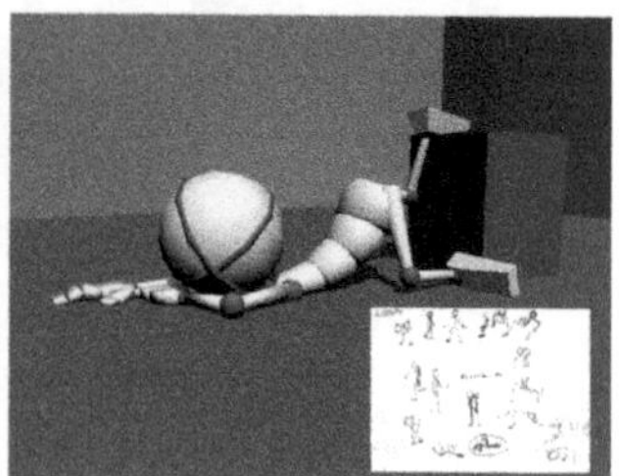

More dynamic poses, based on sketchbook ideas. Note that the first pose is tested from two separate viewpoints before being accepted. (Source: DigiPen student art by Drew Mueller.)

Once you have achieved all that you can with the key drawings, test them in some kind of moving-picture format, viewing them in sync with the audio track if sync sound is what is required. View the pose test over and over again ... sans inbetweens if possible ... until you are sure your poses are right and the timing will work. Make changes to the poses if something isn't working. Focus intently on this as blocking out is probably the most important stage of the animation process—a "point of no return," if you like. It goes without saying that everything you do from this moment on relies entirely on this stage of the production process!

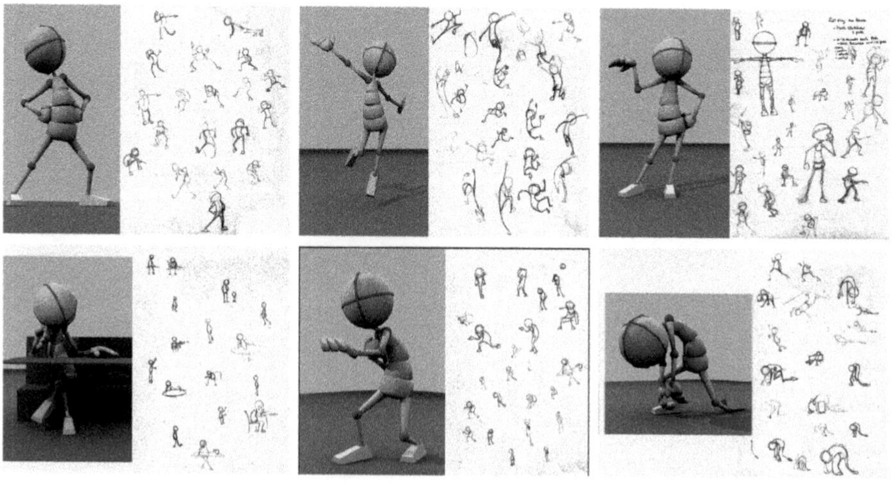

Again, extensive thumbnail poses are worked out before the actual 3D character pose is established. I cannot stress enough the importance of doing this for all styles of animation! (Source: DigiPen student art by William Patrick.)

Assignment

Create key poses for all the scenes in your film, and check that not only the action and timing are what you are looking for, but also that there is broad continuity from scene to scene.

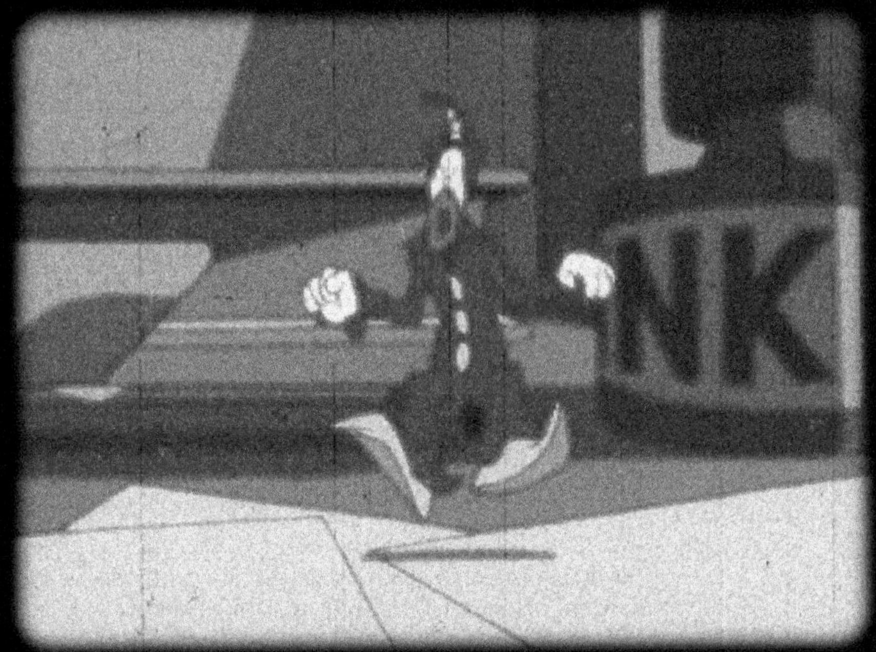

Placement and Timing

We've already discussed placement and timing in Part 1, so this is just a gentle reminder of the things you should start to think about right now.

With keys blocked out and a pose test shot, you will need to start considering the number of in-between positions that will be necessary to link them. By recording the keys to the frame numbers indicated on the exposure sheet, hand-drawn 2D animators will be able to both number their keys and calculate the required in-between drawings. Other animators will just have to judge by seeing the number of frames between one pose timing to the next on the pose test. In case you've forgotten, the following figure is what a typical 2D exposure sheet will look like when everything is doped on two's.

Not matter what your technique for timing turns out to be, don't neglect it!

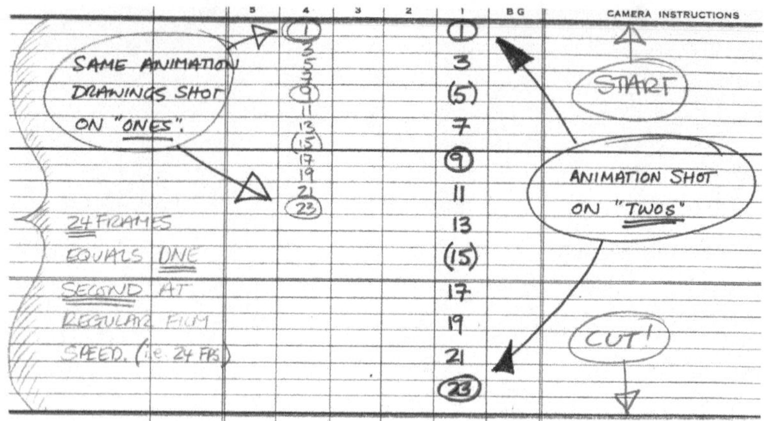

A quick reminder of how long the same images on one's and two's will appear on the exposure sheet!

The best way to know how many frames will work between different key positions will ultimately come entirely from experience—a commodity that most student animators do not yet have. Consequently, to take the faster route to experience, I advise you to study the achievements of the past and see how the great masters from animation's "golden age" tackled it. Part of my own personal pilgrimage was to make my film, *Endangered Species*, where I analyzed and recreated some of the finest classic moments in animation history. The film, part homage, part research, enabled me to study why great animation actually was great animation. But let's first remind ourselves of some core basics we learned earlier.

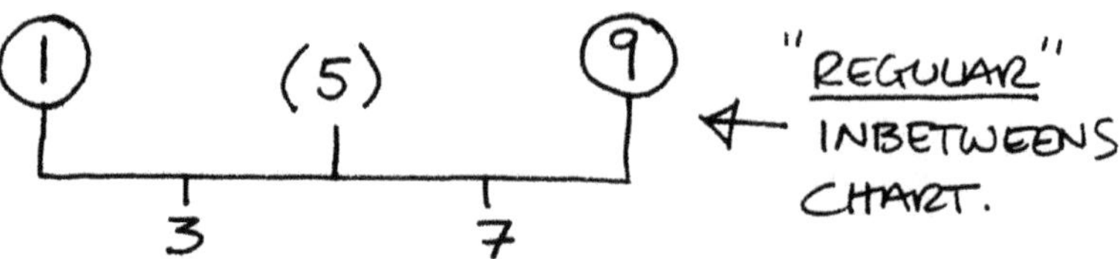

A chart indicating even in-betweens linking key positions on two's.

However, more often than not there will be more in-betweens linking keys, and so we have to next consider whether or not we need to add slow-ins or slow-outs to the action.

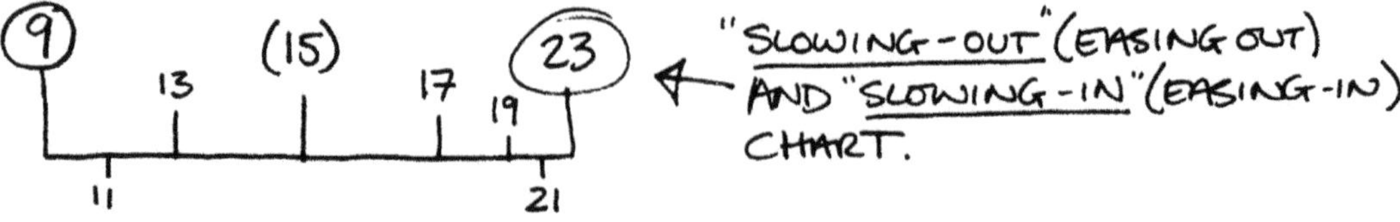

This chart has both slight slow-out and slow-in indications at both ends!

Don't forget that nothing in life moves evenly or in a straight line. All movement either accelerates or decelerates along an arc of some kind. Consequently, as an emergent animator you will need to consider just what effect you want to create between the key poses and how to achieve it. This is where we look to the past for inspiration and information.

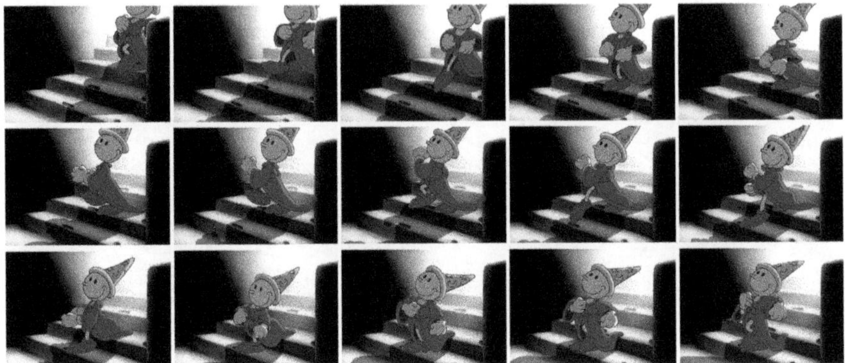

Note the bouncy action of the classic walk, as well as the way the character slows-in and slows-out throughout the up and down moves. Also, everything moves on exaggerated arcs. (Source: *Endangered Species*.)

The discoveries of movement, particularly at the Walt Disney studio between the 1930s and 1960s, has defined the process of great animation ever since. Even fine Pixar movie animation reflects this knowledge in their more contemporary offerings. Therefore, you should examine even more movement from this classic period of animation's history to learn the secrets they knew.

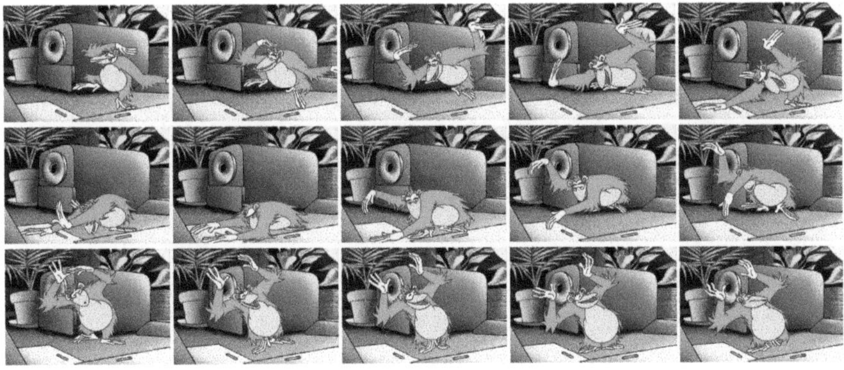

There is very little that is traditionally in-betweened in this fabulous dancing ape sequence. Every frame is virtually a key or an extreme drawing in its own right. Therefore, it is evident that the better and more sophisticated a piece of animation is, the less it relies on traditional in-between positions. (Source: *Endangered Species*.)

Perhaps the major criticism of most poor or rookie animation is that everything moves at the same time on the same keys. What I mean by this is that if a character is walking or running, every part of the torso, arms, legs, and head are in-betweened at the same time, resulting in poor action. But this does not happen in real life. Each part of us moves marginally differently, or at slightly different times and/or with a certain bias to one side or another. This is why observing what is going on with everything that moves around us in our lives is so important.

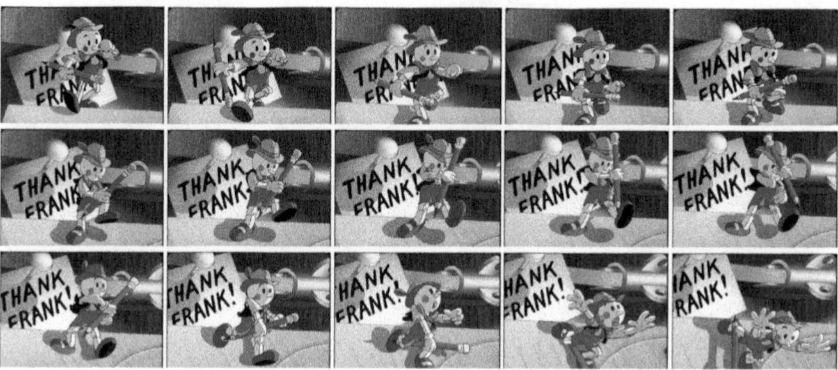

Note the variation in movement as this character begins to fall down a desk top. Most likely the animator did most of the drawings himself and just had an assistant tidy up what was left to do. This action would be nowhere near so dynamic if the animator had thrown out a few random keys and had everything else in-betweened traditionally by his assistant. (Source: *Endangered Species*.)

Assignment

Draft out the placements and timings based on the pose test you previously created. Pay special attention to your envisioned movement from key to key. Note especially where the differences between even, slowing-in, and slowing-out charting approaches can be applied to create more varied and yet more naturalistic action timing.

Two-Dimensional In-Betweening

With all the key poses established, timed out, and charted, it is now time to put in all of your in-betweens. The full process of in-betweening should be familiar to you, if you have worked through the lessons in Part 1 or have consulted either of my previous books, *The Animator's Workbook*, or *Pencils to Pixels: Classical Techniques for Digital Animators* (Focal Press, 2006).

Suffice it to say, in-betweening has always traditionally been viewed as the slog work. It is the labor-intensive, less-creative activity in animation, which is why "master" animators always prefer to have an assistant or in-betweener do the work for them. However, I have always relished

The biggest workload in a traditional, hand-drawn animation studio setting is the in-betweening. (Inbetweeners: Ryal Hansen and Tai Terry.)

in-betweening myself. It is a moment where there is no longer any creative pressure or demands on you. You just have to draw accurately, that is all! Consequently, in-betweening for me is the therapeutic aspect of animation, where I can just "coast" and simply enjoy the process of drawing without thinking (too much, that is).

There is something restful, almost Zen like, about doing in-betweens when there is no time pressure associated with the task . . . at least, if you're working on your own film with no particular time limit!

That said, I don't want to give the impression that the in-betweens can be treated lightly. This is far from the truth. If in-betweens are not accurate or well drawn, they can wreck what may have been an entirely successful animation. With the keys well planned, drawn, and timed out, poorly placed or inaccurate in-betweens can create staccato or, at best, jittery action that will destroy the whole effect. So be accurate, and most of all use superimposition for all the broadly spaced or demanding ones. There is nothing worse than seeing a character's shape squirm around and change simply because the masses and volumes of the character are not consistent from in-between to in-between. Superimposition removes the risk of this, as long as the key points and paths of action are respected and well identified.

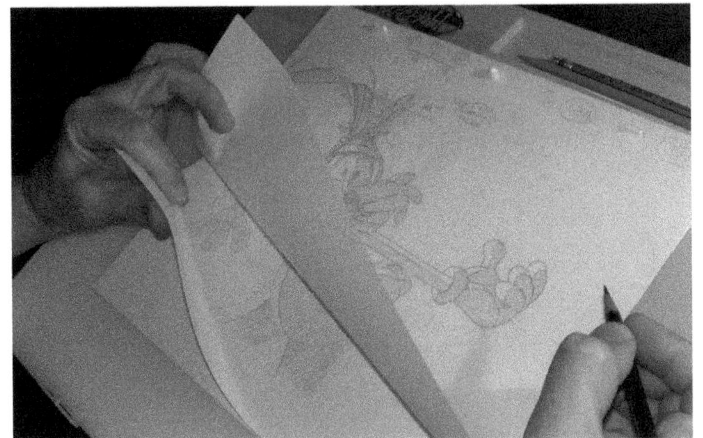

The details with some 2D animation almost demand that you have to constantly flip from one drawing to another, or superimpose the in-between linking the two key drawings.

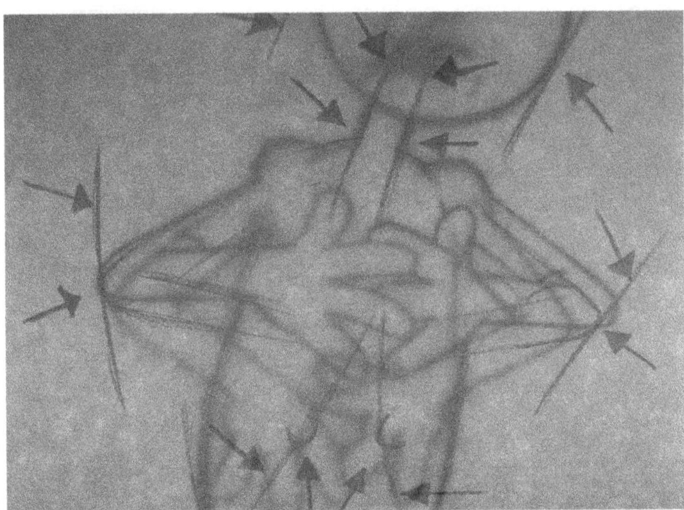

If the key points are not accurately positioned when superimposing, then the whole in-between will be inaccurate.

For the purposes of this book filmmaking course, I have located the in-betweening stage to follow the key pose and key pose testing phases of production. The more disciplined and/or experienced among you might want to handle the in-betweening on a scene-by-scene basis, completing the in-betweens as you work through the film. However, for the less experienced, I strongly recommend pose testing the entire film first, so that before you undertake the time-consuming and demanding volume of in-between drawings, you are certain that the action and scene continuity are well thought through and tested first. It would, of course, be heart-breaking for you to do a great number of in-between drawings, only to find that the essential scene planning and pose positioning was not correct in the first place.

Organization is paramount with all animation projects. Here, a scene production folder and its attached dope sheet are checked before the in-betweens are attempted.

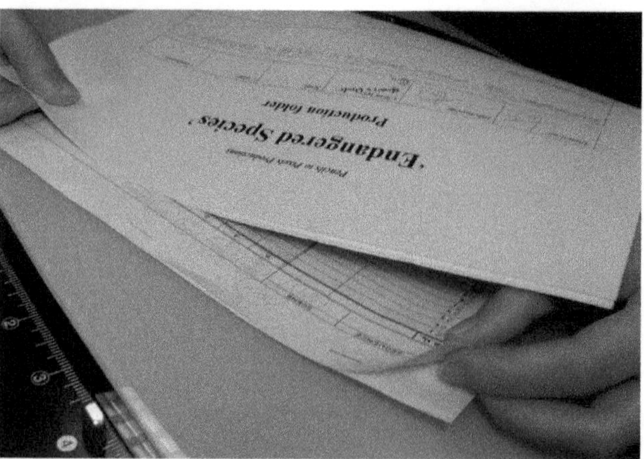

The thing I hate most about animation is having to redo something further down the line. It is demoralizing and you cannot ever capture the spontaneous inspiration that you get when you tackle something for the first time. But redo is something you will most certainly have to do if your planning is awry. Consequently, for absolutely first-time animated filmmakers, I recommend holding back the in-betweening stage until after all the pose testing, timing, and charting are complete.

The empty, expectant lightbox is hinting that less haste and more speed is often the wiser policy!

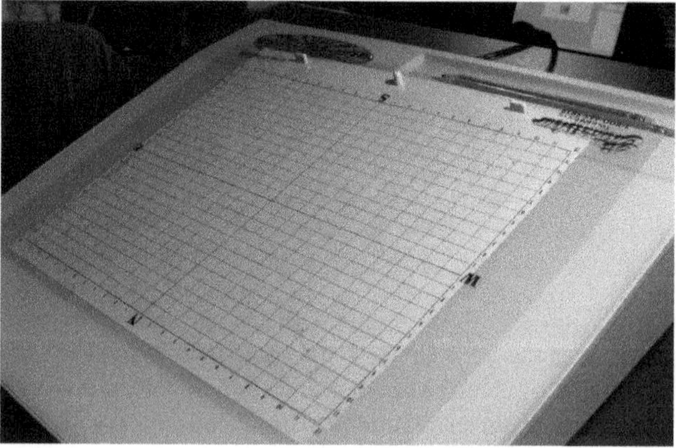

Actually, the only time I would recommend that you perhaps in-between a scene ahead of the others is when you are so inexperienced that you don't actually know, or can't visualize, how fast an action really is going to be when you work out your initial timing and charting from the key poses. In these cases, you might want to in-between your sequence "rough and dirty," meaning you just throw in accurate but very roughly drawn in-betweens as fast as you can for one scene, then shoot it to get an impression of how it looks and how fast it will move.

The rougher you work in the early stages of complicated animation, the faster you can test whether your ideas are working or not!

Armed with one simple test like this, you can then possibly feel better prepared to time and chart out the rest of your keyed action. But don't forget to go back and create more finely drawn and accurate in-betweens to replace the rough ones you did initially. Otherwise, that scene will undoubtedly stand out as sloppily done when the whole film is viewed at the pencil test stage.

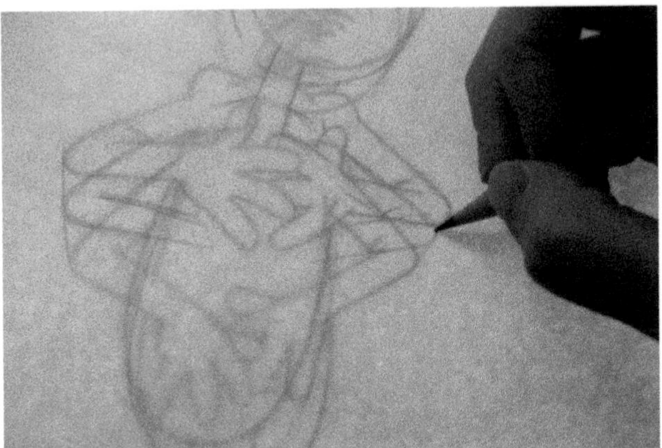

Accuracy, accuracy, accuracy—the core requirement of all in-betweens!

Assignment

Complete all the in-betweens for each stage in your film, as indicated in this chapter lesson.

Rolling, Flipping, and Pencil Testing

The natural extension of the 2D-based in-betweening stage of production is pencil testing your finished drawings once they are complete. Pencil testing is the only way you will ever learn if your animation is working or not, or if the timing is as you imagine it to be or it needs to be. However, you should never neglect the invaluable process of rolling or flipping prior to testing.

You cannot possibly tell if your hand-drawn animation is working unless you learn how to flip!

Flipping, or rolling, will give you a quick impression of how the action is working as you are actually creating it. However, because flipping is essentially a manually driven procedure it will not necessarily give you a perfect sense of the ultimate timing. That said, it will at least give you a good impression of how the action and movement is working prior to subjecting it to a final pencil test.

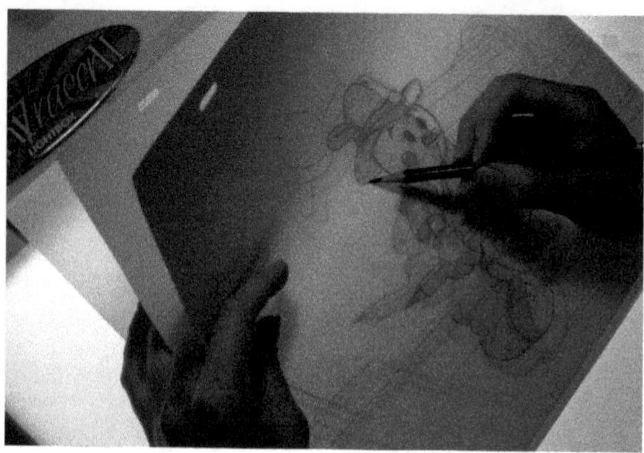

Even when drawing key positions it is important to flip between one or more other key positions to keep form, continuity, and movement consistent. For demonstration purposes, I have shown bottom pegs flipping here, although, as you can see, I use top pegs to animate.

Flipping (Rolling)

For a more comprehensive explanation of all these techniques, please refer to to my book *Animation from Pencils to Pixels*, where I have explained the process extensively on pages 360–365. However, for now, let us accept the fact that flipping (rolling) is a means whereby you can view up to five drawings at once on the drawing board to see how they move and work together. You can flip drawings whether you are using top or bottom pegs, although the technique for doing each of these will be slightly different.

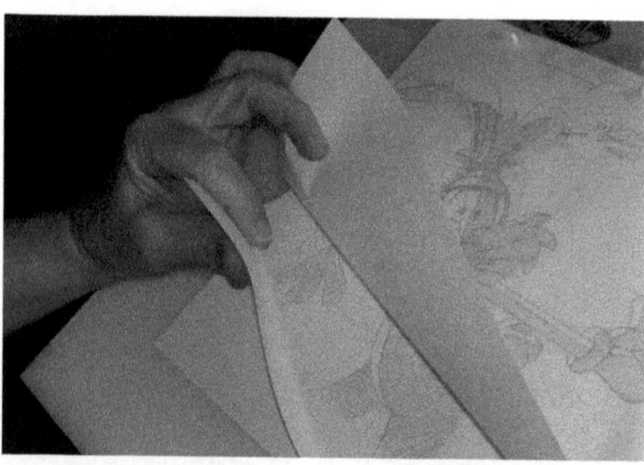

Using top pegs flipping to check things as I do a single in-between.

Using the two-handed technique of top pegs flipping to view five levels of animation drawings at a time.

Flipping is a great way of quickly assessing the placement and accuracy of specific in-betweens as you create them on your lightbox. As previously indicated, you can even flip as you draw in many circumstances. Indeed, it should be an ingrained process that you adopt every time you animate!

Full-Scene Flipping

Full-scene flipping takes the advantages of rolling one stage further, by allowing an animator to view his or her entire scene or comprehensive sequence of animation drawings within the scene if it is a really long one. The technique of full-scene flipping is essentially adopting the principles of the flip book and extending them one stage further. Hold all the drawings together, with the lowest number to the bottom and the highest to the top, and simply flip them from bottom to top to see how the action is working.

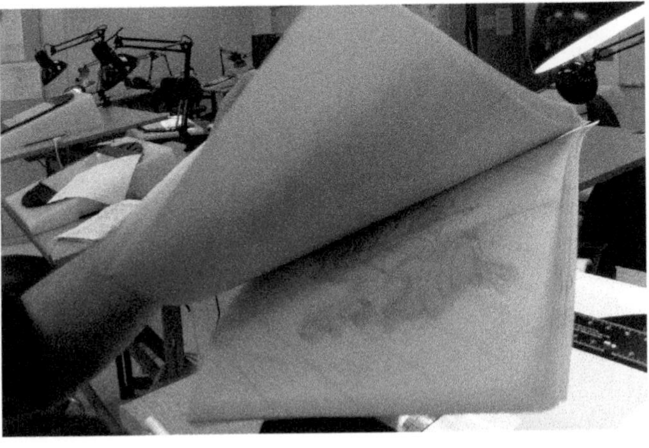

Learn to fan the drawings toward you from bottom to top before you start to flip. It will make the process so much easier.

Clearly, flipping is a wonderful way of knowing if the action is not moving smoothly enough throughout a scene, and it should readily identify any in-between drawings, or even key drawings, that are out of place or incorrectly positioned. Flipping perfectly gives you the broad picture, although it will not give you an ultimate view of any tiny mistakes or inaccurate timing that is occurring. That is where a pencil test comes in.

The basic setup for shooting animation drawings: a digital camera on a stand, hooked up to a computer with software that will capture the images frame by frame. Note the use of a peg bar on the base of the stand for accurate registration while the drawings are being shot.

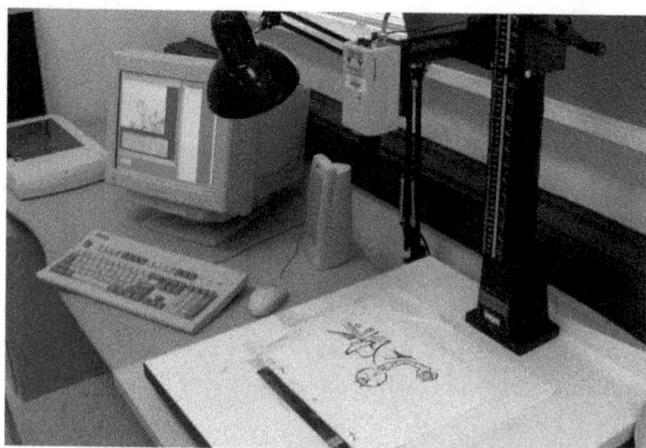

Pencil Test

The pencil test is ultimately the finest method available for testing animation work. To create a pencil test, you essentially need to capture each drawing in numerical sequence and play them back on a screen at the required film speed. There is no clean-up or coloring required at this stage—just your animation pencil drawings shot in the most minimalist way. Yet, stripped down to the bare pencil drawing level at this stage, you will immediately see the flow, continuity of movement, and timing of everything drawing as it is.

When you first see a pencil test with two or more layers, it might take awhile to get used to seeing the lines of one level passing through the lines of another.

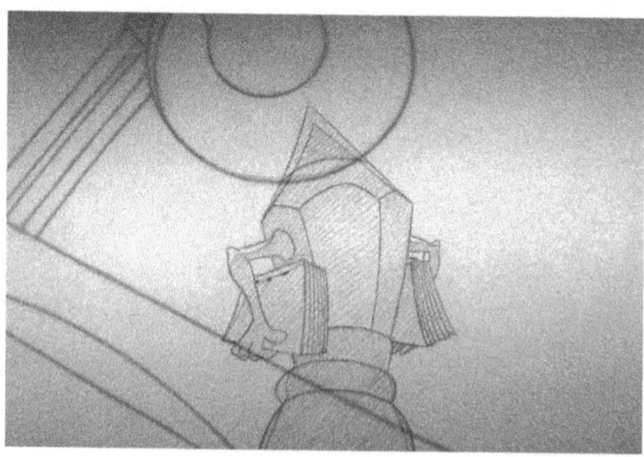

You need to realize now that the first pencil test you attempt is never going to appear as you imagine it to be in your mind! This is true even if you have extensively rolled and flipped your drawings beforehand. There is something very raw and unforgiving about the pencil test. Nothing is covered up with style, line or color, or even music. It is what it is—your pencil drawings moving on the screen in the way you planned them to. You may not have planned them well (although we all think we have at the time!), and therefore the pencil test will reveal your animated failings all too immediately.

Subsequent viewings, over and over again, however, will nevertheless reveal the nature of the weaknesses but also the ways these can be corrected. Consequently, the first pencil test is not an easy thing to watch, unless you are easily pleased, of course! But the pencil test *is* a necessary evil.

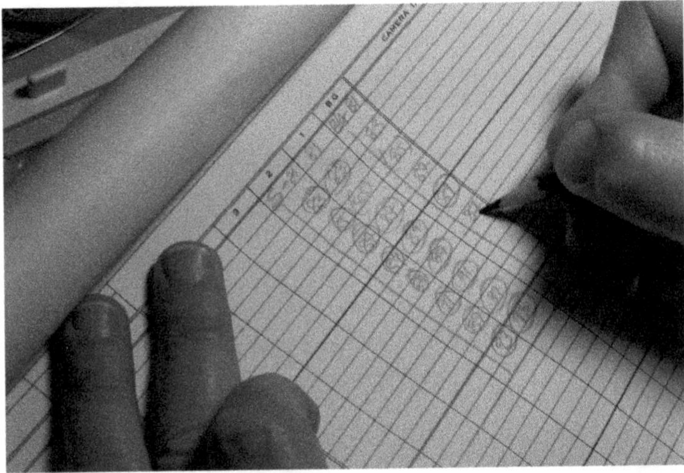

A lot of your thinking is done on the dope sheet before you shoot the animation, but the only accurate test is when you see the pencil test running in real time on a screen or monitor!

Now, if you go into the pencil test stage with an attitude of discovery and learning, the pencil test will hold no fears for you and can actually be your friend. It does not only reveal bad things, it can reveal the good ones too. The pencil test enables you to quickly understand what any number of drawings, at any distance apart, means when seen in real-time playback speed. It shows you the things that work as well as the things that don't work.

Today, the technology to produce a pencil test is so quick and easy that changes and retesting is not such a major chore. I have always used DigiCel's Flipbook to produce mine because it is so easy to use and work with. (ToonBoom Technologies just brought out Pencil Check at the time of writing and it promises to be exceptionally good too.) For example, you can shoot a scene on two's but then find that you would like a little more time in some places and a little less in others. In Flipbook you can cut and paste drawings in the exposure sheet to give you an instant playback of what you need before even touching another drawing!

Using Flipbook to convert drawings shot on one's to two's. (Source: Animation by Katy McCallister.)

Then, with the film giving you timing clues, you can proceed to modify the animation accordingly. In this way, the pencil test is your "teacher" in the art of animation, and you should neither take it lightly nor fear it for the insight it offers you with everything you attempt.

Playing the animation back on the monitor is the real acid test of your work!

I can only repeat that as long as you treat the pencil test as a method of honing and improving your skills as an animator, you will have nothing to fear from it. Go in with the understanding that nothing will be right the first time around, and that you're going to have to fix or modify something. After 40 years of animating, I am still challenged by the pencil test whenever I shoot something I think will be fine. I very rarely "pass" when my tests first appear on the screen!

Art reflects life—the effects of creating a poor pencil test!

Never be afraid to change your thinking on everything if things are just not working. Nothing should be set in stone. You should allow yourself to change your mind. All is merely a process of learning through experience and the pencil test is the best means of gaining experience in this way. Remember that renumbering and readjusting the number of in-betweens and their relative timing and positioning has occurred since the dawn of animation and will continue to do so until it is no more. So, don't feel you have failed if your first pencil test, or even your second or third, is not achieving what you imagined. The great Disney animators of the past used the process of the pencil test as a valuable learning device, where they could try and experiment until they found something that ultimately achieved what they were after, and more than they were after eventually. You must never forget that, like the Holy Grail, the magic of animation is never easily won!

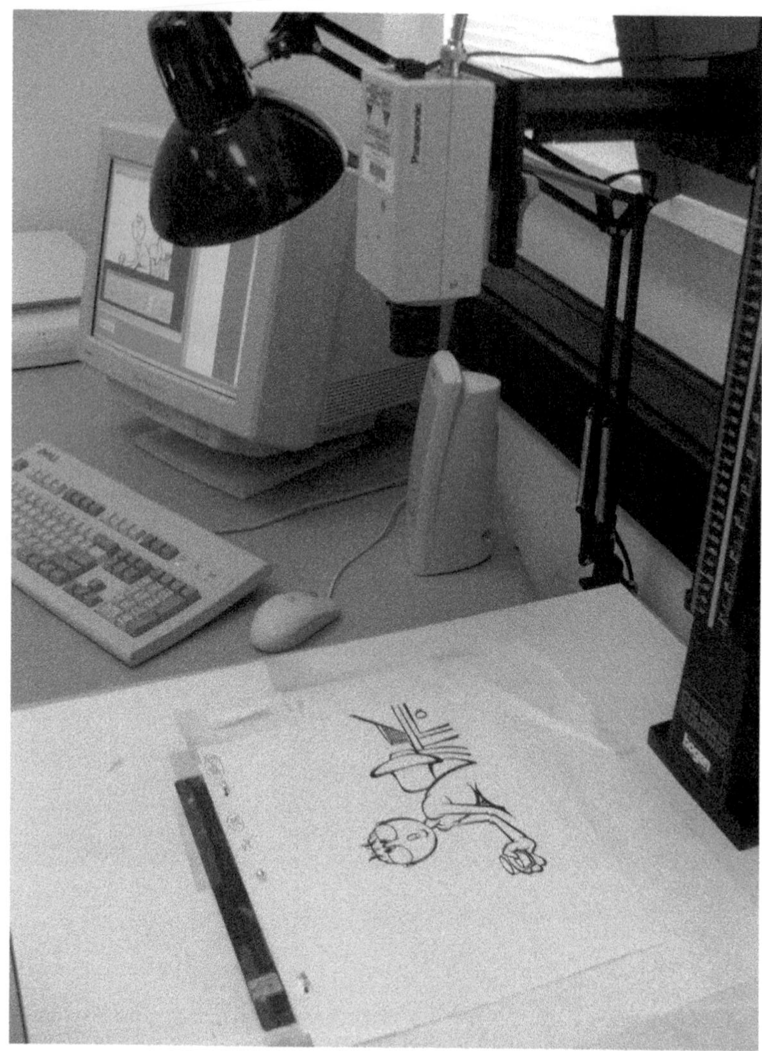

The altar of the Holy Grail!

Assignment

Test (and retest) your animation until everything stands up to the standards and intentions that you first started with.

Clean-Up

Now it is time to take your film to the next level, visually speaking at least. Presumably, at this stage your animation is the best it can ever be. (If not, go back and make it so!) You will have hopefully worked at it and modified it through constant testing and changes, so now it will be as close to perfect as it ever can be. Having gone through that painstaking, extended process, you will want the visual quality of your film to completely support its animated movement. That is where clean-up comes in.

Size isn't everything! At this stage of your production the "quality" of drawing is extremely important!

Using the design approach you created at the concept art and character model stages, you now have to take every penciled animation drawing and redraw them in the original style. It is all too very easy for animators to drift a little off their prescribed character design as they work through keys and more specifically in-betweens, so you will be no different. In a hurry to get your action tested as quickly as possible, it is all too tempting to use a rougher line than you ultimately want, to approximate proportions and volumes of the character without totally locking them down, and to even leave out design details on the costume or character, which are not particularly important when establishing the overall movement. Clean-up is the point where you need to address all these issues.

Cleaning up the traditional way!

Clean-up can be done on top of the original drawings or created on top of new sheets of animation paper that are laid over the originals. Clean-up can be done with a solid black pencil line, an ink line, or even a digital line created directly within the computer. (For the latter you will need to scan your original drawings into your computer, import them into your favorite drawing or painting program, and then work on each one individually to get the consistency of line, form, and design that you arrived at through your original design concepts.) The direct digital technique is becoming more and more popular with contemporary digital animators, especially in the area of Flash or other vector animation approaches.

Vector coloring for a film project pitch. (Source: DigiPen student art.)

I personally prefer to clean-up "traditionally," meaning that I use pencils or pens on paper to do my final clean-up drawings. I then scan these final clean-up drawings directly into my chosen animation program. I still find that I need the tactile feel of a pencil or pen on paper to get the best out of myself. I also love the option of being able to turn the paper in any direction when cleaning up to get each line immaculate, controlled, and styled in exactly the right way. Although modern computer tools and technology do wonderful things, they just can't replace the feel of "real" artwork on a "real" drawing surface as far as I am concerned. Even the wonderful Cintiq drawing tablet does not achieve this, although it really is a fabulous step in the right direction!

There are fabulous advantages to working with modern technology, but for an old-industry die-hard like me, a state-of-the-art Cintiq still doesn't "feel" like paper!

Essentially, clean-up is best approached by drawing on the same sheet of paper that the original animation drawing is created on. The danger of this, though, is that if you mess up the clean-up drawing in this way (especially if you are cleaning up with ink), you are also destroying the original animation drawing and will subsequently have to create it again. This is not such a catastrophe if you have ruined a basic in-between drawing. But if it is a key drawing, then recreating it will be much more challenging. Consequently, I (reluctantly) tend to clean-up on a fresh sheet of animation paper, laid over the original animation drawing.

This is the part of the process that really requires a steady hand!

Whether you work on a rubbed-down original drawing or you lay a fresh sheet of paper over the original drawing for your clean-ups, there are certain things you always need to bare in mind.

Line Quality

Make sure that your cleaned-up line is the same quality of line used in your original character designs. It is tempting to just quickly trace an even, constant line over your character details when the original design style you created featured thick and thin lines that gave added strength and style to the character. However, to do so would result in a loss of quality of your original inspiration, and all for the short-cut convenience of saving a little time! (This does not apply to characters who are originally designed with an even, constant line in the first place, of course!)

Even line inked clean-up.

Also, if you are using a thick and thin line approach, make sure that you consistently follow through from drawing to drawing with it, in keeping with your original design. For example, if you draw your first clean-up drawing with the thick portion of the line under an arm, do not in any circumstance place the thick part of the line above the arm on the next drawing, somewhere else on the next, and so on. This approach will give you a "boiling" (jittery) line that destroys the smoothness of most animation. If, however, you do not want such a highly active and energetic line to define your animation, then you have to be more consistent with your line!

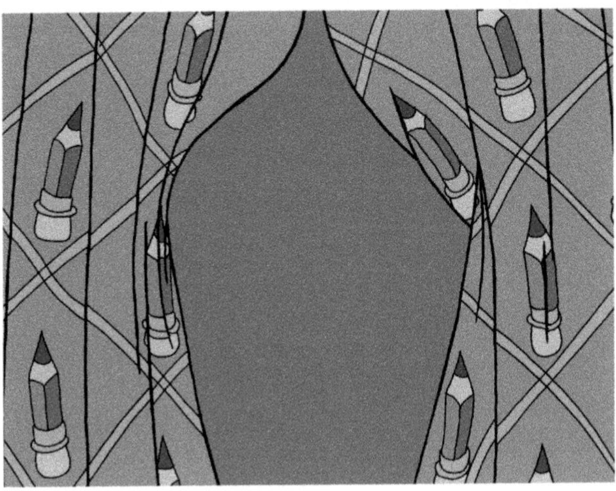

An even line tracing. Note that the edges and folds are a consistent thicker line, whereas the inner design lines are not as thick, providing a different quality to the image.

Join the Lines

Most animation these days is produced digitally and therefore electronic coloring is an absolute certainty. In 99 percent of the cases where digital coloring is used, it is extremely important that all the containing lines of a color area do not have breaks in them. If they do have a break in their boundary, the color fill will flood out to an adjoining color area, or even across the entire screen, and you will have to undo the fill and fix the line before you can color it properly. (Some digital coloring programs automatically fill in the smaller gaps for you, so check the specs.)

See how the color floods out into the screen when there is a gap in the line between the back and tail (circled on the left), whereas when the lines are unbroken the character can be easily colored with no flooding.

Therefore, it is better to catch these errors at the clean-up stage and make sure that every line you create for your character does not have any gaps in it.

Pencil Grain versus Ink Line

Depending on the style of your film's design, you may wish to attempt to create a more grainy pencil line effect, rather than a solid and consistent hard line. This is reasonable from a design point of view, but just remember that in the digital world this can also be a stumbling block at the coloring stage. For example, if you were to significantly enlarge a pencil line side by side with a solid ink one, you will see there are numerous white breaks in the pencil line that are not there in the ink line.

When being drawn, the line breaks are not so evident.

A pencil line style may look more naturalistic when viewed on the screen, but just remember that when you need to color your character, you will need to blow up the image on the screen, frame by frame, so you can paint inside every tiny white speck and crevice that the pencil line creates!

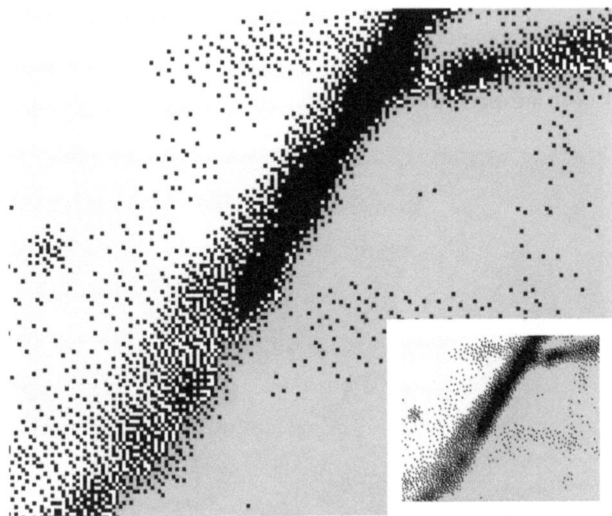

The full-screen image shows a pencil line enlarged to the visible pixel level. Note the white squares (pixels) that will all have to be individually colored! The inset shows what it looks like when we zoom back somewhat. Note how gray and fuzzy it looks.

Clearly this is a time-consuming challenge, although one that you may be prepared to take on. However, if you are aware of this at the outset, you can make a more informed decision on the stylistic approach you take for your film. If you decide you want a pencil-style look to your film but choose not to color in every tiny little white speck within the pencil line work, you'll find that you will get a kind of grayish flickering that can be distracting if everything else is plain, flat color. Therefore, I would suggest that it is wiser to settle for a solid, strong ink line effect wherever possible, at least for your first film.

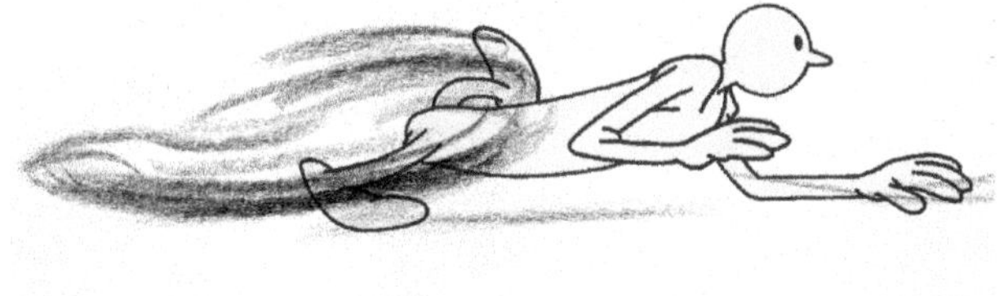

There are times when the use of pencil is a bonus. Here, in a scene emulating the action of the *Roadrunner*, I used soft pencil shading to depict the speed lines! (Source: *Endangered Species*.)

Certainly, when scanning your clean-up drawings after the clean-up is complete, strong and solid black ink lines will copy the best and provide you with the fewest hassles later on.

Shapes, Dimensions, and Volumes

One big danger of 2D animation is that in getting carried away with the animation process, and especially when liberally using squash and stretch in the action, it is very easy to have inconsistent shapes, dimensions, and volumes from animation drawing to animation drawing. For example, in a walk sequence, a common fault is that the lengths and widths of the calves or thighs tend to change shape in length and volume from frame to frame with the work of an inexperienced animator.

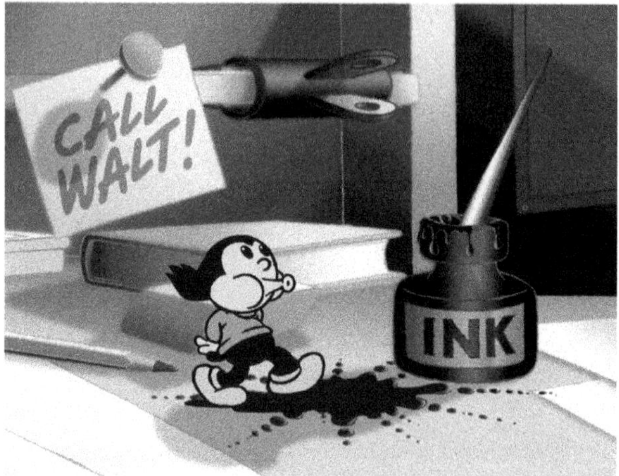

A typical Max Fleischer–style scene from the early days of animation. Note that even the legs on the same drawing have slightly different lengths and volumes! (Source: *Endangered Species*.)

Consequently, when cleaning up this kind of thing, be aware of this danger and try to modify the offending drawings wherever possible. There is, of course, a danger here of distorting the animation by making too many drastic changes in significant areas. So be cautious if you change something too much. A strong tip is to flip your drawings at all times so that you can see that any changes you make are consistent in movement as well as visually.

Never deny the value of flipping, whether you are animating key drawings, in-betweening, or cleaning up!

Describing Volumes

Remember that even the most rudimentary 2D character will imply that there is volume to his or her shape and dimension. For example, the typical cartoon head shape is quite often round in appearance and the rest of the body very basic in shape compared to human shapes and proportions.

Drawn in *Fritz the Cat* style. (Source: *Endangered Species*.)

Many designs need to imply things like thick necks, broad shoulders, bloated stomachs, fat butts, etc. Consequently, you will need to continually create this illusion with the style and approach of the line in your clean-up drawings. Using thick and thin line variations here is especially valuable. I have found that by thickening up the lower part of a rounded nose, for example, gives it shape and body. Of course, using a stronger thick and thin line will produce a more powerful image too!

Sometimes just the merest flick of a thick and thin line can define a facial feature.

A stronger, 'thick & thin' line approach.

Implied Geometry

Often the animation you have created uses perspective and foreshortening to get a "to and from" camera effect. Therefore, be sure that when you clean up these action drawings, you use lines that emphasize the perspective as well as the overlapping volumes within the character. For example, an arm, hand, and finger directed toward the camera can be emphasized or damaged by the selective use of a clean-up line. This is where an awareness of implied geometry comes in.

My personal homage to Richard Williams's Academy Award–winning film, *A Christmas Carol*. (Source: *Endangered Species*.)

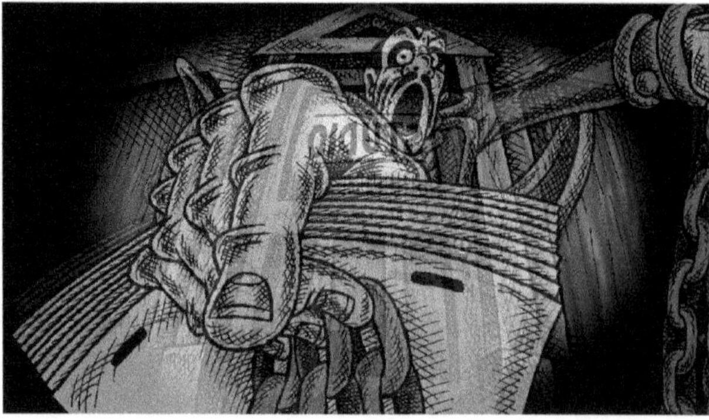

Essentially, implied geometry is a process of drawing where you ensure the audience understands what parts of the drawing are nearer and what parts are farther away. Remember the basic law of perspective states that whatever is nearer to the viewer will appear proportionately larger than what is farther away. You can emphasize this by overlapping the lines of a near element over the lines of one farther away. This will give the audience the illusion that the object is nearer, and in being so, it cuts off part of the more distant element.

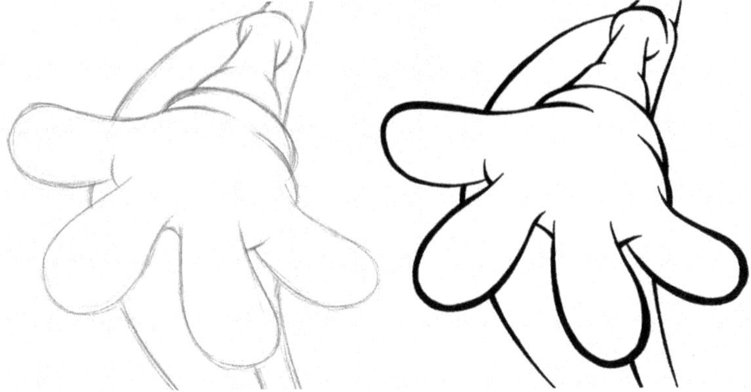

The overlapping lines give the impression of the nearer shapes appearing in front of the ones behind them. By exaggerating the perspective and using strong thick and thin lines in the clean-up, the entire effect can be made even more dramatic!

Follow-Through Lines

Quite often characters are structured using a specific number of overlapping shapes, such as spheres, ovals, etc., to form the entire character design. This was most pronounced in the early days of traditional cartoon animation.

The kind of fat and round design we've seen a million times.

To get a greater understanding of how these characters worked in action, the animators would often leave their construction lines in to identify for the clean-up artist just where these shapes connect and where they continue through to. These were known as *follow-through* construction lines.

Note how the whole design, drawn with a red pencil, is almost entirely made up of circles and linking construction lines.

Clean-up artists often started their process by using a dark pencil to structure everything. These clean-up pencil drawings were then inked onto clear acetate cels, after which they were painted and shot.

The same red animation drawing with the darker cleaned-up lines added. Note how all the follow-through lines are now eliminated.

Consequently, if you are nervous about the structural complications in your own drawings when cleaning up, consider working lightly drawn follow-through lines into your preliminary work. Only when this is all established throughout the scene (and pencil tested!) should you put in your final dark clean-up lines.

Assignment

Clean up your entire pencil-tested animation. As you finish each cleaned-up scene, pencil test it again to see that everything you are doing is consistent and correct before moving on to the next stage.

Scanning

Scanning for modern animators is as important as the animation stand (or rostrum camera in the United Kingdom) was for traditional cell animators. Without either of these essential elements of technology, animators would just not be able to get their drawings up onto the screen.

The animation stand was a huge, precision-made piece of equipment that comprised of a camera tabletop containing both top and bottom panning peg bars, two enormous vertical columns, and a full, movie-standard camera that would rise up and down the columns to film the artwork on the animation table using a whole range of different field sizes.

A traditional rostrum camera, as used before the animation digital age arrived. Preserved by the Animaticus Foundation and on display in the lobby of the DigiPen Institute of Technology.

In the latter days of the industry, somewhere in between the 1980s and 1990s, computers began to be added to drive the whole camera/table mechanism. Before that, everything was done manually, of course.

Today, pretty much anyone can own a scanner or even a digital camera setup if they're lucky. Prices and technology are so accessible that what was once a very major investment for the ambitious professional animator is now the standard equipment that enables anyone to have a professional-level, comprehensive animation studio in their own home.

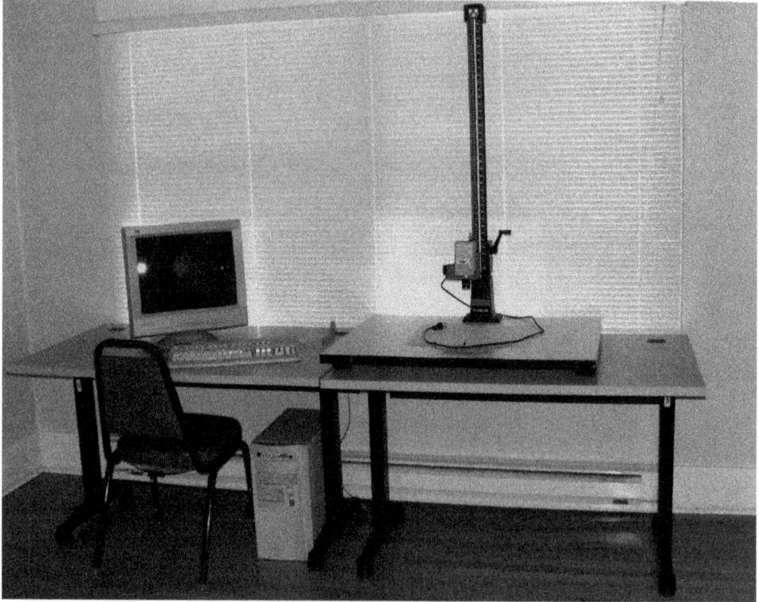

For the luckier among the home bound enthusiasts, a simple digital camera setup!

The only requirement of the scanner for traditional 2D animators is that it scans well and evenly, especially in the line/text bitmap format. Although it is often necessary to scan color imagery for props, backgrounds, or other animation assets, the bulk of scanning for traditional animators simply will be to capture black-and-white line images, frame after frame after frame. Consequently, even the cheapest of scanners should do the trick, as long as they are consistent in their illumination across the scanning area. I have found that for old scanners their illumination tends to fade somewhat toward one edge of the screen, which results in a kind of ugly black, speckly pattern at the offending side of the image.

One of my favorite scanners, the Epson GT 15000, is suitable for movie-scale, 16 field–size productions. (The cardboard box to the right is optional!)

Three "musts" must be born in mind when scanning animation drawings, as follows.

Peg Bar

Since all animation work is created on peg bars for registration purposes, it is very important that you purchase a thin, light, but sturdy peg bar and tape it permanently to the side of the scanner for regular use.

Every scanner will need a portable peg bar taped to it.

It is really essential that each scan is perfectly aligned, otherwise when all the frames are edited together, they will tend to jump and jiggle around in the screen, entirely destroying the smooth look of your animation. The location of the peg bar is therefore extremely important, as you need to make sure that all the field area is covered by the scan and consequently nothing is cut off.

The best way of ensuring a perfectly positioned animation scan is to draw a black-line paper field guide that defines the boundaries of the field area you are using. This is done by first putting the field guide on the pegs of your lightbox. Then you will need to add a fresh sheet of animation paper over it and accurately trace the outline of the field size you are working with.

With the field guide outline positioned over your scanner's glass area, you can then preview scan it.

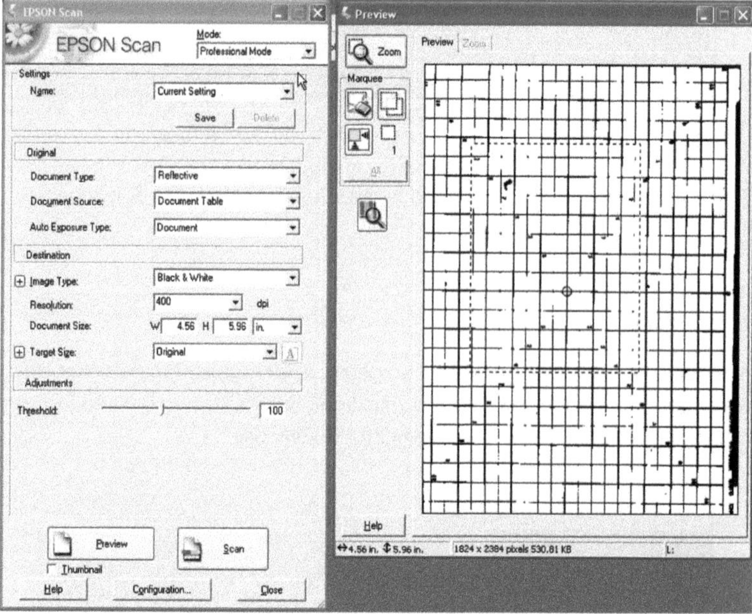

You can always scan your graticule instead of a drawn field guide as long as you can identify the area that you want the animation to be scanned in.

Secure the Field Guide Scanning Area

To make sure the scanner covers the required area, you have to permanently position the guide area for each animation drawing. Most scanners have the ability to scan one image at a time. The secret is to save this feature as a default setting. Staying in the preview mode, drag the dotted line selection area to match the drawn field area. When the framing is perfectly aligned, save it with a name you will always remember.

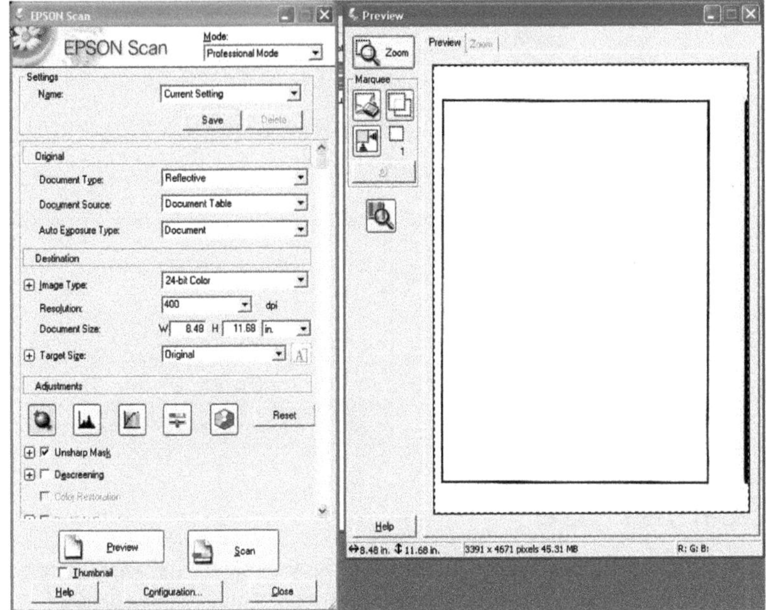

A full scan reveals the maximum scanning area with the drawn field guide inside it.

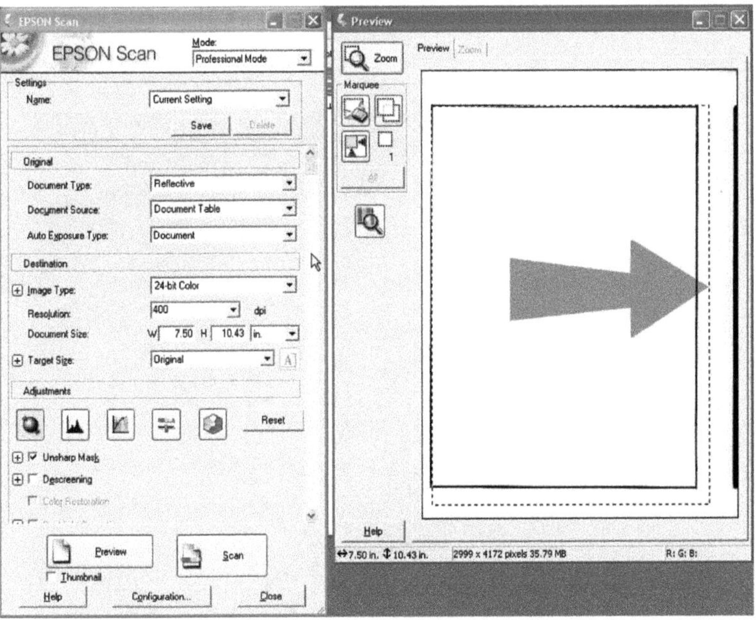

Slowly drag the selection area to match up with the drawn guide.

Saved here as "Setting 7."

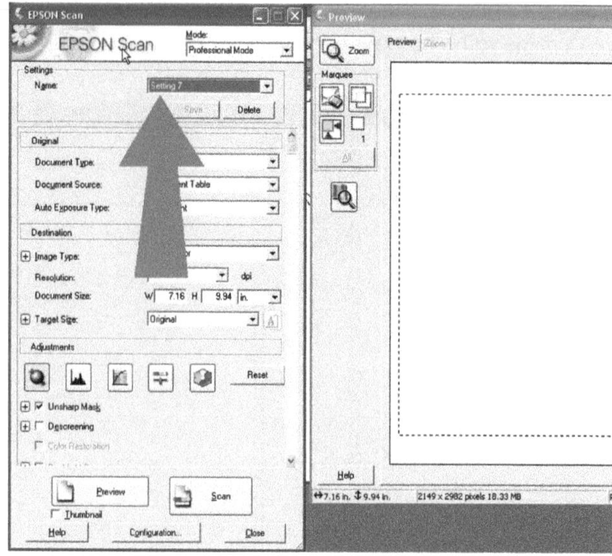

Scanner Size

Before buying a scanner you might like to seriously consider what size of scanner would best suit your needs. Most animators, especially student animators, will probably only be in a position to purchase a standard, high-street style scanner that will work for artwork sized anything up to a standard sheet of letter paper. This means that you will need to work at a 10 field–size framing for everything you do.

A standard office scanner for letter-size papers. This will cope with any framing up to 10 field, or 10.5 field if you're lucky!

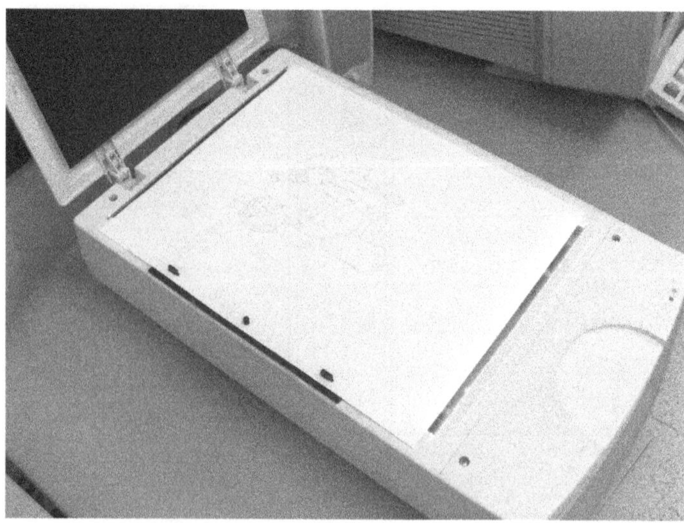

However, if you want to work larger, say a 12 or 16 field (15 field in the United Kingdom), then you will need to purchase a significantly larger scanner such as an 11 × 17-inch one. This, of course, will be significantly more expensive. However, if you intend to be a career animator, or if you are prepared to make a lifelong commitment to your animation work, then it will be a most valuable investment if you want to work with larger formats.

Assignment

Scan all of the animation drawings you have created for your film. However, scan each scene separately and keep the files in separate folders so you can avoid any confusion later in production.

A production folder for keeping all your animation drawings in, together with all the other administrative materials that are required to make an animated film.

When numbering the saved scans, I recommend adding a prefix to the frame number to identify what particular scene it is related to. This is something you may be glad about later when you are working digitally with a huge collection of different files. For example, if you're scanning your first frame from scene 3, I would save the scan as "03_01"; if you are saving drawing 9 from scene 3, I would number that "03_09"; and so on.

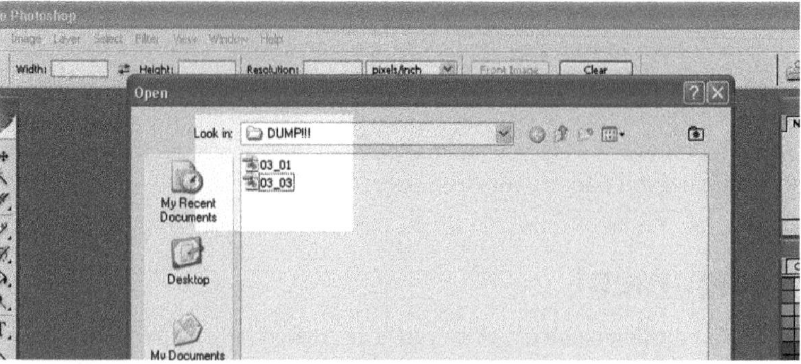

Files should be saved with the scene number first and the drawing number second.

Depending on the animation software you are using, it is most likely that you will need to rotate and resize your scans once they are completed and scanned. For much of my work I actually use Adobe Photoshop, then edit and render my scenes in Adobe Premiere. This way I can rotate and resize my establishing scan (to fit the ultimate screen frame size I wish to render my film in) in one "Actions" process, and then render out all the remaining drawings in the folder using the "Automate/Batch" function.

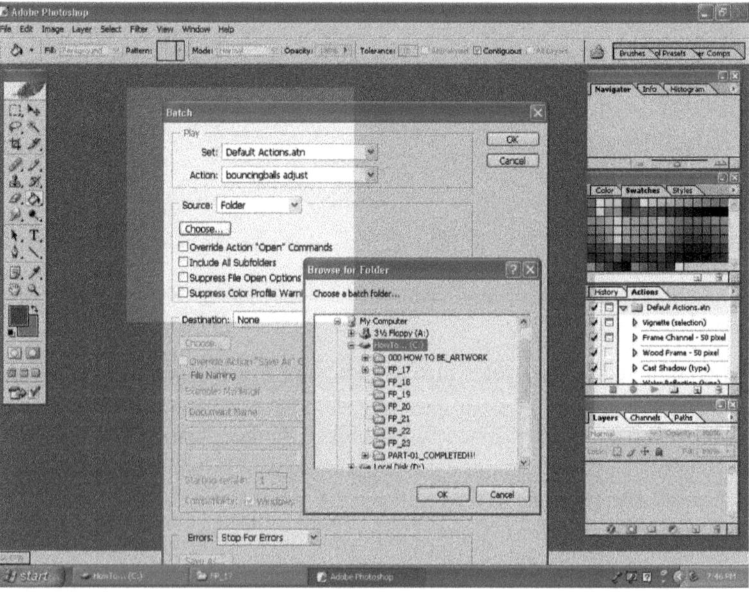

The "Actions" and "Automate/Batch" processes are the answer to an animator's prayers in Adobe Photoshop.

Other programs may, of course, provide a different way of doing this, although perhaps using the Adobe Photoshop process will adequately prepare your scans for any application so they can be imported ready to go.

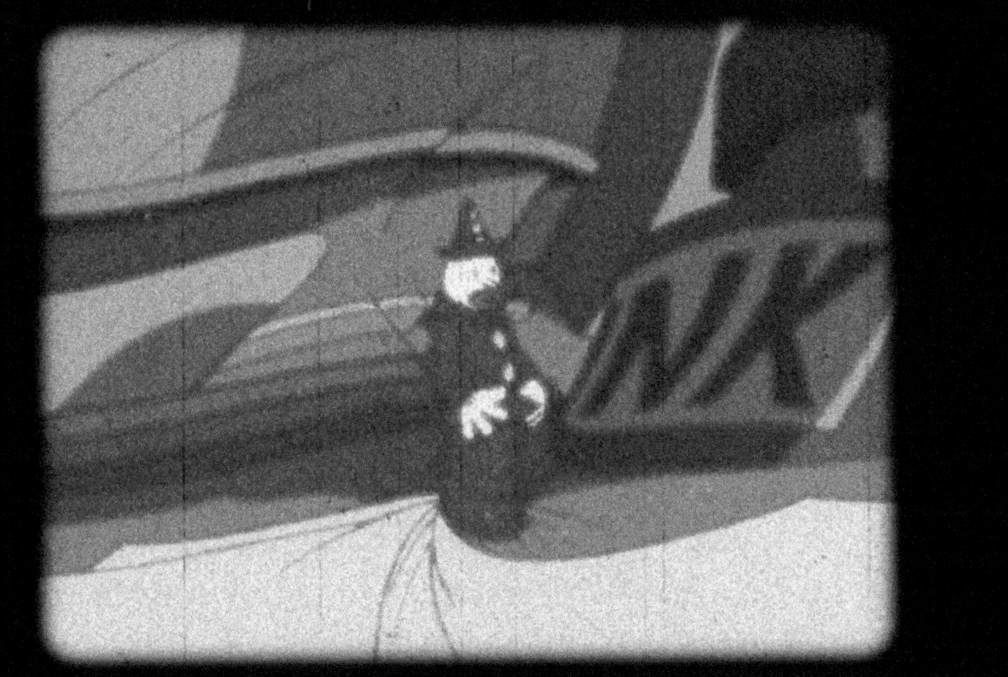

Backgrounds and Environments

Whether artwork is digitally or traditionally created, the background and environment elements within a film are fundamentally important to the way an audience perceives your work. The design may be of the finest quality and the animation superb, but as the background constitutes the majority of the screen area seen in every shot, the quality of it can make or break the way the film looks.

The beauty of digital background art is that it can be quite impactful and multi-dimensional.

Beautifully moody shot, seen in early light. (Source: DigiPen student art by Dan Moyer.)

Backgrounds can be minimalist or extremely elaborate. They can be cartoonish in style or photorealistic. The one thing they have to be is compatible with the styling of your animated characters. For example, unless you are pursuing a totally radical and unorthodox look, you would probably never deliberately choose to have a flat-colored, cartoonish 2D character in a photorealistic setting, or a 2D character in an overtly 3D world.

Pleasing design using 3D toonshading. (Source: DigiPen student art by Jeff Weber.)

Haunting mood for this short 3D-animated film. (Source: DigiPen student art by Sergey Naygel.)

Extensive color and compatibility testing for this character and environment. (Source: DigiPen student art by David Bolton.)

A lot of background painting issues will have been resolved when dealing with basic principles at the concept art, design, and color scripting stages of your film's production. However, the final background art of your film must strongly reflect these approaches, therefore it will pay for you to understand these and more before you begin.

We have dealt with a few of the main principles of color composition in the color script aspect of the production process especially (see FP 10). However, we will return to them, and more, now by way of underlining their importance.

Compositional Color Values

Remember, to achieve the greatest impact and sense of depth in your background art, there must always be significant differences in the color values in the foreground, midground, and background of any environment. The convention is to have foreground objects be the darkest, midground values be neutral, and distant objects be the lightest. It is possible to reverse these to give an entirely different effect.

Excellent example of diminishing values in a picture. (Source: DigiPen student art by Mark Barrett.)

A reverse in values for this painting. (Source: DigiPen student art by Ronald Kury.)

Horizontals and Verticals

It is pretty much universally acknowledged that for most environment art, especially exterior environment art, the horizontals will be significantly lighter in value than the verticals. As with everything, a lot will depend on the light source that affects the picture. But by and large these indications can be implemented for most of the time in your background art.

Light Source and Contrast

Remember that all environments will require three main elements of illumination: highlights, midtones, and shadows.

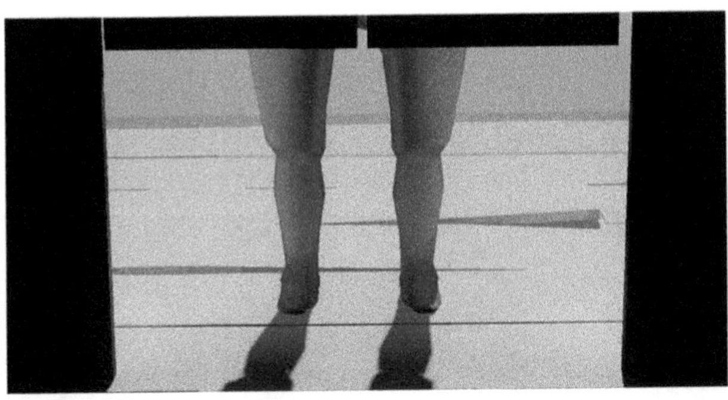

A dramatic use of light and shadow to invoke a mood. (Source: DigiPen student art by Nick Wiley.)

The positioning of these elements will depend entirely on the direction of the main light source in relation to the objects in the scene. Consequently, an exterior landscape on a hot, summer day at noon will have these primal values. However, the same scene viewed at sunrise or sunset will look entirely different.

A bright and clean midday feel. (Source: DigiPen student art by Eric Wiley.)

The same shot with a much cooler, fast-fading light feel. (Source: DigiPen student art by Eric Wiley.)

Interiors are often dominated by a major light source, especially if a single light is on to illumine the scene. However, depending on surfaces and secondary light sources that are there too, there could be a great deal of bounced light and shade that will modify this initial scenario.

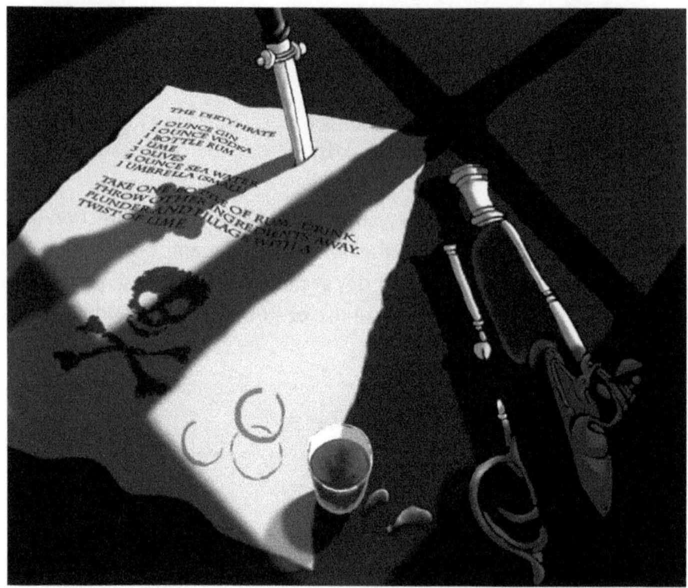

Starkly sketched shadows suggest moonlight flooding into a darkened room through a window. (Source: DigiPen student art by Brian Kent.)

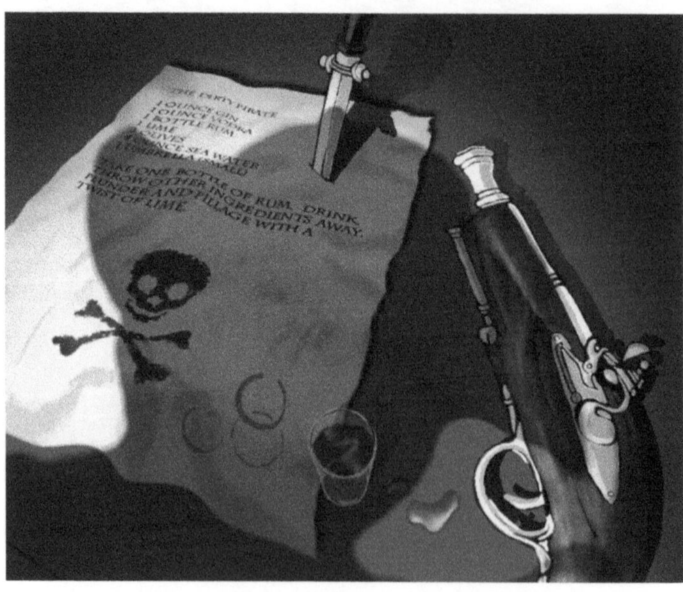

The same shot, but this time light by a softer, interior illumination. (Source: DigiPen student art by Brian Kent.)

Perspective and Lines of Focus

Pretty much all backgrounds will involve some kind of perspective. This is true both for exteriors and interiors.

A starkly lit, bleached scene invoking a strong, unforgiving, sunlit effect. Note how the acute perspective draws us into the center of the shot where the character is. (Source: DigiPen student art by Nick Wiley.)

Panning background layout illustrating interior perspective. (Source: *Endangered Species*.)

The most powerful compositions of all, however, are where the lines of perspective or any other directional lines within the background layout converge to a specific location in the shot. This location is ideally the point where the animated action is going on, fully exploiting these graphic dynamics.

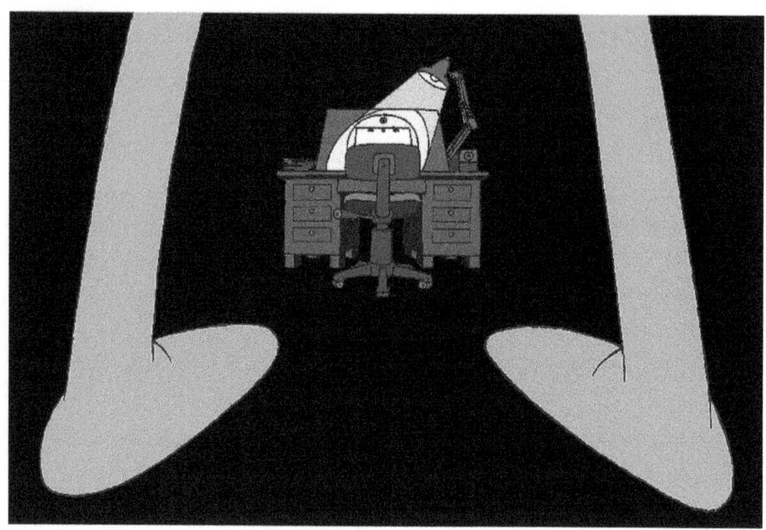

See how the perspective on the feet draws us toward the distant desk. (Source: Early animatic color sketch, *Endangered Species*.)

Verticals in Panning Shots

If you need to create a long, horizontal background for a panning shot, avoid too many verticals, especially closely spaced verticals! This is because there will be the risk of a significant amount of strobing (jittery flickering). This is especially likely if the distance the vertical lines are apart corresponds very closely to the panning distance the artwork is moved frame by frame.

Excellent environment work but could cause strobing problems with poor camerawork decisions due to so many vertical elements (including shadows) in the location. (Source: DigiPen student art by John Hall.)

Strobing can be avoided, however, if:

1. The vertical lines are set further far apart and are randomly spaced.

If the trees were predictably vertical (as they usually are with most background art), then there might be problems with panning in this scene. However, based on observations from real life, this scene is much more photographically acceptable. (Source: DigiPen student art by Jeff Weber.)

2. The lines of the artwork are not perfectly vertical but angled, in varying directions if possible.

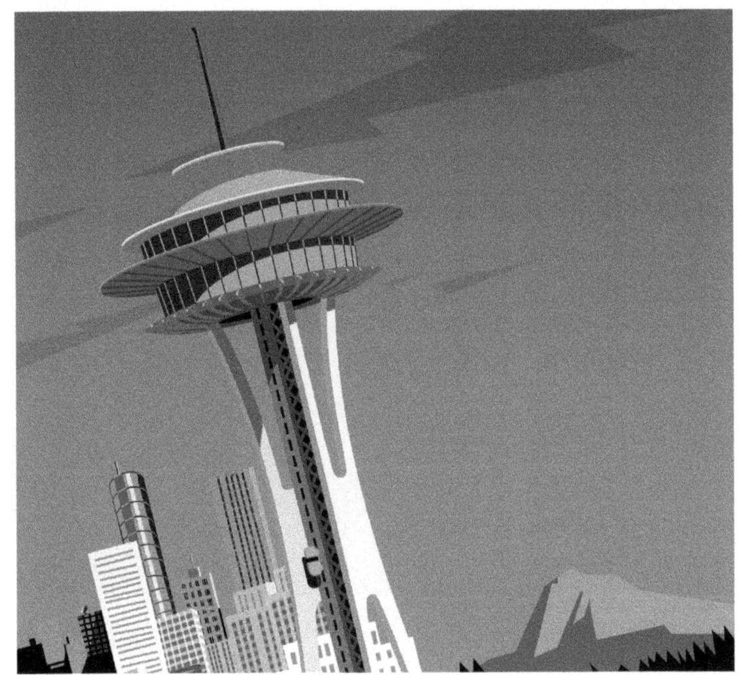

Beautiful illustrative design, and additionally attractive from a camera pan point of view with all the angled verticals. (Source: 2008 2D Or Not 2D Animation Festival poster art by Peter Moehrle.)

Light Against Dark, Dark Against Light

Often poor backgrounds are painted so that the color values behind the character(s) are very similar to the color values selected for the character(s). This makes it very difficult for the audience to differentiate one from the other.

A deliberately underlit scene, illustrating the difficulty of seeing a character with similar color values to that of the background. (Source: DigiPen student art by Greg Attick.)

Therefore, when painting your background always keep in mind this golden rule in terms of clarity: Light objects show up against darker backgrounds, and dark objects show up against lighter backgrounds. Always bear this in mind when selecting background colors and textures that are to go behind the foreground characters.

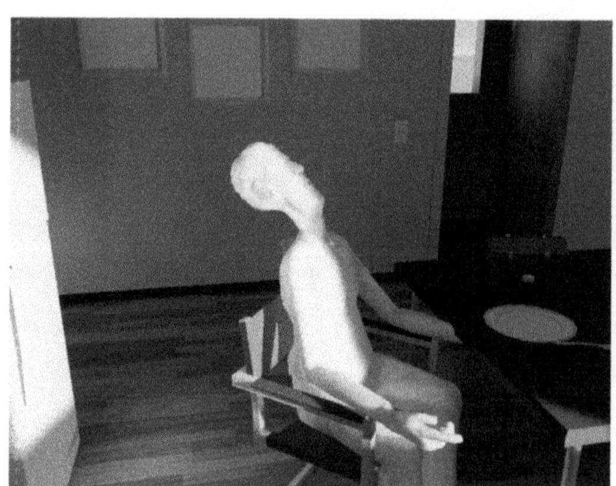

Similar to the previous figure, but these color/lighting tests show how a well-lit character can stand out well against a low-lit background. (Source: DigiPen student art by Greg Attick.)

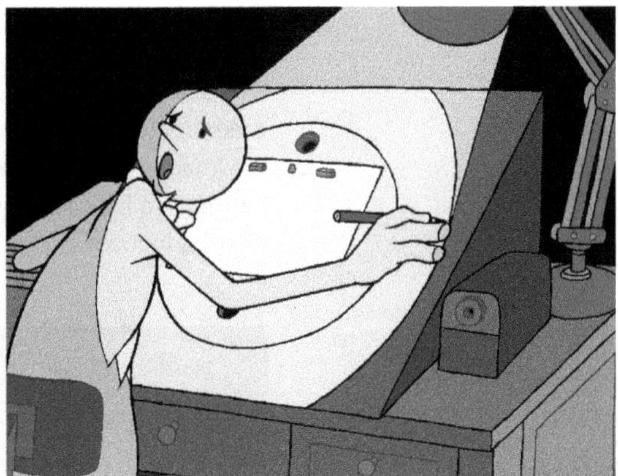

Early color sketches illustrate how the use of a strategically positioned light beam can draw the audiences' eyes to the center of the action. (Note, incidentally, that the frame to the left uses dark gray values instead of pure black to suggest darkness. The frame to the right uses pure black, which is not nearly as elegant or natural to look at.) (Source: First-pass animatic frames, *Endangered Species*.)

Area of Greatest Contrast

When coloring your background, remember the eyes are instinctively drawn to the area of the greater contrast in the scene. Therefore, it might be necessary to implement this fact with your background color work, depending on the particular requirements of the scene in question, of course.

Haunting 3D environment that illustrates how the eyes are indeed drawn to the most intensely lit area. (Source: DigiPen student art by Ryan Miller.)

Use Your Eyes

There are many other rules of painting and/or design that can be found in other books or online tutorials. However, the best teacher of all is through the images you capture with your own eyes! Train yourself to really *see* what happens to light and color values in the world around you, whether that world is indoors or out.

Deep and moody, but note that the eyes are again drawn to the point of greatest illumination. (Source: DigiPen student art by John Hall.)

Also, note how light and shade define form and shape. See, too, how various color values and textures play off one another to define space and dimension. The secrets are constantly all around you, waiting for discovery. You just need to train your eyes, and your consciousness, to see and appreciate them.

Contrasting significantly from the previous illustration, here the eyes are drawn to the darkest shadow area. (Source: DigiPen student art by Eric Wiley.)

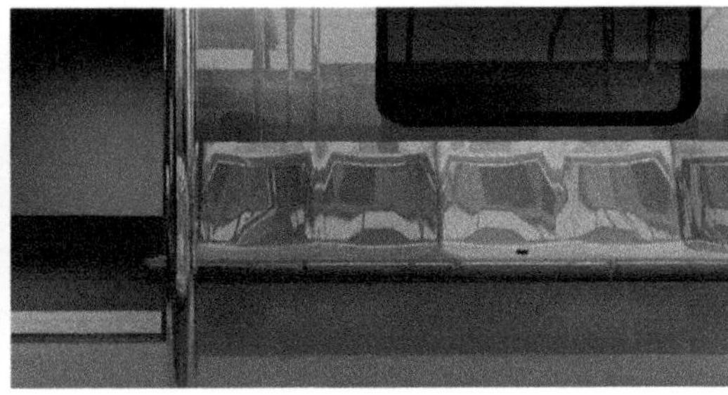

Reflective and differing surfaces define shapes skillfully here. (Source: DigiPen student art by David Vandevord.)

Assignment

Paint all the backgrounds for your film. But as you do so, work with a final colored version of the character(s) required in each scene, so you know exactly what will work and what is not in the final analysis.

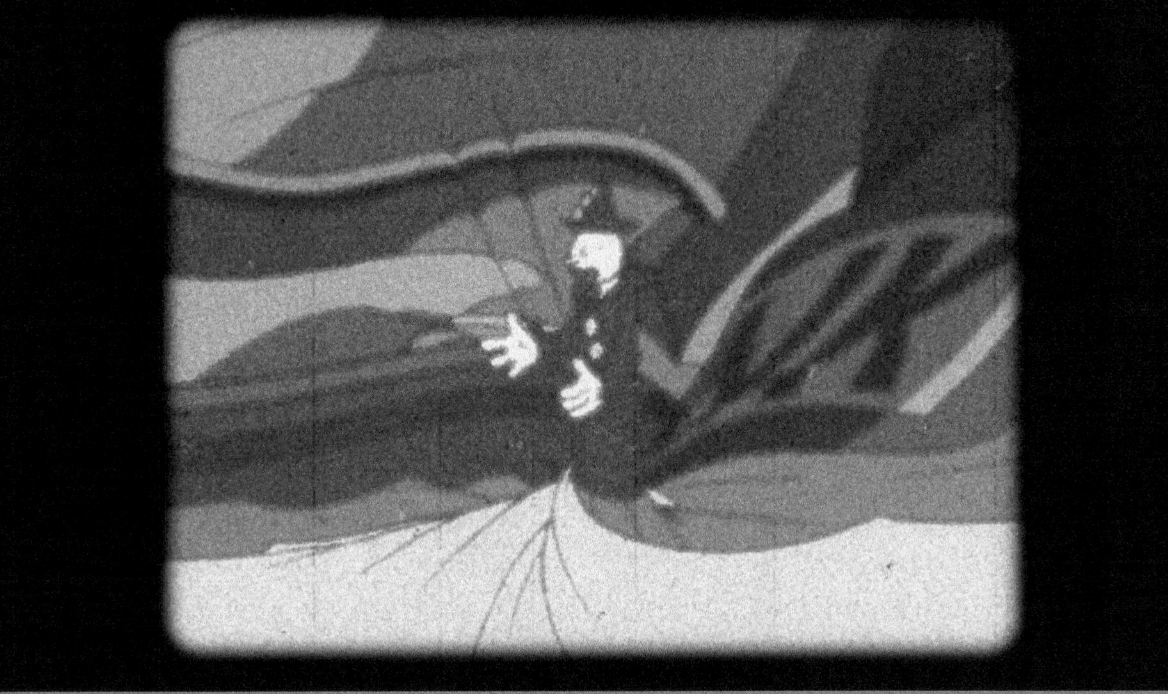

Coloring

Coloring animation once it has been scanned is a relatively easy operation. Of course, a lot depends on the approach and software selected, but by and large, digital coloring is more of a process of tedium than technique. In the old "cell" days, animation drawings used to be hand traced or (later) Xeroxed onto clear acetate sheets called *cells*. These were then painted on the back with opaque paints so that the paint didn't go over the trace lines. The sheets were then turned over again for frame-by-frame shooting over a colored background.

In predigital times, animated images were combined entirely on film using several passes in exposure. In a case where this clown is to be seen on a separately shot background, there would need to be a "male" matte in the shape of the clown's silhouette and a "female" matte in the shape of the background minus the clown's matte. Each one of these, for every frame of film, would need to be hand traced and colored! (Source: *Endangered Species*.)

Nowadays, everything can be handled digitally in one program and ultimately exported as a final movie file. A lot will depend on what software you are using, of course, but a program like Digicel's Flipbook Pro can handle the pencil testing, line tracing, and the coloring aspect of your animation artwork. Similarly, if you are looking to work in a vector environment, then programs like Macromedia's Flash, Cambridge Animation's Animo, or ToonBoom Technology's ToonBoom Studio will give you a similar capability.

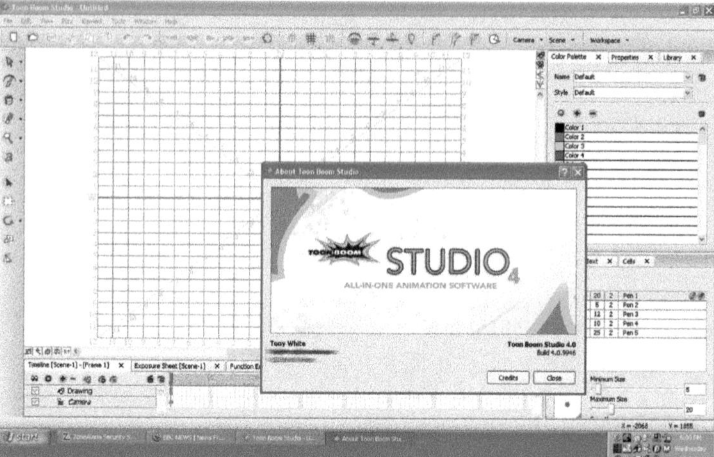

ToonBoom Studio, an answer to every vector animator's prayers!

For ease of operation, I tend to use ToonBoom Studio, but often work with Adobe Photoshop (combined with Adobe Premiere and sometimes Adobe After Effects) to get a more sophisticated illustrative look.

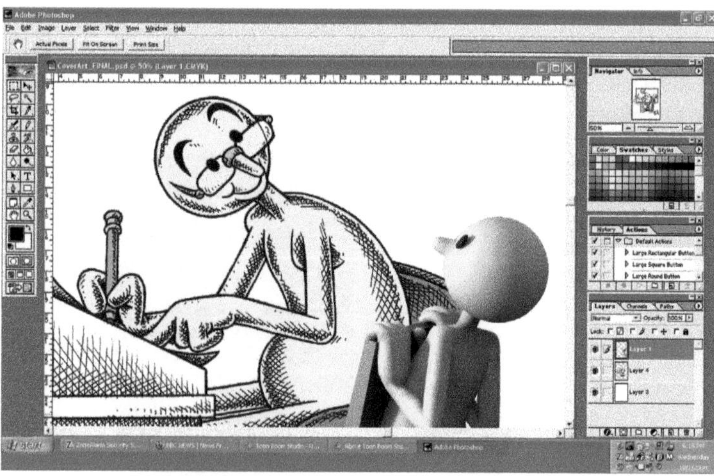

Adobe Photoshop, also an answer to every artist's dreams!

Essentially, once you have inked and scanned your artwork you can import it into whatever program you are able to use. With ToonBoom Studio there is an easy setting on the exposure sheet that lets you import and vectorize all your drawings at once.

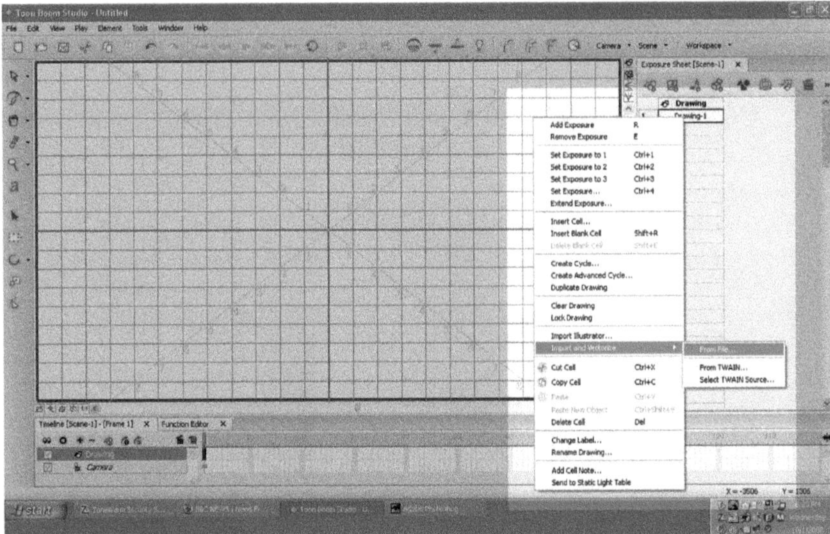

ToonBoom Studio offers a very versatile menu for preparing your work in any way you like for the program's vector environment.

Remember that with Toon Boom Studio you can choose whether you want your drawings imported as one's or two's or even four's or eight's.

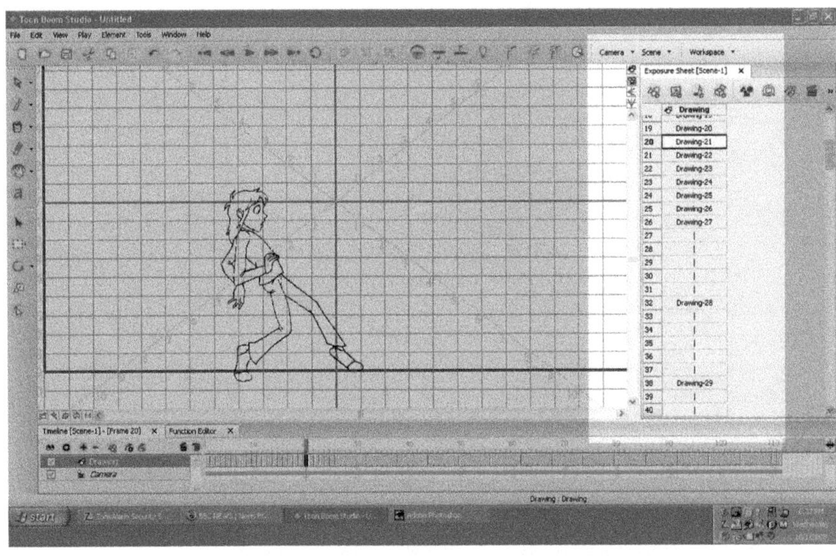

Frame changes can be made individually or as a batch. (Source: Student art by Saille Schumacher.)

Once your drawings are imported, it is really a simple process of coloring the areas of these drawings with the colors you previously chose for your character model and color design work. You can even choose colors by giving them a numerical RGB (red, green, blue) value if you want.

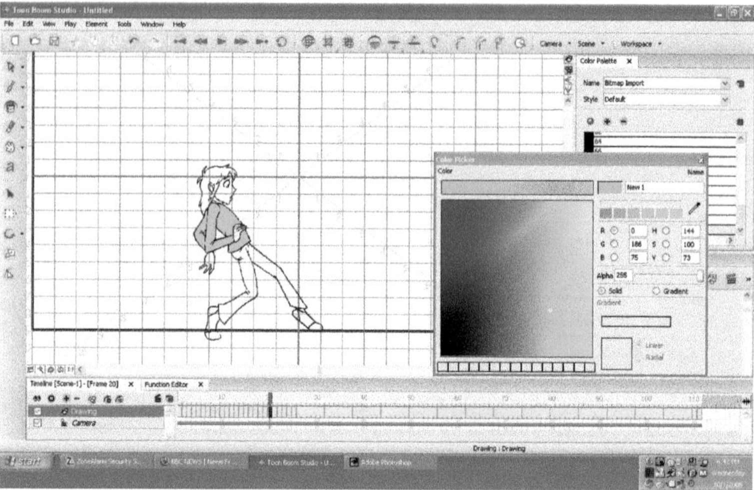

The color palette is easy to use and makes coloring vector animation versatile and very easy. (Source: Student art by Saille Schumacher.)

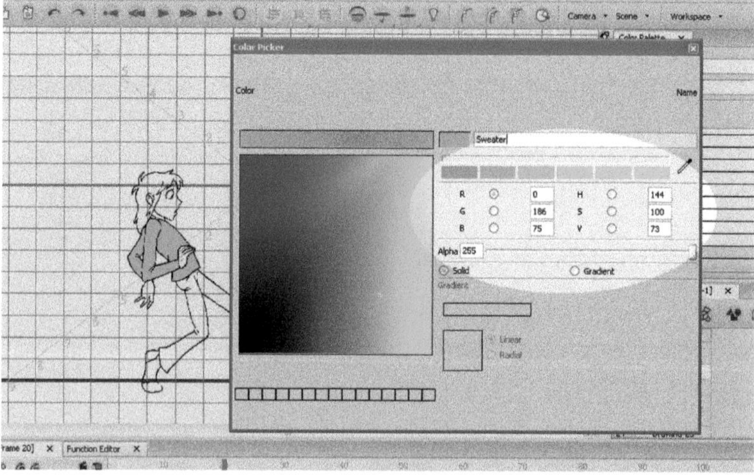

Choose colors by values instead of a regular palette if you like. (Source: Student art by Saille Schumacher.)

Digital coloring is simply a process of selecting the color you want to work with and touching the screen in the area you want the color applied. The color floods out to the boundaries of the drawing area selected.

Just touch the screen with the "Paintbox" tool and the color immediate floods out to fill the area. (Source: Student art by Saille Schumacher.)

Some digital programs allow you to automatically color a sequence of frames in a particular color, as long as the area you want to color is contained in the same area of the screen where the cursor is located on the first touch. More often, you have to manually apply the color on a frame-by-frame basis as the drawings progressively move across the screen. Once you have completed one color you can move onto another color and complete that throughout the sequence. This is repeated until all the colors for all the drawings are completed within the scene.

Unlike the predigital days when cells needed to be colored with paint and brushes, and then left in racks to slowly dry, modern coloring can be done in seconds. (Source: Student art by Saille Schumacher.)

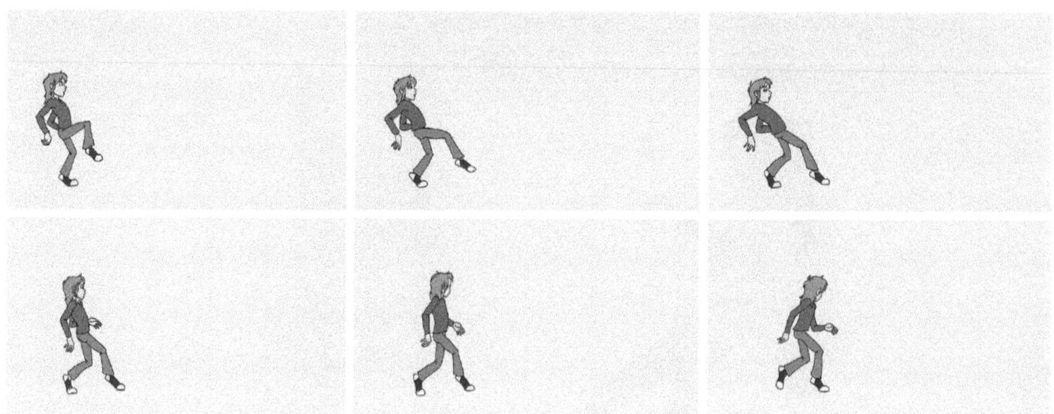

Whether it is 6 drawings or 600, digital coloring makes the big studio opportunities happen on your own desktop. (Source: Student art by Saille Schumacher.)

The only drawback with digital coloring is if your original artwork has gaps in the containing lines, the color being applied will tend to flood out to the surrounding areas, possibly the whole screen in some circumstances!

With a hole in the line of the leg, the color floods out and fills the screen. (Source: Student art by Saille Schumacher.)

That said, it is a relatively simple operation to hand join the gaps before applying color. However, this is a nuisance if you merely want to work quickly through the scene with one color selection after another. Remember, it is much wiser to ensure that you don't have any gaps in your artwork at the clean-up and inking stage. (See chapter FP16 – "Clean—up").

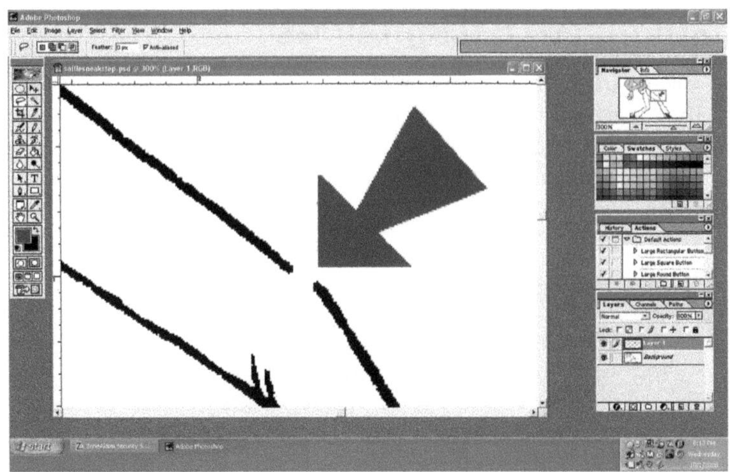

Be sure to fill in all the gaps before you scan, otherwise you'll waste time trying to do it digitally after the color floods. (Source: Student art by Saille Schumacher.)

When dealing with backgrounds, there are two options in terms of coloring; three, if you consider not coloring at all, with perhaps a pure white screen or just black line drawings on white. Most films have colored backgrounds, however, and so the two choices are flat-colored artwork from within the program or importing artwork into the program.

It's rare that animation is seen on blank white screens these days, as clients and investors insist on getting every cent's worth of color in every shot! However, it can happen, and it can be quite refreshing.

Flat-Colored Backgrounds

Flat-colored artwork is treated in exactly the same way as animated drawings are. The line artwork is imported into the program on the lowest layer and colored digitally. It is very difficult to get subtlety with the coloring, but it can be visually exciting, and in keeping with the flat-coloring style of the animation.

Most Web and TV animation strongly relies on flat-colored backgrounds in the digital age. (Source: Art by Katy McAllister.)

Imported Background Artwork

Imported artwork can give you the opportunity of using a traditional, painted background look. As previously discussed, digitally created backgrounds can be as effective as traditionally colored ones, created in any of the specific paint programs that allow for this. With the artwork finished (to the final size of the animation artwork), it is imported, usually in a bitmap format, into the program on the lowest layer.

Moody nighttime atmosphere created in a Macromedia Flash environment. (Source: *Fire Gods*.)

The only drawback with having traditionally styled artwork behind flat-colored animation drawings is that there could be a diversity of style that doesn't fit together comfortably. Too often flat-colored animation drawings on highly painted backgrounds feel out of place, so filmmakers should always adjust their coloring and painting styles to accommodate this to some extent.

This highly original scene is uniquely created using a textured background beneath with flat-colored animation overlaid with transparency to give it a subtle see-through look that echoes an early cave painting style. (Source: *Fire Gods*, by Saille Schumacher.)

Ultimately, whatever kind of visual effect and style of software you choose, the coloring of animation artwork is a vastly less-challenging process than it was in the good-old cell coloring days, where drying of wet paint, the problems of color opacity, and going over line edges were always a challenge. Consequently, animated filmmakers today should be extremely grateful to the pioneers of digital technology for making the painstaking and messy process simple and pain free!

Assignment

Color all your animation drawings from scene to scene and double-check that you haven't missed any colors or colored any particular areas incorrectly.

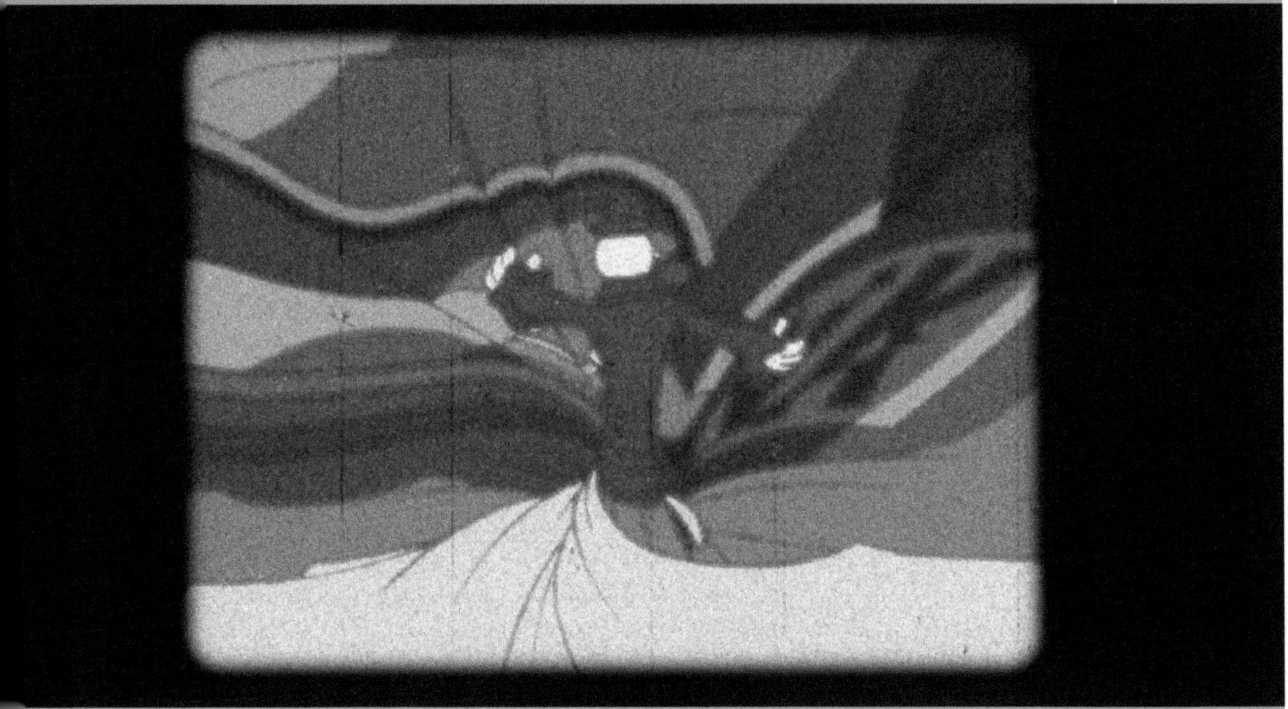

Compositing

With most digital programs today, compositing is taken for granted. With animation placed and colored on differently layers, the background on the bottom layer, and a title or even animated effects on a top layer, it is now comparatively easy to render the whole thing out into a movie format without realizing that you are indeed compositing the scene.

The opening title sequence for *Fire Gods*, where various animation and special effects layers were created in Adobe Photoshop and then rendered out in Adobe Premiere.

Indeed, 99 percent of the time that is probably all you'll ever need to finish your film. However, there are occasions when you'll want to go further than this, and so I would like to just mention a few key compositing approaches you might want to consider.

Layers

Often it is necessary to combine layers of action to create a specific effect. For example, for a recent *Fire Gods* project, I needed to create a long panning scene that required specific levels of the background scenery to move at different speeds from each other. I ended up using three different background layers, two layers of chimney smoke, two layers for machine animation, and one layer of character animation.

Note

The three separate layers of this are discussed and illustrated in MC6 on page 131.

The end of the Industrial Revolution scene in *Fire Gods*, where multiple layers were created to have a multiplane pan to this position; the moving bottles, the seated character, and the slightly transparent smoke were all combined together in Adobe After Effects.

To achieve this specific parallax-layered effect, I used Adobe After Effects, although other programs such as Autodesk's Combustion work equally well. As most people know these days, After Effects is something of a mix between Adobe Photoshop and Adobe Premiere—that is, image-manipulation software combined with movie-editing software. As with Photoshop, After Effects enabled me to remove matted areas of each layer that I didn't want the audience to see via alpha channels. However, in the following figure, I chose blue as my selection color.

The inset shows the initial 3D model of the glassmaker, Dale Chihuly, before he was added into the larger, multilayered scene, including glass hair and a panning composite of a typical Chiluly outdoor exhibition The blue background surrounding the model in the inset was removed, allowing it to be composited into the scene with a minimum of effort. (Source: *Fire Gods*, 3D Model and Animation, Royal Winchester.)

It would be equally possible to use another solid color for these areas. The green-screen approach for live-action and special effects filming is the one you'll probably have heard of most. In this approach, a background environment is shot separately to the actor's action.

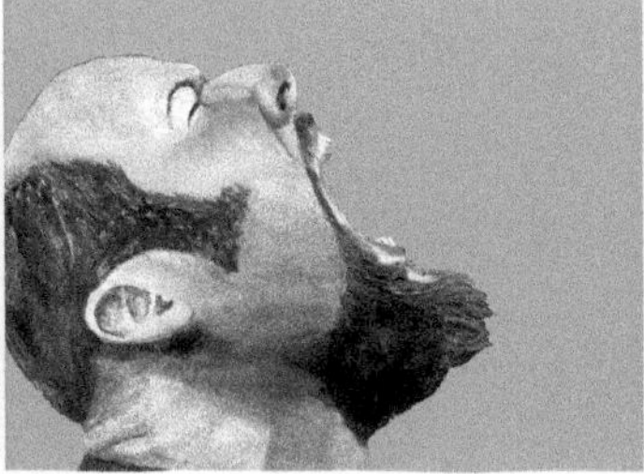

As an experiment to indicate the process of green-screen matting, I took a portrait image (left) with an environment design (right) and proceeded to combine them using a green-screen version of the portrait (center). (Source: DigiPen student art by D. Macdonald [portrait] and J. Ngyuen [environment].)

In conventional filmmaking, the actor is shot against a green-screen background. Everything that is green in that layer can be digitally removed when combined with the required background environment "plate," giving the illusion that the character was actually filmed within it in the first place.

The final composited green-screen piece. (Source: DigiPen student art by D. Macdonald [portrait] and J. Ngyuen [environment].)

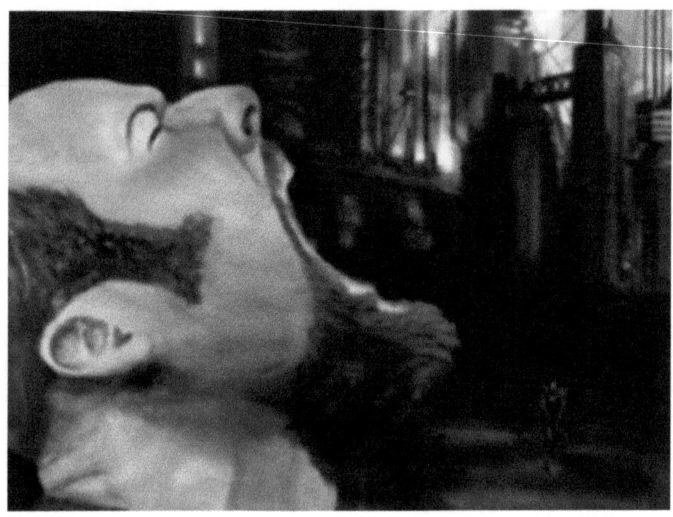

Transparency

Another exciting possibility of compositing your work in separate layers is the fact that you can create things like a transparent visual effect. This is essentially something that is easy to create, whether the object of attention is moving or static. I used the effect in the following figure for an image in my book *Animation from Pencils to Pixels*.

Multiple photographic images composited with transparency over a static background.

I also used transparency for a short sequence in my film *Endangered Species*, where I produced a ghost effect in homage to Richard William's Academy Award–winning TV special, *A Christmas Carol*. The original more effectively created the transparent ghost effect by skillfully compositing the layers on film instead of using digital technology.

The ghost effect, created by making the distant character transparent. (Source: *Endangered Species*.)

However, if you don't have After Effects or a program like it, you can achieve the same effect in something like Adobe Photoshop, then composite everything in a film-editing program like Adobe Premiere.

Cycle Animation

A good way of getting good mileage from your animation is to composite a repeat walk (or run) cycle with a long-panning background action. This is something that digital technology is especially good at. Indeed, I once ran a course that specifically demonstrated how you could do this using Adobe Photoshop.

Although looking complex and hand-crafted, this entire scene (showing the character walking from the far right of the screen to the far left) was actually used creating a simple walk cycle, a background, and a tree overlay! (Source: *Fire Gods*, by Saille Schumacher.)

As scenes are created in layers, it is possible to place the walk action on the upper layer and pan the background artwork past it on the lower layer. For example, I took the last example, and kept the background static and had the animation cycle pan across the shot, frame by frame (see the following figure).

Here, the three individual layers of the previous scene are presented as the tree overlay (covering up the panning walk cycle beneath it), the walk cycle level itself, and the static background. (Source: *Fire Gods*, by Saille Schumacher.)

This gives the very effective illusion of the character walking while the panning background suggests that he is covering a significant amount of ground (i.e., as if the camera is tracking along a scene with the character).

Depth of Field

Lastly, the ultimate sense of depth in a scene can be achieved by manipulating its depth of field. This effectively means changing its focus throughout its various layers. Returning again to our foreground/ background layering approach, it can be very effective if we throw the background out of focus while keeping the foreground action sharp. Occasionally, the opposite is effective too, with the foreground blurred and the background sharp.

Here the background is blurred with the character sharp. (Source: *Fire Gods*, by Monte Michaelis.)

Here he is blurred while the background has been kept sharper. (Source: *Fire Gods*, by Monte Michaelis.)

Titles and Effects

An incredible compositing effect we can utilize is adding titles or animated special effects. Adding titles is self-explanatory. The following figure shows that a titling effect can be achieved at the compositing stage by adding an additional layer on top of everything. The title can be either static or moving, of course. Digital technology is very capable of achieving either without too much struggle.

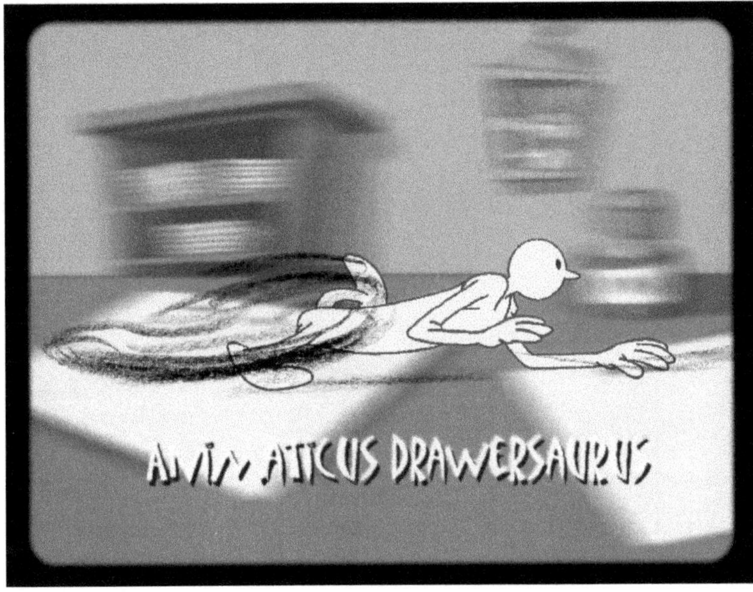

A *Roadrunner* homage sequence. The title is much more visible in the actual sequence as the background is speeding past, highlighting more than is evident here. (Source: *Endangered Species.*)

Assignment

Create any animated effects or titles that you require for your film and then composite them together on layers. If you find that the effects don't work in quite the same way that you envisaged, research other techniques and approaches that might work better for you.

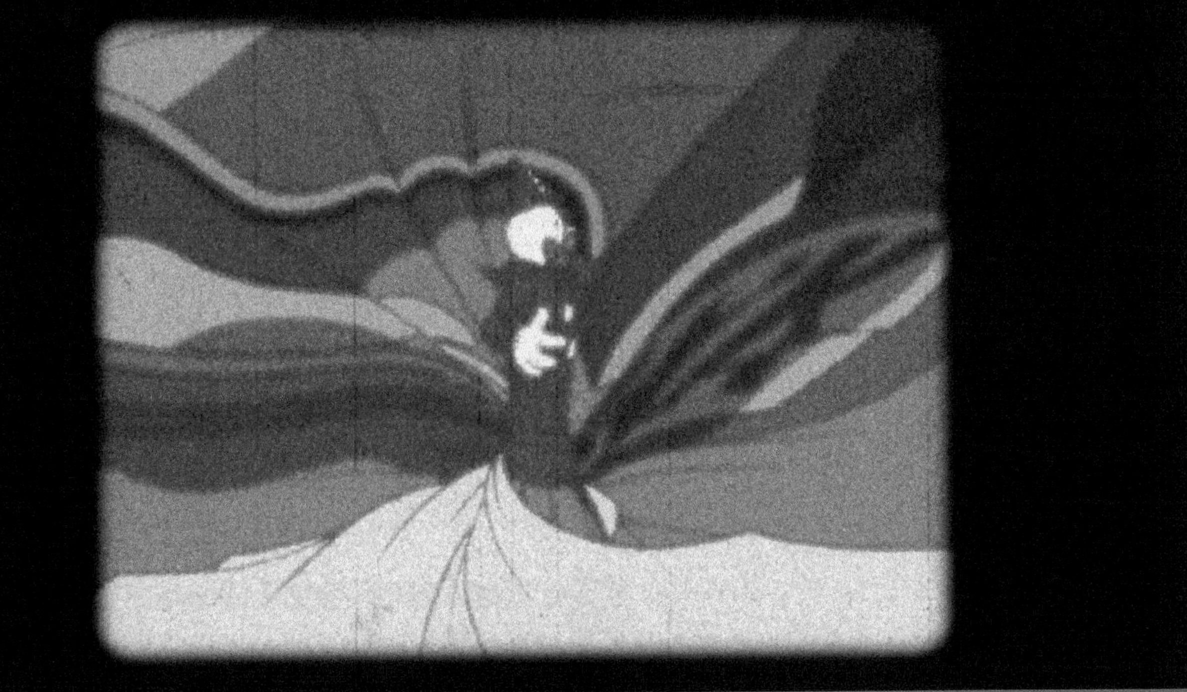

Rendering

Rendering is the stage in production when all the work created so far, and all the data generated during the digital process, are brought together and converted into a film file that can be played back by anyone, at any time, on a standard digital movie player. The file formats most conventionally used are mov (QuickTime) or avi (Windows Media), although there are many others available, especially those for the MP4 format (e.g., video i-Pods).

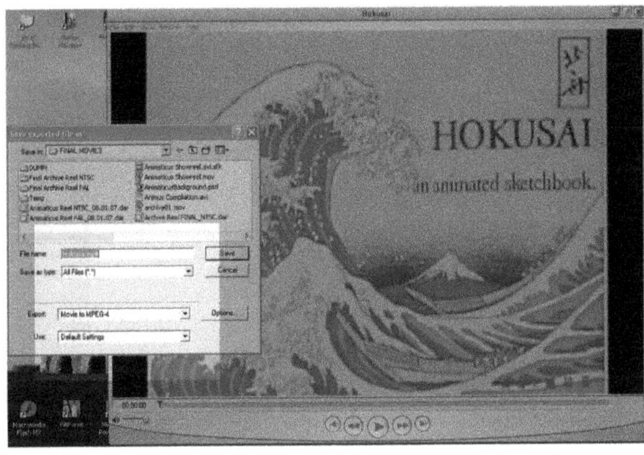

QuickTime 7.5 allows you to export any movie to an MP4 format, which is ideal for today's distribution on the Web via YouTube, blog sites, etc. (Source: The author's own British Academy Award-winning short film, *Hokusai, An Animated Sketchbook*.)

Rendered movie files can be outputted in a number of different shapes, sizes, resolutions, and playing speeds. This means that before you even start animating you really need to consider the size of the screen format you want to use, the quality of image (i.e., resolution) you need to render, and the speed of frames per second (fps) that the film will run at when viewed by your target audience.

Screen Format Ratio

The screen format ratio really has to be decided right up front, before you even begin to put pencil to paper, or cursor to screen. The *screen format ratio* is basically the shape of screen your film will be seen on. For example, if it is for a standard TV or computer monitor, you will need to work in an academy screen format, which is essentially a 4:3 ratio. This means that for every four units of measurement wide, your artwork should be three units high.

Standard academy format.

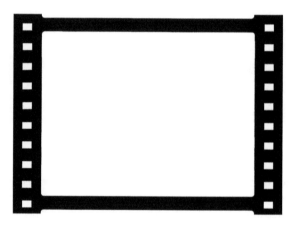

Today, the most common screen format size (outside of regular TV) is widescreen (or 16 × 9 inches), which is a 1.85:1 format. This requires that for every 1.85 units the work area is wide, it has to be 1 unit high. This widescreen format ratio is for cinematic projection; for high-definition TV widescreen the format is 1.78:1.

Widescreen format.

Very similar to widescreen, the high-definition format.

Although these two dimensions are slightly different, they both tend to be generically termed as *widescreen* or *16 × 9* formats. Sometimes they're more generically known as *letterbox* formats.

Resolution

Most TV and computer monitors use a 72-ppi resolution. The measurement ppi means that for every square inch of the screen, there are 72 pixels (or points of light) × 72 pixels that create the image in that area.

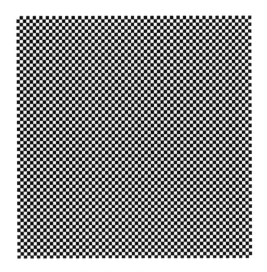

72 × 72 pixels create one square inch of a standard monitor's screen area.

Consequently, for academy format images on most monitors or screens, we are looking at a full-screen image measurement of 720 × 480 pixels (or 720 × 576 pixels for TV in the United Kingdom and other PAL-based regions).

High-definition screens, however, require a larger screen dimension. One of the most standard is 1920 × 1080 pixels. Others can be used also, as long as they conform to a basic 16 × 9 screen ratio.

Frame Rates

When animating and rendering your film, you should also become aware of the fps projection rate required at the point of exhibition. As indicated earlier in this book, the standard projection rate for film is 24 fps. On TV in the United States and other NTSC broadcast regions around the world, 24 fps or, more usually, 30 fps is the requirement. In the United Kingdom and other PAL broadcast regions of the world, the TV projection rate is 25 fps. Computers run at 30 fps and video games at 60 fps (in this case, "fields" per second, which is effectively the equivalent of 30 "frames" per second). Consequently, it is essential to know the correct frame rate for your project *before* you start to draw or create your animation, as well as when you render your final movie footage.

Assignment

Render all your final scenes at the correct screen ratio, resolution, and frame rate for your film's target audience.

Note

You do not have to wait until the very end of your production to render all your final scenes. It is invariably normal practice to render each scene as you finish it and safely store them all for when you complete your entire final render and edit.

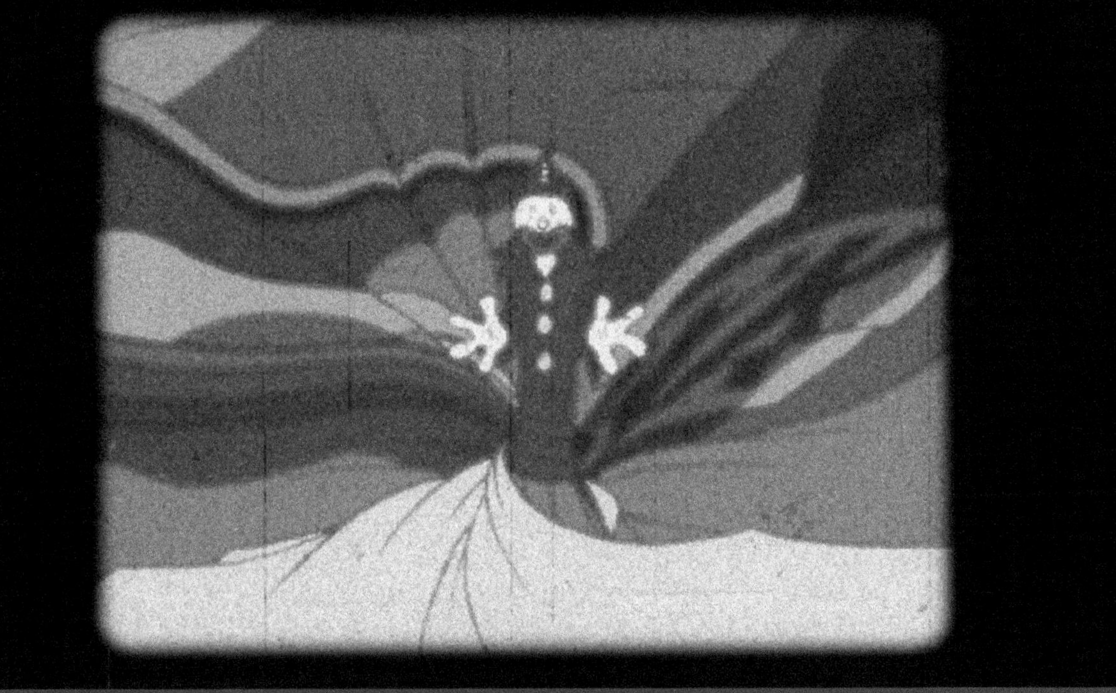

Final Edit

With all the scenes rendered into a standard movie file format that most desktop editing programs will recognize, it is now time to edit everything together to (at last!) create your first film. The final edit stage is also the time to complete the final audio track, for although your final dialog and/or narration may already be recorded, there are things like music and sound effects that you will have to bring to the party too.

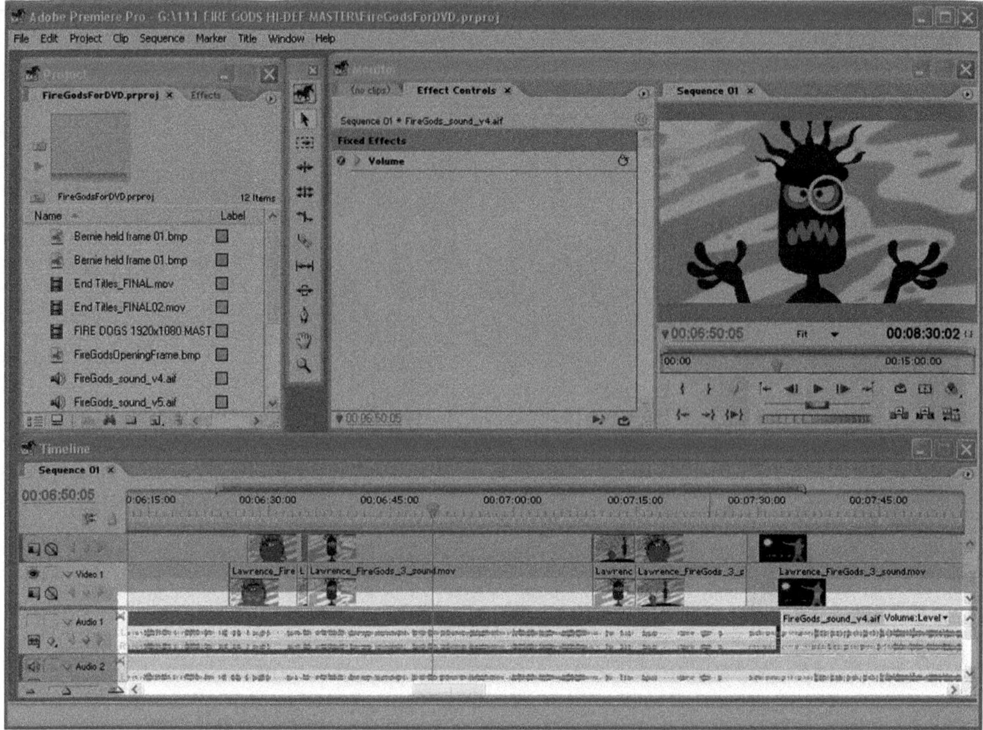

I find that my old faithful standby, Adobe Premiere, does almost everything I need in postproduction. Here, the highlighted audio track timeline allows me to do a rough mix of the final sound elements. (Source: *Fire Gods*.)

Scene Edit

I currently use a PC running a Windows operating system, so I tend to use Adobe Premiere for all my editing tasks. (Mac users will no doubt use Final Cut Pro.) Nevertheless, my version of Premiere Pro v1.5 is more than adequate to illustrate the process, I'm pleased to say.

Note

For the remainder, this is not an actual tutorial for Premiere; I am merely showing you the standard stages I go through to produce a final film.

To edit a film, I upload the separate scene files into the bin provided, then drag-and-drop them in the correct order into the timeline.

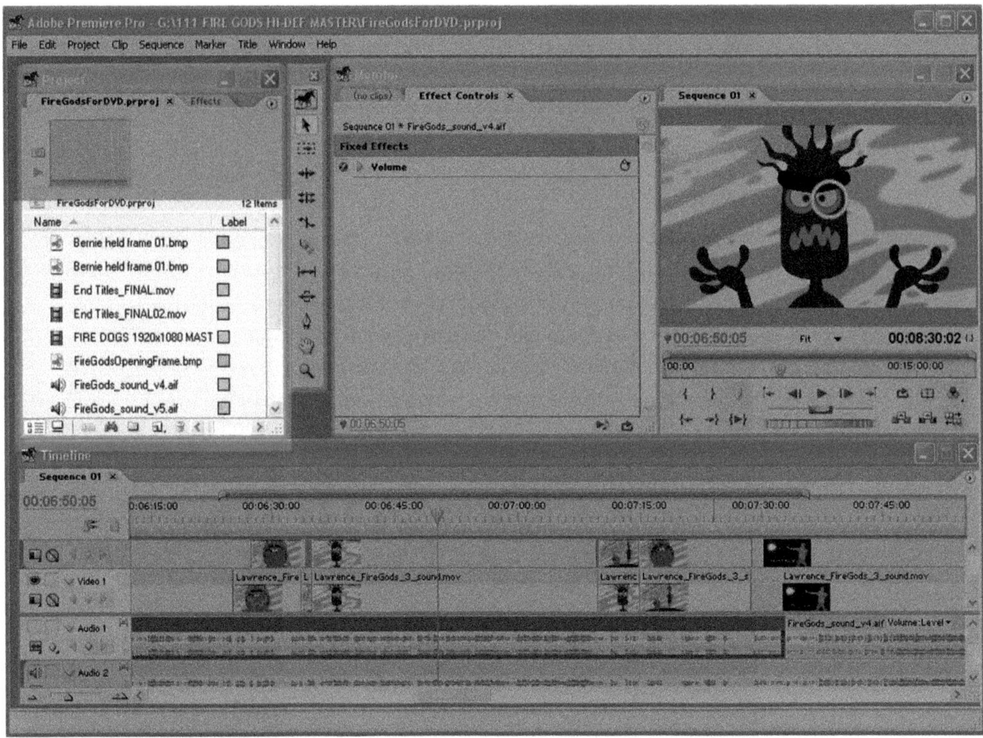

The highlighted area indicates the bin where all my film and audio files are dropped for editing. (Source: *Fire Gods*.)

Next, I import my audio tracks, especially the sound effects tracks, which I will line up with the picture by trial-and-error sliding (also known as scrubbing) to ensure that everything is in sync.

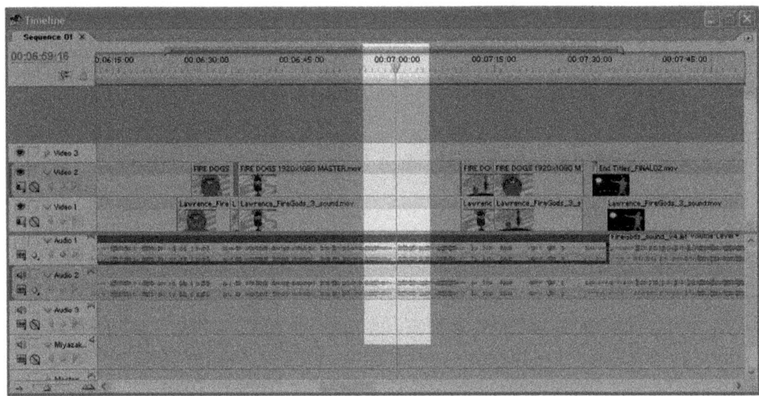
The highlighting indicates where I can scrub along the audio track timeline to identify sounds as I view the picture. (Source: *Fire Gods*.)

With everything lined up and synchronized, I first review my film by clicking the "Play" icon to see it run in the preview screen. Then, if all is well, I do a quick, small-size (say, 360 × 240 pixels) render to ensure that there are indeed no nasty glitches that an in-program preview playback may not reveal.

Note

Sometimes, if your processor speed is slow or your computer's RAM is not large enough to handle the huge volume of data often involved in a full film edit, you will get sticking, or erratic stopping and starting, on the playback that could well conceal a bad edit or a glitch in one of your renders. Rendering this out at a low resolution allows you to test everything without too much investment in time or file size.

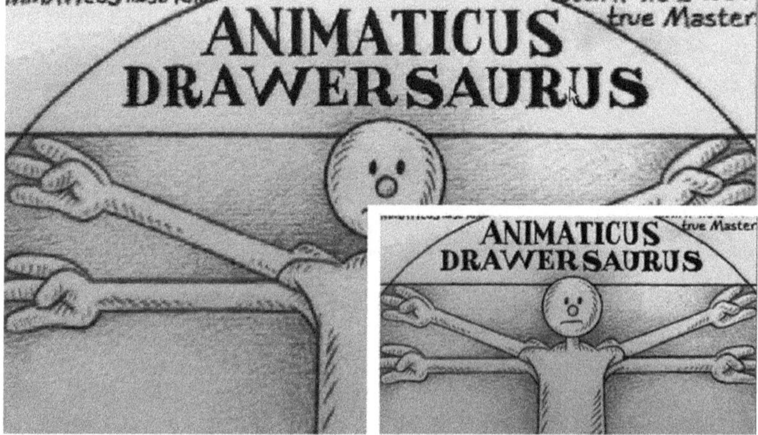

Indicating the difference in relative screen sizes between the (larger) 720 × 480 pixels screen image, I eventually favor the more workable 360 × 240 pixels (inset) that is more practical for quick and glitch-free editing. (Source: *Endangered Species.*)

Music

With all the visuals in place and looking good, I now consider the music content—that is, if I haven't already done so—as well as make a note of the points where I'll need sound effects to support the action.

Note

This can be done sooner, even at the stage when the first animatic is in place.

Music issue is a personal-taste thing. You'll either want music to go with your film or you won't. If you do want music, hopefully you will know someone who can "score" (compose) and record suitable material for you, or else you can find a young professional or student film composer who may want to produce music for you (in exchange for film credits or the opportunity to compose for an animated film). This way you shouldn't need much financial investment to get your music created. Alternatively, you might even be talented enough to do it yourself, or have a large enough budget to afford to pay a professional to do it for you!

Respected Hollywood composer, Hummie Mann.

A good place to check out is Hummie Mann's Pacific Northwest Film Scoring Program in Seattle, WA. Mann is an accomplished professional film composer in his own right and his credits appear in a large number of mainstream Hollywood movies. However, in 1997 he formed the first-ever school for would-be film composers, the Pacific Northwest Film Scoring Program. Now, years later and with many imitators following his lead, this is the premiere school in the world of composition and scoring for films, with many of his students now professionally composing scores in Hollywood.

The home page of the Pacific Northwest Film Scoring Program's web site.

The really exciting thing for student animated filmmakers, however, is the fact that if you have a completed film, Mann will present it to his students for their final project selection. Actually, his students will consider a number of competed films for their final project, but will choose just one that most inspires them musically. With their film selected, the students will then work closely with the chosen filmmaker to create exactly the kind of score that they want for their film. The really big advantage of this though is the fact that the entire finished score will be professionally recorded using a large and accomplished local orchestra. The quality of work produced this way is quite exceptional, and therefore, it is definitely a significant consideration for all student filmmakers working on their initial signature projects.

I used one of Mann's graduate students, Jamie Hall, to compose the music for my film *Endangered Species*, which won a Gold Medal award at the Park City Film Music Festival in 2007! Further information on Mann's film scoring/recording opportunities can be found at *www.pnwfilmmusic.com/default.asp*.

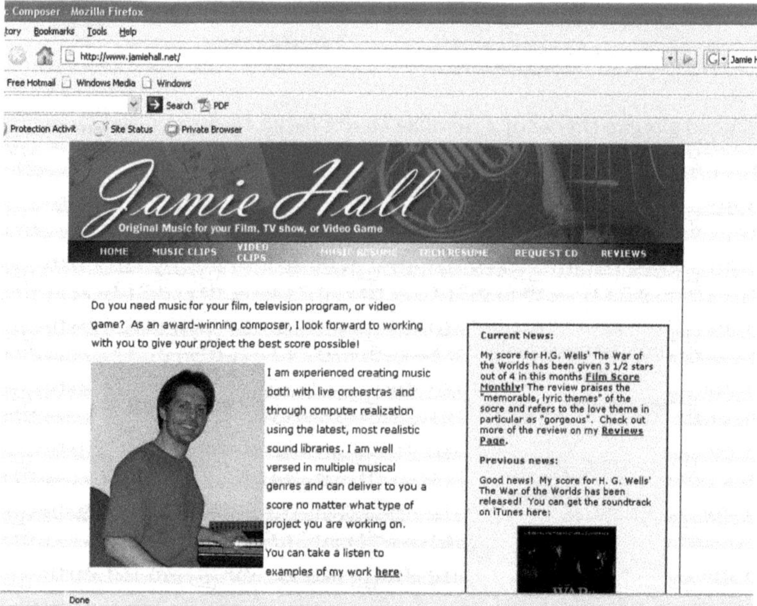

Jamie Hall's home page at *www.jamiehall.net.*

However, if you are not lucky enough to be able to take advantage of this, or the services of an accomplished student or emerging professional composer, you have the options of either having to pay the full price to get a professional to produce the music commercially, use existing music and pay a performing rights fee, or have no music accompaniment at all. That said, unless your film has a distinctly nonmusic capability, I strongly recommend that you somehow find a way of adding music to your film; if it is well performed, it can elevate even the most humble of animated material to the level of impressive—even higher!

Sound Effects

In addition to music, you will also probably need to add sound effects (SFX) to your film to lift the quality of its audio content. For example, if a character slams a door, you will almost certainly need to hear the sound of the door slamming to make it convincing. If a character is running on a muddy surface, you will probably need to hear that surface squelch every time the character's foot hits it.

There are two ways of acquiring sound effects for your audio track: getting them ready-made from a sound effects library or recording them yourself. Online sound effects libraries, such as *www.sounddogs.com*, have a vast supply of sounds that you can listen to online and acquire, either free or for a slight charge if you want them badly enough. With the latter, you at least don't have to step away from your computer to get what you want!

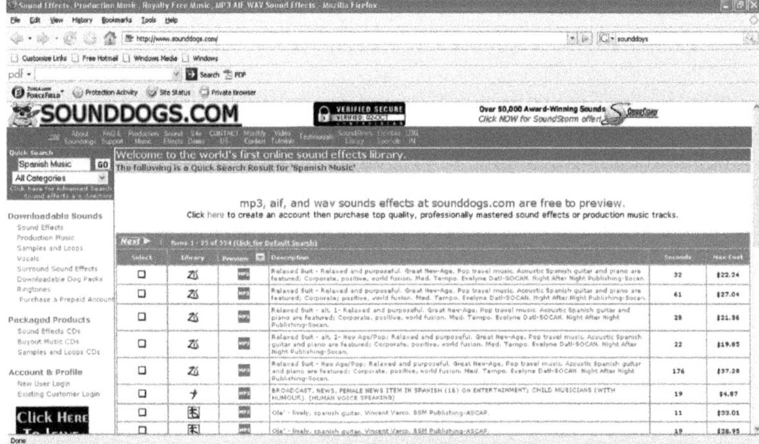

The SoundDogs home page.

Alternatively, if you need sound effects that are entirely original and unique to your film, you will have to work harder to obtain them. These days a reasonably good audio recorder is available for not too much cost (or else you might find someone who will lend you one for your recording purposes).

Most sounds can be created live. However, as you do so, you must always be aware of the ambient sounds that are all around you threatening to spoil the recording. For example, if you want a busy-street sound, it is very easy to point a microphone toward your local main road and record the sounds direct. But, if you want a clean sound of a car starting, but the only place you have to record it is a busy road, you will curse the fact that you can hear the rest of the busy-street ambient sounds that lurk in the background! Planes flying over an otherwise quiet environment can be the cause of much more stress too!

Key sound effects are much better recorded in a Foley studio. Here, footsteps are being recorded in a sound-proofed environment with an assistant walking on gravel in a box!

Another example would be when you want to record the clink of a cup being set down on a saucer. You will, of course, be better off recording it in a perfect sound-free environment, such as a recording studio, than in a busy cafeteria or living room. In any of these kinds of environment, the ambient sound will always tend to drown or subvert the specific sound you are going for.

More Foley effects. This time the sound of a crackling fire is created by the assistant ruffling a plastic bag filled with dry leaves!

The bottom line is that if you do not have a perfect recording environment to record all your "spot" effects sounds in, then you will probably be best advised to bite the bullet and either rent a studio, or else pay for the professional, prerecorded sound effects that are available from sites such as SoundDogs. Remember, you will almost certainly destroy the entire effect of a film you have spent months, or even years, on if the audio material is substandard and distracting.

Final Audio Mix

The last element of your final edit process is the mixing of your soundtrack. *Mixing* means to combine and balance all the sounds you have so they work with the picture and none dominates your audio track to the detriment of the others. The finest sound mixes are produced in a professional audio studio, of course. But you can create a passable final audio track by working with your own film-editing program.

This kind of mid-range college-level equipment will be more than adequate to provide a professional sounding audio track for your film . . . that is, if you can get access to it!

In Premiere, to get the kind of rough mix I am after; I import all my sounds and place them on a number of different audio tracks. Then, using the "Rubber Band" tool, I adjust the volume levels of the various tracks, adding fade-ups and fade-downs at the beginning and end of each audio element where necessary to give smoother transitions.

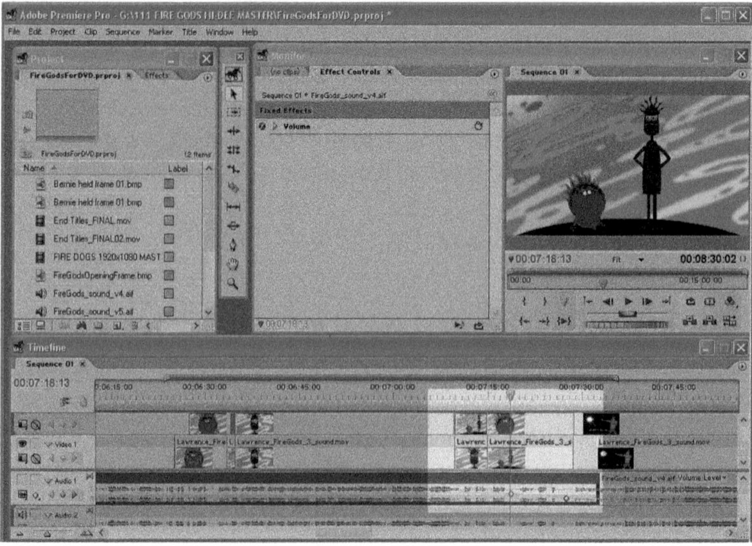

The highlighted area indicates the place in the audio timeline where simple fade-up and fade-downs can be achieved in Adobe Premiere. (Source: *Fire Gods*.)

Remember, you cannot get perfectly balanced audio tracks this way. But you can get reasonably close to that. I would suggest that as a first-time filmmaker you work in Premiere (PC) or Final Cut Pro (Mac) (or whatever film-editing program that works best for you) to create your final foundation track. This actually should be fine for all intents and purposes. However, if you find that your film is promising to be commercially successful and you want to raise it to the highest professional standards, you might just consider paying for a professional sound engineer to recreate your final mix track on professional-level equipment. This is an investment that may well prove worth it in the longer run.

Music and Effects Track

An additional final edit element you might want to consider creating for you film is an M & E (music and effects) track. M & E tracks are used when a film is required to be seen in a number of different foreign languages. So, when creating your final mixed soundtrack, you also need to mix a version where you have the music and effects on one mixed track and the dialog or narrative material on another.

That way, should your film need to be dubbed into different language versions in the future, it will only be the newly recorded foreign language version that needs to be remixed. Remember, the M & E tracks are already mixed on their own level, meaning that it is a comparatively easy job for an audio engineer to blend the new foreign language material later, once it is available.

Assignment

Edit all the final scenes together. Create and mix all the audio elements as one soundtrack too, and then render your final (FINAL!) version of the film.

Oh, and by the way, CONGRATULATIONS! You are now a proven animated filmmaker in your own right! (So, watch out Pixar or Disney!)

Appendix 1: About the Accompanying DVD

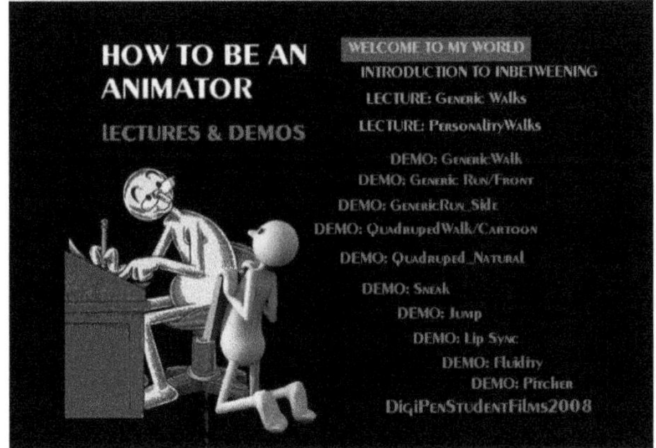

The DVD opening page menu. Click on the subject you wish to see and it will play.

With the DVD that accompanies this book, I've tried to give you the closest experience I can of being in an academy learning environment. Working with the disk space and time limitations that come with this kind of technology, I've tried to pack in as many lectures, samples of test animation, and showings of student work that I can. I've had to leave much out. But hopefully I can make more material available in other ways, specifically through my Desktop Academy web site (*www.desktopacademy.com*). However, the extensive material included here will give you a major insight into the wonderful world of animation education and discovery. It will also hopefully provide you with a sense of what it is like being in a classroom dedicated entirely to the furtherance of animation and what this fabulous art form is capable of achieving. Specifically, the disk contains the following:

WELCOME TO MY WORLD: Filmed introduction to the course and my world of animation.

INTRODUCTION TO IN-BETWEENING: Filmed lecture and demonstration on how accurate and successful in-betweens are created.

GENERIC WALKS: Filmed lecture of the process of creating effective generic walks.

PERSONALITY WALKS: Filmed lecture on how to produce advanced walks with more personality and even eccentricity.

DEMO/GENERIC WALK: Animated example of a generic walk in action.

DEMO/GENERIC RUN—FRONT: Animated example of a generic run, seen from the front.

DEMO/GENERIC RUN—SIDE: Animated example of a generic run, seen from the side.

DEMO/QUADRUPED WALK—CARTOON: Animated example of a cartoon-style quadruped walk.

DEMO/QUADRUPED—NATURAL: Animated example of a real-life quadruped.

DEMO/SNEAK: Animated example of a standard animated sneak.

DEMO/JUMP: Animated example of a generic character running and jumping.

DEMO/LIP SYNC: Animated example of lip synching through a talking pencil.

DEMO/FLUIDITY: Animated example of fluidity in movement.

DEMO/PITCHER: Animated example of a throw, based on the movements of a baseball pitcher.

DIGIPEN STUDENT FILMS 2008: Two outstanding final project films created by DigiPen students in 2008. (The proof of the pudding is in the eating!) One is a graduate team project film, the other a junior individual film. Others can be viewed on the DigiPen Institute of Technology web site at *www.digipen.edu/gallery/art/*.

I believe that the DVD will give you a comprehensive reference work of all the major principles of movement and examples of technique you will need to acquire in order for you to complete this course book. I have tried to distill my several decades of knowledge and experience into spoon-size bites that should enable you to better digest your studies more effectively. You may proceed further through the additional material and opportunities I will continue to add to my Desktop Academy web site. However, I can assure you that everything within the covers of this book and on the DVD will be more than sufficient to make you an animator in your own right. If only I could be cloned and included with each book too, then you'd have my personal feedback on your work at your disposal as well!

Appendix 2: About the Desktop Academy

The logo for the Animaticus Foundation, a non-profit organization that seeks to preserve, teach and evolve the art of traditional, hand-drawn animation.

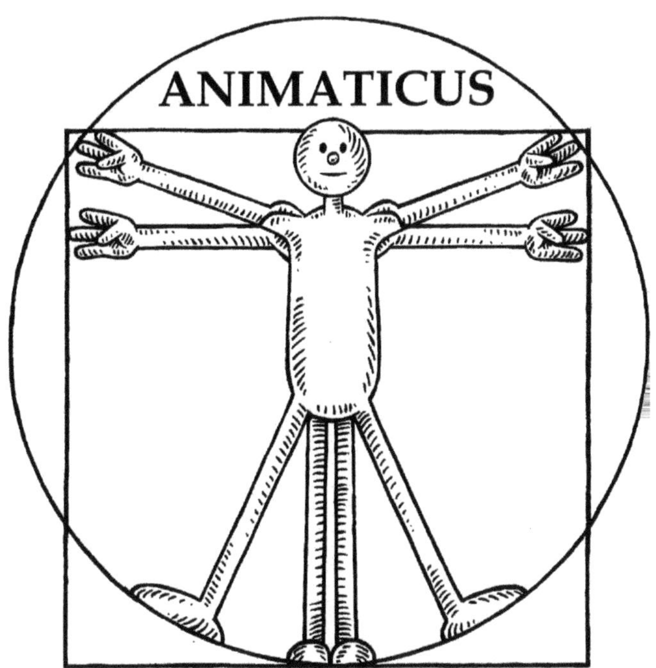

The Desktop Academy is my way of giving you further insight into the animation you will attempt during the course material contained in this book. This online facility will enable you to submit, at reasonable cost, your course work to me for evaluation and a grade. The evaluation involves my viewing your work and giving you feedback on what I feel is good about it and what I feel can be improved. I include concise suggestions and how those improvements can be made. The grading enables you to obtain credits for the ultimate indication of accomplishment, the Diploma of Animated Excellence. This diploma will indicate to potential clients and employers that you have achieved to a very high level of accomplishment all the course material contained in Part 1 of this book, which is no easy accomplishment, I can assure you.

Further details on the diploma and other animation opportunities can be found on the Academy's web site at *www.desktopacademy.com*.

Note

The main focus of the Desktop Academy is to advance the skills of traditional 2D animation in this digital age. However, student animators of all styles and persuasions can enter the Academy's Diploma course, focusing on the animation format of their choice. '2D', '3D', 'Claymation', 'Cut-out' and animators of other persuasions can also submit their work not related to this course work for criticism and review in exchange for a small fee.

Appendix 3: About the Animaticus Foundation

The 2008 poster for the Animaticus Foundation's "2D OR NOT 2D Animation Festival" . . . created by top animation industry concept artist, painter and designer, Peter Moehrle.

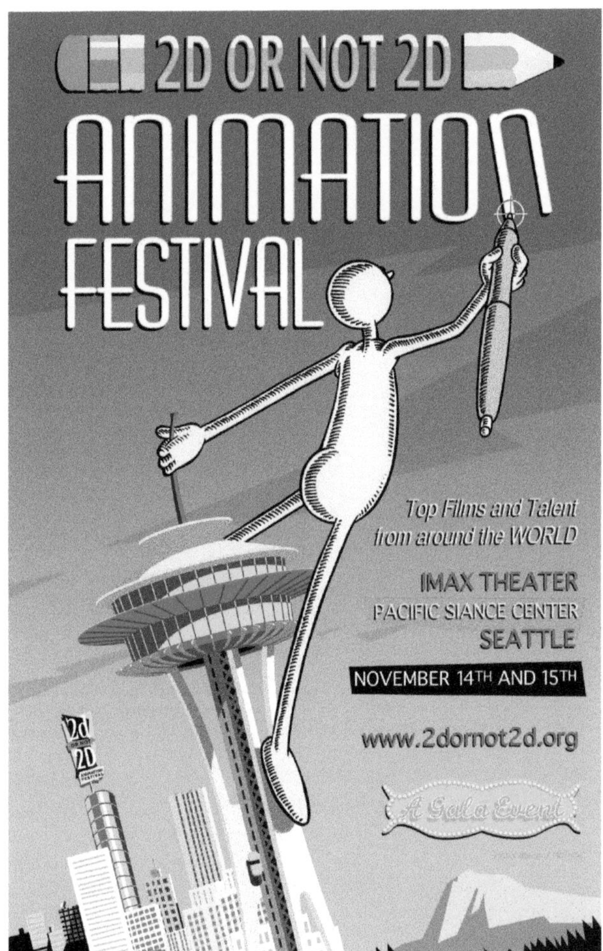

The Desktop Academy of Animation is closely affiliated to The Animaticus Foundation, an official nonprofit organization dedicated to the preservation, education, and evolution of the traditional 2D-animated art form in our digital age. The Animaticus Foundation is host to the annual 2D Or Not 2D Animation Festival, in addition to developing and ultimately producing ground-breaking animated films and allied productions. With sufficient funding, talented students will be partnered with established industry professionals to create a unique apprenticeship through projects that explore new ideas and expression of the animated art form.

Further details about The Animaticus Foundation can be found on the organization's web site at *www.animaticus.com*.

Appendix 4: About the DigiPen Institute of Technology

One of the principal supporters of the work of the Animaticus Foundation is DigiPen Institute of Technology!

When I was asked to be the Program Director and Dean of Fine Art and Animation at the DigiPen Institute of Technology in Redmond, WA, in 2008, I was extremely proud. I had long heard of the school's fast-growing and award-winning reputation in terms of programming and science, but when I joined the faculty of the art department in 2005, the new Bachelor of Fine Arts in Production Animation program was in its infancy. I was, however, immediately impressed by the philosophy of the owner of the school, the truly remarkable Mr. Claude Comair, and of its principle executives, particularly Raymond Yan, chief executive of DigiPen. Even though the school was set in the heart of the digital revolution—indeed, the heart of the games industry to be more specific—this was a learning institution that was committed to producing artists first, then digital maestros second. This effectively means that students at DigiPen spend the first one to two years of their four-year animation experience intensively studying the classic principles of art—drawing, painting, color theory, perspective, composition, and anatomy (human and animal)—before they are even given access to a computer for anything other than logging in to check their class grades! In addition to their formal classes in all these things, students are required to keep up an additional sketchbook of drawing, presenting a minimum of 50 pages per week. This encouragement to keep up their classic art skills is encouraged throughout the program, up until graduation, as the value of this is undeniable, both academically and professionally.

As soon as I began to become a part of this program (by teaching traditional principles of movement through 2D hand-drawn animation to the freshman classes), I was overwhelmed by the quality of artists that were being produced through this program. At the time the school had not graduated anyone in the BFA program, and so all I could do was rave about the program to outsiders without actually having any of the final material to show. However, in 2008, the school saw its first graduates in the spring, and the work I can now show is quite remarkable. Some of this masterly senior work, and much of the remaining school work from freshmen to juniors, is evidenced by a large proportion of the material contained in this book. I think each of these pictures truly does speak a thousand words!

I have no hesitation in saying that I believe that the current program at DigiPen is the best animation program in the country, or will very quickly establish that status if the current evolution of teaching practices consolidates and evolves. A quick examination of the school's web site at *www.digipen.edu* will detail the school's various programs and the BFA in Production Animation program in particular … in addition to science, game design and programming. The art department gallery page will more than confirm what I have said about the quality of the student's animation work. Already the industry is becoming acutely aware of the phenomenon that is DigiPen with many of the current senior students interning at such significant games studios as Arena Net, Bungie, and Microsoft. Our first-time 2008 graduates are already employed full time at many of the major games companies in the Pacific Northwest, and other students have begun to spread further, with one student snapped up by Rhythm & Hues in Hollywood.

DigiPen pioneers the way that all great animators should be taught, and I believe its eventual influence in the animation industry around the world will ultimately be significant. Students of DigiPen are not only prepared extensively for obtaining a job in the industry when they graduate but are additionally expected to be major "movers and shakers" within the industry when their imprint intensifies. We expect nothing less of a DigiPen graduate.

All this is why I am particularly proud of being the Program Director and Dean of Fine Art and Animation at DigiPen. I am proud, too, of working with so many amazing faculty members, each of whom is truly outstanding professional in their own right (and thereby undermining the myth that "those who can't … teach")! Together, I hope we are currently preparing a new generation of artists and animators whose work, in their own way and in their own time, will ultimately rival the wonderful achievements of Disney, Warner Brothers, and Pixar. This particular book-based course in traditionally based animation is very closely allied to the 2D and project programs that from just a small part of the full DigiPen BFA program in production animation!

Appendix 5: Exposure, Exhibitions, and Festivals

"If you animate it, they will come!"

Now that you have made your film, you of course want people to see it! There are a number of exhibition outlets for animated filmmakers these days, but you have to have some degree of perspective on what you can expect. Clearly, unless you have made the most fabulous, feature-length movie that is of the highest professional standard, you are unlikely to attract serious cinematic distribution. Some short films occasionally get a theatrical run with a full-length mainstream movie, but the opportunities are too few to even discuss right here and now and more than likely they are produced by the makers of the main film anyway. Pixar short films are a perfect example of this. Therefore, as an unknown yet emergent filmmaker, I advise you to focus on genuinely attainable opportunities for now, to avoid the pain of rejection later on!

For those wishing a greater depth of information, I have focused more fully on the distribution side of animation in my book, *Animation from Pencils to Pixels: Classical*

Techniques for Digital Animators. However, here are a few potted ideas that may inspire you to research and perhaps take advantage of specific market areas from the get-go.

Short Film Distribution

There is a market for distributing short animated films but it is very limited. Spike and Mike have cornered a market share here, as have the National Film Board of Canada and the AWN-backed "Show of Shows" that tours the USA each year to bring the best of animated short film production to an eager public. That said, it is reasonable to suggest that you may have trouble finding a distributor for your film if it has a running time of something around 20 minutes or less. Nevertheless, it would not hurt for you to investigate possible short-film distributors via the Web, and then see if there is any interest with them for what you intend to offer. Currently, there are a whole number of sites that will screen your film and may even offer you a small fee for every time it is seen!

Television

Unless your film is about 26 minutes long (i.e., a TV half-hour "special" length), there is also little potential for you to exhibit your film in the mainstream. The best chance you have if your film is really short is to find a slot with a more established program that allows for these kinds of short films to be featured. (For example, "The Simpsons" phenomenon started as a small animated insert in "The Tracy Ultiman Show"!) Alternatively, some lesser-known cable stations might possibly show programs that only broadcast animated short films in the first place, or else they may have "filler" spots between their programs that your film might fit into. The reality is that only half-hour TV specials, TV movie-length productions, or long-running 26–minute animated series productions are likely to bring a rewarding opportunity, and a smile of satisfaction on the face of the animated filmmaker!

DVD Sales and Distribution

The best chance of getting your film out to the public, and perhaps make a little money at the same time, is by releasing or distributing your film on a self-published DVD. That said, if your film is much less than 30 minutes, there is realistically little chance of you selling a DVD version of your film in great numbers, unless it is a top-draw, award-winning production with an international appeal. You could include it with a larger, animated film compilation release, where you and other filmmakers could each donate a film to the common cause and share the spoils if it happens to take off later. Alternatively, if your film is good enough and has appeal to a larger audience, then perhaps if you added bonus features, such as a live-action "making of" documentary and an interactive "library" of the film's artwork, it might generate enough interest or value-for-the-money appeal to get enough people to buy your product.

I-Pods, PDAs, Cell Phones, and the Web

Today, there is definite mileage in downloadable entities (such as short animated films) for owners of I-Pods, cell phones, and similar kinds of PDA devices. Everyone these days seems keen to download material from the Web that they can carry around with them and watch in their quieter moments. So your film might just fill that bill for them if it is of sufficient unique interest. You would have to initiate this process, however, by setting up your own custom-made web site, where visitors can preview a clip from your film, purchase it with a credit card, and immediately download it to their various PDA devices via your computer. This is a costly process, of course. But if you are creating a product that the public really likes, it could well be an insightful investment to make on your part.

Festivals

The really best way of getting exposure for your short film is by entering it into the numerous festivals that can be found around the world. There are a whole new generation of exciting festivals for animated films, in addition to the evergreen classics such as Annecy, Ottawa, and Zagreb. My own 2D Or Not 2D Animation Festival attracted over 30 films in 2006, its inaugural year, and then over 65 in 2007. This number of entries went even higher in 2008. Most of these films were clearly worthy of exhibition, and so we were able to screen the vast majority of them to an enthusiastic public. On top of this, our Golden Pencil awards gave eight animated filmmakers increasing status, meaning their films now have a higher profile and pedigree attached to them when they are seeking further exposure through television, DVD, the Web, and the other distribution avenues available. Multiply these eight by all those in the other animation festivals out there, and you'll soon see how attractive festivals are to filmmakers in terms of exposure and word-of-mouth reputation. Additionally, many festivals offer a marketing option, where filmmakers can sell copies of their films to the general public through just giving a small percentage of the sales to the festival organizers, who have given the films the chance of exposure and sales opportunity.

Consequently, for all kinds of filmmakers who wish to seek this kind of exposure through film festivals and film festival awards, I highly recommend

Withoutabox (*www.withoutabox.com*) for providing filmmakers with a unique and incredible service. By opening a free annual filmmaker account with Withoutabox, you give yourself instant access to the majority of film festivals around the world throughout the entire year. Upon joining, you upload all your production information to your account, including "press packs" and other similar promotional material. Then, by simply clicking on a "submission" link for every festival you wish to enter, your information is automatically sent to that festival, confirming your entry. Then, once you have paid your entry fee via the Withoutabox web site at the same time, you simply have to mail your film off to the festival later, ensuring it reaches the organizing offices by the close of the entry date displayed on the site. There is nothing else to do then except wait to hear if your film has been accepted for exhibition, and hopefully later, has won an award!

By paying a little extra, you can directly upload your film to the Withoutabox web site and they will automatically forward it to the festival organizers. I have used the Withoutabox organization repeatedly (both as an independent filmmaker and a festival organizer) and I can only share with you the fact that their organization is absolutely wonderful and second to none!

The really cool thing about Withoutabox is that they list festivals by category for all filmmakers, so it is very easy to identify just the animation-only ones. Additionally, they also list festivals termed Oscar Boosters, which are festivals that if you win an award at you gain an automatic entry into the most prized award out their—the coveted Oscar! (Not easy to do otherwise!) If you can ultimately win an Oscar for your film, your reputation, as well as the reputation of your film, is made!

Appendix 6: Exposure Sheets and Production Folders[1]

Exposure (Dope) Sheets and Production Folders

Although the digital age of animation has well and truly arrived and the traditional processes are pretty much long gone now, except, of course, the importance of pencils and paper, I still find two elements of the past worth clinging to: dope sheets (known as exposure sheets or x-sheets in some quarters) and production folders. It is a popular belief that animators just sit and draw funny cartoons all day long. Well, of course, animation is a lot of that, but it is so much more about time and project management too. A good animator needs a good organized mind as well as an ability to draw. Now that animation scenes can run at a variety of different film speeds, through a variety of different screen formats, and using an infinite number of action and special effects layers in the digital environment, it is so necessary to have your thinking processes working well and consistently. Contemporary animation is now, at its core, an art, a science, and a business management operation all rolled into one!

There are other practical information elements that have to be implemented too. For example, every drawing, layout, and background have to have specific information added so they are not lost or misplaced, creating potential chaos to the production. The necessary information required in these cases would be the sequence, scene, and drawing numbers if it is a series of animation drawings or a layout (with each key also containing the required in-between chart); the sequence, scene, and background numbers, if it is a background; then all this, plus much more, if it is a production folder! Animation paperwork can be scary or tedious when you first see it, but, once explained, dope sheets and production folders can actually become your best friends!

---

[1]Source: From White, T. *Animation from Pencils to Pixels: Classical Techniques for Digital Animators*. Boston: Focal Press, 2006, pp. 349–359. Reprinted by kind permission of Focal Press.

The Dope Sheet

The dope sheet contains all the necessary information about the scene. It might serve as a "note to self" for the animator, but it also is a crucial communications tool for the assistant animator, scene compositor, and anyone else in the project's production line. The dope sheet (often, more than one page per scene) includes the sequence, scene, and page numbers information; phonetic soundtrack breakdown; the scene start and end (cut) points; the animator's action notes; animation layers; drawing order; in-between timings; detailed shooting/scanning instructions; etc. The dope sheet is the one place where you can clearly organize your thoughts and then share them with others in the team. The following figure shows a section of a typical dope sheet.

SEQUENCE	SCENE							SHEET
		5	4	3	2	1	BG	CAMERA INSTRUCTIONS

The top of a sample dope sheet.

Although dope sheets can differ from country to country, or even studio to studio, the essential information presented on them is pretty standard. The first thing to realize is that the dope sheet is comprised of many vertical columns and even more horizontal lines. However, once these columns and lines are understood, the dope sheet soon becomes a friend, rather than an enemy.

The top section has space for the sequence, scene, and page numbers information, together with additional space to write in the scene title, where relevant.

Each of these sections needs to be filled in every time a new dope sheet is used. That way, if the dope sheets ever get scattered or mixed up, this basic information makes it easy to identify and reassemble them without much fuss. That said, it is the remaining information on the dope sheet that is most necessary in the animation process.

Broadly speaking, the narrow, horizontal lines beneath the top information represent every frame of film in the scene. The vertical columns, on the other hand, represent the layers of animation, including the background. Specifically, from left to right in the next figure, these columns indicate your personal notes column, the dialog breakdown column, six columns for the initial animation layers (with digital animation there could be an infinite number of columns but the six represent the maximum levels possible for the old cell animation approach, including background artwork), and then the camera instructions column.

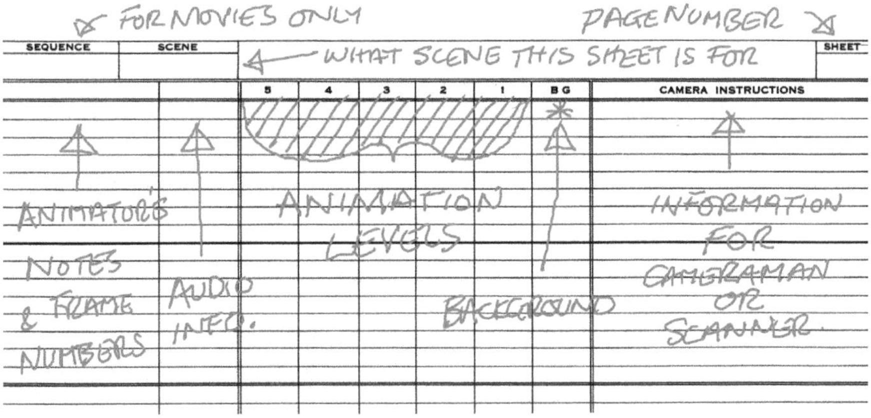

The various areas of a dope sheet.

Frame Lines

The number of frame lines representing the scene to be animated will depend on the speed and the kind of film being used. (If film is even the medium to be used!) Filmicly, there are 16 frames in every foot of 35 mm projected film and 24 projected frames for every second of film time. Therefore, if the animator is working in 35 mm film, every 16th horizontal line on the dope sheet is printed heavier, to identify each foot of film. Additionally, as 24 frames make up a second of film time, each second of film is often represented by a double line. When marking up a dope sheet on any scene I am about to animate, I always indicate each second in a circle on the left column (see the following figure).

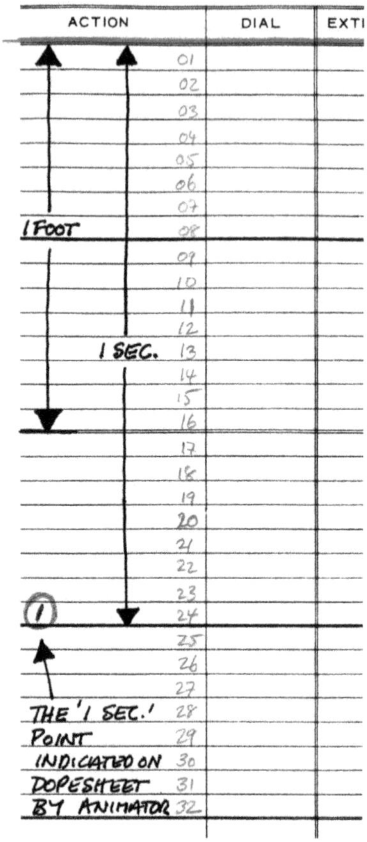

How I mark each second of film on a dope sheet.

Note

You'll need to modify the number of frame lines if you are working in any other film format or a digital environment. Most digital software defaults to 29.97 fps (frames per second) but should be taken as 30 fps for convenience sake.

Remember, too, that whereas U.S. (NTSC format) TV can broadcast films that are produced on both 30 fps and 24 fps, the U.K. (PAL format) TV broadcasts at 25 fps, which means these traditional 35 mm dope sheet markings cannot be applied so easily. Flash animation for the Web can be set to playback at any fps rate required, but the standard is 12 fps. So, as long as you remember the differences in all these formats and tailor the dopes sheets to fit the requirements of your particular production, it is perfectly okay to use the standard dope sheet format and adjust it accordingly.

01	01	01
02	02	02
03	03	03
04	04	04
05	05	05
06	06	06
07	07	07
08	08	08
09	09	09
10	10	10
11	11	11
12	12	12
13	13	13
14	14	14
15	15	15
16	16	16
17	17	17
18	18	18
19	19	19
20	20	20
21	21	21
22	22	22
23	23	23
24	24	24
	25	25
		26
		27
		28
		29
		30

Examples of one second of animation on dope sheets for 24, 25, and 30 fps.

Animator's Notes

Looking at the following figure, the far-left column is described as the animator's personal note column because it is essentially the place where you can make action notes, sketch ideas, outline frame timings, etc., without infringing on the main information sections of the dope sheet. This column is basically an ideas, time, and motion scribble pad, where you can think out loud before beginning the animation process. I also find that writing in the actual frame numbers throughout the scene helps with the drawing numbering/layering compositing process later. I have the sheets preprinted with the repeating numbers 0 through 9 on them; for greater convenience and speed, I only have to add the front number(s) ahead of them each time.

A sample of the top of a completed dope sheet for *Endangered Species*, which was animated at 24 fps throughout.

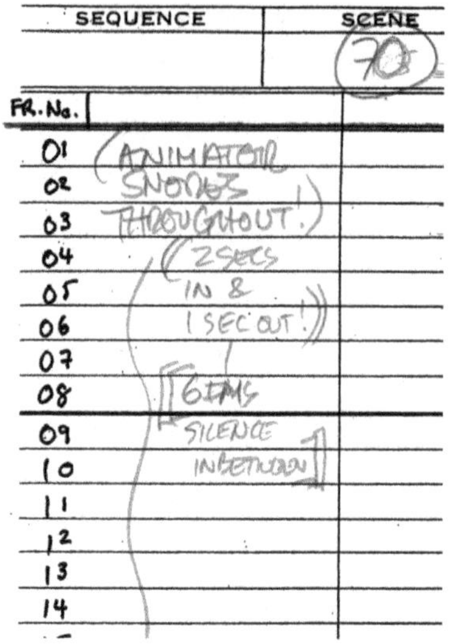

I number my frames throughout the scene for easier compositing later.

Audio Breakdown

The next column is the audio breakdown column. This column contains information that the sound editor has supplied—a frame-by-frame phonetic analysis of the soundtrack, showing exactly on which frame(s) each sound, word, or music beat falls. With phonetic breakdowns, the words are not necessarily spelled as they are written. For example, if the word being analyzed is "caravan," then it could well be phonetically noted as k, aa, rrr, e, v, aa, n. Similarly, "plume" might be broken down as p, l, oo, m and "carbonate" would be k, ah, b, o, n, ay, t. The following figure shows a sample audio breakdown from *Endangered Species*.

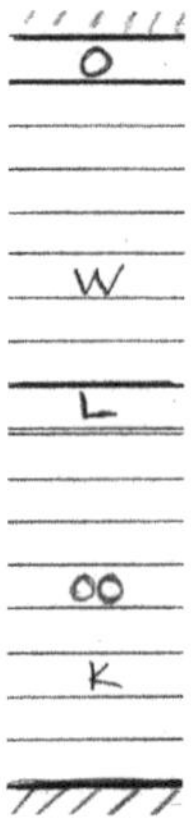

When broken down phonetically, the phrase "Oh, look!" will appear like this on the audio column of a dope sheet.

If the soundtrack is musical and not dialog based, then the breakdown column will display both the music beat (marked as a colored star on the precise frame they fall on) as well as the lyrics broken down phonetically.

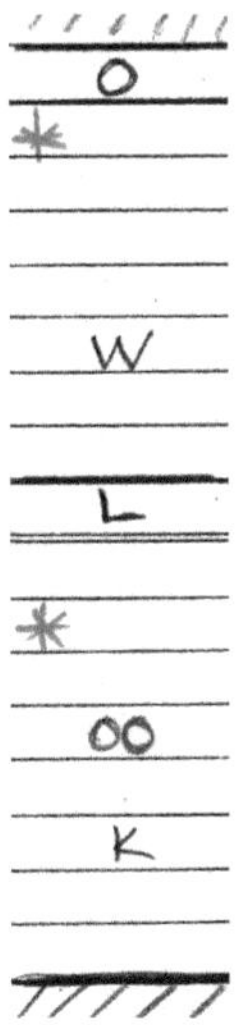

Colored stars mark the musical beat.

If the soundtrack is music-based only and has no lyrics, such as with the original masterpiece *Fantasia*, you would need to write down the sound the music makes in terms that you can recognize and understand. For example, a drum beat could be marked as D---R-U---M if it took up 11 frames, or a trumpet note could be recorded as T-R-U---MP-E----T over 17 frames.

Using different color pencils for different musical instruments, even as single continuous lines drawn down the audio column, with no written, phonetic interpretation at all, is another approach. Obviously, a full-length composition for an entire orchestra cannot be recorded in detail on the narrow, limited column of the dope sheet. But, if at least the main beats and sounds are recorded, you will have enough timing information to choreograph the animation in sync with the music.

Animation Layers

The next six columns are reserved for five layers of animation and the background. As indicated earlier, traditional 2D animators discovered that a finite number of cell layers were possible, as each layer of cell absorbs a significant amount of light and each subsequent layer reduces the illumination of the image below. Digital animators requiring more than five layers of animation will have to create their own custom-made dope sheets or cut and tape two sheets together.

The next figure shows a partially completed layers section. Defining these layers from right to left, we can see that the first, the lowest, is the background. Each scene will more than likely need a new background, although quite often a background can be reused in certain other scenes in the film. Simply write in the BG (background) number here when this decision has been made.

4	3	2	1	EXTRA	CAMERA INS
	M–1	S–1	1	BG 1	
	2	2	2		
	3	3	3		
	4	4	4		
	(5)	(5)	(5)		
	6	6	6		
	7	7	7		
	8	8	8		
	(9)	(9)	(9)		
	10	10	10		

The animation layers for a sample scene.

Then, depending on how many layers the animation needs to be produced on, you will dope (write in) the animation numbers from column 1 moving to the left. Most simple action animation requires only one or two layers. A great deal of animation layer management can be defined through clear thinking at this stage. Each layer of animation defines what needs to move and when and what can remain held without movement. Parts of a character, or even different characters, within a scene can be moved to different layers on specific frames of film when they need to be animated or kept still. However, the best animation keeps held positions and layer juggling to a minimum.

The previous figure illustrates three layers of animation, plus the background. The numbers without any prefix on them represent the main animated action. The other two layers, prefixed by the letter S or the letter M, are additional layers that relate to the main layer. Instead of needlessly writing the letter at the beginning of each one of the numbered drawings in the secondary layers, just write it on the first frame and draw a line down the column in front of all the subsequent numbers in that column, to show that it prefixes all of them.

Every level of animation should be given a different identifying letter. It might even be convenient to make the preceding letter correspond to what the level represents, such as B for the body level, H for the head level, A for the arm level, and so on. However, although desirable for clear identification purposes, this is not always practically possible. If in doubt, use the ascending letters of the alphabet to represent the ascending numbers of the levels—that is

A for column 1, B for column 2, C for column 3, etc. It really doesn't matter what letters are used, as long as none are duplicated. It's also helpful to indicate clearly what each column represents in the scene. This can be very useful when several members of the team are required to access the same scene during its progress through the production. I choose not to put any identifying letter in front of the drawings in the main animation column, as to do so would add extra numbering work, and the more economies that can be made, the better. However, I do meticulously ensure that all the other layers have a logical preceding letter in front of the drawing number.

Shooting or Camera Instructions

In the days when animation was filmed on rostrum cameras, the right-most column was extremely important, as this was where the shooting instructions were always written. Instructions such as field size, track-in (zoom in) and track-out (zoom out), start and end points, special effects, etc. were written here.

Digitally, a great many of these camera instructions are redundant these days, as much of the camera action is either controlled by the digital software at the time or in postproduction. However, it doesn't hurt to write here what you have in mind. The beauty of digital technology is that the best track-in and track-out timing can be better achieved by experimenting at the pencil test or even film editing stage, but, even so, marking up the first intentions on the dope sheet at least provides a starting point. Special effects can be indicated on the dope sheet too, but these also are more often computer generated after the animation stage these days. Even so, this column still is reserved for you to indicate the start and end (cut) frame of the scene, which does apply to all animation whether it is traditionally or digitally created. The camera instruction column may also indicate the frames required for fade-ins or fade-outs at the beginning or end of the scene or layer elements within the scene.

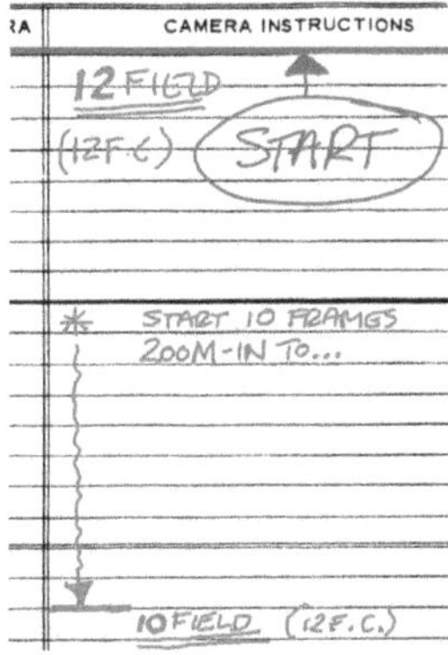

Just some of the information that the cameraman, or the person scanning the artwork, might need.

Rules for Dope Sheets

Regardless of design or production format, it is extremely important that the information indicated by the dope sheet is both clearly thought out and neatly written. The dope sheet is the most important paperwork the professional animator has to work with, as fundamental to animation as a music score is to music. As a result, the dope sheet is an absolute record of your thinking, timing, structure, dialog, and camera planning. To make it more effective, however, it is absolutely essential that the material written on it is clear, concise, and easily understood by anyone who reads it. Here are some additional notes and guidelines for dope sheets:

- Always write clearly and legibly, preferably in block capitals. Write in pencil so notes can be easily erased and changed when necessary.
- Make sure that every page contains the sequence, scene, and page numbers at the top. It is so easy for artwork and dope sheets to get lost or misplaced in the flurry of production.
- Name every level of animation, other than the main level, with a unique prefix letter, whether it's just A, B, C, D, etc., or initials that indicate the content of the layer.
- Remember also that the numbers of each drawing, if animated on two's, should only be odd numbers; animation on one's should include even numbers too.
- Keep the doping of a scene consistent. If you number your drawings by matching frame numbers, then everything should be done that way. Changing your numbering suddenly will create confusion. Sometimes, in reusing particular drawings throughout the scene you cannot avoid changes in numbering. But, if you are aware of the potential confusion, then there is little chance of the confusion arising. (I have seen animators write in arrows in the camera instruction column to indicate that particular numbers are being reused. Similarly, reused numbers can be written in to indicate that they have been used before.)
- Clearly mark the beginning of the scene with a START arrow and end the scene with a similar CUT arrow.
- Write down the appropriate field size at the start of the scene, as well as any camera instructions that are required, even if it seems obvious.
- Make sure that every scene dope sheet is accompanied by a clear field guide, so the cameraperson or scanner knows precisely the area required to be seen.
- For greater clarity, consider using different colored pencils to write different instructions on the dope sheet. For example, I use a black pencil for the animation numbering; a blue pencil for the START and CUT points; red for field size, scanning, or camera instructions; and brown for the audio breakdown notes.

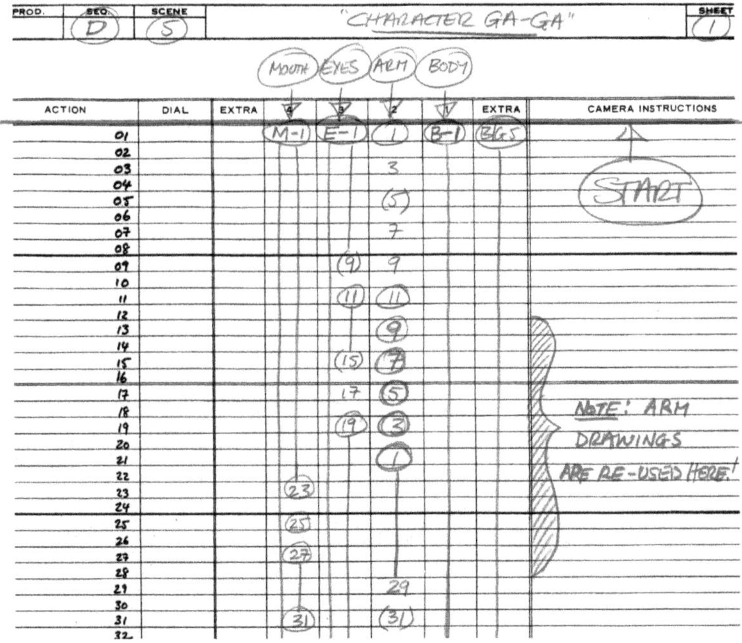

PROD. | SEQ. D | SCENE 5 | "CHARACTER GA-GA" | SHEET 1

ACTION	DIAL	EXTRA	4 (MOUTH)	3 (EYES)	2 (ARM)	1 (BODY)	EXTRA	CAMERA INSTRUCTIONS
01			M-1	E-1	1	B-1	BG5	
02								
03					3			
04								START
05					(5)			
06								
07					7			
08								
09				(9)	9			
10								
11				(11)	(11)			
12								
13					(9)			
14								
15				(15)	(7)			
16								
17				17	(5)			
18								NOTE: ARM
19				(19)	(3)			DRAWINGS
20								
21					(1)			
22								ARE RE-USED HERE!
23			(23)					
24								
25			(25)					
26								
27			(27)					
28								
29					29			
30								
31			(31)		(31)			
32								

Number drawings as consistently as possible and indicate clearly when drawings are reused.

PROD. | SEQ. C | SCENE 9 | "REVEAL" | SHEET 1

ACTION	DIAL	EXTRA	4	3	SMOKE	BIRDS	EXTRA	CAMERA INSTRUCTIONS
01					S-1	B-1	BG9	12FIELD
02								(12F.C.)
03					3	3		
04								START
05					5	(5)		
06								
07					(7)	7		
08								
09					9	(9)		* START 12 FRAMES
10					10	10		
11					11	11		ZOOM-OUT TO...
12					12	12		
13					(13)	(13)		
14					14	14		
15					15	15		
16					16	16		
17					17	(17)		
18					18	18		
19					(19)	19		
20					20	20		
21					21	(21)		10 FIELD
22								
23					23	23		(12F.C.)
24								
25					(25)	(25)		
26								
27					27	27		
28								
29					29	(29)		
30								
31					(31)	31		
32								

Always specify the field and field center on your dope sheets.

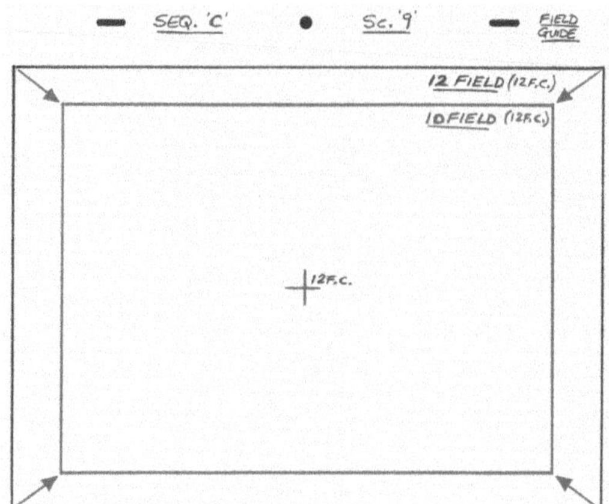

This field guide clearly indicates that the scene starts as a 12 field (12 F.C.) and then tracks-in to a 10 field on the same center line.

The Production Folder

Each scene of animation artwork requires a means of keeping everything together and showing all the detailed requirements of that scene. In 2D animation, that is the production folder, a wrap-around scene file that contains the dope sheets, animation layouts and/or field guide, animation drawings, and background art. The outer cover also needs to communicate specific information about the scene that is both accessible and readable.

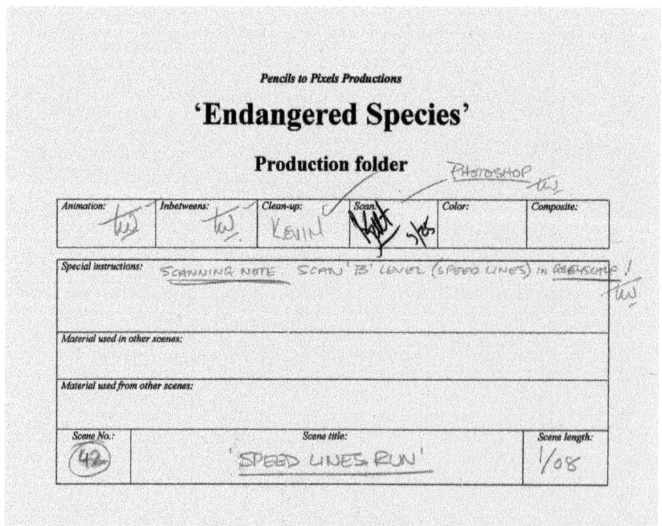

Pencils to Pixels Productions

'Endangered Species'

Production folder

PHOTOSHOP

Animation:	Inbetweens:	Clean-up:	Scan:	Color:	Composite:
TW	TW	KEVIN			

Special instructions: SCANNING NOTE: SCAN 'B' LEVEL (SPEED LINES) IN GREYSCALE! TW

Material used in other scenes:

Material used from other scenes:

Scene No.:	Scene title:	Scene length:
42	'SPEED LINES RUN'	1/08

The cover of a typical production folder, from *Endangered Species*.

A standard production folder needs space to include the production name, sequence number, scene number, footage length (that is, how long in feet and frames the scene is), director's name, animator's name, assistant animator's name, in addition to signature space for the people who created the animation, backgrounds, inking, coloring, checking, scanning/camera, and compositing, which they will fill in as they complete the work in their respective departments. One-person or small-scale operations might not need such an elaborate design, but it can't hurt to have a checklist of activities to complete.

Special Instructions

Each scene has special requirements that lie outside of the usual production process, not necessarily major variations, but some that need to be communicated to the production team beyond any particular department. The cover of the production folder leaves space for additional notes to be added, under the title Special Instructions. This is where you write any additional notes to the relevant members of the production team for any special attention the scene requires. Alternatively, this space could be useful for the director, background artist, special effects animator, and ink and color personnel to write information down too, such as special effects ideas, specific coloring instructions, how the scene needs to be specially composited, etc.

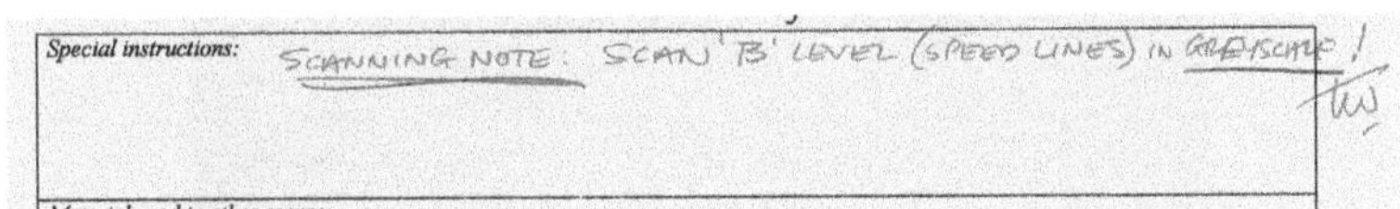
Special instructions: SCANNING NOTE: SCAN 'B' LEVEL (SPEED LINES) IN GREYSCALE !

Special instructions should be included on the production folder.

Material Used from Other Scenes

In larger productions especially, it is common to share artwork from one scene to another. Animation drawings, background artwork, and other elements can be saved as library material for other parts in the story. With low-budget productions, this is actively encouraged to cut down on time and budget costs. Therefore, it is important to know what material needs to be used from other scenes when a new scene is being created or completed. This section in the production folder facilitates this, with the relevant recycled artwork and scene number it is taken from included here.

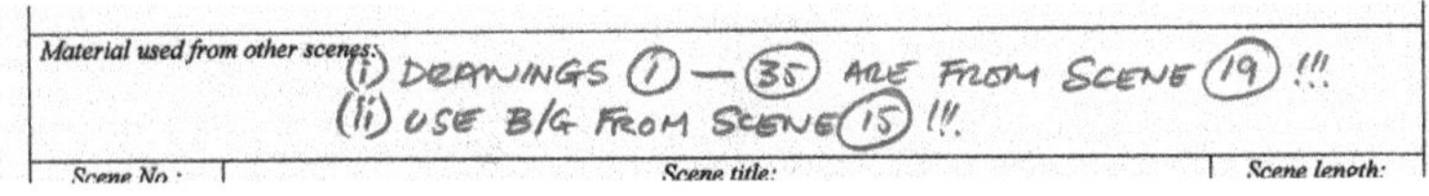
Material used from other scenes: (i) DRAWINGS 1 — 35 ARE FROM SCENE 19 !!!
(ii) USE B/G FROM SCENE 15 !!.

Indicate material from other scenes that can be used in this one.

Material Used in Other Scenes

For the same reasons, it is possible to say what material from the current scene can be used in other scenes. With such information on the production folder, team members further down the line know what artwork needs to be saved and moved into the appropriate scene(s) when the time comes.

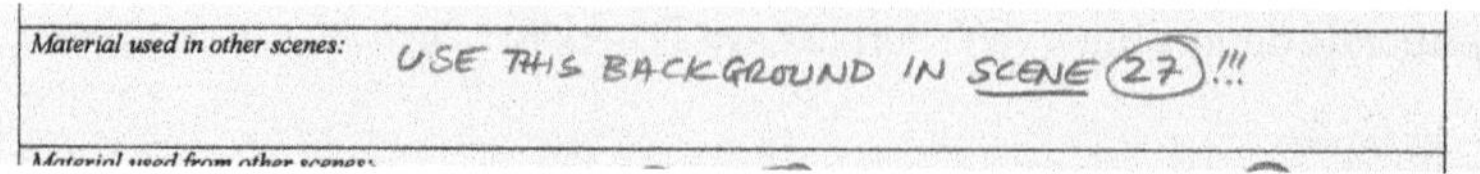
Material used in other scenes: USE THIS BACKGROUND IN SCENE (27)!!!

Indicate any material from this scene that will be used in others.

Attached Dope Sheet

The scene dope sheet should be included with the scene production folder. The safest and most certain way of doing this (so that the dope sheet and the folder do not ever get separated) is to staple the dope sheet to the inside of the production folder. If this is done in the correct orientation, it will be possible to read the cover of the folder, open it, and see the information on the dope sheet from the same point of view.

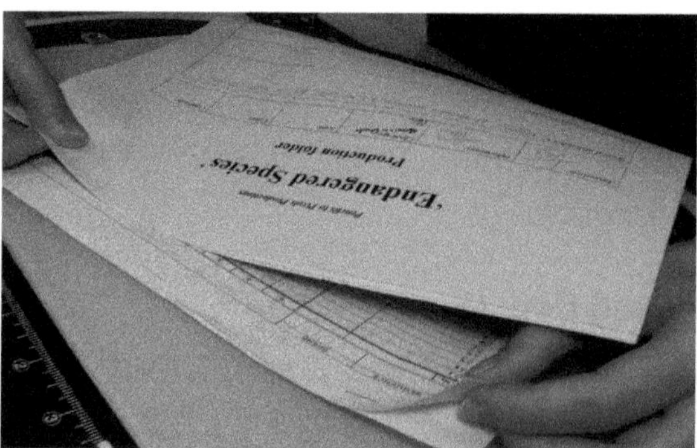

The production folders and dope sheets for *Endangered Species* were all printed on standard 11 × 17–inch paper, stapled together at the top, and then folded over lengthwise. The production folder was copied on ivory-colored paper to differentiate it from the white dope sheet pages.

Appendix 7: Glossary

A

Above-the-Line Costs: Costs found in a film budget that include all expenditures over and above the production costs of the crew, facilities, and regular budget expenditures, such as for the producer, director, and principal cast.

Academy: Standard 4:3 format screen ratio, used in all TV work and many films.

Accent Sounds: Parts in an audio track that have a special significance or emphasis, on which the animator can hang a particular pose or key movement.

Aerial Image: Film process of combining live action with animation, where the animation is filmed conventionally on a rostrum camera, with top lighting, while the live action is simultaneously backprojected into the camera lens.

Agency: Advertising agency, the organization responsible for a company's advertising strategy, scripted ideas, marketing, and advertising production.

Agent: *See* Artist's Rep.

Analog Tape: Recording tape that reproduces sound or picture by a magnetic tape process.

Animation Characters: Imagined characters who are conceived by a designer and are brought to life by an animator's skill.

Animation Layout: Accurate drawing that plots out the size and placement of animated action within a scene, prior to animation taking place.

Animator: *See* Key Animator.

Answer Print: The final color-graded film print, containing the soundtrack and picture combined.

Anticipation: A reactive action in the opposite direction to the main action, which precedes the main action and provides added impact or impetus to it.

Arc: Curved path of action through which an animated movement travels.

Art Director: Artist who is responsible for conceiving the overall visual styling of a film.

Artist's Rep: Agent who presents an artist's or animator's work to prospective clients.

Artwork: All the created visual material that makes up an animated film.

Assistant Animator: Junior (or trainee) animator who assists the key animator in putting in the major in-betweens of a scene. At the highest level, the assistant animator is someone who is effectively the business manager of the key animator in all production work, doing pretty much everything for him or her other than the creation of key drawings for animation.

Atmos: Background sound effects that need to be added to the audio track of the film to give the scene a natural-sounding atmosphere (e.g., traffic sounds, birds singing, city drone, etc.).

B

Background Designs: The styling of artwork that will not move in a scene.

Background Layout: Accurate drawing that depicts everything in a scene that is to appear in the background, prior to the background art being created.

Backgrounds: Finished artwork that depicts all that does not move in an animation scene, mostly found behind the animated action.

Bar Sheet: Printed master sheet in traditional 2D animation that enables the sound editor to plot out the phonetic content (and timings) of an audio track, frame by frame.

Below-the-Line Costs: All budgeted costs, other than those indicated in above-the-line costs.

BETA: Format of industry-standard videotape used for certain broadcast-quality TV productions.

Bid: Budgeting estimate presented to an agency by a production company when pitching for a contract to produce a commercial.

Bi-pack: Traditional method of combining live action with animation in the camera.

Blank Leader: Black, white, or colored film strip that a film editor adds to the beginning or end of a scene or sequence.

Blue- or Green-Screen Background: Method of filming live action that enables the actors to be separated from the background and composited with another live-action or animation background later.

Boiling: Used to describe the kind of flickering that occurs when a number of animated images that contain differing textures are filmed together in an animation sequence.

Boiling can also occur when there is extensive cross-hatching involved from drawing to drawing, or if the lines of each drawing are vastly different in form and substance.

Breakdown Drawing: The first in-between drawing that is created by the animator (or assistant animator) between two keys.

Breaking It Down: The process where a sound editor, or animator, produces a frame-by-frame (phonetic) analysis of an audio track that contains dialog, narration, or song lyrics. May also include a similar analysis of the beats and main instrumentation found in a music track.

Budget: Estimated costs of a production based on a known script and visual stylings.

Burning-in: Traditional film process of superimposing a brighter image onto a previously exposed darker one by means of running the film back and shooting the image to be superimposed as white (or a bright color) against a pure black background (e.g., adding a white title to a previously created film sequence).

C

Camera Instruction Sheets: *See* Dope Sheets.

Camera Operator: Skilled individual who operates the rostrum camera.

Cash Flow: Projection of how much, and when, the finances estimated in the budget will need to be accessed throughout the actual production schedule.

Cell Paints: Traditionally used color paints that are applied to the back of cells once the animation has been traced onto them.

Cell Punch: Engineered, precision instrument that creates registration holes in animation paper and cells.

Cells: Sheets of clear acetate onto which the animation drawings are inked, traced, or xeroxed and painted.

Cell xeroxing: Method of copying drawn artwork onto cells using a photocopying machine.

Center of Gravity: The inner point within a character where all his or her volume, weight, and mass are centrally focused.

Character Design: The visual interpretation of a character who is to be animated.

Charts: Drawn indicators, written on the key drawings by the animator, to show the assistant animator (or in-betweener) where the required number of in-betweens need to be positioned.

Checker: Member of the 2D animation team who meticulously checks the animation artwork and dope sheets prior to them being filmed or scanned.

Checking: The process undertaken by the checker.

Cinemascope (Scope): 2.35:1 film screen ratio, which is achieved by using a special anamorphic lens on the camera and projector. They are pretty much exclusively reserved for large-scale, epic movies.

Clean-up: The process undertaken by the clean-up artist.

Clean-up Artist: The member of an animation team who converts rough animation drawings into finely inked, finished artwork that reflects the design style of the film and are ready to be traced or scanned.

Click Track: Guide musical soundtrack, which contains a metronome beat, allowing the animator to time and pace the action prior to the final soundtrack being recorded. (Note: As the click track has to provide the animator with a precise timing of the action, it is essential that the final music arrangement is recorded at the same beat as the guide track, otherwise the animation and the music will not be synchronized.)

Color Designs: Approved colorings of the various animated characters/elements featured in the film.

Color Gels: Colored, transparent cells that are laid over the animation artwork in traditional 2D animation to provide a mood change (e.g., a deep blue over a scene will give a nighttime feel).

Color Grading: Fine-tuning color adjustments made to a film once everything has been completed.

Color Model: Color design of an animated character or object that defines the precise colors that are to be used when the artwork is complete.

Commissioning Editor: Individual employed by television companies to seek out, identify, and sign up new projects for TV broadcasting.

Composer: Individual responsible for writing and arranging the musical content of the proposed film.

Compositing: The procedure of combining various separate filmic elements (e.g., live action with animation, layers of animation with other layers of animation and special effects, etc.) through a digital or film optical-editing process.

Copy: Written material contained in an advertising script.

Copyright Agreement: Legal document that enables filmmakers to work with intellectual property that is not their own.

Copywriter: Member of an advertising agency creative team who is responsible for the writing of a script.

Corporate Sponsorship: Finance from a major industrial corporation or business entity that can help finance the production for a film in exchange for the goodwill or publicity value that such an association can bring to the company.

Creative Team: Members of the agency personnel who are related to the visual and written content of a particular commercial (e.g., art director and copywriter).

Cushion-in/Cushion-out: *See* Slow-in/Slow-out.

Cut: The point in a film where one scene ends and another begins.

Cut Outs: Animation artwork that is cut out and moved under the camera, frame by frame.

Cutting: The process undertaken by the editor when assembling all the scenes in a film together.

Cutting Copy: A double-head presentation of the production whereby all selected scenes are projected on one strip of film, while the soundtrack is played on another.

Cycle Animation: A process of economizing on animation whereby the action ends where it began and therefore can be repeated over and over again (e.g., in walks and runs).

D

Dailies: *See* Rushes.

Dead Zone: The first six frames of a scene where the human brain cannot detect either image or movement.

Design: *See* Design Concept.

Design Concept: The overall visual look of the film.

Designer: Member of the production team who is responsible for the design content of the film.

Design Stage: The phase in the production schedule (at the beginning of the film) when all the design work is undertaken.

Development Package: A collection of presentation material that will allow investors the opportunity of assessing the production from every angle (e.g., script, designs, budget, cash flow, legal tie-ups, etc.).

Dialog: All the spoken material contained in the soundtrack.

Diffusion Filter: A filter that is placed over the lens of the camera when shooting that creates a soft, diffused look to the scene.

Digital Tape: Tape that records sounds or pictures digitally (as opposed to analog tape).

Director: Member of the production team who is responsible for the overall interpretation, styling, structuring, and timing of the film.

Dissolve: The moment in a film where one scene fades out as another scene fades in.

Distribution Rights: An agreement arranged between a producer and a distributor whereby the right to distribute the film through specific markets is legally obtained.

Distributor: The individual who distributes a film through various markets (e.g., cinemas, network TV, cable and satellite TV, retail video, etc.).

Dope Sheets: Printed sheets that allow the animator to communicate to the rostrum cameraman how the animation drawings are to be filmed.

Double Bounce: Style of animated walk where the character's body bounces up and down twice during one step.

Double Take: An animated character's exaggerated reaction to an event that has just taken place in a scene.

Double-head: The film when picture and soundtrack are projected separately.

Drag: Where one part is delaying behind the main action (e.g, the hand dragging behind as the arm swings through on a walk).

Drawing Board: Artist's work surface.

Dub: Process of mixing the music, dialog, and sound effects onto one soundtrack.

E

Edit: The process of joining all the scenes of a film together, in conjunction with the soundtrack.

Editor: Creative member of the production team who supervises the edit.

Edit Suit: Facility where all the visual elements of a film are edited, or dubbed, together.

Electric Pencil Sharpener: Important and time-saving component of the animator's toolkit.

Establishing Shot: Scene at the beginning of a film that establishes the story's setting.

Exposure Sheets: *See* Dope Sheets.

Exposure Test: A test undertaken by the rostrum cameraman to ascertain the correct exposure of a scene (or the special effects within it).

Extra Charges: Costs that are incurred outside of the original budget which are brought about as a result of an agency, or client, requesting changes that lie outside of the original script requirements.

F

Feature Film: Full-length movie seen in the cinema or on TV.

Field Center: The central point within a field guide from which all measurements are made.

Field Size: Area on the animation artwork that the camera will see.

Film Lawyer: A legal practitioner who specializes in film work (very important).

Film Optical: The process of joining live action with animation, or of adding graphics, titles, dissolves, or visual effects to an existing piece of film.

Film Size: Defines the width of film stock being used (e.g., 35 mm, 16 mm, 8 mm, Super 8, etc.).

Film Stock: Defines the nature of film stock being used (e.g., color, black-and-white, film speed, etc.).

Final Shoot: Stage of filming where the finished, color animation artwork is shot.

Final Track: Stage of recording when the soundtrack is complete and approved.

Fixed Costs: Overheads contained in the budget (e.g., rent, rates, leases, etc.).

Follow-through: Where one part of an action continues to move (catch up) when the main action ceases (e.g., a cape of a running figure continues to carry forward, then settles to a halt after the figure has stopped.)

Footage: Length of a film, or sequence, in feet and frames.

Footage Rate: Amount of film footage required to be completed each week by the animator/assistant animator in order that the schedule and budget be met.

Frames per Second (FPS): Rate of speed that the film is projected: 24 frames per second (cinema and U.S. TV) or 25 frames per second (British TV).

Frame: Name of an individual image contained in a strip of film.

Freeze: A hold—a moment where an animated character stops moving and remains that way for a specific number of frames.

Frosted Cells: Diffused-looking acetate that can be drawn on with regular pencils. When the drawing is complete, the frosted cell can be sprayed with lacquer, which causes it to become clear, like standard cells.

Funny Money: Term given to film finance derived from unorthodox sources (e.g., private investors, with a private interest in the nature of the film envisaged).

FX: Abbreviated form, meaning effects (visual or sound).

G

Graded Print: A color-corrected film still at the double-head stage.

Graticule: Precision-drafted guide for allowing the animator to calculate and define the field sizes of various pieces of animation artwork.

Green- or Blue-Screen Background: Method of filming live action that enables the actors to be separated from the background and composited with another live-action or animation background later.

Guide Track: A roughly recorded soundtrack that gives the animator an idea of what the final track will be like (often used at the Leica Reel stage).

H

Hand Tracing: Process whereby the animation is traced (by brush or pen) onto the cell by an inker.

Harry: Electronic device for editing/combining live-action film and animation on videotape.

High-Definition (Hi-Def): TV system that uses 1000 lines on the screen, as opposed to 625 (United Kingdom) or 525 (United States).

Highlight: An illuminated effect, featured on one part of the animated image, which suggests that a bright light is being shone on it (e.g., the opposite side to that of a shadow).

Highlight Run: An effects element used in composited animation that creates an illumined effect on the brighter side of an animated image.

Hit: Strong emphasis created in the animated action (usually in synchronization with an important sound on the soundtrack).

Hot Spot: Area on the animation artwork that is overexposed due to uneven lighting on the rostrum camera tabletop.

I

In-Between Drawings: Drawings that are created between two previously existing drawings in accordance with the instructions of the animator/assistant animator.

In-Betweener: A trainee animator who is required to produce only in-between drawings.

In-Betweening: The process of doing in-betweens.

Independent Filmmaker: Filmmaker (usually a producer) who creates a film independently of established film production sources (e.g., TV companies, major distributors, etc.).

Inker: Member of the film production team who is responsible for transferring the animation drawing onto animation cells.

Inking: The process undertaken by an inker.

K

Key Animator: Skilled artist with the ability to bring life to inanimate drawings.

Key Drawing: A major animation drawing created by the animator that indicates an extreme of movement.

Key Frames: Color presentation artwork that indicates the design look that those particular sequences of animation will have in the final film.

L

Lab: Film-processing laboratory.

Layout Drawing: Detailed sketch that indicates everything that appears in a scene.

Leica Reel: Filmed layout drawings that are shown in sync with the approved soundtrack.

Lightbox: Backlit work surface that is used by most members of the animation team.

Line Drawing: Pencil drawing that contains no color or shading.

Line of Action: An invisible line within a character pose that defines the main dynamic of that pose.

Lip Sync: The drawing of animated mouth movements that move in synchronization with the soundtrack.

Literary Rights Agreement: Negotiated legal arrangement that allows the filmmaker the right to use an existing book, or published story, for the basis of a film script.

Live Action: The filming of actors or natural scenery in real time as opposed to drawn or animated artwork.

Location: Place where filmed action takes place.

M

Mag Track: Soundtrack that is recorded onto magnetic film stock that is the same size as the film stock used for the picture (e.g., 35 mm, 16 mm, etc.).

Mark-Up: Percentage of profit indicated in the budget.

Match Cut: An editing device where a character is in a set position at the end of one scene and in the identical position at the start of the next scene, where maybe the background is entirely different. A match cut can work with a static image or a moving sequence.

Match Lines: Lines on animation drawings indicating where an animated character is matching to an object on the background that is intended to appear in the foreground (and therefore beyond which the animation cell must not be painted).

Matte: Artwork or similar device used in combining one or more filmic images that blots out background material, leaving a precise, unexposed area into which the image that is to be composited in will fit.

Matte Run: An effects element used in compositing work that carries the required matting artwork.

Merchandising: A means by which extra revenue may be obtained for film finance (where the rights in animated characters may be sold, so as to produce toys, games, books, etc.).

Mix: *See* Dissolve.

Model Sheets: Design sheets that depict the structure of the approved animation characters from every conceivable angle.

Moviola: Machine used for viewing film at the double-head stage.

Multiplane Camera: Specialized camera that offers the opportunity of filming different (and separate) levels of animation in a scene, giving the illusion of 3D depth.

Mute: Action that contains no soundtrack.

N

Neg Cutting: A process that requires the careful editing of the film's negative once the final shoot and edit are approved.

Negative Pick-up: Distribution deal that states that the distributor need not pay the film's producer any money until the final negative is delivered.

NTSC: TV broadcast system used in the United States and other countries (525 lines).

O

Optical Track: Visual soundtrack stripe that is found along the edge of an answer (or combined) print.

Option Agreement: Negotiated legal arrangement that allows the filmmaker to purchase the right to develop copyright material for a specific length of time prior to the film receiving production finance and the full rights being obtained.

Overlapping Action: Technique used by the animator to create a more fluid look to the action.

P

Pack Shot: Scene (usually at the end of a commercial) that presents the product that is being advertised.

Paintbox: An electronic painting device that allows film images to be enhanced or changed once they are transferred to videotape.

Painter: Member of the film production team who is responsible for painting the animation drawings once they have been transferred onto the cell by the inker.

PAL: A TV broadcast system used in the United Kingdom and other countries (625 lines).

Pan: A film action take that requires the camera to travel across the artwork to create movement.

Paper/Cell Rack: Part of the studio equipment that allows wet painted cells to dry individually.

Passing Position: The midway position between two extreme key positions in an animated walk.

Path of Action: The central line along which and action takes place (e.g., the center of gravity in a ball as it bounces, or a character as he or she runs or walks).

Peg Bar: The registration device on which punched animation paper or cells are placed.

Peghole Reinforcements: Adhesive paper/plastic reinforcements that are affixed around the paper or cell punch holes, preventing them from tearing inadvertently.

Pegholes: Specific holes that are punched into animation paper or cells to aid the precise registration of drawings.

Pencil Test: A filmed interim motion test of the animation produced while the drawings are still at the pencil stage.

Percentage Exposure: A special effects technique that requires one aspect of the artwork within a scene to be filmed at less than 100 percent exposure.

Photo-rotos: Photographic prints, taken frame by frame, from live-action negative to enable the animator to register animation drawings to the movements in a live-action/animation film combination.

Pilot Film: Short presentation sequence of finished animation, created specifically to show potential investors what the overall film will look like.

Producer: Key member of the production team responsible for ensuring that the film is created on time and budget, and who negotiates all distribution (and incidental) deals with outside interests.

Production Company: The organization responsible for the production of a film.

Production Folders: Preprinted folders containing all the camera instructions required by the animator, together with all the information relating to the creation of that scene.

Production Line: The processes involved in the production of a film.

Production Team: All the relevant personnel required to produce an animated film.

Projector: Equipment required for the projection of all film in cinematic conditions.

R

Recording Session: Event that occurs when the film soundtrack is being recorded.

Registration: The process of ensuring that each animation drawing is in perfect register with the rest in the scene.

Renderer: Member of the film production team who is responsible for applying the textured shaping to flat-colored, animation artwork, creating more of a 3D design look.

Rendering: The work undertaken by a renderer.

Rostrum Camera: Specialized film camera that undertakes the shooting of animation artwork in a vertical format.

Rotoprints: *See* Photo-rotos.

Rotoscope: Device invented by Max Fleischer for tracing live action, frame by frame.

Rotoscoping: The process of tracing live action so that it looks like 2D-animated action.

Rough Animation: Loosely drawn animation that allows the animator to rapidly check the action prior to any detailed and time-consuming drawing being applied to the animation work.

Rushes: The first processed film print, often received the day after the animation artwork has been shot.

S

Safe Titling: Area within the full academy field size, within which all titling can be viewed on a TV monitor without it being cut off around the edges or distorted by the TV screen.

Sales Agent: Agent who is able to take a film development package and sell it to established film financiers on behalf of the film's producer (receiving, as a fee, a percentage of the production budget).

Scene: An individual sequence of visual action that occurs (with many others) within a film.

Scene Planning: The process by which a director plots a sequence of scenes to tell a story. The process of assigning timing and levels to 2D animation on a dope sheet.

Scene Slate: A device shot at the beginning of a scene, which indicates the relevant production, sequence, and scene numbers of the material being filmed.

Schedule: An analysis of the timing and stages required in order that a film be successfully completed.

Screenplay: A written description of the story, dialog, and visual concept of the film, created prior to its production.

Script: *See* Screenplay.

Scrubbing: A method of manually dragging a cursor of a pointer along a timeline in order to see a specific section of a film or hear a specific section of audio track.

Sequence: Collection of scenes that relate a specific phase of the film's storyline.

SFX: Abbreviation for sound effects.

Shadow: An area superimposed onto an animated image that suggests a shaded effect over everything that is furthermost from an illumined light source.

Shadow Run: An effects element used in compositing work that carries the required shadowing material.

Show Reel: Collection of previous work collated on videotape by the production company, showing the best of their work in the hope of attracting future work from potential clients.

Slash Animation: Old style of animation, in precell days, where the character was animated on the lower level and the background was drawn on an upper level with holes cut in it to allow the action to show through.

Slug: *See* Blank Leader.

Sneak: Traditional technique of producing tip-toe walks with animated characters.

Sound Bench: Workplace used by editors to produce a breakdown of soundtracks.

Soundtrack: All the recorded audio material used in any film.

Stagger: Animation technique used to create a trembling, shaking, or juddering visual effect.

Steinbeck: Machine used for viewing film at the double-head stage, utilizing a flatbed format.

Sticking: A process where a film being viewed on a computer monitor stops, glitches, or locks up due to an overload of data being processed or a computer's RAM capability being too low.

Sting: Short, sharp note or chord in the soundtrack used to make a dramatic musical emphasis of the film's action.

Storyboard: Visual interpretation of the script, produced by way of a series of small drawings, depicting the content of each scene's action.

Storyline: Brief written outline of a film's dramatic content.

Strobing: A jittery, visual affect on the screen, usually produced by having too many vertical lines in an even panning shot. Can also occur when an animated character moves on two's while the background pans on one's.

Studio: Place in which the production team works.

Studio Overheads: Costs relating to the noncreative needs of a production studio (e.g., administrative, telephones, electricity, etc.).

Superimposition (Animation): The process of taking 2D animation drawings off the pegs, then laying one on top of the other, so as to more clearly create a new in-between.

Superimposition (Title): The process of overlaying an image on top of a previously filmed scene (e.g., a title over a product shot in a commercial or a light effect through a window at night).

Sync: The perfect interrelation between sound and picture in a scene (e.g., lip sync).

Synopsis: *See* Storyline.

T

Telecine: Facility suit used for the electronic transfer of film imagery to videotape.

Theatrical Film: Feature-length film to be shown in cinema outlets.

Three-dimensional Animation (3D): Animation using models, puppets, and/or solid objects.

Thumbs/Thumbnails: Very simple, fast-drawn sketches that represent initial ideas for animation poses, or as storyboard frames when visualizing a storyline.

Tiling: The process of scanning extra-large artwork in sections, then compositing it back together again by overlapping and merging the layers within a computer program such as Photoshop.

Top-lit/Backlit Shoot: The dual shooting of animation intended for live-action/animation composited work: The first where the animation artwork is shot top-lit against a blue-screen or plain background, and the second where the same artwork is shot in silhouette against backlit, white light.

Tracebacks: Procedure where portions within an animation drawing (that are not moving) are precisely traced back from the previous drawing.

Tracer: *See* Inker.

Tracing Down: Process of transferring the drawing of a background layout onto a ready-stretched sheet of watercolor or cartridge paper that is ready for coloring.

Track: *See* Soundtrack.

Track Breakdown: The process whereby the sound editor analyses every individual sound on a track, frame by frame.

Transfer: The transferring of the soundtrack from the original recording tape to the relevant mag track indicated.

Treatment: Document that outlines the director's concept for the film at the early, predevelopment stage.

Triple Bidding: Procedure undertaken by many advertising agencies whereby three competing production companies are invited to bid on a specific commercial script.

Truck- (Track-) In: Action where the camera moves in on the artwork.

Truck- (Track-) Out: Action where the camera pulls out from the artwork.

TV Cut-Off: Area within the field size that represents the outer portion of the artwork that will be automatically cut off when viewed on a TV monitor.

Two-dimensional Animation (2D): All animation that is produced on a two-dimensional plane (e.g., drawn artwork).

V

Voiceover: Recorded voice that is heard offscreen.

Voice Talent: Actor/actress used for voiceover recordings.

W

Wedge Test: A range of varying exposure tests produced before a final shoot where percentage exposures are being used.

Weight: Technique in animation that gives the animated character a real sense of heaviness.

Widescreen: Cinematic screen ratio where a standard academy format is reduced at the top and bottom to give the picture an extended landscape look.

Wooden: A word used by animators to describe a character's action when it lacks weight, energy, or flexibility.

Z

Zip Pan: The technique of extremely fast panning across animation artwork.

Zoom: A fast truck-in or truck-out.

"THE END?." . . . I think that will be up to you!

Index

B

C

E

F

G

H

I

J

K

L

U

V

W

X

Z

Milton Keynes UK
Ingram Content Group UK Ltd.
UKHW050457071024
449327UK00015B/411